# TAKING SIDES

Clashing Views on Controversial

# Issues in Science, Technology, and Society

**SIXTH EDITION**

# TAKING SIDES

Clashing Views on Controversial

# Issues in Science, Technology, and Society

**SIXTH EDITION**

**Selected, Edited, and with Introductions by**

**Thomas A. Easton**
*Thomas College*

**McGraw-Hill/Dushkin**
**A Division of The McGraw-Hill Companies**

Photo Acknowledgment
Cover image: M. Freeman/PhotoLink/Getty Images

Cover Art Acknowledgment
by Maggie Lytle



Manufactured in the United States of America

Sixth Edition

1234567890DOCDOC0987654

Library of Congress Cataloging-in-Publication Data
Main entry under title:
Taking sides: clashing views on controversial issues in science, technology, and society/selected, edited, and with introductions by Thomas A. Easton.—6th ed.
Includes bibliographical references and index.
1. Science—Social aspects. 2. Technology—Social aspects. I. Easton, Thomas A., *comp.*
306.45

0-07-291713-X
ISSN: 1098-5417

Printed on Recycled Paper

# Preface

Those who must deal with scientific and technological issues—scientists, politicians, sociologists, business managers, and anyone who is concerned about a neighborhood dump or power plant, government intrusiveness, expensive space programs, or the morality of medical research, among many other issues—must be able to consider, evaluate, and choose among alternatives. Making choices is an essential aspect of the scientific method. It is also an inescapable feature of every public debate over a scientific or technological issue, for there can be no debate if there are no alternatives.

The ability to evaluate and to select among alternatives—as well as to know when the data do not permit selection—is called critical thinking. It is essential not only in science and technology but in every other aspect of life as well. *Taking Sides: Clashing Views on Controversial Issues in Science, Technology, and Society* is designed to stimulate and cultivate this ability by holding up for consideration 19 issues that have provoked substantial debate. Each of these issues has at least two sides, usually more. However, each issue is expressed in terms of a single question in order to draw the lines of debate more clearly. The ideas and answers that emerge from the clash of opposing points of view should be more complex than those offered by the students before the reading assignment.

The issues in this book were chosen because they are currently of particular concern to both science and society. They touch on the nature of science and research, the relationship between science and society, the uses of technology, and the potential threats that technological advances can pose to human survival. And they come from a variety of fields, including computer and space science, biology, environmentalism, law enforcement, and public health.

**Organization of the book** For each issue, I have provided an *issue introduction,* which provides some historical background and discusses why the issue is important. I then present two selections, one pro and one con, in which the authors make their cases. Each issue concludes with a *postscript* that brings the issue up to date and adds other voices and viewpoints. I have also provided relevant Internet site addresses (URLs) on the *On the Internet* page that accompanies each part opener. At the back of the book is a listing of all the *contributors to this volume,* which gives information on the scientists, technicians, professors, and social critics whose views are debated here.

Which answer to the issue question—yes or no—is the correct answer? Perhaps neither. Perhaps both. Students should read, think about, and discuss the readings and then come to their own conclusions without letting my or their instructor's opinions (which perhaps show at least some of the time!) dictate theirs. The additional readings mentioned in both the introductions and the postscripts should prove helpful. It is worth stressing that the issues covered in this book are all *live* issues; that is, the debates they represent are active and ongoing.

**Changes to this edition** This sixth edition represents a considerable revision. There are nine completely new issues: "Should Society Restrict the Publication of Unclassified but "Sensitive" Research?" (Issue 1); "Do Environmentalists Overstate Their Case?" (Issue 6); "Will Hydrogen Replace Fossil Fuels for Cars?" (Issue 7); "Do Vaccines Cause Autism?" (Issue 9); "Should DDT Be Banned Worldwide?" (Issue 10); "Should We Expand Efforts to Find Near-Earth Objects?" (Issue 11); "Should NASA Continue to Pursue Manned Space Exploration?" (Issue 13); "Does the Internet Strengthen Community?" (Issue 14); and "Does the War on Terrorism Threaten Privacy?" (Issue 15).

The issue on the search for extraterrestrial intelligence (Issue 12) has been retitled and given two new essays, bringing the issue up to debate and changing the focus. In addition, for three of the issues retained from the previous edition, one reading has been replaced to update the debate: "Should Society Act Now to Halt Global Warming?" (Issue 5); "Will Screens Replace Pages?" (Issue 16); and "Is the Use of Animals in Research Justified?" (Issue 17). In all, there are 23 new selections. The book's introduction and the issue introductions and postscripts for the retained issues have been revised and updated where necessary.

**A word to the instructor** An *Instructor's Manual with Test Questions* (multiple-choice and essay) is available through the publisher for the instructor using *Taking Sides* in the classroom. It includes suggestions for stimulating in-class discussion for each issue. A general guidebook, *Using Taking Sides in the Classroom,* which discusses methods and techniques for integrating the pro-con approach into any classroom setting, is also available. An online version of *Using Taking Sides in the Classroom* and a correspondence service for *Taking Sides* adopters can be found at `http://www.dushkin.com/usingts/`.

*Taking Sides: Clashing Views on Controversial Issues in Science, Technology, and Society* is only one title in the Taking Sides series. If you are interested in seeing the table of contents for any of the other titles, please visit the Taking Sides Web site at `http://www.dushkin.com/takingsides/`.

**Thomas A. Easton**
*Thomas College*

# Contents In Brief

# Contents

Richard J. Clifford, a professor of biblical studies, argues that although modern creationism is flawed, excluding the Bible and religion from American public education is indefensible. He maintains that schools should be places where religious beliefs are treated with respect. Professor of political science Marjorie George argues that the U.S. Constitution and the Supreme Court have created a solid wall between the educational system and religion. Despite the efforts of creationists to find ways around or through that wall, she holds, religion "can play no role in the classroom."



Lester R. Brown, founder of the Worldwatch Institute, and Worldwatch researchers Gary Gardner and Brian Halweil argue that population growth is straining the Earth's ability to support humanity and that population must therefore be stabilized. Stephen Moore, director of the Cato Institute, argues that the population-control ethic is a threat both to freedom and to the principle that every human life has intrinsic value.



The Intergovernmental Panel on Climate Change states that global warming appears to be real, with strong effects on sea level, ice cover, and rainfall patterns to come, and that human activities—particularly emissions of carbon dioxide—are to blame. Neuroscience researcher Kevin A. Shapiro argues that past global warming predictions have been wrong and that the data do not support calls for immediate action to reduce emissions of carbon dioxide.



Environmental journalist Ronald Bailey argues that the natural environment is not in trouble, despite the arguments of many environmentalists that it is. He holds that the greatest danger facing the environment is not human activity but "ideological environmentalism, with its hostility to economic growth and technological progress." David Pimentel, a professor of insect ecology and agricultural sciences, argues that those

**NO: John Merchant,** from "Expanded and Updated from: A New Direction in Space," *IEEE Technology and Society* (Winter 1994) *222*

Conservative writer John Derbyshire contests that although manned space flight is expensive, it is a romantic enterprise with a place in the American spirit. John Merchant, a retired staff engineer at Loral Infrared and Imaging Systems, argues that it will be much cheaper to develop electronic senses and remotely operated machines humans can use to explore other worlds.

## PART 5 THE COMPUTER REVOLUTION 233

### Issue 14. Does the Internet Strengthen Community? 234

**YES: John B. Horrigan,** from "Online Communities: Networks that Nurture Long-Distance Relationships and Local Ties," Pew Internet & American Life Project (October 2001) *236*

**NO: Jonathon N. Cummings, Brian Butler, and Robert Kraut,** from "The Quality of Online Social Relationships," *Communications of the ACM* (July 2002) *244*

John B. Horrigan asserts that when people go online, they form both relationships with distant others who share their interests and strengthen their involvement with their local communities. Jonathon N. Cummings, Brian Butler, and Robert Kraut maintain that online communication is less valuable for building strong social relationships than more traditional face-to-face and telephone communication.

### Issue 15. Does the War on Terrorism Threaten Privacy? 254

**YES: J. Michael Waller,** from "Fears Mount over 'Total' Spy System," *Insight on the News* (December 24, 2002) *256*

**NO: Stuart Taylor, Jr.,** from "How Civil-Libertarian Hysteria May Endanger Us All," *National Journal* (February 22, 2003) *261*

Writer J. Michael Waller describes objections to the Defense Department's proposed effort to search through government and commercial databases in search of patterns of behavior that can identify terrorists ("Total Information Awareness") and argues that it indeed threatens a severe invasion of privacy. Stuart Taylor, Jr., contests that the objectors have their priorities wrong: curbing "government powers in the name of civil liberties [exacts] too high a price in terms of endangered lives."

### Issue 16. Will Screens Replace Pages? 266

**YES: Steve Ditlea,** from "The Real E-Books," *Technology Review* (July/August 2000) *268*

**NO: Stephen Sottong,** from "E-Book Technology: Waiting for the 'False Pretender'," *Information Technology & Libraries* (June 2001) *276*

Writer Steve Ditlea argues that computers can simplify publishing, improve access to readers, and enhance the reading experience and that e-books are becoming both practical and popular. Librarian Stephen Sottong argues that e-books are not cheap, readable, or durable enough to replace paper books and that they pose special problems for libraries.

# Introduction

## Analyzing Issues in Science and Technology

As civilization enters the twenty-first century, it cannot escape science and technology. Their fruits—the clothes we wear, the foods we eat, the tools we use—surround us. They also fill us with both hope and dread for the future, for although new discoveries promise us cures for diseases and other problems, new insights into the wonders of nature, new gadgets, new industries, and new jobs (among other things), the past has taught us that technological developments can have unforeseen and terrible consequences.

Those consequences do *not* belong to science, for science is nothing more (or less) than a systematic approach to gaining knowledge about the world. Technology is the application of knowledge (including scientific knowledge) to accomplish things we otherwise could not. It is not just devices such as hammers and computers and jet aircraft, but also management systems and institutions and even political philosophies. And it is of course such *uses* of knowledge that affect our lives for good and ill.

We cannot say, "for good *or* ill." Technology is neither an unalloyed blessing nor an unmitigated curse. Every new technology offers both new benefits and new problems, and the two sorts of consequences cannot be separated from each other. Automobiles provide rapid, convenient personal transportation, but precisely because of that benefit, they also create suburbs, urban sprawl, crowded highways, air pollution, and even global climate change.

## Optimists vs. Pessimists

The inescapable pairing of good and bad consequences helps to account for why so many issues of science and technology stir debate in our society. Optimists focus on the benefits of technology and are confident that we will be able to cope with any problems that arise. Pessimists fear the problems and are sure their costs will outweigh any possible benefits.

Sometimes the costs of new technologies are immediate and tangible. When new devices—steamship boilers or space shuttles—fail or new drugs prove to have unforeseen side-effects, people die. Sometimes the costs are less obvious.

The proponents of technology answer that if a machine fails, it needs to be fixed, not banned. If a drug has side-effects, it may need to be refined or its permitted recipients may have to be better defined (the banned tranquilizer thalidomide is famous for causing birth defects when taken early in pregnancy; it is apparently quite safe for men and nonpregnant women).

## Certainty vs. Uncertainty

Another root for the debates over science and technology is uncertainty. Science is by its very nature uncertain. Its truths are provisional, open to revision.

Unfortunately, most people are told by politicians, religious leaders, and newspaper columnists that truth is certain. They therefore believe that if someone admits uncertainty, their position is weak and they need not be heeded. This is, of course, an open invitation for demagogues to prey upon fears of disaster or side-effects or upon the wish to be told that the omens of greenhouse warming and ozone holes (etc.) are mere figments of the scientific imagination.

## Natural vs. Unnatural

Still another source of controversy is rooted in the tendency of new ideas—in science and technology as in politics, history, literary criticism, and so on—to clash with preexisting beliefs or values. These clashes become most public when they pit science against religion and "family values." When heart transplants were new, at least one religious group rejected them on the grounds that they were a kind of cannibalism. The group changed its mind later, but the battle between evolution and creationism still stirs passions a century and a half after Darwin first said human beings had nonhuman predecessors. It is nearly as provocative to suggest that homosexuality is a natural variant of human behavior (rather than a twisted choice of evil over good), or that there might be a genetic component to intelligence or aggressiveness (perhaps detectable as an innate difference between groups such as blacks and whites), or that the traditional mode of human reproduction might be expanded with in vitro fertilization, cloning, or even genetic engineering.

Many new developments are rejected as "unnatural." For most people, "natural" seems to mean any device or procedure to which they have become accustomed. Very few realize how "unnatural" are such ordinary things as circumcision and horseshoes and baseball.

The search for and the application of knowledge is perhaps the human species' single most defining characteristic. Other creatures also use tools, communicate, love, play, and reason. Only humans have embraced change. We are forever creating variations on our religions, languages, politics, and tools. Innovation is as natural to us as building dams is to a beaver.

## Voodoo Science

Public confusion over science and technology is increased by several factors. One is the failure of public education. In 2002, the Committee on Technological Literacy of the National Academy of Engineering and the National Research Council published a report (*Technically Speaking: Why All Americans Need to Know More about Technology*) that said that although the United States is defined by and dependent on science and technology, "its citizens are not equipped to make well-considered decisions or to think critically about technology. As a society, we are not even fully aware of or conversant with the technologies we use every day."

A second factor is the willingness of some to mislead. Alarmists stress awful possible consequences of new technology without paying attention to actual evidence, they demand certainty when it is impossible, and they reject the new because it is untraditional or even "unthinkable." And then there are the marketers, hypesters, fraudsters, activists, and even legitimate scientists and critics who oversell their claims. Robert L. Park, author of *Voodoo Science: The Road from Foolishness to Fraud* (Oxford University Press, 2002) lists seven warning signs "that a scientific claim lies well outside the bounds of rational scientific discourse" and should be viewed warily:

- The discoverer pitches his claim directly to the media, without permitting peer review.
- The discoverer says that a powerful establishment is trying to suppress his or her work.
- The scientific effect involved is always at the very limit of detection.
- Evidence for a discovery is only anecdotal.
- The discoverer says a belief is credible because it has endured for centuries.
- The discoverer has worked in isolation.
- The discoverer must propose new laws of nature to explain an observation.

## The Soul of Science

The standard picture of science—a world of observations and hypotheses, experiments and theories, a world of sterile white coats and laboratories and cold, unfeeling logic—is a myth of our times. It has more to do with the way science is presented by both scientists and the media than with the way scientists actually do their work. In practice, scientists are often less orderly, less logical, and more prone to very human conflicts of personality than most people suspect.

The myth remains because it helps to organize science. It provides labels and a framework for what a scientist does; it may thus be especially valuable to student scientists who are still learning the ropes. In addition, it embodies certain important ideals of scientific thought. It is these ideals that make the scientific approach the most powerful and reliable guide to truth about the world that human beings have yet devised.

## The Ideals of Science: Skepticism, Communication, and Reproducibility

The soul of science is a very simple idea: *Check it out.* Scholars used to think that all they had to do to do their duty by the truth was to say "According to . . . " some ancient authority such as Aristotle or the Bible. If someone with a suitably illustrious reputation had once said something was so, it was so. Arguing with authority or holy writ could get you charged with heresy and imprisoned or burned at the stake.

This attitude is the opposite of everything that modern science stands for. As Carl Sagan says in *The Demon-Haunted World: Science as a Candle in the Dark* (Random House, 1995, p. 28), "One of the great commandments of science is, 'Mistrust arguments from authority.'" Scientific knowledge is based not on authority but on reality itself. Scientists take nothing on faith. They are *skeptical.* When they want to know something, they do not look it up in the library or take others' word for it. They go into the laboratory, the forest, the desert—wherever they can find the phenomena they wish to know about—and they ask those phenomena directly. They look for answers in the book of nature. And if they think they know the answer already, it is not of books that they ask, "Are we right?" but of nature. This is the point of "scientific experiments"—they are how scientists ask nature whether their ideas check out.

This "check it out" ideal is, however, an ideal. No one can possibly check everything out for himself or herself. Even scientists, in practice, look things up in books. They too rely on authorities. But the authorities they rely on are other scientists who have studied nature and reported what they learned. In principle, everything those authorities report can be checked. Observations in the lab or in the field can be repeated. New theoretical or computer models can be designed. What is in the books can be confirmed.

In fact, a good part of the official "scientific method" is designed to make it possible for any scientist's findings or conclusions to be confirmed. Scientists do not say, "Vitamin D is essential for strong bones. Believe me. I know." They say, "I know that vitamin D is essential for proper bone formation because I raised rats without vitamin D in their diet, and their bones turned out soft and crooked. When I gave them vitamin D, their bones hardened and straightened. Here is the kind of rat I used, the kind of food I fed them, the amount of vitamin D I gave them. Go thou and do likewise, and you will see what I saw."

*Communication* is therefore an essential part of modern science. That is, in order to function as a scientist, you must not keep secrets. You must tell others not just what you have learned by studying nature, but how you learned it. You must spell out your methods in enough detail to let others repeat your work.

Scientific knowledge is thus *reproducible* knowledge. Strictly speaking, if a person says, "I can see it, but you can't," that person is not a scientist. Scientific knowledge exists for everyone. Anyone who takes the time to learn the proper techniques can confirm it. They don't have to believe in it first.

---

As an exercise, devise a way to convince a red-green colorblind person, who sees no difference between red and green, that such a difference really exists. That is, show that a knowledge of colors is reproducible, and therefore scientific, knowledge, rather than something more like belief in ghosts or telepathy.

Here's a hint: Photographic light meters respond to light hitting a sensor. Photographic filters permit light of only a single color to pass through.

# The Standard Model of the Scientific Method

As it is usually presented, the scientific method has five major components. They include *observation, generalization* (identifying a pattern), stating a *hypothesis* (a tentative extension of the pattern or explanation for why the pattern exists), and *experimentation* (testing that explanation). The results of the tests are then *communicated* to other members of the scientific community, usually by publishing the findings. How each of these components contributes to the scientific method is discussed briefly below.

## Observation

The basic units of science—and the only real facts the scientist knows—are the individual *observations*. Using them, we look for patterns, suggest explanations, and devise tests for our ideas. Our observations can be casual, as when we notice a black van parked in front of the fire hydrant on our block. They may also be more deliberate, as what a police detective notices when he or she sets out to find clues to who has been burglarizing apartments in our neighborhood.

## Generalization

After we have made many observations, we try to discern a pattern among them. A statement of such a pattern is a *generalization*. We might form a generalization if we realized that every time there was a burglary on the block, that black van was parked by the hydrant.

Cautious experimenters do not jump to conclusions. When they think they see a pattern, they often make a few more observations just to be sure the pattern holds up. This practice of strengthening or confirming findings by *replicating* them is a very important part of the scientific process. In our example, the police would wait for the van to show up again and for another burglary to happen. Only then might they descend on the alleged villains.

## The Hypothesis

A tentative explanation suggesting why a particular pattern exists is called a *hypothesis*. In our example, the hypothesis that comes to mind is obvious: The burglars drive to work in that black van.

The mark of a good hypothesis is that it is *testable*. The best hypotheses are *predictive*. Can you devise a predictive test for the "burglars use the black van" hypothesis?

Unfortunately, tests can fail even when the hypothesis is perfectly correct. How might that happen with our example?

Many philosophers of science insist on *falsification* as a crucial aspect of the scientific method. That is, when a test of a hypothesis shows the hypothesis to be false, the hypothesis must be rejected and replaced with another.

## The Experiment

The *experiment* is the most formal part of the scientific process. The concept, however, is very simple: An experiment is nothing more than a test of a hypothesis. It is what a scientist—or a detective—does to check an idea out.

If the experiment does not falsify the hypothesis, that does not mean the hypothesis is true. It simply means that the scientist has not yet come up with the test that falsifies it. The more times and the more different ways that falsification fails, the more probable it is that the hypothesis is true. Unfortunately, because it is impossible to do all the possible tests of a hypothesis, the scientist can never *prove* it is true.

Consider the hypothesis that all cats are black. If you see a black cat, you don't really know anything at all about all cats. If you see a white cat, though, you certainly know that not all cats are black. You would have to look at every cat on Earth to prove the hypothesis. It takes just one to disprove it.

This is why philosophers of science say that *science is the art of disproving,* not proving. If a hypothesis withstands many attempts to disprove it, then it may be a good explanation of what is going on. If it fails just one test, it is clearly wrong and must be replaced with a new hypothesis.

However, researchers who study what scientists actually do point out that the truth is a little different. Almost all scientists, when they come up with what strikes them as a good explanation of a phenomenon or pattern, do *not* try to disprove their hypothesis. Instead, they design experiments to *confirm* it. If an experiment fails to confirm the hypothesis, the researcher tries another experiment, not another hypothesis.

Police detectives may do the same thing. Think of the one who found no evidence of wrongdoing in the black van but arrested the suspects anyway. Armed with a search warrant, he later searched their apartments. He was saying, in effect, "I *know* they're guilty. I just have to find the evidence to prove it."

The logical weakness in this approach is obvious, but that does not keep researchers (or detectives) from falling in love with their ideas and holding onto them as long as possible. Sometimes they hold on so long, even without confirmation of their hypothesis, that they wind up looking ridiculous. Sometimes the confirmations add up over the years and whatever attempts are made to disprove the hypothesis fail to do so. The hypothesis may then be elevated to the rank of a *theory, principle,* or *law.* Theories are explanations of how things work (the theory of evolution *by means of* natural selection). Principles and laws tend to be statements of things that happen, such as the law of gravity (masses attract each other, or what goes up comes down) or the gas law (if you increase the pressure on an enclosed gas, the volume will decrease and the temperature will increase).

## Communication

Each scientist is obligated to share her or his hypotheses, methods, and findings with the rest of the scientific community. This sharing serves two purposes. First, it supports the basic ideal of skepticism by making it possible for others to say, "Oh, yeah? Let me check that." It tells those others where to see what the scientist saw, what techniques to use, and what tools to use.

Second, it gets the word out so that others can use what has been discovered. This is essential because science is a cooperative endeavor. People who work thousands of miles apart build with and upon each other's discoveries, and some of the most exciting discoveries have involved bringing together information from very different fields, as when geochemistry, paleontology, and astronomy came together to reveal that what killed off the dinosaurs 65 million years ago was apparently the impact of a massive comet or asteroid with the Earth.

Scientific cooperation stretches across time as well. Every generation of scientists both uses and adds to what previous generations have discovered. As Isaac Newton said, "If I have seen further than [other men], it is by standing upon the shoulders of Giants" (Letter to Robert Hooke, February 5, 1675/6).

The communication of science begins with a process called "peer review," which typically has three stages. The first occurs when a scientist seeks funding—from government agencies, foundations, or other sources—to carry out a research program. He or she must prepare a report describing the intended work, laying out background, hypotheses, planned experiments, expected results, and even the broader impacts on other fields. Committees of other scientists then go over the report to see whether the scientist knows his or her area, has the necessary abilities, and is realistic in his or her plans.

Once the scientist has the needed funding, has done the work, and has written a report of the results, that report will go to a scientific journal. Before publishing the report, the journal's editors will show it to other workers in the same or related fields and ask whether the work was done adequately, the conclusions are justified, and the report should be published.

The third stage of peer review happens after publication, when the broader scientific community gets to see and judge the work.

This three-stage quality-control filter can, of course, be short-circuited. Any scientist with independent wealth can avoid the first stage quite easily, but such scientists are much, much rarer today than they were a century or so ago. Those who remain are the object of envy. Surely it is fair to say that they are not frowned upon as are those who avoid the later two stages of the "peer review" mechanism by using vanity presses and press conferences.

On the other hand, it is certainly possible for the standard peer review mechanisms to fail. By their nature, these mechanisms are more likely to approve ideas that do not contradict what the reviewers think they already know. Yet unconventional ideas are not necessarily wrong, as Alfred Wegener proved when he tried to gain acceptance for the idea of continental drift in the early twentieth century. At the time, geologists believed the crust of the Earth—which was solid rock, after all—did not behave like liquid. Yet Wegener was proposing that the continents floated about like icebergs in the sea, bumping into each other, tearing apart (to produce matching profiles like those of South America and Africa), and bumping again. It was not until the 1960s that most geologists accepted his ideas as genuine insights instead of hare-brained delusions.

## The Need for Controls

Many years ago, I read a description of a wish machine. It consisted of an ordinary stereo amplifier with two unusual attachments. The wires that would normally be connected to a microphone were connected instead to a pair of copper plates. The wires that would normally be connected to a speaker were connected instead to a whip antenna of the sort we usually see on cars.

To use this device, one put a picture of some desired item between the copper plates. It could be a photo of a person with whom one wanted a date, a lottery ticket, a college, anything. One test case used a photo of a pest-infested cornfield. One then wished fervently for the date, a winning ticket, a college acceptance, or whatever else one craved. In the test case, that meant wishing that all the cornfield pests should drop dead.

Supposedly the wish would be picked up by the copper plates, amplified by the stereo amplifier, and then sent via the whip antenna wherever wish-orders have to go. Whoever or whatever fills those orders would get the message, and then. . . . Well, in the test case, the result was that when the testers checked the cornfield, there was no longer any sign of pests.

What's more, the process worked equally well whether the amplifier was plugged in or not.

I'm willing to bet that you are now feeling very much like a scientist—skeptical. The true, dedicated scientist, however, does not stop with saying, "Oh, yeah? Tell me another one!" Instead, he or she says something like, "Mmm. I wonder. Let's check this out." (Must we, really? After all, we can be quite sure that the wish machine does not work because if it did, it would be on the market. Casinos would then be unable to make a profit for their backers. Deadly diseases would not be deadly. And so on.)

Where must the scientist begin? The standard model of the scientific method says the first step is observation. Here, our observations (as well as our necessary generalization) are simply the description of the wish machine and the claims for its effectiveness. Perhaps we even have an example of the physical device itself.

What is our hypothesis? We have two choices, one consistent with the claims for the device, one denying those claims: The wish machine always works, or the wish machine never works. Both are equally testable, but perhaps one is more easily falsifiable. (Which one?)

How do we test the hypothesis? Set up the wish machine, and perform the experiment of making a wish. If the wish comes true, the device works. If it does not, it doesn't.

Can it really be that simple? In essence, yes. But in fact, no.

Even if you don't believe that wishing can make something happen, sometimes wishes do come true by sheer coincidence. Therefore, if the wish machine is as nonsensical as most people think it is, sometimes it will *seem* to work. We therefore need a way to shield against the misleading effects of coincidence. We need a way to *control* the possibilities of error.

Coincidence is not, of course, the only source of error we need to watch out for. For instance, there is a very human tendency to interpret events in such a way as to agree with our preexisting beliefs, our prejudices. If we believe in wishes, we therefore need a way to guard against our willingness to interpret near misses as not quite misses at all. There is also a human tendency not to look for mistakes when the results agree with our prejudices. That cornfield, for instance, might not have been as badly infested as the testers said it was, or a farmer might have sprayed it with pesticide whether the testers had wished or not, or the field they checked might have been the wrong one.

We would also like to check whether the wish machine does indeed work equally well plugged in or not, and then we must guard against the tendency to wish harder when we know it's plugged in. We would like to know whether the photo between the copper plates makes any difference, and then we must guard against the tendency to wish harder when we know the wish matches the photo.

Coincidence is easy to protect against. All that is necessary is to repeat the experiment enough times to be sure we are not seeing flukes. This is one major purpose of replication.

Our willingness to shade the results in our favor can be defeated by having someone else judge the results of our wishing experiments. Our eagerness to overlook "favorable" errors can be defeated by taking great care to avoid any errors at all; peer reviewers also help by pointing out such problems.

The other sources of error are harder to avoid, but scientists have developed a number of helpful *control* techniques. One is "blinding." In essence, it means setting things up so the scientist does not know what he or she is doing.

In the pharmaceutical industry, this technique is used whenever a new drug must be tested. A group of patients are selected. Half of them—chosen randomly to avoid any unconscious bias that might put sicker, taller, shorter, male, female, homosexual, black, or white patients in one group instead of the other—are given the drug. The others are given a dummy pill, or a sugar pill, also known as a placebo. In all other respects, the two groups are treated exactly the same. Drug (and other) researchers take great pains to be sure groups of experimental subjects are alike in every way but the one way being tested. Here that means the only difference between the groups should be which one gets the drug and which one gets the placebo.

Unfortunately, placebos can have real medical effects, apparently because we *believe* our doctors when they tell us that a pill will cure what ails us. We have faith in them, and our minds do their best to bring our bodies into line. This mind-over-body "placebo effect" seems to be akin to faith healing.

*Single Blind.* The researchers therefore do not tell the patients what pill they are getting. The patients are "blinded" to what is going on. Both placebo and drug then gain equal advantage from the placebo effect. If the drug seems to work better or worse than the placebo, then the researchers can be sure of a real difference between the two.

*Double Blind.* Or can they? Unfortunately, if the researchers know what pill they are handing out, they can give subtle, unconscious cues. Or they may interpret any changes in symptoms in favor of the drug. It is therefore best to keep the researchers in the dark too; since both researchers and patients are now blind to the truth, the experiment is said to be "double blind." Drug trials often use pills that differ only in color or in the number on the bottle, and the code is not broken until all the results are in. This way nobody knows who gets what until the knowledge can no longer make a difference.

Obviously, the double-blind approach can work only when there are human beings on both sides of the experiment, as experimenter and as experimental subject. When the object of the experiment is an inanimate object such as a wish machine, only the single-blind approach is possible.

With suitable precautions against coincidence, self-delusion, wishful thinking, bias, and other sources of error, the wish machine could be convincingly tested. Yet it cannot be perfectly tested, for perhaps it works only sometimes, when the aurora glows green over Copenhagen, in months without an "r," or when certain people use it. It is impossible to rule out all the possibilities, although we can rule out enough to be pretty confident as we call the gadget nonsense.

Very similar precautions are essential in every scientific field, for the same sources of error lie in wait wherever experiments are done, and they serve very much the same function. However, we must stress that no controls and no peer review system, no matter how elaborate, can completely protect a scientist—or science—from error.

Here, as well as in the logical impossibility of proof (experiments only fail to disprove) and science's dependence on the progressive growth of knowledge (its requirement that each scientist make his or her discoveries while standing on the shoulders of the giants who went before, if you will) lies the uncertainty that is the hallmark of science. Yet it is also a hallmark of science that its methods guarantee that uncertainty will be reduced (not eliminated). Frauds and errors will be detected and corrected. Limited understandings of truth will be extended.

Those who bear this in mind will be better equipped to deal with issues of certainty and risk.

Something else to bear in mind is that argument is an inevitable part of science. The combination of communication and skepticism very frequently leads scientists into debates with each other. The scientist's willingness to be skeptical about and hence to challenge received wisdom leads to debates with everyone else. A book like this one is an unrealistic portrayal of science only because it covers such a small fraction of all the arguments available.

## Is Science Worth It?

What scientists do as they apply their methods is called *research.* Scientists who perform *basic or fundamental research* seek no specific result. Basic research is motivated essentially by curiosity. It is the study of some intriguing aspect of nature for its own sake. Basic researchers have revealed vast amounts of detail about the chemistry and function of genes, explored the behavior of electrons in semiconductors, revealed the structure of the atom, discovered radioactivity, and opened our minds to the immensity in both time and space of the universe in which we live.

*Applied or strategic research* is more mission-oriented. Applied scientists turn basic discoveries into devices and processes, such as transistors, computers, antibiotics, vaccines, nuclear weapons and power plants, and communications and weather satellites. There are thousands of such examples, all of which are answers to specific problems or needs, and many of which were quite surprising to the basic researchers who first gained the raw knowledge that led to these developments.

It is easy to see what drives the movement to put science to work. Society has a host of problems that cry out for immediate solutions. Yet there is also a need for research that is not tied to explicit need because such research undeniably supplies a great many of the ideas, facts, and techniques that problem-solving researchers then use in solving society's problems. Basic researchers, of course, use the same ideas, facts, and techniques as they continue their probings into the way nature works.

In 1945—after the scientific and technological successes of World War II—Vannevar Bush argued in *Science, the Endless Frontier* (Washington, DC: National Science Foundation, 1990) that science would continue to benefit society best if it were supported with generous funding but not controlled by society. On the record, he was quite right, for the next half-century saw an unprecedented degree of progress in medicine, transportation, computers, communications, weapons, and a great deal more.

There have been and will continue to be problems that emerge from science and its applications in technology. Some people respond like Bill Joy, who argues in "Why the Future Doesn't Need Us," *Wired* (April 2000), that some technologies—notably robotics, genetic engineering, and nanotechnology—are so hazardous that we should refrain from developing them. On the whole, however, argue those like George Conrades ("Basic Research: Long-Term Problems Facing a Long-Term Investment," *Vital Speeches of the Day,* May 15, 1999), the value of the opportunities greatly outweighs the hazards of the problems. Others are less sanguine. David H. Guston and Kenneth Keniston ("Updating the Social Contract for Science," *Technology Review,* November/December 1994) argue that despite the obvious successes of science and technology, public attitudes toward scientific research also depend on the vast expense of the scientific enterprise and the perceived risks. As a result, the public should not be "excluded from decision making about science." That is, decisions should not be left to the experts alone.

Conflict also arises over the function of science in our society. Traditionally, scientists have seen themselves as engaged in the disinterested pursuit of knowledge, solving the puzzles set before them by nature with little concern for whether the solutions to these puzzles might prove helpful to human enterprises such as war, health care, and commerce, among many more. Yet again and again the solutions found by scientists have proved useful. They have founded industries. And scientists love to quote Michael Faraday who, when asked by politicians what good the new electricity might be, replied: "Someday, sir, you will tax it."

Not surprisingly, society has come to expect science to be useful. When asked to fund research, it feels it has the right to target research on issues of social concern, to demand results of immediate value, and to forbid research it deems dangerous or disruptive.

Private interests such as corporations often feel that they have similar rights in regard to research they have funded. For instance, tobacco companies have displayed a strong tendency to fund research that shows tobacco to be safe and to cancel funding for studies that come up with other results, which might interfere with profits.

One argument for public funding is that it avoids such conflict-of-interest issues. Yet politicians have their own interests, and their control of the purse strings—just like a corporation's—can give their demands a certain undeniable persuasiveness.

## Public Policy

The question of targeting research is only one way in which science and technology intersect the broader realm of public policy. Here the question becomes how society should allocate its resources in general: toward education or prisons? health care or welfare? research or trade? encouraging new technologies or cleaning up after old ones?

The problem is that money is finite. Faced with competing worthy goals, we must make choices. We must also run the risk that our choices will turn out to have been foolish.

## The Purpose of This Book

Is there any prospect that the debates over the proper function of science, the acceptability of new technologies, or the truth of forecasts of disaster will soon fall quiet? Surely not, for some of the old issues will forever refuse to die (think of evolution vs. creationism), and there will always be new issues to debate afresh. Some of the new issues will strut upon the stage of history only briefly, but they will in their existence reflect something significant about the way human beings view science and technology. Some will remain controversial as long as has evolution or the population explosion (which has been debated ever since Thomas Malthus' 1798 "Essay on the Principle of Population"). Some will flourish and fade and return to prominence; early editions of this book included the debate over whether the last stocks of smallpox virus should be destroyed; they were not, and the war on terrorism has brought awareness of the virus and the need for smallpox vaccine back onto the public stage. The loss of the space shuttle *Columbia* reawakened the debate over whether space should be explored by people or machines. Some issues will remain live but change their form, as has the debate over government interception of electronic communications. And there will always be more issues than can be squeezed into a book like this one—think, for instance, of the debate over whether nonlethal weapons are better than lethal ones (discussed by Mark Wheelis in "'Nonlethal' Chemical Weapons: A Faustian Bargain," *Issues in Science and Technology,* Spring 2003; Eric Adams, "Shoot to Not Kill," *Popular Science,* May 2003).

Since almost all of these science and technology issues can or will affect the conditions of our daily lives, we should know something about them. We can begin by examining the nature of science and a few of the current controversies over issues in science and technology. After all, if one does not know what science, the scientific mode of thought, and their strengths and limitations are, one cannot think critically and constructively about any issue with a scientific or technological component. Nor can one hope to make informed choices among competing scientific, technological, or political and social priorities.

# On the Internet . . .

## Science and Technology Policy

The Federal Office of Science and Technology Policy advises the President on how science and technology affects domestic and international affairs.

http://www.ostp.gov/

## Institute for Creation Research

According to the developers of this site, the Institute for Creation Research (ICR) is a major center of scientific creationism.

http://www.icr.org

## Committee for the Scientific Investigation of Claims of the Paranormal

The Committee for the Scientific Investigation of Claims of the Paranormal encourages the critical investigation of paranormal and fringe-science claims from a responsible, scientific point of view and disseminates factual information about the results of such inquiries to the scientific community and the public. It also promotes science and scientific inquiry, critical thinking, science education, and the use of reason in examining important issues, and it also publishes the *Skeptical Inquirer.*

http://www.csicop.org

## Science and Creationism

The National Academy of Sciences maintains this page of links and resources on science and creationism.

http://www.nationalacademies.org/evolution/

PART 1

# The Place of Science and Technology in Society

*The partnership between human society and science and technology is an uneasy one. Science and technology offer undoubted benefits, in both the short and long term, but they also challenge received wisdom and present us with new worries, perhaps especially when they fall into the wrong hands. The issues in this section deal with, whether access to scientific and technological information should be controlled, the conflict between science and traditional elements of society, and the debate over creationism versus evolution.*

- Should Society Restrict the Publication of Unclassified but "Sensitive" Research?
- Is Science a Faith?
- Should Creationism and Evolution Get Equal Time in Schools?

# ISSUE 1

## Should Society Restrict the Publication of Unclassified but "Sensitive" Research?

**YES: Lewis M. Branscomb,** from "The Changing Relationship between Science and Government Post-September 11," Chapter 2 in Albert H. Teich, Stephen D. Nelson, and Stephen J. Lita, eds., *Science and Technology in a Vulnerable World* (Washington, DC: Committee on Science, Engineering, and Public Policy, American Association for the Advancement of Science, 2002)

**NO: Charles M. Vest,** from "Response and Responsibility: Balancing Security and Openness in Research and Education," *Report of the President for the Academic Year* 2001–2002 (Cambridge, MA: Massachusetts Institute of Technology, 2002)

### ISSUE SUMMARY

**YES:** Lewis M. Branscomb asserts that because the results of much scientific research have the potential to aid terrorists, there is a need to control the publication and distribution of "sensitive but unclassified" information.

**NO:** Charles M. Vest maintains that the rapid progress of science and technology depends critically on openness of publication of and access to research results.

The fall of 2001 was remarkable for two events. One was the al Qaeda use of hijacked airliners to destroy the World Trade Towers in New York City. The other was the still-mysterious appearance of anthrax spores in the mail. The two do not seem to have been related, but together they created a climate of fear and mistrust. Part of that fear and mistrust was aimed at science and technology, for the al Qaeda terrorists had used computers and the Internet for communicating with each other, and whoever was responsible for the anthrax scare obviously knew too much about anthrax. One response was the Bush Administration's March 2002 declaration that some information—notably the results of scientific research, especially in the life sciences—might not be classified in the ways long familiar to researchers in nuclear physics (for instance), but it could still be considered "sensitive" and thus worthy of restrictions on publication and dissemination. The Department of Defence (DoD) announced—and promptly dropped—plans to restrict the use and spread of unclassified DoD-funded research. However, a National Academy of Sciences report on agricultural bioterrorism that contained no classified information was censored on the insistence of the Department of Agriculture "to keep potentially dangerous information away from enemies of the United States." National security experts warned "that the current system of openness in science could lead to dire consequences." [See Richard Monastersky, "Publish and Perish?" *Chronicle of Higher Education* (October 11, 2002).] However, many have objected to inventing and attempting to restrict the new "sensitive but unclassified" category of information. Steven Teitelbaum, president of the Federation of American Societies for Experimental Biology, said, "information should be either classified or not classified."

In July 2002, researchers announced that they had successfully assembled a polio virus from biochemicals and the virus's gene map. Members of Congress called for more care in releasing such information, and the American Society for Microbiology (ASM) began to debate voluntary restrictions on publication. By August, the ASM had policy guidelines dictating that journal submissions that contain "information . . . that could be put to inappropriate use" be carefully reviewed and even rejected. The ASM policy has met surprisingly little active resistance, for though "New Antiterrorism Tenets Trouble Scientists," [Peg Brickley, *The Scientist* (October 28, 2002)], many researchers see the need for restraint. However, many say, there is a need for new rules to be very clear [see David Malakoff, "Researchers See Progress in Finding the Right Balance," *Science* (October 18, 2002)].

In April 2002, the American Association for the Advancement of Science (AAAS) held its annual Colloquium on Science and Technology Policy. The papers in the resulting book [*Science and Technology in a Vulnerable World,* Albert H. Teich, Stephen D. Nelson, and Stephen J. Lita, eds. (AAAS, 2002)] included Lewis M. Branscomb's argument that because the results of much scientific research have the potential to aid terrorists, there is a need to control the publication and distribution of "sensitive but unclassified" information. Other essays discussed the impact of such controls on science and the university culture, but none had quite the thrust of Charles M. Vest's report to the MIT community, in which he insisted that openness in science must preempt fears of the consequences of scientific knowledge falling into the wrong hands. Indeed, MIT forbids classified research on campus, relegating it instead to satellite laboratories.

**Lewis M. Branscomb**

**YES**

# The Changing Relationship between Science and Government Post-September 11

The events of September 11, 2001 came as a great shock to the American people. But the anticipation of that day goes back a long time. Exactly 25 years ago Harvard professor Gerald Holton . . . describe[d] three kinds of terrorism. Type I is traditional terrorism by an individual or small group of people who are determined to wreak havoc for reasons of their own. It is not connected with any government. Type II terrorism is conducted by a dysfunctional state, unable to deal with the rest of the world through normal interstate relationships. This state engages in terrorism either against its own people or against others. Type III terrorism occurs when the Type I terrorist (a stateless terrorist group) finds that it can get resources and technical support from a Type II terrorist state.

We now face Type III terrorism. We must understand that the source of our vulnerability to terrorism is not the terrorists themselves. Our vulnerability is generated by our economic, social, and political systems. . . . If you have a highly competitive market economy, everyone is driven to greater efficiency. But the public also wants stability. Stability, with only small perturbations, is built into the system. But this does not work unless you have a peaceful, obedient society that does not threaten to exploit these vulnerabilities. This society cannot avoid threats to leverage that very hyper-efficiency.

## University-Government Relationships

University-government relationships have changed with every major war. Before and during World War II, and even for some time after, everyone understood that you dropped what you were doing when your country needed you. The science and technology community was totally dedicated to defeating the enemy, which was known and identifiable. Everyone pulled together in the expectation of unconditional surrender by the enemy. The war would have an end point, after which there would be peaceful life and civil society again.

The Cold War was somewhat different, in that it was of indefinite duration. But it was similar because the opponent was a state, which was well-known and well-recognized. We produced an unresilient (but effective) strategy called mutually assured destruction (MAD). The military and foreign policy people had the responsibility to manage that problem. Society had to support it, but it did not really upset our civil life. The military-industrial complex ran the "war." Academic support was primarily through the basic research agencies (such as the Office of Naval Research, the Air Force Office of Scientific Research, the Army Research Office, and the Defense Advanced Research Projects Agency).

The war on terrorism is different. We have an unknown enemy in our midst, and the duration is indefinite. We are creating vulnerabilities all the time. Unless we do something different, it is going to get worse.

The universities need to support the nation in this war, building on their traditional values. But we need some significant changes. Catastrophic terrorism is the ultimate in asymmetric warfare. We depended on S&T [science and technology] to compensate for the asymmetry in the Cold War, when Soviet forces greatly outnumbered ours. We compensated by having our forces technically superior. But, now, each terrorist threat is in some ways a new war. Terrorists are technically competent and may be armed with weapons of mass destruction. To what extent can S&T compensate for this asymmetry? What is the role of and the effect on the universities? . . .

## Countering Terrorism

There are three ways to counter terrorism. One, you can reduce the incentives that create and motivate terrorists. This approach clearly falls in the category of foreign and military policies, international relations and alliances, and intelligence. S&T can certainly contribute here, through technical means and gathering intelligence and through social science studies. The ideal solution would be to make this a peaceful world in which the number of individuals willing to kill themselves to destroy societies was greatly reduced. But that is very hard to do.

Another way is to detect and arrest the terrorists. This is essentially a police function. This may be the cheapest of the three, but it is the one that bears most heavily on civil rights and civil liberties.

The third way is to harden the target society, that is, make it more difficult for the terrorists to attack. We do this by detecting their preparations, intercepting their plans, making the targets less vulnerable, limiting the damage they can do, and enhancing the recovery. Industry has a role to play in this area. But we must motivate industry to reduce the vulnerabilities inherent in our society.

## The Nature of the Vulnerabilities

We credit science and technology not only for creating an efficient economy, but also for creating the weapons that terrorists use. These weapons are based on the same technologies we use domestically for beneficial purposes. Our S&T strategy to address this has to be very sophisticated. It has to use the very S&T that creates the vulnerabilities to lessen those vulnerabilities.

One of our biggest problems is that the critical elements of our infrastructure are deeply linked. When one part is attacked, we see a domino effect on the other parts. The three most obvious infrastructure elements are energy, communications, and transportation. If you bring down any one of these three, the other two are affected. For example, if you bring the energy sector down, you cannot communicate and you cannot travel. There is a lot you cannot do. Terrorists understand that, and we must deal with this reality. We have to consider the threat of multiple, simultaneous attacks on our infrastructure.

Another problem was brought on by deregulation, by getting the federal government out of the markets. Over the last decade, we have introduced more competition, particularly in the energy area, by deregulating. One result of that is a significant increase in vulnerability.

The threats are now more varied than simply the weapons of mass destruction. They include bioterrorism, chemical warfare, nuclear attack, and radiation contamination. All of these threats affect infrastructure issues. They come together in the cities where people are, because people are the targets. In cities we face the key issue of managing the warnings of an attack, as well as the attack itself. We also have to support the first responders.

And, finally, of course, our defense has to address the issues of intelligence and borders. One of the unfortunate characteristics of almost every feature of security and defense, whether security against crime or against minor acts of terrorism, is based on a single, thin wall. We try to check people coming into the country, but once they are legally in, they are in. We can put a fence around a critical facility, but if you can overcome it, you are in. That is characteristic of most of our systems, even in the computer area. Computer security has the same thin wall, and it does not work. We need a lot of technical tools to address this. They include sensor systems, data systems and networks, biomedical vaccines, chemical warfare treatments, and biometrics for efficient identification. Some of these involve cross-cutting issues and human factors-decision systems.

Terrorism, to a greater degree than any problem before, calls for a new way of thinking about the nature of the threats and how to deal with them. It calls for systems engineering and analysis. It calls for strategy-driven goals for the research program and the creation of new capabilities. Basic research will help us develop the strategy we need. It will not give us the answers to the current problem, but it will tell us how to change the questions.

## Basic Research

Basic research, if it removes ignorance in critical areas, can give us a whole new way to approach this problem and make it easier to solve. That, in my view, is the critical role of basic research. But when you think about it, the government is not well-structured to do anything that is built on a systems strategy that cuts across all the current missions and areas of technical activity in the country. Countering terrorism is going to touch on every discipline in the universities, not just technical areas. Importantly, this time we have to pay attention to what the social sciences and humanities have to contribute.

Many different fields will need to address the many requirements of the war on terrorism. Developing sensors and dealing with hazardous materials will involve chemistry, physics, and engineering. Nuclear and radiological threats will be addressed by nuclear science. Bioterrorism will need the biomedical sciences and medical services. Threats against energy will be on the agenda of the physical facilities themselves, their infrastructure links, engineering, and information technology. Transportation and distribution are in the realm of engineering. Protecting our water, food, and agriculture will need people from biology and chemistry. Cyberattacks will be met by information science and engineering. Cities and people will be protected by the social and behavioral sciences. Infrastructure linkages will be taken care of by systems analysis and systems engineering people.

The political world has always been skeptical about the contributions of the social sciences and humanities. There are areas of which social science cannot give actionable advice, but there are many other areas where it absolutely can. Social scientists have studied the terrorism problem in great detail and have things to tell us that are very important.

## R&D Capability and Mobilization

The big difficulty is that the government and the universities are "stovepiped," with different areas in technical work segregated into different organizations; financed by specific agencies. In the government, we do not have to create an S&T capability. We have fabulous S&T capability. It is nurtured by agencies born out of World War II and the Cold War. These agencies have massive capability to mobilize American science and technology. They are well-known: the National Institutes of Health [NIH], the National Science Foundation [NSF], the U.S. Departments of Energy (DOE), Defense and the National Aeronautics and Space Administration. These are big organizations devoted to a technical enterprise. But they do not, with the possible exception of the Department of Defense and some of DOE, have the mission of domestic security against terrorism. That mission is in agencies like the Federal Emergency Management Agency, the U.S. Customs Service, the Immigration and Naturalization Service, the U.S. Coast Guard, and the U.S. Department of Transportation. The latter is a technical agency, but it has never had a very strong research and development (R&D) capability. There are many other agencies, as well as state and local governments, in this situation. So the customers for science and technology are agencies with very little R&D experience.

Most of the U.S. R&D capability is in the hands of agencies that do not have the mission of countering terrorism. So how can we put all that together? When you go to the universities to get work done in physics, you know where to go. But if you want to solve a more complex problem, the universities are not internally structured, in most cases, to work on it. The implementation of any strategy depends on the federal government, which is capable of deploying most of the nation's capability (except that in the private sector).

We do not want to disrupt the present S&T capability. Instead, we are going to have to create an architecture for defining not only a strategy for using S&T in counterterrorism and managing its execution, but we also have to help the President manage that process. This requires linked-systems approaches and intersectional collaboration (involving the federal government, states, cities, and industry). It will be a challenge. We are not very experienced in this area. But most counterterrorism research must be interdisciplinary and in a systems context. We have our work cut out for us. As I said above, government science agencies tend to be stovepiped. Interdisciplinary work is hard to peer review. But many counterterrorism problems cut across agency lines. The university structure is also poorly adapted to a systems context and multidisciplinary work. We may need some institutional innovations, both in government and in the universities.

The universities have many resources. They have research capability for creating new options and competencies. They have links to local government and industry. They have access to students and colleagues around the world. And they have relevant capability in the social sciences and humanities. But the universities have needs too. They need more research resources. They need to continue to have access to foreign resources and students, the freedom to share technical information, and acceptable levels of security. They need to be able to admit students and collaborate with foreign scientists without irrational restrictions. And they need to be able to handle and deal with the very difficult and unclear question of how sensitive information should be handled in the research community.

## Possible Effects of a New Strategy

Positive effects could come out of all this. . . . Important agencies of the government may learn how to use the research capacity of the country. We could also broaden the base of support, with new sources and levels of funding. . . .

[T]he right research strategy will benefit "dual use" technologies. We can define problems to address civil as well as security needs. For example, we could develop better ways to detect an infection prior to seeing clinical symptoms. We can also develop ways to make needed capabilities affordable. New probes and sensors that identify and track containers reduce costs in time and money in normal commercial shipping. This has wide application. We can also find new ways to deal with natural disasters. This would include advancements in communications, robotics, and even clothing for firefighters and hazardous materials specialists. We could also improve threat characterization for first responders. . . .

The good news is that basic research may emerge out of this to be seen as a strategic necessity. We may see a new balance between the physical and health sciences. Because the problem is so ill defined, we need an open-ended, imaginative, creative way of thinking about it. This will only come out of the basic research community, which has been substantially funded by the traditional civilian agencies (NSF, NIH, DOE, etc.).

The bad news is that as agencies re-label a large part of their programs as counterterrorism, they invite constraints. The research may be the same, but it may now be labeled as defending the country, and, therefore, critically important to national security. So Congress, knowing that the universities are so important, may put constraints on communication, publication, and the like, beyond what ought to be done. Legislation and agency policy may place information restrictions on grants. Indeed, counterterrorism is a preempting budget priority. So if you cannot re-label your program as counterterrorism, then that part of your budget may suffer. I hope this will not be the case.

We must look seriously at the government's inability to manage cross-cutting research programs. Counterterrorism requires a systems approach. The systems approach demands capability at the top level of government to develop national research programs. This will help with maximizing interdisciplinary research, but it is going to put additional burdens on the White House Office of Science and Technology Policy, the Office of Homeland Security, and others. But it is very important that we have a strong, visionary capability to lead the definition of how S&T can help in this area. If successful, we can apply this approach to sustainable development, climate change, and other areas that challenge our quality of life.

## Control of Information

The control of sensitive information is a big issue. This is a quote from *The Economist,* which I think is very perceptive.

> Knowledge is power. Those who possess it have always sought to deny it to their enemies. . . . But exactly what knowledge needs to be controlled depends on who those enemies are. Nor is the control of knowledge without cost.
>
> A free society should regard it as a last resort. Scientists cannot build on each other's results if they do not know them. And governments are frequently tempted to hide not only what is dangerous, but also what is embarrassing. That can result in dangers of its own.[1]

Unfortunately, the present state of government controls on information is chaotic. The system of military secret classification is not adapted to the terrorist threat. The U.S. Department of Health and Human Services has no legal authority to classify information as "secret." This means that information that could be extraordinarily dangerous if it were publicly known to the terrorists is not protected. We have to protect this information in some way until the rules are worked out as to how this will be done routinely. The term "sensitive but unclassified" is likely to be applied to much university work, even though it has no clear definition. We see serious, legitimate dilemmas about what should, in fact, be published. Add to this the Patriot Act (PL 107-56), which authorizes intrusion into the Internet, servers, answering machines, and other telecommunication equipment. (It also requires colleges to turn over student records, and requires the National Center for Education Statistics to turn over data in response to a warrant.)

This poses the question, but it does not give the answer, of how this will be done. Ultimately, we need to resolve a lot of open issues with respect to the government's view of sensitive information.

Security and intelligence on university campuses is a much more difficult problem now than during the Cold War. Public interest in security lapses at universities, real or imagined, will be intense. Terrorist threats are extraordinarily diverse and of indefinite duration. The public will expect research universities to track students who may be perceived as threats.

## Conclusion

I think the scientific community is going to have to engage in a long debate. It should have started before September 11 because this debate has to do with things besides terrorism. It has to do with the moral and ethical responsibility of individual scientists and engineers. We all must think about how they can relate our activity in science, our communication, and all the things we do in a way that we believe benefits the long-term public interest.

Must the culture of science evolve to discourage its misuse? If so, in what ways? Is there a consensus on the expectations scientists place on themselves now? I believe that thoughtful self-constraint is the only way to maintain the creativity of science and still protect the country.

## Note

1. Secrets and lives. 2002. *The Economist,* March 9.

NO 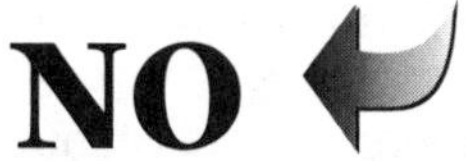

**Charles M. Vest**

# Response and Responsibility: Balancing Security and Openness in Research and Education

## Openness and Security

The ability of our nation to remain secure in the face of both traditional military threats and international terrorism while maintaining the excellence and pace of American science and technology requires a delicate balance. It depends first and foremost on effective dialogue and joint problem solving by those responsible for maintaining our security and those who lead our scientific, engineering, and higher education communities.

Our immediate impulse when threatened is to wall ourselves off and to regulate the release of information of potential use to our enemies. This is understandable, and frequently justified, but in today's complicated world, the security issues raised regarding research and education do not lend themselves to simple responses—especially when long-term consequences are considered. Why?

The future health, economic strength, and quality of life in America, and indeed the world, depend on the continued rapid advance of science and technology, and on the education of scientists and engineers at the most advanced levels. The rapid progress of science and technology, and the advanced education of scientists and engineers, in turn, depends critically on openness of process, openness of publication, and openness of participation within our institutions and across national boundaries.

Historically, our nation and world have faced many challenges to peace and security. Now we face a constant threat of determined terrorists. Their immediate objectives are to kill large numbers of people, or to cause terror, panic, or disruptions of our lives and economy.

As we respond to the reality of terrorism, we must not unintentionally disable the quality and rapid evolution of American science and technology, or of advanced education, by closing their various boundaries. For if we did, the irony is that over time this would achieve in substantial

From the Report of the President for the Academic Year 2001–2002 Cambridge MA: Massachusetts Institute of Technology, 2001. 

measure the objectives of those who disdain our society and would do us harm by disrupting our economy and quality of life.

Americans are learning that the balance between protection of our lives and of our liberties is as difficult to strike as it is essential that we do so. I believe that it is equally imperative that we strike the right balance between security and the openness of our scientific research and education. But I conclude that we must rely very heavily on maintaining that openness.

In the year since the murderous attacks in New York, Washington, and Pennsylvania, the experience of MIT and other leading research-intensive universities [was] primarily one of calm and reasoned interaction and consultation with the federal government on such matters as the admission of international students and scholars, the openness of scientific research, and the control of dangerous chemical and biological agents.

However, the discussion of these issues and the establishment of a regulatory environment associated with homeland security are far from over. It therefore seems timely to address some of the fundamental issues and long-term consequences of our decisions.

Before doing so, let me make clear that, although it is not the topic of this essay, MIT and our sister institutions take very seriously our responsibility to serve our nation by applying our talents and capabilities to the protection of human life and infrastructure in our homeland and throughout the world. . . .

## International Students

A matter of current debate, legislation, and policy implementation is the degree to which our university campuses should remain open to international students and scholars. Who should receive student visas? Should there be limitations on what foreign-born students can study? What criteria should be applied when answering such questions?

American research universities hold deep and long-standing values of openness in scientific research and education. Yet we must test these values and their implications against the realities of the catastrophic terrorist acts that left 3,000 dead within our borders in a single, horrific day. The fact is that an environment requiring careful evaluation of these values and their security implications had developed well before September 11, 2001.

For decades, the outward diffusion of people, ideas, and collaboration from our universities has been celebrated as important and timely. This diffusion has been accelerated by the Internet and the World Wide Web, and by the rapid evolution of globalization and internationalization. These forces of openness and outward pull are now opposed by concerns about their possible implications for our vulnerability to terrorism and for the nation's broader posture regarding export controls on certain technologies and information.

Clearly, the resolution of these issues requires an ongoing, substantive dialogue between the academic community and the Federal Government. In my view, during the past twelve months, such a dialogue has begun and in general has proceeded well toward reasoned resolution of several core issues. Nonetheless, the underlying sense of partnership is fragile and is vulnerable to political winds that can shift in a moment. It would be devastating to our long-term national interest if substantive dialogue and mutual problem solving were not continued. . . .

- The openness of U.S. research universities to foreign students and scholars has been overwhelmingly successful in building the excellence of our institutions, enhancing the educational experience of our students, contributing to American industry and academia, furthering the advancement of nations around the world, and disbursing good will toward and understanding of our system and values.
- Nationally, the proportion of foreign students in science and engineering doctoral programs continues to grow. This, however, is largely a reflection of problems in our secondary educational system coupled with a popular culture that does not promote or value the dedication and long years of hard work required for success in these fields.
- Our openness to international students and scholars has been questioned or reviewed many times throughout our history, including during the most recent decades.

We now find ourselves in perilous times that require that we consider, in partnership with our Federal government, whether our openness to foreign students requires modification. Indeed, statutory requirements for such determinations are already in place. We have the harsh reality that a few of those responsible for the bombing of the World Trade Center in 1993, and the mass killings in New York, Washington and Pennsylvania last year, entered this country on student visas. We also have the concern that future catastrophic terrorism—unlike that committed to date—might require advanced scientific knowledge or materials that could be acquired in university classrooms or laboratories.

Thus two questions are raised: Should we track the whereabouts of foreign students, and should there be restrictions on what they study?

## Tracking International Students

Students and visiting scholars must be issued visas by U.S. consular officers around the world after they have been admitted to study at a U.S. university. The consuls have the responsibility for judging the appropriateness of admitting each such student. This is the proper division of labor—universities evaluate academic credentials, and federal officials in the State Department determine admissibility to the United States.

It is broadly agreed that once students arrive in this country universities should maintain and provide to the government fundamental "directory information" including whether each individual is enrolled and what area of study he or she is pursuing. It certainly is legitimate for the government to track non-immigrant students and scholars, and determine whether they are pursuing the purposes for which they were admitted. Despite numerous comments by journalists and politicians to the contrary, the higher education community has supported, and continues to support, such tracking.

The problem has been that this information, which is already collected by the universities, gets buried in a vast amount of paper that cannot be processed or analyzed in a timely manner. A new computer system, SEVIS (Student and Exchange Visitor Information System), is under rapid development to correct this situation. MIT supports the deployment of SEVIS, and so does every major higher education association.

## Sensitive Areas of Study

Presidential Decision Directive No. 2, issued by President Bush in October 2001, requires that the federal government, in consultation with the higher education community, determine "sensitive areas of study" that should be off limits to students from certain nations. Even this is not a new concept. There has existed for some time a State Department system called Mantis that is alerted when a potential student from certain countries applies to study in a field that appears on the Technology Alert List, e.g., nuclear engineering, lasers, sensors, ceramics, radar, electronic guidance systems, or munitions. The State Department must then generate a specific opinion as to whether the student should be granted a visa.

Nonetheless, I am deeply concerned about where implementation of this directive could lead. The basic framework, developed by the White House in consultation with agencies such as the State Department and the Department of Justice, and with considerable discussion with the higher education community, is fundamentally sound. The core of this framework is the Interagency Panel on Advanced Science and Security (IPASS). The proposed task of IPASS is widely understood to be to determine whether students or scholars applying to enter the U.S. will engage in research activities that provide access to advanced science or technology of direct relevance to the development, deployment, or delivery of weapons of mass destruction.

This framework, if I have accurately portrayed it, has two important positive features. First, it establishes a high-level review panel, rather than generating a list of specific subjects or courses considered off limits. Second, it applies to matters associated with weapons of mass destruction, which, as I will explain later in this essay, seems appropriate to me. Third, it places this judgment with the admitting authorities *at the time of visa application,* thus maximizing the openness of our institution to students once they are properly admitted to the U.S.

Where could the IPASS framework go wrong and unreasonably disrupt the basic workings of research universities? I would suggest the following potentialities as troubling or inappropriate:

- Moving beyond criteria that are based rather narrowly on weapons of mass destruction.

- Expanding criteria to cover academic courses and classes, rather than very specific research and development activities.
- Applying new academic restrictions to students after they have begun to study at the institution for which they were properly granted a visa.

Indeed, the MIT Ad Hoc Committee on Access to and Disclosure of Scientific Information, chaired by former U.S. Secretary of the Air Force Sheila E. Widnall, in its report *In the Public Interest,* recommended that "No foreign national granted a visa by the U.S. government should be denied access to courses, research or publications generally available on campus."

This Committee further stated, "The well-being of our nation will ultimately be damaged if education, science, and technology suffer as a result of any practices that indiscriminately discourage or limit the open exchange of ideas.

"We recommend that no classified research should be carried out on campus; that no student, graduate or undergraduate, should be required to have a security clearance to perform thesis research; and that no thesis research should be carried out in [intellectual] areas requiring access to classified materials."

## Scientific Materials and Information

Terrorism to date has been decidedly low-tech, although its worst instances have been very sophisticated organizationally. Truck bombs, commandeering of commercial aircraft, and credit card fraud appear to have been the primary tools used by those who have done us great harm. The materials they used have been things such as fertilizer, diesel fuel, and off-the-shelf chemicals. None of this has involved scientific or technical information that is advanced, or difficult to obtain. This is an important observation, although no guarantee of the future course of events. Indeed, the as-yet undetermined origin of anthrax attacks in the U.S. gives rise to important concerns.

The nebulous, diffuse nature of terrorism makes a simple prescription for the responsibilities of academic institutions impossible. Nonetheless, let me suggest a basic framework for thinking about it, by parsing the issues among the most commonly discussed mechanisms for terrorist attacks of a technological nature.

This framework reflects the nature of the information and materials required:

- The use of ***nuclear weapons and missiles*** is a singular matter. The information required to construct a nuclear weapon is acquired over many years. It is generally not the stuff of classroom learning; rather it is largely sophisticated know-how developed by experience, testing, and advanced computational simulation. Most nations can only acquire the critical components and materials required for construction of a nuclear weapon by illegal means.

- ***Cyberterrorism*** is the use of computer and communication technology to disrupt, corrupt, or disable our military or commercial IT systems. Potentially it could directly weaken our national security, or it could bring havoc to our economy. The information required by a cyberterrorist can be presumed to be of varying degrees of sophistication, but generally available. It is largely the stuff of hacking. The materials, in this case, are computers and access to the Internet. Having said this, cybersecurity is an urgent issue in all domains of industry, education, and government. It imposes additional administrative burdens and regulatory costs on all organizations, and it calls for more computer scientists and mathematicians who are U.S. citizens, trained to protect our information infrastructure.
- ***Bioterrorism*** could involve the propagation of disease and the defeat or disruption of therapies to counter it. The information required is likely to be available in published literature. Some experientially gained know-how might be involved, but it could generally be obtained by a wide variety of experiences in laboratories, medical establishments, or pharmaceutical companies. Some specialized equipment or facilities might be required, but they would likely have widespread applicability to legitimate activities. This situation is distinctly unlike the case of nuclear weapons and poses some of the most vexing issues. The needed biological materials may or may not be readily available.
- ***Chemical or explosive attacks*** are somewhat less commonly discussed, but are, in my view, among the things we should be most worried about. The information required for many forms is readily available, even to the layperson. Some dangerous agents are difficult to obtain, but others can be purchased off the shelf. The terrible destruction of lives by an angry American at the Alfred P. Murrah Building in Oklahoma City and the use of Sarin gas in Tokyo are prime examples.

Having reviewed these categories, I would say that nuclear weaponry seems to be an almost singular case. Critical knowledge and know-how should be, and is, highly restricted by the normal security classification processes of the Department of Defense and the Department of Energy. These are not things that students should be required to access in the conduct of university research; they cannot be taught in a normal classroom. It is an area that, in my view, is appropriate for reasoned decision-making by IPASS. But we should depend primarily on our well-established classification and security mechanisms.

I do not believe that cyberterrorism, bioterrorism or the use of chemical explosives pose threats that could in a meaningful way be countered or avoided by restrictions on what is taught in our university classrooms, or on the country of origin of our students. This is basic knowledge, and as in most instances in life, basic knowledge can be used for good or ill. The knowledge of what makes a virus virulent is also the key to medical therapies and disease prevention. This may be an uncomfortable reality, but it is a reality.

The ***material*** (as distinct from the information) needed to cause terror by chemical or biological means is a different matter. It is a clear responsibility of universities to not be a ***source*** of such materials for use by those who would do harm. Access to pathogens and dangerous chemicals must be carefully restricted and monitored in the normal course of doing science. Inventories should be minimized. Location, quantities, and security should be maintained effectively and accurately. We are working hard to establish best practice in this regard at MIT.

It is the further responsibility of universities to educate all of their research and laboratory students about security issues regarding their materials and equipment. This should be integrated with education and training regarding the health, safety, and environmental responsibilities of laboratory practice. Things as basic as not working alone in chemical and biological laboratories must be reinforced.

## Select Agents

The term "select agent" came into the scientific vernacular when, on June 12, 2002, the President signed into law the Public Health Security and Bioterrorism Preparedness and Response Act of 2002 (H.R. 3448, Pub. L. 107-188).

As a first step in this law, all researchers in the life sciences were required to report to their institution and to the government (Department of Health and Human Services) by September 10 their inventory of 40 "select agents" that might be used as bioweapons. Other provisions of the law will include similar reporting requirements for potentially lethal agricultural materials and security measures for laboratories that keep such agents. In addition, only those researchers determined to have a legitimate need will be allowed access to these materials, which will not be available to students or scholars from countries that are considered to be sponsors of terrorism or to people with histories of mental illness or felony or drug convictions.

By and large, the academic community has treated this as a reasonable approach and, of course, will comply with the law. But even this seemingly straightforward approach is not without a huge potential price to be paid in the advancement of science, and therefore in our health and welfare. The MIT Ad Hoc Committee on Access to and Disclosure of Scientific Information was deeply concerned about the path down which we may be starting, noting that the Secretary of Health and Human Services has the statutory power to expand the list of select agents. The Committee expressed the view that we could soon arrive at a level of restriction of access to materials by our students, faculty, or staff on the basis of their citizenship, for example—something that would be incompatible with our principles of openness, and would cause us to withdraw from the corresponding research topics on our campus.

## Publication of Scientific Information

The most difficult challenge as we balance prudent measures to maintain our security with the openness that is so essential to America's basic principles, to the excellence of our universities, and to the conduct of science, is associated with publishing information in the life sciences.

Why is this so complicated?

Science is a collective endeavor. Science increasingly is an international endeavor. The weight of these two statements is compounding at lightning speed as the complexity of science increases, and because, like all of society, scientists are tied together through the Internet. Science progresses not just by singular discoveries, but also by the independent verification and interactive discussion of discoveries. Knowledge is honed through ongoing dialogue that takes unexpected twists and turns. It thrives in openness, and suffers in isolation.

Thus, in fields such as microbiology, the very nature of science, when combined with the dual nature of information—i.e., its use for good or for ill—presents a challenge in an environment filled with well-justified concern about terrorism. . . .

## In Conclusion

The debate about security and openness is not new. In 1958 Norbert Wiener opined, "To disseminate information about a weapon . . . is to make practically certain that it will be used." As if in rejoinder, Edward Teller said in 1987 that "Secrecy is not compatible with science, but it is even less compatible with democratic procedure." These statements by two brilliant scientists with experience in defense work reflect the fact that virtually all science and engineering knowledge, or most other knowledge for that matter, can be used for good or ill.

This certainly does not mean that we can wash our hands of the responsibility to address hard questions about the safety and security of our fellow citizens. But in an age when the "weapon" may be a truckload of explosives, a computer virus, a commandeered aircraft, or finely milled bacterial spores, "dissemination of information" is a nebulous matter. And in an age when the rapid advance of science and technology is essential to sustaining our health, economy, and quality of life, Teller's observation is of crucial importance.

Traditional American values of openness in education and research must prevail. But this will be possible only if we in research universities contribute our talents to maintaining the security of our homeland, and if the Federal government and academia maintain a respectful, substantive, and effective dialogue between those who do science and those who are charged with protecting the nation.

# POSTSCRIPT

## Should Society Restrict the Publication of Unclassified but "Sensitive" Research?

It is a frustrating truth that science and technology offer both threat and promise, even in the context of terrorism. William B. Bonvillian and Kendra V. Sharp ["Homeland Security Technology," *Issues in Science and Technology* (Winter 2001–2002)] note that the need to detect terrorists before they can do damage requires "accelerated technology development and deployment." Yet the same science and technology, in the wrong hands, can aid the terrorists.

It is worth noting that "Even before the terrorist attacks of 2001, White House directives and agencies used the label SBU [sensitive but unclassified] to safeguard from public disclosure information that does not meet the standards for classification." [See Genevieve J. Knezo, "'Sensitive but Unclassified' and Other Federal Security Controls on Scientific and Technical Information: History and Current Controversy" (Congressional Research Service Report for Congress, April 2, 2003).] Yet, says Ronald M. Atlas, ["National Security and the Biological Research Community," *Science* (October 25, 2002)], the controversy is far from settled and "is likely to continue until we have a national debate and reach consensus on how to balance the traditional openness of science with national security in the new age of bioterrorism." The presidents of the National Academies of Sciences and Engineering and the Institute of Medicine issued a statement that same month that said that although "No restrictions may be placed upon the conduct or reporting of federally funded fundamental research that has not received national security classification," the research community should work closely with the federal government to determine which presently unclassified research should be classified. Early in 2003, the National Academies and the Center for Strategic and International Studies hosted a meeting that concluded researchers had better exercise self-restraint before the government imposes restraint. At the workshop, the editors of a number of major scientific journals indicated that they were following the American Society for Microbiology's lead in watching for security issues, and a group of editors and prominent scientists issued a "Statement on Scientific Publication and Security" that stressed that while both editors and authors bear responsibility to the public for the consequences of publication, scientific publication must include sufficient details for replication of the work; the very research that may be most helpful to terrorists is also likely to be most helpful to fighting terrorists; and when "on occasion an editor may conclude that the potential harm of publication outweighs the potential societal benefits . . . the paper should be modified, or not be published." [See Donald Kennedy, "Two Cultures" (editorial), *Science* (February 21, 2003).]

Are there other possible answers besides restricting—voluntarily or otherwise—publication of potentially hazardous work? John D. Steinbruner and Elisa D. Harris ["Controlling Dangerous Pathogens," *Issues in Science and Technology* (Spring 2003)] call for a global body that could oversee and regulate potentially dangerous disease research. Robert H. Sprinkle proposes "The Biosecurity Trust" (*Bioscience,* March 2003): The Trust would be "a transnational, nongovernmental life-sciences organization" whose goals would be "First, to keep safe, or to make safe, the work of well-intentioned life scientists. Second, to maximize the chance that directors of malicious research-and-development efforts worldwide would cite as chief among their frustrations chronic trouble attracting and retaining, or even successfully coercing, sufficient numbers of life scientists willing to pursue illegal and immoral ends or to keep completely quiet about the true purpose of efforts assisted or observed. Third, to complement existing and evolving legal safeguards, rather than to replace or preempt them. Fourth, to foster the adaptation of the most forceful elements of the modern life-sciences ethical tradition, the Nuremberg principles, to nonmedical situations, specifically to weaponeering by life scientists and to environmental endangerment. Fifth, to enrich the capacity to understand and manage biosecurity compromise, such as through the promotion of microbial-ecological education and research."

# ISSUE 2

## Is Science a Faith?

**YES: Daniel Callahan,** from "Calling Scientific Ideology to Account," *Society* (May/June 1996)

**NO: Richard Dawkins,** from "Is Science a Religion?" *The Humanist* (January/February 1997)

### ISSUE SUMMARY

**YES:** Bioethicist Daniel Callahan argues that science's domination of the cultural landscape unreasonably excludes other ways of understanding nature and the world and sets it above any need to accept moral, social, and intellectual judgment from political, religious, and even traditional values.

**NO:** Biologist Richard Dawkins maintains that science "is free of the main vice of religion, which is faith" because it relies on evidence and logic instead of tradition, authority, and revelation.

Science and technology have come to play a huge role in human culture, largely because they have led to vast improvements in nutrition, health care, comfort, communication, transportation, and humanity's ability to affect the world. However, science has also enhanced understanding of human behavior and of how the universe works, and in this it frequently contradicts what people have long thought they knew. Furthermore, it actively rejects any role of God in scientific explanation.

Many people therefore reject what science tells us. They see science as just another way of explaining how the world and humanity came to be; in this view, science is no truer than religious accounts. Indeed, some say science is just another religion, with less claim on followers' allegiance than other religions that have been divinely sanctioned and hallowed by longer traditions. Certainly, they see little significant difference between the scientist's faith in reason, evidence, and skepticism as the best way to achieve truth about the world and the religious believer's faith in revelation and scripture.

The antipathy between science and religion has a long history. In 1616 the Catholic Church attacked the Italian physicist Galileo Galilei (1564–1642) for teaching Copernican astronomy and, thus, contradicting the teachings of the Church; when invited to look through the telescope and see the moons of Jupiter for themselves, the Church's representatives reportedly refused (Pope John Paul II finally pardoned Galileo in 1983). On the other side of the conflict, the French Revolution featured the destruction of religion in the name of rationality and science, and the worship of God was officially abolished on November 10, 1793.

To many people, the conflict between science and religion is really a conflict between religions, or faiths, much like those between Muslims and Hindus or between conservative and liberal Christians. This view often becomes explicit in the debates between creationists and evolutionists.

The rejection of science is also evident among those who see science as denying both the existence of God and the importance of "human values" (meaning behaviors that are affirmed by traditional religion). This leads to a basic antipathy between science and religion, especially conservative religion, and especially in areas—such as human origins—where science and scripture seem to be talking about the same things but are contradicting each other. This has been true ever since evolutionary theorist Charles Darwin first published *On the Origin of Species by Means of Natural Selection* in 1859. Today, Michael Ruse can still title an essay "Is Evolution a Secular Religion?" (*Science,* March 7, 2003); his answer is that "Today's professional evolutionism is no more a secular religion than is industrial chemistry" but there is also a "popular evolutionism" that treads on religious ground and must be carefully distinguished.

Religious people are not the only ones who see in science a threat to "human values." Science also contradicts people's preferences, which are often based less on religion than on tradition and prejudice. For instance, science insists that no race or gender is superior to another; that homosexuality is natural, not wicked; that different ways of living deserve respect; and that it is possible to have too many children and to cut down too many trees. It also argues that religious proscriptions that may have once made sense are no longer relevant (the Jewish practice of not eating pork, for example, is a good way to avoid trichinosis; however, says science, so are cooking the meat at higher temperatures and not feeding pigs potentially contaminated feed).

Many people feel that there is a baby in the bathwater that science pitches out the window. Science, they say, neglects a very important side of human existence embodied in that "human values" phrase. Daniel Callahan sees this side as the source of moral, political, and intellectual judgment, which science by its dominance of society tends to evade. Science, he argues in the following selection, has become an ideology in its own right, as intolerant as any other, and it sorely needs judgment or criticism to keep it from steamrollering the more human side of life.

In the second selection, Richard Dawkins maintains that science differs profoundly from religion in its reliance on evidence and logic—not on tradition, authority, and revelation—and is therefore to be trusted much more.

**Daniel Callahan**

# Calling Scientific Ideology to Account

I come to the subject of science and religion with some complex emotions and a personal history not irrelevant to my own efforts to think about this matter. It seems appropriate for me to lay this history out a bit to set the stage for the argument I want to make. For the first half of my life, from my teens through my mid-thirties, I was a serious religious believer, a church member (Roman Catholic), and someone whose identity as both a person and as an intellectual had a belief in God at its center. During that time I had little contact with the sciences; literature and philosophy caught my imagination. I was a fine example, for that matter, of the gap between the two cultures that C. P. Snow described, caught up as I was in the humanities and generally ignorant about science. I spent most of my time among humanists and religious believers (though believers of a generally liberal kind).

All of that changed in my late thirties. Two events happened simultaneously. The first was a loss of my religious faith, utterly and totally. I ceased to be a theist, became an atheist, and so I remain today. I did not, however, have any revolt against organized religion (as it is sometimes pejoratively called) or the churches; nor did I lose respect for religious believers. They just seem to me wrong in their faith and mistaken in their hope. The second event was my discovery of the field of biomedical ethics, seemingly a fertile area for my philosophical training and an important window into the power of the biomedical sciences to change the way we think about and live our lives. With this new interest I began spending much of my time with physicians and bench scientists and worked hard to understand the universe of science that I was now entering (through the side door of biomedical ethics).

Meanwhile, as I was undergoing my own personal changes, the relationship between science and religion was shifting in the country as well. When I was growing up, there was still considerable debate about religion and science, with some believers arguing that there was a fundamental incompatibility between them and others holding that they were perfectly congenial. Some scientists, for their part, wrote books about religion, saying that they had found God in their science. Others, of a more positivistic bent, thought that science had forever expunged the notion of a God and that science would eventually offer an explanation of everything.

This debate seemed to subside significantly in the 1970s and 1980s. Science came almost totally to win the minds and emotions of educated Americans, and technological innovation was endlessly promoted as the key to both human progress and economic prosperity, a most attractive combination of doing good and doing well. While public opinion polls and church attendance figures, not to mention the gestures of politicians, showed the continuing popularity of religion, it was science that had captured the academy, the corridors of economic power, and high-brow prestige in the media. There remained, to be sure, skirmishes here and there over such issues as the teaching of creationism in the schools, particularly in the Bible Belt, and mutterings about the "religious Right" and its opposition to abortion, embryo and fetal research, and the like. Although there had been some bursts of anti-technology sentiments as part of the fallout of the 1960s culture wars, they had little staying power. The "greening of America" soon ran into a drought.

Science, in short, finally gained the ascendancy, coming to dominate the cultural landscape as much as the economic marketplace. This was the world of science I entered and in which I still remain enmeshed. My reaction to the news in May 1995 that a religious group, with the help of Jeremy Rifkin, was entering a challenge to the patenting of life was one of rueful bemusement: what a quixotic gesture, almost certainly doomed to failure but not, perhaps, before a round of media attention. Such battles make good copy, but that's about it.

The specific issue of the patenting of life deserves discussion, and someone or other would have raised it. Yet it hardly signals a new struggle between science and religion. It is neither that central an issue, nor did it appear even to galvanize a serious follow-up response among most religious groups. Congress, moreover, has given no indication that it will take up the issue in any serious way. In other words, it appears to have sunk as an issue as quickly as it arose.

Yet I confess to a considerable degree of uneasiness here. Science should not have such easy victories. It needs to have a David against its Goliath. This is only to say that scientific modernism—that is, the cultural dominance of science—desperately needs to have a serious and ongoing challenger. By that I mean the challenge of a different way of looking at nature and the world, one capable of shaking scientific self-satisfaction and complacency and resisting its at-present overpowering social force. Science needs, so to speak, a kind of loyal opposition.

This kind of opposition need not and should not entail hostility to the scientific method, to the investment of money in scientific research, or to the hope that scientific knowledge can make life better for us. Not at all. What it does entail is a relentless skepticism toward the view that science is the single and greatest key to human progress, that scientific knowledge is the only valid form of knowledge, and that some combination of science and the market is the way to increased prosperity and well-being for all. When religion can only fight science with the pea-shooters of creationism and antipatenting threats, it has little going for it. That response surely does not represent a thoughtful, developed, and articulate counterbalance to the hold of science on modern societies.

I say all of this because what I discovered upon entering the culture of science—that is, scientism—was something more than a simple commitment to the value and pursuit of scientific knowledge. That is surely present, but it is also accompanied socially by two other ingredients, science as ideology and science as faith.

## Science as Ideology

By science as ideology I mean that constellation of values that, for many, constitutes a more or less integrated way of interpreting life and nature, not only providing a sense of meaning but also laying out a path to follow in the living of a life. At the core of that ideology is a commitment to science as the most reliable source of knowledge about the nature of things and to technological innovation as the most promising way to improve human life. Closely related features of that ideology are an openness to untrammeled inquiry, limited by neither church nor state, skepticism toward all but scientifically verifiable claims, and a steady revision of all knowledge. While religion should be tolerated in the name of toleration rather than on grounds of credibility, it should be kept in the private sphere, out of the public space, public institutions, and public education. The ideology of scientism is all-encompassing, a way of knowing, and, culturally embodied, a way of living.

By science as faith I mean the ideology of science when it includes also a kind of non-falsifiable faith in the capacity of science not simply to provide reliable knowledge but also to solve all or most human problems, social, political, and economic. It is non-falsifiable in the sense that it holds that any failure to date of science to find solutions to human problems says nothing at all about its future capacity to do so; such solutions are only a matter of time and more refined knowledge. As for the fact that some of the changes science and technology have wrought are not all good, or have both good and bad features, science as faith holds that there is no reason in principle that better science and new knowledge cannot undo earlier harm and avoid future damage. In a word, no matter what science does, better science can do even better. No religious believer, trying to reconcile the evil in the world with the idea of a good and loving God, can be any more full of hope that greater knowledge will explain all than the scientific believer. And there is no evidence that is allowed to count against such a belief, and surely not religious arguments.

It is at just this point that I, the former religious believer, find it hard to confidently swallow the ideology of science, much less the serene faith of many of its worshippers. I left one church but I was not looking to join another. Nonetheless, when I stepped into the territory of science that appeared to be exactly the demand: If you want to be one of us, have faith. Yet a perspective that aims to supply the kind of certain metaphysical and ethical knowledge once thought limited to religion and to provide the foundations for ways of life seems to me worthy of the same kind of wariness that, ironically, science first taught me to have about religion. If science warns us to be skeptical of traditionalism, of settled but unexamined views, of knowledge claims poorly based on hard evidence, on acts of faith that admit of no falsifiability, why should I not bring that same set of attitudes to science itself? That interesting magazine, *The Skeptical Inquirer,* dedicated to getting the hard facts to debunk superstition, quackery, and weird claims by strange groups, does not run many articles devoted to debunking science or claims made in behalf of the enlightenment it can bring us. (I believe it has yet to publish even one such article, but I may be wrong about that.)

Maybe that is not so surprising. Such rebelliousness seems utterly unacceptable to scientism, utterly at odds with its solemn pieties and liturgical practices. To question the idea of scientific progress, to suggest that there are valid forms of nonscientific knowledge, to think that societies need something more than good science and high technology to flourish is to risk charges of heresy in enlightened educated circles every bit as intimidating as anything that can be encountered in even the most conservative religious groups. The condescension exhibited toward the "religious Right" surely matches that once displayed by Christianity toward "pagans." Even a Republican-dominated, conservative Congress knows it can far better afford politically to drastically cut or eliminate funding for the National Endowments for the Humanities and the Arts than for the National Science Foundation or the National Institutes of Health.

Now I come to the heart of my problem with the ideology and faith of scientism. Like any other human institution and set of practices, science needs to be subject to moral, social, and intellectual judgment; it needs to be called to task from time to time. Ideally that ought to be done by institutions that have the cultural clout to be taken seriously and by means of criteria for judgment that cannot themselves easily be called into question. Religion itself has always had this notion as part of its own self-understanding: It believes that it—churches, theologies, creeds—stands under the higher judgment of God and recognizes that it can itself fall into idolatry, the worship of false gods. One might well complain that the churches have seemed, in fact, exceedingly slow in rendering negative judgment upon themselves. Even so, they have the idea of such judgment and on occasion it has indeed been exercised.

Unfortunately—and a profound misfortune it is—science no longer has seriously competitive ways of thinking or institutions that have a comparable prestige and power. Science no longer has a counterweight with which it must contend, no institution or generally persuasive perspective that can credibly pass judgment on scientific practices and pretensions. No secular force or outlook or ideology exists to provide it. Religion once played that role: Popes, prelates, and preachers could once rain some effective fire and brimstone down on science, often enough mistakenly yet sometimes helpfully. But religion, too concerned to protect its own turf, too unwilling to open its eyes to new possibilities and forms of knowledge, offered mainly condemnation along with, now and then, some lukewarm support. Moreover, the gradual secularizing of the cultures of the developed countries of the world, relegating religion to the domestic sphere, took away religion's platform to speak authoritatively to public life. Scientific modernism was there to fill the gap, and it has been happy to do so. It is not possible to utter prayers in public schools, but there are no limits to the homage that can be lavished upon science and its good works.

The absence of a counterweight to the ideology of science has a number of doleful effects. It helps to substantiate the impression that there is no alternative, much less higher, perspective from which to judge science and its works. If you are the king of the hill, all things go your way and those below you are fearful or hesitant to speak out. It helps as well to legitimate the mistaken belief that all other forms of knowledge are not only inferior but that they are themselves always subject to the superior judgment of science. Accordingly, claims of religious knowledge of a credible kind were long ago dismissed by science. At its best, science is benignly tolerant of religion, patting it on the head like a kindly but wiser grandparent. At its worst, it can be mocking and dismissive. The kinds of knowledge generated by the humanities fare a little better, but not all that much.

From the perspective of my own field, bioethics, it is distressing to see the way that claims for the value or necessity of scientific research are treated with an extraordinary deference, usually going unquestioned. A recent federal panel on embryo research, for instance, set the issue up as a struggle between the moral status of the embryo, on the one hand, and that of the "need" (not just desire on the part of researchers) for embryo research, on the other. In a fine display of nuanced, critical thinking, the panel took apart excessive claims for the rights of embryos, urging "respect" but allowing research. As for the claims of research, they were accepted without any doubts or hesitations at all; they seemed self-evident to the panel, not in need of justification. Even Henry VIII, the king of his hill, hardly got that kind of deference, even from those luckless wives he had beheaded. In a culture saturated with the ideology of science, there seems hardly any forceful voice to call it to account.

If there was a loyal opposition, it would not let the claims and triumphalism of the scientific establishment go unchallenged. It would treat that establishment with respect, but it would fully understand that it is an *establishment*, intent on promoting its own cause and blowing its own horn, critical of its opponents and naysayers, and of course never satisfied with the funds available to it (funds that, if forthcoming in greater quantity, will someday find a cure for cancer, discover the molecular basis for disease, give us cheap energy generated by cold fusion, etc., etc.). A loyal opposition would bring to science exactly the same cool and self-critical eye that science itself urges in the testing of scientific ideas and hypotheses. One of the great intellectual contributions of science has been its methodological commitment to self-criticism and self-revision; and that is one reason it came to triumph over religion, which has not always shown much enthusiasm for skepticism about its key doctrines.

But if self-criticism and self-revision are at the heart of the scientific method, then a good place to begin employing them is at home, on the scientific ideology that culturally sustains the whole apparatus. A loyal opposition would do this not only to temper exaggerated self-congratulations on the part of science but also to keep science itself scientific.

The insuperable limitation of the scientific method is that it cannot be used to criticize the ideology of science or its methods. To try to do so only begs the question of its validity. In the end, we judge that method more by its fruits and consequences than by its a priori validity. The problem here is that science cannot tell us what consequences we ought to want, what kind of knowledge we need, or what uses are best for the knowledge that science demonstrates. Science, that is, is far more helpful with our means than our ends. Good science cannot tell us how to organize good societies or develop good people (or even tell us how to define "good") or tell us what is worth knowing. There is no scientific calculus to tell us how much a society should invest in scientific research; that is a matter of prudence.

It is here that the other forms of knowledge ought and must come into play: the knowledge developed by the humanities or the "soft" social sciences; the political values and structures created by democratic societies, built upon argument, some consensus, and some compromise. My own domain, that of the humanities, was long ago intimidated by science. It does not complain about the grievous disparity between research resources lavished upon it in comparison with science. Those humanists who dare enter the church of science and mutter to its high priests are given the back of the scientific hand, quickly labeled as cranks or, black mark of black marks, Luddites. The scientific establishment should help to encourage and support other forms of knowing and should be willing to learn from them; that would be to display the openness and creativity it touts as its strength. It does not, however, take the fingers of even one hand to count the number of Nobel laureates in science who have petitioned Congress for stronger support for the humanities.

What is a proper role for religion in a society captured by the ideology of science? Its most important role, the one it has played from time to time with other principalities and powers, would be simply to urge some humility on science and to call it to task for pretentiousness and power grabbing. Science ought to stand under constant moral judgment, and there is an important role for religion to play in formulating some of the criteria for such judgment. It is thus proper for religion to remind science of something religion should always be reminding itself of as well: Neither science nor religion are whole and entire unto themselves. Religion stands under the judgment of God (it tells us), and science stands under the judgment of the collective conscience of humankind (which religion does *not* tell us). Religion can remind the world, and those in science, that the world can be viewed from different perspectives. And it can remind that world, including science, what it means to attempt, as does religion, to make sense of everything in some overall coherent way. There is no need to agree with the way in which religion comprehends reality in order to be reminded of the human thirst for some sense of coherence and meaning in the world.

There has always been an aspect of science that overlaps with supernatural religion. That is the kind of natural piety and awe that many scientists feel in the face of the mysteries and beauty of the natural world. This can be called a kind of natural religion, and some scientists easily make the move from the natural to the supernatural, even if many of their more skeptical colleagues—who also share the sense of natural awe—do not follow them in taking that step. This natural awe frequently expresses itself in a hesitation to manipulate nature for purely self-interested ends, whether economic or medical. The concern of ecologists for the preservation of biodiversity, the hesitations of population geneticists about germ-line therapy, the worry of environmentalists about the protection of tropical forests or of biologists for the preservation of even rare species, all testify to that kind of natural piety. It is here that there is room for an alliance between science and religion, between that science that sees the mystery and unprobed depths of the natural world and that religion that sees nature as the creation and manifestation of a beneficent god.

It is important, for that matter, that science find allies in its desire to keep its natural piety alive and well. The primary enemies of that piety are the casual indifference of many human beings to nature and the more systematic despoiling of nature carried out in the name of the market, human betterment, or the satisfying of private fantasies and desires. Environmentalism has long been torn by a struggle that pits conservationists against preservationists. Conservationists believe that the natural world can be cultivated for human use and its natural resources protected if care is taken. Preservationists, and particularly the "deep ecologists," are hostile to that kind of optimism, holding that nature as it is needs to be protected, not manipulated or exploited. Conservationism has a serious and sober history and has been by no means oriented toward a crude exploitation of nature. But it is a movement that has often been allowed to shade off into that kind of technological optimism that argues that whatever harm scientific progress and technological innovation cause, it can just as readily be undone and corrected by science.

This is the ideology of science taken to extremes, but a common enough viewpoint among those who see too much awe of nature, too much protectionism, as a threat to economic progress. Religion could well throw its weight behind responsible conservation, and it would not hurt a bit if some theologians and church groups took up the cause of deep ecology. That is an unlikely cause to gain great support in an overcrowded world, and particularly in the poverty-stricken parts of that world. But it is a strong countercurrent worth introducing into the larger stream of efforts to preserve and respect nature. A little roughage in the bowels helps keep things moving.

Perhaps the cultural dominance of science is nowhere so evident as in a feature of our society frequently overlooked: the powerful proclivity to look to numbers and data as the key to good public policy. Charts, tables, and graphs are the standard props of the policy analyst and the legislator. This is partly understandable and justifiable. With issues of debate and contention, hard data is valuable. It can help to determine if there is a real problem, the dimensions of that problem, and the possible consequences of different solutions. But the soft underside of the deification of data is the too frequent failure to recognize that data never tells its own story, that it is always subject to, and requires, interpretation.

There is no data that can carry out that work. On the contrary, at that point we are thrown back upon our values, our way of looking at the world and society, and our different social hopes and commitments. The illusion of the inherent persuasiveness of data is fostered by scientism, which likes to think that there can be a neutral standpoint from which to assess those matters that concern us, that scientific information plays that role, and that the answer to any moral and social battles is simply more and better information.

The dominance of the field of economics in social policy itself tells an interesting story: the need to find a policy discipline that has all the trapping of science in its methods and that can capture its prestige. It is a field that aspires to be a science and that speaks the culturally correct language of modeling, hypothesis testing, and information worship. And it has been amply rewarded for its troubles, recently gaining the blessing of a Nobel prize for its practitioners to signal its status as a science, and for many years capturing the reins of public power and office in a way unmatched by any other academic discipline.

There is a prestigious government Council of Economic Advisors. There is not now, and probably never will be, a Council of Philosophical Advisors, or Historical Advisors, or Humanistic Advisors. But then, that is likely to be the fate of any field that cannot attach itself to the prestige of science. It will lack social standing, just as religion now lacks serious intellectual standing. Note that I say "intellectual standing." There is no doubt that religion can still have a potent political status or that religion can from time to time make trouble for science (or, more accurately, make trouble for the agendas of some scientists, for example, for those who would like to do embryo research). But in the larger and more enduring world of dominant ideas and ideologies, science sits with some serenity, and much public adulation, in an enviable position. It is interesting to note what no one seems to have noticed. In the demise of communism as a political philosophy and a set of political regimes, one of its features has endured nicely: its faith in science. That is the one feature it shared with the Western capitalist democracies that triumphed over it. It is also, let it be noted, a key feature of a market ideology, the engine of innovation, a major source of new products, and—in its purported value neutrality—a congenial companion for a market ideology that just wants to give people the morally neutral gift of freedom of economic choice, not moralisms about human nature and the good society of a kind to be found in the now-dead command economies of the world.

Allow me to end as I began. There was a time when I hoped my own field, bioethics, might serve as the loyal opposition to scientific ideology, at least its biomedical division. In its early days, in the 1960s and 1970s, many of those first drawn to it were alarmed by the apparently unthinking way in which biomedical knowledge and technologies were being taken up and disseminated. It seemed important to examine not only the ethical dilemmas generated by a considerable portion of the scientific advances but also to ask some basic questions about the moral premises of the entire enterprise of unrelenting biomedical progress. That latter aspiration has yet to be fulfilled. Most of those who have come into the field have accepted scientific ideology as much as most scientists, and they have no less been the cultural children of their times, prone to look to medical progress and its expansion of choice as a perfect complement to a set of moral values that puts autonomy at the very top of the moral hierarchy. Nothing seems to so well serve the value of autonomy as the expanded range of human options that science promises to deliver, whether for the control of procreation or the improvement of health or the use of medical means to improve our lives. Not many people in bioethics, moreover, care to be thought of as cranks, and there is no faster way to gain that label than to raise questions about the scientific enterprise as a whole. Bioethicists have, on the whole, become good team players, useful to help out with moral puzzles now and then and trustworthy not to probe basic premises too deeply. Unless one is willing to persistently carry out such probes, the idea of a loyal opposition carries no weight.

Can religion, or bioethics, or some other social group or force in our society call science to account when necessary? Can it do so with credibility and serious credentials? Can it do so in a way that helps science to do its own work better, and not simply to throw sand in the eyes of scientists? I am not sure, but I surely hope so. I can only say, for my part, that I left one church and ended in the pews of another one, this one the Church of Science. In more ways than one—in its self-confidence, its serene faith in its own value, and its ability to intimidate dissenters—it seems uncomfortably like the one I left. How can it be made to see that about itself?

NO 

**Richard Dawkins**

# Is Science a Religion?

It is fashionable to wax apocalyptic about the threat to humanity posed by the AIDS virus, "mad cow" disease, and many others, but I think a case can be made that *faith* is one of the world's great evils, comparable to the smallpox virus but harder to eradicate.

Faith, being belief that isn't based on evidence, is the principal vice of any religion. And who, looking at Northern Ireland or the Middle East, can be confident that the brain virus of faith is not exceedingly dangerous? One of the stories told to young Muslim suicide bombers is that martyrdom is the quickest way to heaven—and not just heaven but a special part of heaven where they will receive their special reward of 72 virgin brides. It occurs to me that our best hope may be to provide a kind of "spiritual arms control": send in specially trained theologians to deescalate the going rate in virgins.

Given the dangers of faith—and considering the accomplishments of reason and observation in the activity called science—I find it ironic that, whenever I lecture publicly, there always seems to be someone who comes forward and says, "Of course, your science is just a religion like ours. Fundamentally, science just comes down to faith, doesn't it?"

Well, science is not religion and it doesn't just come down to faith. Although it has many of religion's virtues, it has none of its vices. Science is based upon verifiable evidence. Religious faith not only lacks evidence, its independence from evidence is its pride and joy, shouted from the rooftops. Why else would Christians wax critical of doubting Thomas? The other apostles are held up to us as exemplars of virtue because faith was enough for them. Doubting Thomas, on the other hand, required evidence. Perhaps he should be the patron saint of scientists.

One reason I receive the comment about science being a religion is because I believe in the fact of evolution. I even believe in it with passionate conviction. To some, this may superficially look like faith. But the evidence that makes me believe in evolution is not only overwhelmingly strong; it is freely available to anyone who takes the trouble to read up on it. Anyone can study the same evidence that I have and presumably come to the same conclusion. But if you have a belief that is based solely on faith, I can't examine your reasons. You can retreat behind the private wall of faith where I can't reach you.

From Richard Dawkins, "Is Science a Religion?" *The Humanist* (January/February 1997).

Now in practice, of course, individual scientists do sometimes slip back into the vice of faith, and a few may believe so single-mindedly in a favorite theory that they occasionally falsify evidence. However, the fact that this sometimes happens doesn't alter the principle that, when they do so, they do it with shame and not with pride. The method of science is so designed that it usually finds them out in the end.

Science is actually one of the most moral, one of the most honest disciplines around—because science would completely collapse if it weren't for a scrupulous adherence to honesty in the reporting of evidence. (As [famous magician] James Randi has pointed out, this is one reason why scientists are so often fooled by paranormal tricksters and why the debunking role is better played by professional conjurors; scientists just don't anticipate deliberate dishonesty as well.) There are other professions (no need to mention lawyers specifically) in which falsifying evidence or at least twisting it is precisely what people are paid for and get brownie points for doing.

Science, then, is free of the main vice of religion, which is faith. But, as I pointed out, science does have some of religion's virtues. Religion may aspire to provide its followers with various benefits—among them explanation, consolation, and uplift. Science, too, has something to offer in these areas.

Humans have a great hunger for explanation. It may be one of the main reasons why humanity so universally has religion, since religions do aspire to provide explanations. We come to our individual consciousness in a mysterious universe and long to understand it. Most religions offer a cosmology and a biology, a theory of life, a theory of origins, and reasons for existence. In doing so, they demonstrate that religion is, in a sense, science; it's just bad science. Don't fall for the argument that religion and science operate on separate dimensions and are concerned with quite separate sorts of questions. Religions have historically always attempted to answer the questions that properly belong to science. Thus religions should not be allowed now to retreat from the ground upon which they have traditionally attempted to fight. They do offer both a cosmology and a biology; however, in both cases it is false.

Consolation is harder for science to provide. Unlike Religion, science cannot offer the bereaved a glorious reunion with their loved ones in the hereafter. Those wronged on this earth cannot, on a scientific view, anticipate a sweet comeuppance for their tormentors in a life to come. It could be argued that, if the idea of an afterlife is an illusion (as I believe it is), the consolation it offers is hollow. But that's not necessarily so; a false belief can be just as comforting as a true one, provided the believer never discovers its falsity. But if consolation comes that cheap, science can weigh in with other cheap palliatives, such as pain-killing drugs, whose comfort may or may not be illusory, but they do work.

Uplift, however, is where science really comes into its own. All the great religions have a place for awe, for ecstatic transport at the wonder and beauty of creation. And it's exactly this feeling of spine-shivering, breath-catching awe—almost worship—this flooding of the chest with ecstatic wonder, that modern science can provide. And it does so beyond the wildest dreams of saints and mystics. The fact that the supernatural has no place in our explanations, in our understanding of so much about the universe and life, doesn't diminish the awe. Quite the contrary. The merest glance through a microscope at the brain of an ant or through a telescope at a long-ago galaxy of a billion worlds is enough to render poky and parochial the very psalms of praise.

Now, as I say, when it is put to me that science or some particular part of science, like evolutionary theory, is just a religion like any other, I usually deny it with indignation. But I've begun to wonder whether perhaps that's the wrong tactic. Perhaps the right tactic is to accept the charge gratefully and demand equal time for science in religious education classes. And the more I think about it, the more I realize that an excellent case could be made for this. So I want to talk a little bit about religious education and the place that science might play in it.

I do feel very strongly about the way children are brought up. I'm not entirely familiar with the way things are in the United States, and what I say may have more relevance to the United Kingdom, where there is state-obliged, legally enforced religious instruction for all children. That's unconstitutional in the United States, but I presume that children are nevertheless given religious instruction in whatever particular religion their parents deem suitable.

Which brings me to my point about mental child abuse. In a 1995 issue of the *Independent,* one of London's leading newspapers, there was a photograph of a rather sweet and touching scene. It was Christmas time, and the picture showed three children dressed up as the three wise men for a nativity play. The accompanying story described one child as a Muslim, one as a Hindu, and one as a Christian. The supposedly sweet and touching point of the story was that they were all taking part in this nativity play.

What is not sweet and touching is that these children were all four years old. How can you possibly describe a child of four as a Muslim or a Christian or a Hindu or a Jew? Would you talk about a four-year-old economic monetarist? Would you talk about a four-year-old neo-isolationist or a four-year-old liberal Republican? There are opinions about the cosmos and the world that children, once grown, will presumably be in a position to evaluate for themselves. Religion is the one field in our culture about which it is absolutely accepted, without question—without even noticing how bizarre it is—that parents have a total and absolute say in what their children are going to be, how their children are going to be raised, what opinions their children are going to have about the cosmos, about life, about existence. Do you see what I mean about mental child abuse?

Looking now at the various things that religious education might be expected to accomplish, one of its aims could be to encourage children to reflect upon the deep questions of existence, to invite them to rise above the humdrum preoccupations of ordinary life and think *sub specie alternitatis.*

Science can offer a vision of life and the universe which, as I've already remarked, for humbling poetic inspiration far outclasses any of the mutually contradictory faiths and disappointingly recent traditions of the world's religions.

For example, how could any child in a religious education class fail to be inspired if we could get across to them some inkling of the age of the universe? Suppose that, at the moment of Christ's death, the news of it had started traveling at the maximum possible speed around the universe outwards from the earth? How far would the terrible tidings have traveled by now? Following the theory of special relativity, the answer is that the news could not, under any circumstances whatever, have reached more than one-fiftieth of the way across one galaxy—not one-thousandth of the way to our nearest neighboring galaxy in the 100-million-galaxy-strong universe. The universe at large couldn't possibly be anything other than indifferent to Christ, his birth, his passion, and his death. Even such momentous news as the origin of life on Earth could have traveled only across our little local cluster of galaxies. Yet so ancient was that event on our earthy time-scale that, if you span its age with your open arms, the whole of human history, the whole of human culture, would fall in the dust from your fingertip at a single stroke of a nail file.

The argument from design, an important part of the history of religion, wouldn't be ignored in my religious education classes, needless to say. The children would look at the spell-binding wonders of the living kingdoms and would consider Darwinism alongside the creationist alternatives and make up their own minds. I think the children would have no difficulty in making up their minds the right way if presented with the evidence. What worries me is not the question of equal time but that, as far as I can see, children in the United Kingdom and the United States are essentially given *no* time with evolution yet are taught creationism (whether at school, in church, or at home).

It would also be interesting to teach more than one theory of creation. The dominant one in this culture happens to be the Jewish creation myth, which is taken over from the Babylonian creation myth. There are, of course, lots and lots of others, and perhaps they should all be given equal time (except that wouldn't leave much time for studying anything else). I understand that there are Hindus who believe that the world was created in a cosmic butter churn and Nigerian peoples who believe that the world was created by God from the excrement of ants. Surely these stories have as much right to equal time as the Judeo-Christian myth of Adam and Eve. . . .

When the religious education class turns to ethics, I don't think science actually has a lot to say, and I would replace it with rational moral philosophy. Do the children think there are absolute standards of right and wrong? And if so, where do they come from? Can you make up good working principles of right and wrong, like "do as you would be done by" and "the greatest good for the greatest number" (whatever that is supposed to mean)? It's a rewarding question, whatever your personal morality, to ask as an evolutionist where morals come from; by what route has the human brain gained its tendency to have ethics and morals, a feeling of right and wrong?

Should we value human life above all other life? Is there a rigid wall to be built around the species *Homo sapiens,* or should we talk about whether there are other species which are entitled to our humanistic sympathies? Should we, for example, follow the right-to-life lobby, which is wholly preoccupied with *human* life, and value the life of a human fetus with the faculties of a worm over the life of a thinking and feeling chimpanzee? What is the basis of this fence we erect around *Homo sapiens*—even around a small piece of fetal tissue? (Not a very sound evolutionary idea when you think about it.) When, in our evolutionary descent from our common ancestor with chimpanzees, did the fence suddenly rear itself up?

. . . [S]cience could give a good account of itself in religious education. But it wouldn't be enough. I believe that some familiarity with the King James version of the Bible is important for anyone wanting to understand the allusions that appear in English literature. Together with Book of Common Prayer, the Bible gets 58 pages in the *Oxford Dictionary of Quotations.* Only Shakespeare has more. I do think that not having any kind of biblical education is unfortunate if children want to read English literature and understand the provenance of phrases like "through a glass darkly," "all flesh is as grass," "the race is not to the swift," "crying in the wilderness," "reaping the whirlwind," "amid the alien corn," "Eyeless in Gaza," "Job's comforters," and "the widow's mite."

I want to return now to the charge that science is just a faith. The more extreme version of this charge—and one that I often encounter as both a scientist and a rationalist—is an accusation of zealotry and bigotry in scientists themselves as great as that found in religious people. Sometimes there may be a little bit of justice in this accusation; but as zealous bigots, we scientists are mere amateurs at the game. We're content to *argue* with those who disagree with us. We don't kill them.

But I would want to deny even the lesser charge of purely verbal zealotry. There is a very, very important difference between feeling strongly, even passionately, about something because we have thought about and examined the evidence for it on the one hand, and feeling strongly about something because it has been internally revealed to us, or internally revealed to somebody else in history and subsequently hallowed by tradition. There's all the difference in the world between a belief that one is prepared to defend by quoting evidence and logic and a belief that is supported by nothing more than tradition, authority, or revelation.

# POSTSCRIPT

## Is Science a Faith?

The conflict between science and religion is deep and broad. The root reason may be simply that science says, "Check it out—don't take anyone's word for the truth," while religion says, "Take the word of your preacher or your scripture. Believe—but don't even *think* about checking." Scientific skepticism is always a threat to established authority. It challenges old truths. It revises and replaces beliefs, traditions, and power structures.

Does this mean that science is a threat to society? Those who share the beliefs under attack often think so. They may believe that the Bible or the Koran is a much better guide to the nature of the world than science is. They may believe in crystal power and magic spells. They may tie knots in their electric cords to trim the size of their electric bills. They may even be postmodernist university professors who say that science is just a "useful myth," no different from any other fiction. As Mano Singham writes in "The Science and Religion Wars," *Phi Delta Kappan* (February 2000), "In the triangle formed by science, mainstream religion, and fringe beliefs, it is the conflict between science and fringe beliefs that is usually the source of the most heated, acrimonious, and public debate." There are also those, like Callahan, who wish that there were some segment of society with sufficient stature to sit in judgment over science, to criticize it, and perhaps to rein it in, certainly to keep it from arrogantly quashing other views, such as those of religion. And although most Americans welcome the benefits of science and technology, they are often very leery of the unrestricted inquiry that characterizes science and challenges tradition. See, for example, Janet Raloff, "When Science and Beliefs Collide," *Science News* (June 8, 1996); Gerald Holton, *Einstein, History, and Other Passions: The Rebellion Against Science at the End of the Twentieth Century* (Addison-Wesley, 1996); and "Science Versus Antiscience?" *Scientific American* (January 1997). Some scientists even feel threatened by the conflict between their professional and private beliefs. Some have therefore spent a great deal of effort searching for ways to reconcile science and religion. For instance, Leon Lederman and Dick Teresi write about the quest for the most fundamental fragment of the atom in *The God Particle* (Dell, 1994). Stephen Hawking, in *A Brief History of Time* (Bantam Books, 1988), expresses the thought that science might lead humanity to "know the mind of God."

Can these scientists be speaking in more than metaphorical terms? Perhaps not, for science deals in observable reality, which can provide at best only hints of a designer, creator, or God. Science cannot provide *direct* access to God, at least as people currently understand the nature of God. Still, it is not only creationists who see signs of design. Some scientists find the impression of design quite overwhelming, and many feel that science and religion actually have a great deal in common. Harvard University astronomer and evangelical Christian Owen Gingerich says that both are driven by human beings' "basic wonder and desire to know where we stand in the universe." It is therefore not terribly surprising to find the two realms of human thought intersecting very frequently or to find many people in both realms concerned with reconciling differences. See Gregg Easterbrook, "Science and God: A Warming Trend?" *Science* (August 15, 1997).

On the other hand, some scientists find attempts to reconcile science and religion strange at best. Eugenie Scott, of the National Center for Science Education, insists that "science is just a method" and that people who see God in the complexity of biology or astronomy are "going beyond their data" and misusing science "to validate their positions." Paul Gross, former director of the Woods Hole Marine Biological Laboratory and coauthor of *Higher Superstition: The Academic Left and Its Quarrels with Science* (Johns Hopkins University Press, 1994), even finds those who see God in science frightening. More recently, Gross, Norman Levitt, and Martin W. Lewis coedited *The Flight from Science and Reason* (New York Academy of Sciences, 1997) to consider the opposition to the scientific, rational approach to the world that now finds wide expression in many nonscientific academic areas.

Are such views no more than an illustration of Callahan's contention that science—or "scientism"—has become an ideology and a faith as intolerant of others as any religion? Certainly some feel that science can provide many of the same rewards as religion. See Chet Raymo's *Skeptics and True Believers: The Exhilarating Connection Between Science and Religion* (Walker, 1998), in which he seeks a kind of spirituality without belief, finding all the awe, wonder, and mystery anyone could wish in the universe revealed by science. Michael Shermer, in "The Shamans of Scientism," *Scientific American* (June 2002), adds that "it is scientism's shamans who command our veneration" today, and scientists are "the premier mythmakers of our time."

# ISSUE 3

## Should Creationism and Evolution Get Equal Time in Schools?

**YES: Richard J. Clifford,** from "Creationism's Value?" *America* (March 11, 2000)

**NO: Marjorie George,** from "And Then God Created Kansas? The Evolution/Creationism Debate in America's Public Schools," *University of Pennsylvania Law Review* (January 2001)

### ISSUE SUMMARY

**YES:** Richard J. Clifford, a professor of biblical studies, argues that although modern creationism is flawed, excluding the Bible and religion from American public education is indefensible. He maintains that schools should be places where religious beliefs are treated with respect.

**NO:** Professor of political science Marjorie George argues that the U.S. Constitution and the Supreme Court have created a solid wall between the educational system and religion. Despite the efforts of creationists to find ways around or through that wall, she holds, religion "can play no role in the classroom."

It has long been an article of faith for scientists that teleological questions ("why" questions that presume there is an intent behind the phenomena they study) should not be asked, largely because "intent" implies an intender, which is generally taken to mean divine will. As a result, there is a continuing between the forces of faith and the forces of reason. Conservative Christians in the southern United States, Texas, and California have mounted vigorous campaigns to require public school biology classes to give equal time to both biblical creationism and Darwinian evolution. For many years, this meant that evolution was hardly mentioned in high school biology textbooks.

For a time, it looked like evolution had scored a decisive victory. In 1982 federal judge William K. Overton struck down an Arkansas law that would have required the teaching of straight biblical creationism, with its explicit talk of God the Creator, as an unconstitutional intrusion of religion into a government activity: education. But the creationists have not given up. They have returned to the fray with something they call "scientific creationism," and they have shifted their campaigns from state legislatures and school boards to local school boards, where it is harder for lawyers and biologists to mount effective counterattacks. "Scientific creationism" tries to show that the evolutionary approach is incapable of providing satisfactory explanations. For one thing, it says that natural selection relies on random chance to produce structures whose delicate intricacy really could only be the product of deliberate design. Therefore, there must have been a designer. There is no mention of God—but, of course, that is the only possible meaning of "designer" (unless one believes in ancient extraterrestrial visitors). For an excellent presentation of the various threads in the debate over intelligent design, see Robert T. Pennock, *Intelligent Design Creationism and Its Critics: Philosophical, Theological, and Scientific Perspectives* (MIT Press, 2001).

William Johnson, associate dean of academic affairs at Ambassador University in Big Sandy, Texas, offered another argument for replacing the theory of evolution in a 1994 speech reprinted in "Evolution: The Past, Present, and Future Implications," *Vital Speeches of the Day* (February 15, 1995). He argued that the triumph of Darwin's theory "meant the end of the traditional belief in the world as a purposeful created order . . . and the consequent elimination of God from nature has played a decisive role in the secularization of Western society. Darwinian theory broke man's link with God and set him adrift in a cosmos without purpose or end." Johnson suggested that evolution—and perhaps the entire scientific approach to nature—should be abandoned in favor of a return to religion because of the untold damage it has done to the human values that underpin society.

In 1999, the Kansas Board of Education deleted evolution—as well as much other science that would support the idea of an Earth and universe older than 6,000 years—from coverage in state competency tests. Since most teachers could be expected to focus their efforts on material their students would need to score well on the tests, and since the Board had vocal anti-evolution, pro-creation members, the Board's move was widely seen as supporting the anti-evolution, pro-creation agenda.

In the following selections, Richard J. Clifford argues that modern creationism is flawed in that it fails to recognize both that the Bible holds many versions of creation and that those who composed those versions did not think the same way as modern scientists. However, he maintains that excluding the Bible and religion from American public education is indefensible. Marjorie George, on the other hand, argues that the U.S. Constitution and the Supreme Court have created a solid wall between the educational system and religion for a very good reason: in order to protect independent thinking. Despite the efforts of creationists to find ways around or through that wall, she asserts, creationism and religion have no place in public education.

**Richard J. Clifford**

# YES

# Creationism's Value?

"The whole battle is hotting up," declared Ken Ham to The New York Times (12/1/99). A disillusioned science teacher turned creationist, Ham opposes the theory of evolution. He proposes instead a literal reading of the first chapter of the Book of Genesis: God created the world in six days. This interpretation has broader implications, for there is "a culture war hotting up in America between Christian morality and relative morality, which is really the difference between a creation-based philosophy and an evolution-based one." To a creationist like Ken Ham, even the common conservative view that a "day" in Genesis 1 stands for a time-span of eons is unacceptable, for it would attribute error to the Bible and reduce morality to human whim.

Creationists, who have been in and out of the public eye since the Scopes trial in 1925, had some major successes [recently]. In August 1999 the Kansas Board of Education deleted almost every mention of evolution from the state's science curriculum, and in October the Kentucky Board of Education voted to substitute the phrase "change over time" for "evolution." Oklahoma officials recently decreed that textbooks must include a disclaimer on the certainty of evolution.

What, then, should be thought of creationism? Is it a courageous stand for open-mindedness toward the Bible in an educational culture that excludes the biblical perspective? Or is it an attempt to impose an idiosyncratic view of the Bible and of science? At first glance, the creationist proposal seems reasonable: Present students with two theories, evolution and creationism, and let them make up their own minds. A second look, however, shows that the proposal contains two assumptions that virtually all professionally trained biblical scholars and scientists completely reject: that Genesis 1, interpreted literally, is the only or at least the standard biblical creation account, and that the six-day creation story in Genesis 1 is a rival to the modern theory of evolution. These assumptions show that creationism fundamentally misunderstands the Bible and the relation of science and religion.

The majority of biblical scholars, theologians of the mainstream churches, and philosophers of science hold an alternative view that will be summarized here under three headings: creation in the Bible, the differences between biblical and modern views of creation and the relation of religion and science.

## Creation in the Bible

The strongest biblical argument against creationism is that Genesis 1 is only one of many creation accounts in the Bible, and these biblical accounts are too distinctive to be harmonized. The cosmogony found in the second and third chapters of Genesis tells a very different story than Genesis 1. Here are a few of these differences. Creation in Genesis 2 proceeds at an unspecified pace that surely lasts longer than a week, whereas in Genesis 1 all takes place within six days. In Genesis 1, the man and the woman are created at the same time, whereas in Genesis 2 the man is created earlier than the woman. In Genesis 1, the animals are created before the man, which is the opposite of the order in Genesis 2.

Other creation accounts—in the Psalms, Isaiah 40–66, Job and Proverbs—also differ from one another and from Genesis 1. Psalms 77, 89 and 93, for example, depict creation as a cosmic battle with the forces of chaos; God's victory is the act of creation. Isaiah 40–55 uses creation-by-combat to interpret the reconstruction of Israel after the sixth-century exile. Israel's new creation is portrayed through a grand analogy—just as in olden times God brought Israel into being by vanquishing Sea (the Red or Reed Sea) and bringing the people to Canaan, so today he is bringing Israel into being by vanquishing Desert and bringing the people to Zion (see especially Isa. 43:16–21). Creation-by-combat is common in the Bible (and in the literature of Israel's neighbors). The creation-by-word in Genesis 1 is unique in the Old Testament and to make it the biblical standard, as creationists do, is gratuitous on purely biblical grounds.

## Biblical and Modern Views of Creation

As the above examples suggest, creation in the Bible differs markedly from modern conceptions—a point that is neglected by creationism. There are important differences in the process, in the world that emerges and in the manner of reporting.

1. *The process of creation.* Ancient Near Eastern writers imagined creation on the model of human making or of natural activity. For example, the gods formed the world as an artisan works clay, or as a king's word makes things happen, or as a warrior defeats an enemy. Biblical writers did not draw the modern dichotomous distinction between "nature" and human beings, and they used psychic and social analogies to explain non-human phenomena. Today, influenced by scientific and evolutionary thinking, we understand creation as the (impersonal) interaction of physical forces extending over eons.
2. *The product or world that emerges.* For the ancients, creation issued in a *populated* universe. Human society was normally the term of biblical accounts. Ancient cosmogonies explained the institutions and practices of contemporary society. The first appearance of a reality was a privileged time when the imprint of the divine maker was freshest. Hence, to know the origin of a thing was in some

sense to know its essence. For moderns, on the other hand, creation is usually thought of in terms of the planets and stars. If life is mentioned, it is usually life in its most primitive forms. Human society and culture do not usually come into consideration.

3. *The manner of reporting and the criteria of truth.* The Bible often describes creation as a drama, whereas contemporary thinkers write scientific reports. The description in each case follows upon a particular conceptualization of creation, either "impersonal" or "dramatic." Each has its own criteria of truth. Scientific reports explain new data by new hypotheses, discarding old hypotheses when they do not adequately explain the data. There can be only *one* true account. Ancients, on the other hand, had many cosmogonies. They were not bothered, for example, by the impossibility of harmonizing the first and second chapters of Genesis. Their only requirement was verisimilitude—does the cosmogony make sense as a story? Ancients were less interested in how creation happened than in what the gods or God intended.

The Bible must be read in light of its difference—"The past is a foreign country; they do things differently there." Biblical cosmologists were not scientists or historians in the current meaning of those terms. They were people of faith seeking understanding by exploring the *origins* of their world. Instead of using the genre of the scientific essay that we would employ, they told and retold stories of origin, altering details or even recasting them entirely for the one purpose of explaining the world that God made. To read their stories of origins as if they were modern scientific reports is to misinterpret both the Bible and science.

## Relation of Science and Theology

The third problem with creationism is that it reads biblical cosmogonies and scientific reports with the same literalness. Ian G. Barbour, who is professor of physics, professor of religion and Bean Professor of Science, Technology and Society at Carleton College in Minnesota, criticized such undifferentiated reading in his Gifford Lectures of 1989–91, published as *Religion and Science: Historical and Contemporary Issues* (1997, Part II, No. 4). Barbour argues that the models for relating science and religion are ultimately four: 1) conflict, 2) independence, 3) dialogue and 4) integration. Under the conflict model, Barbour groups both creationism and its great nemesis, the scientific materialism that holds that the scientific method is the *only* method and that matter is the fundamental reality. Each of these claims that science and theology make competing literal statements about the same domain, the history of nature. But, says Barbour, this mixes different levels of discourse. Scientific materialism starts from science but ends up making broad philosophical claims without acknowledging its shift. Biblical creationism moves from theology to make claims about science, again without recognizing its jump to a new level of discourse. Neither school owns up to its shifting methodology.

The models most commonly used in mainstream Christian theology are the third and the fourth, dialogue and integration. It turns out that dialogue is the model favored by many contemporary Roman Catholic thinkers—for example, John Paul II, Ernan McMullin, David Tracy, and the late Karl Rahner. Dialogue notices the presuppositions and the limit-questions of each area, and it is careful about methodology. Integration goes a step further, seeking some kind of integration between the content of theology and the content of science. The writings of Pierre Teilhard de Chardin (1881–1955) provide examples of this model. Whether we prefer the model of dialogue or integration, we have to be aware of the differences between the aims and methods of science and of theology. We cannot flatten out these differences as creationists do, nor can we do away with the differences between biblical literature and our own.

## Value of Creationism

What ought one to think, then, of creationists and their project? First of all, we should recognize that creationists are human beings like ourselves, who earnestly seek religious meaning in the Bible. Moreover, if we are to be practical, we need to be aware that criticizing them will likely have no effect whatsoever. Creationists are constantly attacked and have become inured to it. The best approach, therefore, is positive—to show how a non-fundamentalist reading of the creation accounts can be religiously meaningful. Biblical creation stories reveal a God who is intent on making the world beautiful for the human race and also reveal what the world will be like at the end of time. God defeats chaos and is shown as the God of life, order and beauty.

Nonetheless, we must criticize the creationist project, even as we recognize its sincerity. This criticism will have a political dimension in addition to its epistemological one. As George Marsden has pointed out in *Fundamentalism and American Culture: The Shaping of Twentieth-Century Evangelicalism 1870–1925* (1980), American fundamentalism has a political goal—the preservation or restoration of a nondenominational conservative Christian culture. It is clear from the pressure they have exerted on state school boards that creationists share that political agenda. Opponents of creationism must, therefore, not only criticize it as an idea but also actively oppose creationists' strategy of imposing their religious views on others.

The debate about creationism in public schools can, however, have a happy outcome. American public education has traditionally excluded the Bible and religion from its curriculum. This exclusion of so central an aspect of human life and history has always been indefensible on purely academic grounds. The attempt to force schools to teach creationism can be a wake-up call to public educators. In November 1999 the National Bible Association and the First Amendment Center, with the support of 20 national organizations, ranging from the American Association of School Administrators to the Union of American Hebrew Congregations, published a booklet on teaching the Bible in public schools. Avoiding what it calls "two failed models"—advocacy of one religion or making schools into "religion-free zones"—the booklet suggests an approach in which "public schools neither inculcate nor inhibit religion but become places where religion and religious conviction are treated with fairness and respect." That approach is the best response to creationism.

# NO 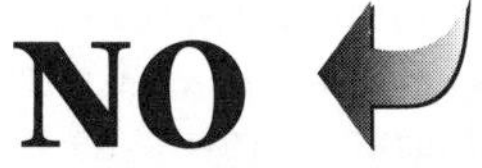

**Marjorie George**

# And Then God Created Kansas?

## Introduction

Kansas has recently become embroiled in a fierce debate over the minds of the state's children, specifically regarding what those children will learn in their public school science classrooms. At first glance, a science curriculum does not seem like a subject of great controversy, but it continues to be one in Kansas and other communities across the country. The controversy hinges specifically on the role evolution should play in science classrooms, but also reflects the broader debate over what role schools should play in students' moral development.

Today many parents are worried about sending their children to public schools. In addition to being concerned about their children's classroom education, parents are also concerned about violence, premarital sex, and drug use. Increasingly, a variety of people are suggesting that problems outside the classroom are due to a lack of morality among young people and communities are turning to religion to provide a solution.

The Bill of Rights of the United States Constitution, however, begins: "Congress shall make no law respecting an establishment of religion, or prohibiting the free exercise thereof. . . ." The Supreme Court has made it clear that the Establishment Clause of the First Amendment of the Constitution erects a high "wall between church and state." The Court has also emphasized that the law itself need not "establish" religion in order to violate the Clause, but may "be one 'respecting' the forbidden objective while falling short of its total realization."

The Court has created a large barrier preventing the inclusion of religion in government, in theory making the government entirely separate from religious institutions. In public schools, however, the two have coexisted in a variety of ways, including recitation of prayers before and after football games and graduation ceremonies, the posting of the Ten Commandments on school walls, the recital of the Lord's Prayer at the beginning of the day, and the teaching of creationism in science classes.

The inclusion or exclusion of religion from public education introduces unique difficulties and often calls for a delicate balancing of interests.

From Marjorie George, "And Then God Created Kansas? The Evolution/Creationism Debate in America's Public Schools," *University of Pennsylvania Law Review*, vol. 149 (January 2001).  Notes omitted.

This is due to the school's role as both educator and guardian during school hours, the involuntary nature of students' attendance at school, and the students' impressionability. The Court keeps these concerns in mind as it monitors compliance with the Establishment Clause in public elementary and secondary schools. Given that public schools are under the control of state and local governments, the Court cautions that "[c]ourts do not and cannot intervene in the resolution of conflicts which arise in the daily operation of school systems and which do not directly and sharply implicate basic constitutional values." At the same time, the Court reiterated that the protection of the fundamental rights guaranteed in the First Amendment within the confines of the public school is essential and that it will not hesitate to protect them when necessary. Schools must avoid not only being a source of indoctrination, but also destroying the students' private beliefs.

While religion in public schools has generally been the subject of public attention and legal action in the United States, the feud regarding creationism and evolution began when Charles Darwin published his theories of evolution in 1859. The debate soon moved into the classroom and first caught the attention of the public in 1927 in the famous *Scopes* "Monkey Trial" in Tennessee. In the aftermath of the Monkey Trial, fourteen states considered anti-evolution statutes in 1927, but only two, Mississippi and Arkansas, enacted such statutes. Since that time, additional statutes attempting to limit the discussion of evolution in public school classrooms have been introduced and enacted. The two challenges to these laws that reached the Supreme Court were both successful, with the Court in each case finding a violation of the Establishment Clause because the statute at issue constituted a prohibited establishment of religion. As laws limiting the teaching of evolution in school or requiring the teaching of creationism in school have been struck down, proponents of creationism have looked for new and original ways to circumvent these decisions. Efforts to come up with new methods to fight the teaching of evolution in public schools are receiving additional attention since many school boards are now controlled by Christian conservatives who generally favor the teaching of creationism in public schools. . . .

## I. How the Creationism Debate Evolved

The teaching of creationism is unique from most other issues involving religion in public schools because it combines the individual's religious beliefs with classroom education. Science teachers are often told to instruct students on subjects which conflict with either their scholarly understanding of evolution or their personal religious beliefs.

The debate to some extent is about the reliability of science itself. In many respects, science is the study of hypotheses and theories—trying to develop explanations for what is not understood. The theory of evolution explains changes in living things over time. The National Academy of Sciences explains that "[t]he concept of biological evolution is one of the most important ideas ever generated by the application of scientific methods to the natural world." Scientists rely on a wide range of scientific evidence, including the fossil record, common structures, the distribution of species, and similarities in development, to support the theory of evolution and simultaneously debunk the creationists' theory of the relatively short history of the earth.

Creationists, on the other hand, believe that God created Earth and the living things on it, as explained in the Bible. Specific views vary—some creationists agree that the Earth is indeed very old, while others claim that the Earth and universe are relatively young and that a catastrophic event, such as a great flood, led to many of the changes on Earth. Many "old Earth" creationists believe that evolution may have played a role in the development of living things since their creation, whereas most "young Earth" creationists believe that God created living things basically in their current form.

In their ongoing battle against evolution, creationists argue that because there are no eyewitnesses regarding what occurred at the beginning of time and at every stage since, creationism is just as likely an explanation as evolution. In fact, creationists argue that there is written evidence supporting their position—the Bible. Scientists counter that failure to physically see a scientific phenomenon does not make it unfounded. Many generally accepted scientific theories cannot be witnessed, such as the existence of atoms and the Earth's movement around the sun, yet scientists infer their existence through the use of "extensive observation and experimentation."

The public school debate regarding evolution and creationism did not begin in earnest until the early 1920s when Christian conservatives, led by William Jennings Bryan, began a crusade against the teaching of evolution. As a result of their efforts, by 1930 twenty state legislatures had debated anti-evolution laws, and three (Tennessee, Mississippi, and Arkansas) had passed laws prohibiting the teaching of evolution in public schools.

The establishment of anti-evolution laws quickly led to a battle for popular opinion between the American Civil Liberties Union, which was recruiting a volunteer teacher to test the Tennessee law, and the World's Christian Fundamentalist Association, whose goal was to restore traditional religious values. John T. Scopes, a high school science teacher in Dayton, Tennessee, came forward to be the defendant in the case. He was charged with violating the Tennessee Anti-Evolution Act of 1925, which made it unlawful to teach any scientific theory that denies the story of the divine creation of man taught in the Bible, and instead posits that man evolved from animals. In creating the legislation, the lawmakers attempted to counteract the increased emphasis on evolution that arose in the late nineteenth and early twentieth centuries as a result of scientists' increasing reliance on Darwin's theory of natural selection.

The stage was then set for the great debate that would ultimately be known as the Monkey Trial. Two of the greatest orators of the time were pitted against one another: Clarence Darrow on behalf of John T. Scopes and William Jennings Bryan on behalf of the prosecution. Due to the throngs of curious spectators, the trial was conducted outside; the very unusual proceeding even included Darrow calling opposing counsel Bryan as an expert witness on the Bible.

In the end, Scopes was convicted and fined $100. The Tennessee Supreme Court reversed the conviction solely on technical grounds, carefully noting that the anti-evolution law was consistent with the Tennessee Constitution. The Tennessee Law remained valid, and anti-evolutionists were able to solidify their position throughout the United States.

Following the *Scopes* decision, the controversy remained somewhat dormant until momentum began to shift against the creationists in the 1950s. First, the influence of scientists greatly increased as their numbers grew approximately tenfold from 1925 to 1960. Second, scientists' funding levels jumped concomitantly with their numbers. Finally, the major catalyst that refocused Americans' attentions on science was the Soviet Union's successful launching of the first satellite, Sputnik, in 1957. This new attention to science returned evolution to the public consciousness.

## II. The Supreme Court Speaks up

### A. "Monkey Laws" Unconstitutional

In 1968, the U. S. Supreme Court had its first opportunity to consider an anti-evolution statute. In *Epperson v. Arkansas,* the Court held that an Arkansas state law prohibiting the teaching of evolution in public schools violated the Establishment Clause. The Arkansas anti-evolution statute, which was passed in 1928, prohibited any public school teacher from "teach[ing] the doctrine or theory that mankind descended or ascended from a lower order of animals." The Court found that the state lawmakers had an unconstitutional religious purpose in passing the law, as they acted as a result of an "upsurge of 'fundamentalist' religious fervor." By the time of the *Epperson* decision there had been a clear shift in public opinion since the *Scopes* decision and the national popular press openly greeted and embraced the Court's decision.

### B. Turning the Tables and Applying the *Lemon* Test

After the Court held in *Epperson* that a state could not prevent teachers from discussing evolution in the classroom, partisans on both sides leapt at the remaining openings in the debate. The *Epperson* decision "did not address either restrictions on the nature of such discussion [about the theory of evolution] or the constitutionality of teaching creationism." Not accepting rejection, the Arkansas legislature passed a new law in 1981 mandating that "[p]ublic schools within [the] State shall give balanced treatment to creation-science and to evolution-science." The Western District of Arkansas stridently rejected this most recent attempt by the Arkansas legislature to limit the teaching of evolution in public schools.

The Supreme Court has subsequently considered a series of cases that address issues relating to religion in public schools and has held unconstitutional the use of religious school teachers in public schools; a moment of silence for school prayer; the display of a copy of the Ten Commandments on public classroom walls; and the daily reading of the Bible. In 1986, in *Edwards v. Aguillard,* the Court considered another state law that dealt with the teaching of evolution and creationism in the public schools. Instead of simply outlawing the teaching of evolution, however, the anti-evolutionists adopted a new approach. Much like the second Arkansas act, which was found unconstitutional by the district court, Louisiana's Creationism Act forbade the teaching of the theory of evolution in public schools unless accompanied by instruction in "creation-science." This approach was symbolic of a broader movement to recast creationism as scientific in order to obtain broader support and satisfy critics.

The Supreme Court held that the Louisiana Creationism Act violated the Establishment Clause. In rejecting the statute, the Court utilized a three-prong test introduced in *Lemon v. Kurtzman* to determine whether legislation comports with the Establishment Clause. Since the adoption of the *Lemon* test, the Supreme Court and lower courts have used it systematically. *Lemon* provides that a statute is unconstitutional if any of the three prongs of the test are violated: first, the legislature must have adopted the law with a secular purpose; second, the statute's principal or primary effect must be one that neither advances nor inhibits religion; and third, the statute must not result in excessive government entanglement with religion. . . .

## III. Skirting the Court's Rulings: Trying to Bring Creationism Back to Public Schools

### A. . . . A Turn Toward Religion

. . . The debate about teaching evolution and creationism in public schools has not diminished; in fact, it now seems stronger than ever. This comes as no surprise when considering a recent Gallup poll that indicates that 44% of Americans consider themselves creationists and believe that God created humans in their present form within the last 10,000 years. Given these beliefs, some parents want their children to rely more on religion; they also may not want their children taught lessons that run counter to their religious teachings.

In its simplest terms, the Bible recounts how God created the Earth in seven days and put all creatures on Earth as they now exist. The theory of evolution, on the other hand, asserts that all life is a product of complex change, which ferrets out weak and reinforces strong characteristics. These explanations in their basic forms run directly counter to one another. Biblical literalists—those who believe that the Bible is a literal telling of creation in seven days—claim that evolution is an unproven theory that is simply wrong and should not be taught in the public schools. Most scientists, on the other hand, state that evolution is a foundational part of a science education, whereas creationism is a solely religious notion that should not be taught in the public schools. While supporters of evolution have won important battles, the war is far from over.

## B. New Approaches and Variations on Old Themes

Supporters of creationism have chosen various approaches in their attempts either to bring creationism into the classroom or remove evolution. One basic philosophy that arises under all four approaches discussed below is that evolution is speculative and unfounded. For example, both Alabama and Oklahoma require a disclaimer in biology textbooks stating that evolution is a controversial theory. A similar law in Tangipahoa, Louisiana mandated that teachers read a disclaimer immediately before teaching evolution in public school science classes. The Fifth Circuit held that law unconstitutional in August 1999.

### *1. Creationism as Science*

One relatively new approach to introducing creationism into public school science curricula is to argue that the scientific basis for creationism is just as strong as that for evolution. Creationists have developed their own scientific evidence to bolster their claims and dispute those of the evolutionists. In fact, a number of organizations exist solely to further this approach. One such group, Answers in Genesis, contends: "The account of origins presented in Genesis is a simple but factual presentation of actual events and therefore provides a reliable framework for scientific research into the question of the origin and history of life, mankind, the Earth, and the universe."

The most successful attempt to introduce creationism as science in public schools is based on the "theory of intelligent design." This theory is not based on one specific religious philosophy or a particular religious story, but on the general notion "that the world and its creatures are far too complex to have arisen through random patterns of evolution and must be the product of some intelligent designer." The intelligent design theory was recently thrust into the public spotlight by *Of Pandas and People,* a science textbook incorporating this approach. Many communities across the country have publicly debated the adoption of this textbook, once again stirring the evolution versus creationism debate.

### *2. Evolution as Religion*

The flipside to the approach that defends creationism by claiming it is a valid scientific theory is to attack evolution as a form of religion itself—"secular humanism." The general argument is that although creationism is based on religious beliefs, evolution is as well. Just as teachers cannot be compelled to teach creationism because it violates the Establishment Clause, teachers similarly could not be compelled to teach evolution if it were classified as a religion.

Little chance exists, however, that the Supreme Court will view evolution as a form of religion. . . .

### *3. Competing Theories as Source for Debate*

The third approach, which has gained momentum recently, provides that children should be taught both evolution and creationism so that they may determine for themselves which is more accurate. This argument is actually incorporated in both approaches discussed above: creationism as science and evolution as religion. These two approaches contend that creationism stands on the same ground as evolution and should therefore receive equal treatment in public school science curricula. One need not adopt either of the approaches, however, to believe that both evolution and creationism should be presented to children. Nevertheless, many of the arguments for teaching both evolution and creationism hinge on some of the fundamental positions presented above.

Legally, this approach is promising to supporters of creationism because the Supreme Court specifically left the door open for this type of science education. In *Edwards,* the Court limited its holding: "We do not imply that a legislature could never require that scientific critiques of prevailing scientific theories be taught." First, the Court would have to believe that the critiques were scientific and not religious. Second, any such law would still have to satisfy the three prongs of the *Lemon* test, and the Court's rulings concerning the religious nature of creationism would establish a difficult burden for the state to overcome.

***4. Discourage or Prohibit the Teaching of Evolution***

Closely related to encouraging debate is a final approach that, in theory, does not involve creationism at all—discouraging the introduction of evolution. As will be further discussed in the examination of Kansas's actions below, states have accomplished this end by removing the requirement from their state curriculum that evolution be taught. In the last four years, six other states—Arizona, Alabama, Illinois, New Mexico, Texas, and Nebraska—"have tried to remove evolution from state science standards or water down the concepts, with varying degrees of success."

This approach avoids a weakness in the three other possibilities. In theory, it avoids the Supreme Court holding that creationism is a religious doctrine. If creationism is not introduced in any way, then the proponents can argue religion is not being "established"; therefore the *Lemon* test will not even come into play.

## C. Evolution and Creationism in Kansas

The Kansas science curriculum became the focus of international media attention in August 1999 when the Kansas State Board of Education voted to adopt newly drafted standards. The controversy arose because of the Board's earlier rejection of standards drafted by the state's science curriculum committee—a committee comprised of scientists, educators, and citizens created for this specific purpose. The original set of standards was based on the National Science Education Standards ("NSES"), a general framework drafted by the National Academy of Sciences. The NSES include evolution as a "unifying concept" in science, linking cosmology, geology, physics, and biology.

Evolution opponents immediately addressed the Board to voice their outrage at the standards. In response to these objections, board member Steve Abrams presented a new set of standards. These standards were the result of the efforts of Celtie Johnson, an avid opponent of evolution. Ms. Johnson organized a group of creationists from Kansas and Missouri and together they drafted the standards. The standards approved in August 1999 were primarily based on the work of Johnson's group:

> [T]he board approved science standards that contained references to microevolution, or adaptation, but no mention of macroevolution, or change from one species to another. The revised version no longer lists evolution as one of science's unifying concepts. The revised standards also omit many references to the age of Earth. There is no longer any mention of the big-bang theory.

The standards also contain other, more subtle references to the underlying ideas and arguments made by proponents of creationist science. For example, as a general principle for "teaching with tolerance and respect," they wrote that "[n]o evidence or analysis of evidence that contradicts a current science theory should be censored." The standards also include "examples anyone familiar with the debate would recognize as favorites of creationists, such as the volcanic explosion of Mount St. Helens in 1980, a catastrophe they say proves Earth can undergo monumental changes in short periods of time."

Of course, these standards do not outlaw the teaching of macroevolution in public schools; macroevolution simply is not a "required" concept and will not be included on state-wide standardized tests. Some teachers are worried that the uncertain status of evolution will only bring more controversy and challenges both to the classroom and to a subject already wrought with tension. Now when a teacher chooses to teach evolution, which many science teachers assure they will continue to do, they will face criticisms and questions about their choice. These criticisms will not just come from students, which is natural and expected in classroom discussions, but also from other teachers and the community at large. Many science teachers strongly believe that teaching evolution is not optional, and one high school biology teacher said, "If I teach biology without evolution I'd be doing an injustice to students, and to myself."

## D. Do Kansas's Standards Violate the Constitution?

The Kansas School Board's effort to reduce the prominence of evolution in its science curriculum standards rests on shaky legal ground. The school board's action is consistent with other efforts to limit or prevent the teaching of evolution in public schools without coming in direct conflict with the Supreme Court's Establishment Clause jurisprudence. The Court, however, has always interpreted the Establishment Clause to prevent not only the favoring of one religion over another, but also the favoring of religion generally over irreligion. The Court has been particularly vigilant in Establishment Clause cases involving compulsory public education.

### *1. Applying the* Lemon *Test*

The constitutionality of the new Kansas science standards turns on satisfaction of the three prongs of the *Lemon* test. If the standards fail even one of the three prongs, then they would be found to violate the Establishment Clause.

**a. No Secular Purpose** Under the *Lemon* test, the first consideration is whether the school board adopted the standards with a secular purpose. The Court has said that a "governmental intention to promote religion is clear when the State enacts a law to serve a religious purpose." Although this is a close case, it is unlikely that Kansas would be able to overcome the very high bar set by the Court. The school board members' stated purpose is to ensure that their students were being taught "good science." The Court would likely find this purpose to be a sham, just as it found "academic freedom" in *Edwards,* "promotion of moral values" in *Schempp,* and "education[] function" in *Stone* all to be shams.

The Court has made clear in its previous decisions that the historical context of the debate about evolution is relevant when determining whether the decisionmakers acted with a religious purpose. The Court has acknowledged the obvious reason for limiting the teaching of evolution. In *Epperson,* where the state law forbade the teaching of evolution in public schools, the Court expressed its concern that the law "was confined to an attempt to blot out a particular theory because of its supposed conflict with the Biblical account, literally read." Defenders of the Kansas School Board's science standards would certainly argue that the situation in Kansas is substantially different from the state law at issue in *Epperson* because the standards simply de-emphasize the reliance on evolution. Thus, unlike the state law in *Epperson,* the Kansas standards do not attempt "to blot out a particular theory." However, the concern is the same: that the board is acting to restrict the teaching of a certain "body of knowledge . . . for the sole reason that it is deemed to conflict with a particular religious doctrine."

The de-emphasis of evolution in the Kansas curriculum certainly appears to be due to its conflict with religious beliefs, particularly those of Bible literalists. First, if the concerns were really for "good science," why would the standards drafted by the state's science curriculum committee—a committee composed of scientists, educators, and citizens—be rejected without any explanation? The committee was created precisely for the purpose of drafting these standards because these individuals were believed to have the necessary knowledge and skills. Second, a striking similarity exists between the Creation Science Association draft standards and the exact wording in the modified standards proposed by school board members Harold Voth, Steve Abrams, and Scott Hill. Kansas Citizens for Science compared the adopted standards with those of the creationist group and found "that excluding the introduction, 40 of 42 changes to the standards written by Abrams, Voth and Hill were contained verbatim in one or both of the creationist documents." Third, Celtie Johnson, the woman who first presented board member Abrams with the alternative Creation Science Association standards, was primarily motivated by religious reasons. Johnson also claims that she "was motivated by a search for truth," but her conception of truth is that evolution is a completely unfounded theory, and she "firmly believes in the biblical account of creation." Fourth, although the final version of the standards did not contain any discussion about creationism, it does contain components of the arguments in favor of creationism. Finally, Abrams admits that creationist scholars influenced those elements he included in the standards.

**b. Primary Effect That Advances or Inhibits Religion** . . . [T]he Court will only consider the remaining two prongs of the test, primary effect and excessive entanglement, if it finds a secular purpose for the law. In this case, therefore, the consideration would need to go no further. If the Court finds a secular purpose, such as good science, and does not regard it as a sham, the Court would next need to find the Kansas science standards' "principal or primary effect [as] one that neither advances nor inhibits religion." The Court has never before reached these prongs in a case involving the teaching of evolution and creationism in the public schools and often does not reach these prongs in other cases involving the Establishment Clause and public schools.

In *Wallace v. Jaffree,* although the Court found the purpose of the statute to be religious and therefore violative of the Establishment Clause, Justice Powell, in his concurring opinion, did note "that the 'effect' of a straightforward moment-of-silence statute is unlikely to 'advanc[e] or inhibi[t] religion.'" The Court's main consideration with regard to this prong of the *Lemon* test would be "the effect on the minds and feelings of immature pupils." Justice Powell concluded that the likelihood of children thinking about religion in such a circumstance was very small. In *Board of Education v. Mergens,* the Court noted again the significance of the students' age in determining the effect of a requirement that meeting space be provided to religious student organizations. In that case the Court concluded that the students would understand that while permitting student speech on campus, the school was not endorsing it.

The situation in Kansas is arguably different from those discussed above in several ways. First, the science standards apply to all students, not only those who may be deemed mature enough to understand the state's role. Second, the teachers are directly involved in the teaching of the science curriculum, unlike both of the situations above, where the school merely allows a moment of silence and where teachers are not at all involved in the meetings. Finally, the state's involvement in limiting the teaching of certain subjects contrary to some citizens' religious beliefs "threatens to convey a message of state support for religion to students and to the general public."

**c. Excessive Entanglement with Religion** The Court's considerations under the third and final prong are very similar to those under the "effect" prong. The Court will consider the "character and purposes of the institutions that are benefited, the nature of the aid that the State provides, and the resulting relationship between the government and the religious authority." The Court has held laws relating to religion in public schools to pass these two prongs only when they were very narrowly focused and when they necessitated very limited teacher involvement.

If the Kansas science standards reached the third prong, they would likely survive. If the purpose and effects are both found to be secular, then the entanglement will likely be slight. Furthermore, the Court is usually concerned about entanglement—demonstrated in the factors listed above—with regard to direct financial or other benefits to religious institutions, typically religious schools.

## Conclusion

The Court has made clear that creationism does not have a place in public classrooms. In concluding that the Louisiana Creationism Act was unconstitutional, the Court disparagingly noted:

> [I]t is not happenstance that the legislature required the teaching of a theory that coincided with this religious view [that God was responsible for the creation of humankind]. . . . The legislation therefore sought to alter the science curriculum to reflect endorsement of a religious view that is antagonistic to the theory of evolution.

Nonetheless, the debate continues. While states may no longer pass laws forbidding the teaching of evolution or demanding equal treatment for creationist theories, they may attack the issue in other ways. The approaches are varied and sometimes creative, but they continue to arise.

The wall preventing such entanglement between religion and public education must remain high with regard to the science curriculum, in part because concerns surrounding the teaching of science are closely related to other public school curriculum issues. If science classes in high schools can be tailored not to offend certain people's religious beliefs, then other courses may be next: history (no Holocaust?), English (no Mark Twain's *Huckleberry Finn?*), health (no sex education?). In order to protect independent thinking, religious beliefs must not be allowed to determine the curriculum of public school courses.

The real concern here is the education of school children. "[N]o law [shall be made] respecting an establishment of religion," including laws affecting public schools. While religion on the periphery may not offend the Supreme Court's requirements for separation, it can play no role in the classroom.

# POSTSCRIPT

## Should Creationism and Evolution Get Equal Time in Schools?

Early in 2001, a new Kansas Board of Education took office and promptly put evolution back in the curriculum. See Eugene Russo, "Fighting Darwin's Battles," *The Scientist* (March 19, 2001). Yet the battle is hardly won. Not even Pope John Paul II's 1996 announcement that "new knowledge leads us to recognize that the theory of evolution is more than a hypothesis" had much impact. In 2002, the Cobb County [Georgia] School Board amended its curriculum policy to encourage the teaching of creationism; see "Georgia County Approves Policy To Undermine Science Instruction, "*Church & State* (November 2002). Eugenie C. Scott, "Antievolutionism: Changes and Continuities," *Bioscience* (March 2003), says that "Claims that evolution is a theory in crisis, that evolution is incompatible with Christianity, and that it is only fair to teach 'both sides'" appeared at the very beginning of the evolution–creationism debate (the 1925 Scopes trial) and have continued to "appear in any arena in which the antievolution movement is active."

The debate has at times turned abusive, as it did in May 1996, when biologists attempting to inform the Ohio House Education Committee of how thoroughly the evidence supports the theory of evolution were heckled, jeered, and shouted down. See Karen Schmidt, "Creationists Evolve New Strategy," *Science* (July 26, 1996). The rhetoric on the other side is not always much better. Virginia Barbour, "Science and Myth," *Lancet* (April 20, 2002), says that "intellectual laziness is the most charitable explanation for not accepting the evidence for evolution." See also John Rennie, "15 Answers to Creationist Nonsense" (*Scientific American,* July 2002).

The late Stephen Jay Gould, in "The Persistently Flat Earth," *Natural History* (March 1994), makes the point that irrationality and dogmatism serve the adherents of neither science nor religion well: "The myth of a war between science and religion remains all too current and continues to impede a proper bonding and conciliation between these two utterly different and powerfully important institutions of human life."

Many Americans appear to agree with Gould. For example, Dudley Barlow, in "The Teachers' Lounge: Kansas Junta Repudiated," *Education Digest* (May 2000), contends that most Americans are willing to give creationism space in public education because "it is good to expose students to several different ways of thinking about complex ideas." However, the battle continues (see Mano Singham, "The Science and Religion Wars," *Phi Delta Kappan* [February 2000] and Randy Moore, "The Revival of Creationism in the United States," *Journal of Biological Education* [Winter 2000]) and even shows sign of spreading abroad. In Turkey, for instance, teachers of evolution are receiving e-mailed death threats, and a legislator is trying to get evolution taken out of the schools. See Robert Koenig, "Creationism Takes Root Where Europe, Asia Meet," *Science* (May 18, 2001).

Early in 2001 a new Kansas Board of Education took office and promptly put evolution back in the curriculum. See Eugene Russo, "Fighting Darwin's Battles," *The Scientist* (March 19, 2001).

# On the Internet . . .

## Worldwatch Institute

The Worldwatch Institute is dedicated to fostering the evolution of an environmentally sustainable society, one in which human needs are met in ways that do not threaten the health of the natural environment or the prospects of future generations.

http://www.worldwatch.org

## Facing the Future: People and the Planet

Facing the Future strives to educate people about critical global issues, including population growth, poverty, overconsumption, and environmental destruction.

http://www.facingthefuture.org

## Global Warming

The Environmental Protection Agency maintains this site to summarize the current state of knowledge about global warming.

http://www.epa.gov/globalwarming/

## Intergovernmental Panel on Climate Change

The Intergovernmental Panel on Climate Change (IPCC) was formed by the World Meteorological Organization (WMO) and the United Nations Environment Programme (UNEP) to assess any scientific, technical, and socioeconomic information that is relevant to the understanding of the risk of human-induced climate change.

http://www.ipcc.ch

## National Renewable Energy Laboratory

The National Renewable Energy Laboratory (NREL) is the leading center for renewable energy research in the United States.

http://www.nrel.gov

## Heritage Foundation

The Heritage Foundation is a think tank whose mission is to formulate and promote conservative public policies based on the principles of free enterprise, limited government, individual freedom, traditional American values, and a strong national defense.

http://www.heritage.org

# PART 2

## The Environment

*As the damage that human beings do to their environment in the course of obtaining food, wood, ore, fuel, and other resources has become clear, many people have grown concerned. Some of that concern is for the environment—the landscapes and living things with which humanity shares its world. Some of that concern is more for human welfare; it focuses on the ways in which environmental damage threatens human health or even human survival.*

*Some environmental issues are well known. These include over-population, global warming, and the impact of environmentalism on individual freedoms and property rights. All have provoked extensive debate over details and degrees of certainty, over what can or should be done to prevent future difficulties, and even over whether or not the issues are real.*

- Do We Face a "Population Problem"?
- Should Society Act Now to Halt Global Warming?
- Do Environmentalists Overstate Their Case?
- Will Hydrogen Replace Fossil Fuels for Cars?

# ISSUE 4

## Do We Face a "Population Problem"?

**YES: Lester R. Brown, Gary Gardner, and Brian Halweil,** from "Sixteen Impacts of Population Growth," *The Futurist* (February 1999)

**NO: Stephen Moore,** from "Body Count: Population and Its Enemies," *National Review* (October 25, 1999)

### ISSUE SUMMARY

**YES:** Lester R. Brown, founder of the Worldwatch Institute, and Worldwatch researchers Gary Gardner and Brian Halweil argue that population growth is straining the Earth's ability to support humanity and that population must therefore be stabilized.

**NO:** Stephen Moore, director of the Cato Institute, argues that the population-control ethic is a threat both to freedom and to the principle that every human life has intrinsic value.

In 1798 the British economist Thomas Malthus published his *Essay on the Principle of Population.* In it, he pointed with alarm at the way the human population grew geometrically (a hockey-stick curve of increase) and at how agricultural productivity grew only arithmetically (a straight-line increase). It was obvious, he said, that the population must inevitably outstrip its food supply and experience famine. Contrary to the conventional wisdom of the time, population growth was not necessarily a good thing. Indeed, it led inexorably to catastrophe. For many years, Malthus was something of a laughingstock. The doom he forecast kept receding into the future as new lands were opened to agriculture, new agricultural technologies appeared, new ways of preserving food limited the waste of spoilage, and the birth rate dropped in the industrialized nations (the "demographic transition"). The food supply kept ahead of population growth and seemed likely—to most observers—to continue to do so. Malthus's ideas were dismissed as irrelevant fantasies.

Yet overall population kept growing. In Malthus's time, there were about 1 billion human beings on Earth. By 1950—when Warren S. Thompson worried that civilization would be endangered by the rapid growth of Asian and Latin American populations during the next five decades (see "Population," *Scientific American* [February 1950])—there were a little over 2.5 billion. In 1999 the tally passed 6 billion. By 2025 it will be over 8 billion. Statistics like these, which are presented in *World Resources 2000–2001,* a biennial report of the World Resources Institute in collaboration with the United Nations Environment and Development Programmes (Oxford University Press, 2000), are positively frightening. The Worldwatch Institute's yearly *State of the World* reports (W. W. Norton) are no less so. By 2050 the UN expects the world population to be about 9 billion (see *World Population Prospects: The 2002 Revision* (UN, February 2003) (http://www.un.org/esa/population/publications/wpp2002/WPP2002-HIGHLIGHTSrev1.PDF). While global agricultural production has also increased, it has not kept up with rising demand, and—because of the loss of topsoil to erosion, the exhaustion of aquifers for irrigation water, and the high price of energy for making fertilizer (among other things)—the prospect of improvement seems exceedingly slim to many observers.

Some people are still laughing at Malthus and his forecasts of doom, which two centuries never saw come to pass. Among the scoffers are Julian Simon, a "cornucopian" economist who believes that the more people we have on Earth, the more talent we have available for solving problems, and that humans can indeed find ways around all possible resource shortages. See his essay "Life on Earth Is Getting Better, Not Worse," *The Futurist* (August 1983).

But more and more people—including some economists—are coming to realize that Malthus's error lay not in his prediction but in his timing. He was quite correct to say that a growing population must inevitably outrun its food supply. The only question is how long human ingenuity can stave off the day of reckoning.

Can population really go as high as many predict? If it does, can the world possibly supply the food and other resources that so many people will need? There are famines, water shortages, and other resource-related problems in the world today. Won't they grow far worse long before we approach the 10 billion mark in 2050? Paul R. Ehrlich and Anne H. Ehrlich, in "The Population Explosion: Why We Should Care and What We Should Do About It," *Environmental Law* (Winter 1997), state, "Population growth may be the paramount force moving humanity inexorably towards disaster." It is essential, they contend, to reduce the impact of population in terms of both numbers and resource consumption.

In the following selection, Lester R. Brown, Gary Gardner, and Brian Halweil share the Ehrlichs' concern. "What is needed," they say, "is an all-out effort to lower fertility . . . while there is still time." In the second selection, Stephen Moore argues that Malthus has long been wrong and will remain so and that all indicators are steadily improving thanks to the human talent for solving problems. He maintains that attempts to restrict family size are an assault on human freedom and on the principle that every human life has intrinsic value.

**Lester R. Brown, Gary Gardner, and Brian Halweil**

# Sixteen Impacts of Population Growth

The world's population has doubled during the last half century, climbing from 2.5 billion in 1950 to 5.9 billion in 1998. This unprecedented surge in population, combined with rising individual consumption, is pushing our claims on the planet beyond its natural limits.

The United Nations projects that human population in 2050 will range between 7.7 billion and 11.2 billion people. We use the United Nations' middle-level projection of 9.4 billion (from *World Population Prospects: The 1996 Revision*) to give an idea of the strain this "most likely" outcome would place on ecosystems and governments in the future and of the urgent need to break from the business-as-usual scenario.

Our study looks at 16 dimensions or effects of population growth in order to gain a better perspective on how future population trends are likely to affect human prospects:

## Impacts on Food and Agriculture

### 1. Grain Production

From 1950 to 1984, growth in the world grain harvest easily exceeded that of population. But since then, the growth in the grain harvest has fallen behind that of population, so per-person output has dropped by 7% (0.5% a year), according to the U.S. Department of Agriculture.

The slower growth in the world grain harvest since 1984 is due to the lack of new land and to slower growth in irrigation and fertilizer use because of the diminishing returns of these inputs.

Now that the frontiers of agricultural settlement have disappeared, future growth in grain production must come almost entirely from raising land productivity. Unfortunately, this is becoming more difficult. The challenge for the world's farmers is to reverse this decline at a time when cropland area per person is shrinking, the amount of irrigation water per person is dropping, and the crop yield response to additional fertilizer use is falling.

## 2. Cropland

Since mid-century, grain area—which serves as a proxy for cropland in general—has increased by some 19%, but global population has grown by 132%. Population growth can degrade farmland, reducing its productivity or even eliminating it from production. As grain area per person falls, more and more nations risk losing the capacity to feed themselves.

The trend is illustrated starkly in the world's four fastest-growing large countries. Having already seen per capita grain area shrink by 40%–50% between 1960 and 1998, Pakistan, Nigeria, Ethiopia, and Iran can expect a further 60%–70% loss by 2050—a conservative projection that assumes no further losses of agricultural land. The result will be four countries with a combined population of more than 1 billion whose grain area per person will be only 300–600 square meters—less than a quarter of the area in 1950.

## 3. Fresh Water

Spreading water scarcity may be the most underrated resource issue in the world today. Wherever population is growing, the supply of fresh water per person is declining.

Evidence of water stress can be seen as rivers are drained dry and water tables fall. Rivers such as the Nile, the Yellow, and the Colorado have little water left when they reach the sea. Water tables are now falling on every continent, including in major food-producing regions. Aquifers are being depleted in the U.S. southern Great Plains, the North China Plain, and most of India.

The International Water Management Institute projects that a billion people will be living in countries facing absolute water scarcity by 2025. These countries will have to reduce water use in agriculture in order to satisfy residential and industrial water needs. In both China and India, the two countries that together dominate world irrigated agriculture, substantial cutbacks in irrigation water supplies lie ahead.

## 4. Oceanic Fish Catch

A fivefold growth in the human appetite for seafood since 1950 has pushed the catch of most oceanic fisheries to their sustainable limits or beyond. Marine biologists believe that the oceans cannot sustain an annual catch of much more than 93 million tons, the current take.

As we near the end of the twentieth century, overfishing has become the rule, not the exception. Of the 15 major oceanic fisheries, 11 are in decline. The catch of Atlantic cod—long a dietary mainstay for western Europeans—has fallen by 70% since peaking in 1968. Since 1970, bluefin tuna stocks in the West Atlantic have dropped by 80%.

With the oceans now pushed to their limits, future growth in the demand for seafood can be satisfied only by fish farming. But as the world turns to aquaculture to satisfy its needs, fish begin to compete with livestock and poultry for feedstuffs such as grain, soybean meal, and fish meal.

The next half century is likely to be marked by the disappearance of some species from markets, a decline in the quality of seafood caught, higher prices, and more conflicts among countries over access to fisheries. Each year, the future oceanic catch per person will decline by roughly the amount of population growth, dropping to 9.9 kilograms (22 pounds) per person in 2050, compared with the 1988 peak of 17.2 kilograms (37.8 pounds).

### 5. Meat Production

When incomes begin to rise in traditional low-income societies, one of the first things people do is diversify their diets, consuming more livestock products.

World meat production since 1950 has increased almost twice as fast as population. Growth in meat production was originally concentrated in western industrial countries and Japan, but over the last two decades it has increased rapidly in East Asia, the Middle East, and Latin America. Beef, pork, and poultry account for the bulk of world consumption.

Of the world grain harvest of 1.87 billion tons in 1998, an estimated 37% will be used to feed livestock and poultry, producing milk and eggs as well as meat, according to the U.S. Department of Agriculture. Grain fed to livestock and poultry is now the principal food reserve in the event of a world food emergency.

Total meat consumption will rise from 211 million tons in 1997 to 513 million tons in 2050, increasing pressures on the supply of grain.

## Environment and Resources

### 6. Natural Recreation Areas

From Buenos Aires to Bangkok, dramatic population growth in the world's major cities—and the sprawl and pollution they bring—threaten natural recreation areas that lie beyond city limits. On every continent, human encroachment has reduced both the size and the quality of natural recreation areas.

In nations where rapid population growth has outstripped the carrying capacity of local resources, protected areas become especially vulnerable. Although in industrial nations these areas are synonymous with camping, hiking, and picnics in the country, in Asia, Africa, and Latin America most national parks, forests, and preserves are inhabited or used for natural resources by local populations.

Migration-driven population growth also endangers natural recreation areas in many industrial nations. Everglades National Park, for example, faces collapse as millions of newcomers move into southern Florida.

Longer waiting lists and higher user fees for fewer secluded spots are likely to be the tip of the iceberg, as population growth threatens to eliminate the diversity of habitats and cultures, in addition to the peace and quiet, that protected areas currently offer.

## 7. Forests

Global losses of forest area have marched in step with population growth for much of human history, but an estimated 75% of the loss in global forests has occurred in the twentieth century.

In Latin America, ranching is the single largest cause of deforestation. In addition, overgrazing and overcollection of firewood—which are often a function of growing population—are degrading 14% of the world's remaining large areas of virgin forest.

Deforestation created by the demand for forest products tracks closely with rising per capita consumption in recent decades. Global use of paper and paperboard per person has doubled (or nearly tripled) since 1961.

The loss of forest areas leads to a decline of forest services. These include habitat for wildlife; carbon storage, which is a key to regulating climate; and erosion control, provision of water across rainy and dry seasons, and regulation of rainfall.

## 8. Biodiversity

We live amid the greatest extinction of plant and animal life since the dinosaurs disappeared 65 million years ago, at the end of the Cretaceous period, with species losses at 100 to 1,000 times the natural rate. The principal cause of species extinction is habitat loss, which tends to accelerate with an increase in a country's population density.

A particularly productive but vulnerable habitat is found in coastal areas, home to 60% of the world's population. Coastal wetlands nurture two-thirds of all commercially caught fish, for example. And coral reefs have the second-highest concentration of biodiversity in the world, after tropical rain forests. But human encroachment and pollution are degrading these areas: Roughly half of the world's salt marshes and mangrove swamps have been eliminated or radically altered, and two-thirds of the world's coral reefs have been degraded, 10% of them "beyond recognition." As coastal migration continues—coastal dwellers could account for 75% of world population within 30 years—the pressures on these productive habitats will likely increase.

## 9. Climate Change

Over the last half century, carbon emissions from fossil-fuel burning expanded at nearly twice the rate of population, boosting atmospheric concentrations of carbon dioxide, the principal greenhouse gas, by 30% over preindustrial levels.

Fossil-fuel use accounts for roughly three-quarters of world carbon emissions. As a result, regional growth in carbon emissions tend to occur where economic activity and related energy use is projected to grow most rapidly. Emissions in China are projected to grow over three times faster than population in the next 50 years due to a booming economy that is heavily reliant on coal and other carbon-rich energy sources.

Emissions from developing countries will nearly quadruple over the next half century, while those from industrial nations will increase by

30%, according to the Intergovernmental Panel on Climate Change and the U.S. Department of Energy. Although annual emissions from industrial countries are currently twice as high as from developing ones, the latter are on target to eclipse the industrial world by 2020.

### 10. Energy

The global demand for energy grew twice as fast as population over the last 50 years. By 2050, developing countries will be consuming much more energy as their populations increase and become more affluent.

When per capita energy consumption is high, even a low rate of population growth can have significant effects on total energy demand. In the United States, for example, the 75 million people projected to be added to the population by 2050 will boost energy demand to roughly the present energy consumption of Africa and Latin America.

World oil production per person reached a high in 1979 and has since declined by 23%. Estimates of when global oil production will peak range from 2011 to 2025, signaling future price shocks as long as oil remains the world's dominant fuel.

In the next 50 years, the greatest growth in energy demands will come where economic activity is projected to be highest: in Asia, where consumption is expected to grow 361%, though population will grow by just 50%. Energy consumption is also expected to increase in Latin America (by 340%) and Africa (by 326%). In all three regions, local pressures on energy sources, ranging from forests to fossil fuel reserves to waterways, will be significant.

### 11. Waste

Local and global environmental effects of waste disposal will likely worsen as 3.4 billion people are added to the world's population over the next half century. Prospects for providing access to sanitation are dismal in the near to medium term.

A growing population increases society's disposal headaches—the garbage, sewage, and industrial waste that must be gotten rid of. Even where population is largely stable—the case in many industrialized countries—the flow of waste products into landfills and waterways generally continues to increase. Where high rates of economic and population growth coincide in coming decades, as they will in many developing countries, mountains of waste will likely pose difficult disposal challenges for municipal and national authorities.

## Economic Impacts and Quality of Life

### 12. Jobs

Since 1950, the world's labor force has more than doubled—from 1.2 billion people to 2.7 billion—outstripping the growth in job creation. Over the next half century, the world will need to create more than 1.9 billion jobs in the developing world just to maintain current levels of employment.

While population growth may boost labor demand (through economic activity and demand for goods), it will most definitely boost labor supply. As the balance between the demand and supply of labor is tipped by population growth, wages tend to decrease. And in a situation of labor surplus, the quality of jobs may not improve as fast, for workers will settle for longer hours, fewer benefits, and less control over work activities.

As the children of today represent the workers of tomorrow, the interaction between population growth and jobs is most acute in nations with young populations. Nations with more than half their population below the age of 25 (e.g., Peru, Mexico, Indonesia, and Zambia) will feel the burden of this labor flood. Employment is the key to obtaining food, housing, health services, and education, in addition to providing self-respect and self-fulfillment.

## 13. Income

Incomes have risen most rapidly in developing countries where population has slowed the most, including South Korea, Taiwan, China, Indonesia, and Malaysia. African countries, largely ignoring family planning, have been overwhelmed by the sheer numbers of young people who need to be educated and employed.

If the world cannot simultaneously convert the economy to one that is environmentally sustainable and move to a lower population trajectory, economic decline will be hard to avoid.

## 14. Housing

The ultimate manifestation of population growth outstripping the supply of housing is homelessness. The United Nations estimates that at least 100 million of the world's people—roughly equal to the population of Mexico—have no home; the number tops 1 billion if squatters and others with insecure or temporary accommodations are included.

Unless population growth can be checked worldwide, the ranks of the homeless are likely to swell dramatically.

## 15. Education

In nations that have increasing child-age populations, the base pressures on the educational system will be severe. In the world's 10 fastest-growing countries, most of which are in Africa and the Middle East, the child-age population will increase an average of 93% over the next 50 years. Africa as a whole will see its school-age population grow by 75% through 2040.

If national education systems begin to stress lifelong learning for a rapidly changing world of the twenty-first century, then extensive provision for adult education will be necessary, affecting even those countries with shrinking child-age populations.

Such a development means that countries which started population-stabilization programs earliest will be in the best position to educate their entire citizenry.

### 16. Urbanization

Today's cities are growing faster: It took London 130 years to get from 1 million to 8 million inhabitants; Mexico City made this jump in just 30 years. The world's urban population as a whole is growing by just over 1 million people each week. This urban growth is fed by the natural increase of urban populations, by net migration from the countryside, and by villages or towns expanding to the point where they become cities or they are absorbed by the spread of existing cities.

If recent trends continue, 6.5 billion people will live in cities by 2050, more than the world's total population today.

## Actions for Slowing Growth

As we look to the future, the challenge for world leaders is to help countries maximize the prospects for achieving sustainability by keeping both birth and death rates low. In a world where both grain output and fish catch per person are falling, a strong case can be made on humanitarian grounds to stabilize world population.

What is needed is an all-out effort to lower fertility, particularly in the high-fertility countries, while there is still time. We see four key steps in doing this:

**Assess Carrying Capacity** Every national government needs a carefully articulated and adequately supported population policy, one that takes into account the country's carrying capacity at whatever consumption level citizens decide on. Without long-term estimates of available cropland, water for irrigation, and likely yields, governments are simply flying blind into the future, allowing their nations to drift into a world in which population growth and environmental degradation can lead to social disintegration.

**Fill the Family-Planning Gap** This is a high-payoff area. In a world where population pressures are mounting, the inability of 120 million of the world's women to get family-planning services is inexcusable. A stumbling block: At the International Conference on Population and Development in Cairo in 1994, the industrialized countries agreed to pay one-third of the costs for reproductive-health services in developing countries. So far they have failed to do so.

**Educate Young Women** Educating girls is a key to accelerating the shift to smaller families. In every society for which data are available, the more education women have, the fewer children they have. Closely related to the need for education of young females is the need to provide equal opportunities for women in all phases of national life.

**Have Just Two Children** If we are facing a population emergency, it should be treated as such. It may be time for a campaign to convince couples everywhere to restrict their childbearing to replacement-level fertility.

# NO 

**Stephen Moore**

# Body Count: Population and Its Enemies

At a Washington reception, the conversation turned to the merits of small families. One woman volunteered that she had just read Bill McKibben's environmental tome, *Maybe One,* on the benefits of single-child families. She claimed to have found it "ethically compelling." I chimed in: "Even one child may put too much stress on our fragile ecosystem. McKibben says 'maybe one.' I say, why not none?" The response was solemn nods of agreement, and even some guilt-ridden whispers between husbands and wives.

McKibben's acclaimed book is a tribute to the theories of British economist Thomas Malthus. Exactly 200 years ago, Malthus—the original dismal scientist—wrote that "the power of population is . . . greater than the power in the earth to produce subsistence for man." McKibben's application of this idea was to rush out and have a vasectomy. He urges his fellow greens to do the same—to make single-child families the "cultural norm" in America.

Now, with the United Nations proclaiming that this month we will surpass the demographic milestone of 6 billion people, the environmental movement and the media can be expected to ask: Do we really need so many people? A recent AP headline lamented: "Century's growth leaves Earth crowded—and noisy." Seemingly, Malthus has never had so many apostles.

In a rational world, Malthusianism would not be in a state of intellectual revival, but thorough disrepute. After all, virtually every objective trend is running in precisely the opposite direction of what the widely acclaimed Malthusians of the 1960s—from Lester Brown to Paul Ehrlich to the Club of Rome—predicted. Birth rates around the world are lower today than at any time in recorded history. Global per capita food production is much higher than ever before. The "energy crisis" is now such a distant memory that oil is virtually the cheapest liquid on earth. These facts, collectively, have wrecked the credibility of the population-bomb propagandists.

Yet the population-control movement is gaining steam. It has won the hearts and wallets of some of the most influential leaders inside and outside government today. Malthusianism has evolved into a multi-billion-dollar industry and a political juggernaut.

Today, through the U.S. Agency for International Development (AID), the State Department, and the World Bank, the federal government pumps some 350 million tax dollars a year into population-containment activities. The Clinton administration would be spending at least twice that amount if not for the efforts of two Republican congressmen, Chris Smith of New Jersey and Todd Tiahrt of Kansas, who have managed to cut off funding for the most coercive birth-reduction initiatives.

Defenders of the U.N. Population Fund (UNFPA) and other such agencies insist that these programs "protect women's reproductive freedom," "promote the health of mothers," and "reduce infant mortality." Opponents of international "family planning," particularly Catholic organizations, are tarred as anti-abortion fanatics who want to deprive poor women of safe and cheap contraception. A 1998 newspaper ad by Planned Parenthood, entitled "The Right Wing Coup in Family Planning," urged continued USAID funding by proclaiming: "The very survival of women and children is at stake in this battle." Such rhetoric is truly Orwellian, given that the entire objective of government-sponsored birth-control programs has been to invade couples' "reproductive rights" in order to limit family size. The crusaders have believed, from the very outset, that coercion is necessary in order to restrain fertility and avert global eco-collapse.

The consequences of this crusade are morally atrocious. Consider the one-child policy in China. Some 10 million to 20 million Chinese girls are demographically "missing" today because of "sex-selective abortion of female fetuses, female infant mortality (through infanticide or abandonment), and selective neglect of girls ages 1 to 4," according to a 1996 U.S. Census Bureau report. Girls account for over 90 percent of the inmates of Chinese orphanages—where children are left to die from neglect.

Last year, Congress heard testimony from Gao Xiao Duan, a former Chinese administrator of the one-couple, one-child policy. Gao testified that if a woman in rural China is discovered to be pregnant without a state-issued "birth-allowed certificate," she typically must undergo an abortion—no matter how many months pregnant she is. Gao recalled, "Once I found a woman who was nine months' pregnant but did not have a birth-allowed certificate. According to the policy, she was forced to undergo an abortion surgery. In the operating room, I saw how the aborted child's lips were sucking, how its limbs were stretching. A physician injected poison into its skull, and the child died and was thrown into the trash can."

The pro-choice movement is notably silent about this invasion of women's "reproductive rights." In 1989, Molly Yard, of the National Organization for Women, actually praised China's program as "among the most intelligent in the world." Stanford biologist Paul Ehrlich, the godfather of today's neo-Malthusian movement, once trumpeted China's population control as "remarkably vigorous and effective." He has congratulated Chinese rulers for their "grand experiment in the management of population."

Last summer, Lisa McRee of *Good Morning America* started an interview with Bill McKibben by asking, in all seriousness, "Is China's one-child policy a good idea for every country?" She might as well have asked whether every country should have gulags.

Gregg Easterbrook, writing in the Nov. 23, 1998 *New Republic*, correctly lambasted China for its "horrifying record on forced abortion and sterilization." But even the usually sensible Easterbrook offered up a limp apology for the one-child policy, writing that "China, which is almost out of arable land, had little choice but to attempt some degree of fertility constraint." Hong Kong has virtually no arable land, and 75 times the population density of mainland China, but has one of the best-fed populations in the world.

These coercive practices are spreading to other countries. Brian Clowes writes in the *Yale Journal of Ethics* that coercion has been used to promote family planning in at least 35 developing countries. Peru has started to use sterilization as a means of family planning, and doctors have to meet sterilization quotas or risk losing their jobs. The same is true in Mexico.

In disease-ridden African countries such as Nigeria and Kenya, hospitals often lack even the most rudimentary medical care, but are stocked to the rafters with boxes of contraceptives stamped "UNFPA" and "USAID." UNFPA boasts that, thanks to its shipments, more than 80 percent of the women in Haiti have access to contraceptives; this is apparently a higher priority than providing access to clean water, which is still unavailable to more than half of the Haitian population.

Population-control groups like Zero Population Growth and International Planned Parenthood have teamed up with pro-choice women in Congress—led by Carolyn Maloney of New York, Cynthia McKinney of Georgia, and Connie Morella of Maryland—to try to secure $60 million in U.S. funding for UNFPA over the next two years. Maloney pledges, "I'm going to do whatever it takes to restore funding for [UNFPA]" this year.

Support for this initiative is based on two misconceptions. The first is the excessively optimistic view that (in the words of a *Chicago Tribune* report) "one child zealotry in China is fading." The Population Research Institute's Steve Mosher, an authority on Chinese population activities, retorts, "This fantasy that things are getting better in China has been the constant refrain of the one-child apologists for at least the past twenty years." In fact, after UNFPA announced in 1997 that it was going back into China, state councillor Peng Peiyun defiantly announced, "China will not slacken our family-planning policy in the next century."

The second myth is that UNFPA has always been part of the solution, and has tried to end China's one-child policy. We are told that it is pushing Beijing toward more "female friendly" family planning. This, too, is false. UNFPA has actually given an award to China for its effectiveness in population-control activities—activities far from female-friendly. Worse, UNFPA's executive director, Nafis Sadik, is, like her predecessors, a longtime apologist for the China program and even denies that it is coercive. She is on record as saying—falsely—that "the implementation of the policy is purely voluntary. There is no such thing as a license to have a birth."

Despite UNFPA's track record, don't be surprised if Congress winds up re-funding it. The past 20 years may have demonstrated the intellectual bankruptcy of the population controllers, but their coffers have never been more flush.

American billionaires, past and present, have devoted large parts of their fortunes to population control. The modern-day population-control movement dates to 1952, when John D. Rockefeller returned from a trip to Asia convinced that the teeming masses he saw there were the single greatest threat to the earth's survival. He proceeded to divert hundreds of millions of dollars from his foundation to the goal of population stabilization. He was followed by David Packard (co-founder of Hewlett-Packard), who created a $9 billion foundation whose top priority was reducing world population. Today, these foundations are joined by organizations ranging from Zero Population Growth (ZPG) to Negative Population Growth (which advocates an optimal U.S. population size of 150 million–120 million fewer than now) to Planned Parenthood to the Sierra Club. The combined budget of these groups approaches $1 billion.

These organizations tend to be extremist. Take ZPG. Its board of directors passed a resolution declaring that "parenthood is not an inherent right but a privilege" granted by the state, and that "every American family has a right to no more than two children."

"Population growth is analogous to a plague of locusts," says Ted Turner, a major source of population-movement funding. "What we have on this earth today is a plague of people. Nature did not intend for there to be as many people as there are." Turner has also penned "The Ted Commandments," which include "a promise to have no more than two children or no more than my nation suggests." He recently reconsidered his manifesto, and now believes that the voluntary limit should be even lower—just *one* child. In Turner's utopia, there are no brothers, sisters, aunts, or uncles.

Turner's $1 billion donation to the U.N. is a pittance compared with the fortunes that Warren Buffett (net worth $36 billion) and Bill Gates (net worth roughly $100 billion) may bestow on the cause of population control. Buffett has announced repeatedly that he views overpopulation as one of the greatest crises in the world today. Earlier this year, Gates and his wife contributed an estimated $7 billion to their foundation, of which the funding of population programs is one of five major initiatives.

This is a massive misallocation of funds, for the simple reason that the overpopulation crisis is a hoax. It is true that world population has tripled over the last century. But the explanation is both simple and benign: First, life expectancy—possibly the best overall numerical measure of human well-being—has almost doubled in the last 100 years, and the years we are tacking on to life are both more active and more productive. Second, people are wealthier—they can afford better health care, better diets, and a cleaner environment. As a result, infant-mortality rates have declined nearly tenfold in this century. As the late Julian Simon often explained, population growth is a sign of mankind's greatest triumph—our gains against death.

We are told that this good news is really bad news, because human numbers are soon going to bump up against the planet's "carrying capacity." Pessimists worry that man is procreating as uncontrollably as John B. Calhoun's famous Norwegian rats, which multiply until they die off from lack of sustenance. Bill McKibben warns that "we are adding another

New York City every month, a Mexico every year, and almost another India every decade."

But a closer look shows that these fears are unfounded. Fact: If every one of the 6 billion of us resided in Texas, there would be room enough for every family of four to have a house and one-eighth of an acre of land—the rest of the globe would be vacant. (True, if population growth continued, some of these people would eventually spill over into Oklahoma.)

In short, the population bomb has been defused. The birth rate in developing countries has plummeted from just over 6 children per couple in 1950 to just over 3 today. The major explanation for smaller family sizes, even in China, has been economic growth. The Reaganites were right on the mark when, in 1984, they proclaimed this truth to a distraught U.N. delegation in Mexico City. (The policy they enunciated has been memorably expressed in the phrase "capitalism is by far the best contraceptive.") The fertility rate in the developed world has fallen from 3.3 per couple in 1950 to 1.6 today. These low fertility rates presage declining populations. If, for example, Japan's birth rate is not raised at some point, in 500 years there will be only about 15 Japanese left on the planet.

Other Malthusian worries are similarly wrongheaded. Global food prices have fallen by half since 1950, even as world population has doubled. The dean of agricultural economists, D. Gale Johnson of the University of Chicago, has documented "a dramatic decline in famines" in the last 50 years. Fewer than half as many people die of famine each year now than did a century ago—despite a near-quadrupling of the population. Enough food is now grown in the world to provide every resident of the planet with almost four pounds of food a day. In each of the past three years, global food production has reached new heights.

Overeating is fast becoming the globe's primary dietary malady. "It's amazing to say, but our problem is becoming overnutrition," Ho Zhiqiuan, a Chinese nutrition expert, recently told *National Geographic*. "Today in China obesity is becoming common."

Millions are still hungry, and famines continue to occur—but these are the result of government policies or political malice, not inadequate global food production. As the International Red Cross has reported, "the loss of access to food resources [during famines] is generally the result of intentional acts" by governments.

Even if the apocalyptic types are correct and population grows to 12 billion in the 21st century, so what? Assuming that human progress and scientific advancement continue as they have, and assuming that the global march toward capitalism is not reversed, those 12 billion people will undoubtedly be richer, healthier, and better fed than the 6 billion of us alive today. After all, we 6 billion are much richer, healthier, and better fed than the 1 billion who lived in 1800 or the 2 billion alive in 1920.

The greatest threat to the planet is not too many people, but too much statism. The Communists, after all, were the greatest polluters in history. Economist Mikhail Bernstam has discovered that market-based economies are about two to three times more energy-efficient than Communist, socialist, Maoist, or "Third Way" economies. Capitalist South Korea has three times the population density of socialist North Korea, but South Koreans are well fed while 250,000 North Koreans have starved to death in the last decade.

Government-funded population programs are actually counterproductive, because they legitimize command-and-control decision-making. As the great development economist Alan Rufus Waters puts it, "Foreign aid used for population activities gives enormous resources and control apparatus to the local administrative elite and thus sustains the authoritarian attitudes corrosive to the development process."

This approach usually ends up making poor people poorer, because it distracts developing nations from their most pressing task, which is market reform. When Mao's China established central planning and communal ownership of agriculture, tens of millions of Chinese peasants starved to death. In 1980, after private ownership was established, China's agricultural output doubled in just ten years. If Chinese leaders over the past 30 years had concentrated on rapid privatization and market reform, it's quite possible that economic development would have decreased birth rates every bit as rapidly as the one-child policy.

The problem with trying to win this debate with logic and an arsenal of facts is that modern Malthusianism is not a scientific theory at all. It's a religion, in which the assertion that mankind is overbreeding is accepted as an article of faith. I recently participated in a debate before an anti-population group called Carrying Capacity Network, at which one scholar informed me that man's presence on the earth is destructive because *Homo sapiens* is the only species without a natural predator. It's hard to argue with somebody who despairs because mankind is alone at the top of the food chain.

At its core, the population-control ethic is an assault on the principle that every human life has intrinsic value. Malthusian activists tend to view human beings neither as endowed with intrinsic value, nor even as resources, but primarily as consumers of resources. No wonder that at last year's ZPG conference, the Catholic Church was routinely disparaged as "our enemy" and "the evil empire."

The movement also poses a serious threat to freedom. Decisions on whether to have children—and how many—are among the most private of all human choices. If governments are allowed to control human reproduction, virtually no rights of the individual will remain inviolable by the state. The consequence, as we have seen in China, is the debasement of human dignity on a grand scale.

Another (true) scene from a party: A radiant pregnant woman is asked whether this is her first child. She says, no, in fact, it is her sixth. Yuppies gasp, as if she has admitted that she has leprosy. To have three kids—to be above replacement level—is regarded by many as an act of eco-terrorism.

But the good news for this pregnant woman, and the millions of others who want to have lots of kids, is that the Malthusians are simply wrong. There is no moral, economic, or environmental case for small families. Period.

If some choose to subscribe to a voluntary one-child policy, so be it. But the rest of us—Americans, Chinese, and everybody else—don't need or want Ted Turner or the United Nations to tell us how many kids to have. Congress should not be expanding "international family planning" funding, but terminating it.

Congress may want to consider a little-known footnote of history. In time, Thomas Malthus realized that his dismal population theories were wrong. He awoke to the reality that human beings are not like Norwegian rats at all. Why? Because, he said, man is "impelled" by "reason" to solve problems, and not to "bring beings into the world for whom he cannot provide the means of support." Amazingly, 200 years later, his disciples have yet to grasp this lesson.

# POSTSCRIPT

## Do We Face a "Population Problem"?

Janet Raloff, in "Can Grain Yields Keep Pace?" *Science News* (August 16, 1997), notes that many experts believe that although there are genuine difficulties in continuing to produce a food supply that is adequate to feed a growing world population, it can be done. She quotes Gurdev S. Khush, the chief rice breeder at the International Rice Research Institute in Manila, Republic of the Philippines, as saying, "If we manage our resources properly and continue to put money into research, we should be able to meet world food needs for at least the next 30 years." On the other hand, Russell Hopfenberg and David Pimentel, "Human Population Numbers as a Function of Food Supply," *Environment, Development and Sustainability* (No. 3, 2001), say that population grows to meet its food supply. Increasing food production will therefore result in a larger population. To control population, we can either increase "food production and allow biological mechanisms such as malnutrition and disease to limit the population by means of an increased death rate [or] cap the increases in food production and thereby halt the increases in population by means of a reduced birth rate." Since developed nations have lower birth rates, others see the solution in relieving world poverty; see Frederick Turner, "Make Everybody Rich," *Independent Review* (Summer 2002).

Resources and population come together in the concept of "carrying capacity," defined very simply as the size of the population that the environment can support, or "carry," indefinitely, through both good years and bad. It is not the size of the population that can prosper in good times alone, for such a large population must suffer catastrophically when droughts, floods, or blights arrive or the climate warms or cools. It is a long-term concept, where "long term" means not decades or generations, nor even centuries, but millennia or more.

What is Earth's carrying capacity for human beings? It is surely impossible to set a precise figure on the number of human beings the world can support for the long run. As Joel E. Cohen discusses in *How Many People Can the Earth Support?* (W. W. Norton, 1996), estimates of Earth's carrying capacity range from under a billion to over a trillion. The precise number depends on our choices of diet, standard of living, level of technology, willingness to share with others at home and abroad, and desire for an intact physical, chemical, and biological environment, as well as on whether or not our morality permits restraint in reproduction and our political or religious ideology permits educating and empowering women. The key, Cohen stresses, is human choice, and the choices are ones we must make within the next

50 years. Phoebe Hall, "Carrying Capacity," *E Magazine* (March/April 2003), notes that even countries with large land areas and small populations, such as Australia and Canada, can be overpopulated in terms of resource availability.

Andrew R. B. Ferguson, in "Perceiving the Population Bomb," *World Watch* (July/August 2001), sets the maximum sustainable human population at about 2 billion. Sandra Postel, in the Worldwatch Institute's *State of the World 1994* (W. W. Norton, 1994), says, "As a result of our population size, consumption patterns, and technology choices, we have surpassed the planet's carrying capacity. This is plainly evident by the extent to which we are damaging and depleting natural capital" (including land and water).

Yet there is hope. The United Nations Development and Environment Programmes, with the World Bank and World Resources Institute, analyzed world ecosystems and concluded that although there are many signs of trouble, once overuse is controlled many ecosystems can recover. See *World Resources 2000–2001—People and Ecosystems: The Fraying Web of Life* (World Resources Institute, 2000).

# ISSUE 5

## Should Society Act Now to Halt Global Warming?

**YES: Intergovernmental Panel on Climate Change,** from "Climate Change 2001: The Scientific Basis," A Report of Working Group I of the Intergovernmental Panel on Climate Change (2001)

**NO: Kevin A. Shapiro,** from "Too Darn Hot?" *Commentary* (June 2001)

### ISSUE SUMMARY

**YES:** The Intergovernmental Panel on Climate Change states that global warming appears to be real, with strong effects on sea level, ice cover, and rainfall patterns to come, and that human activities—particularly emissions of carbon dioxide—are to blame.

**NO:** Neuroscience researcher Kevin A. Shapiro argues that past global warming predictions have been wrong and that the data do not support calls for immediate action to reduce emissions of carbon dioxide.

Scientists have known for more than a century that carbon dioxide and other "greenhouse gases" (including water vapor, methane, and chlorofluorocarbons) help prevent heat from escaping the earth's atmosphere. In fact, it is this "greenhouse effect" that keeps the earth warm enough to support life. Yet there can be too much of a good thing. Ever since the dawn of the industrial age, humans have been burning vast quantities of fossil fuels, releasing the carbon they contain as carbon dioxide. Because of this, some estimate that by the year 2050, the amount of carbon dioxide in the air will be double what it was in 1850. By 1982 an increase was apparent. Less than a decade later, many researchers were saying that the climate had already begun to warm. Now there is a strong consensus that the global climate is warming and will continue to warm. There is less agreement on just how much it will warm or what the impact of the warming will be on human (and other) life. See Spencer R. Weart, "The Discovery of the Risk of Global Warming," *Physics Today* (January 1997).

The debate has been heated. The June 1992 issue of *The Bulletin of the Atomic Scientists* carries two articles on the possible consequences of the greenhouse effect. In "Global Warming: The Worst Case," Jeremy Leggett says that although there are enormous uncertainties, a warmer climate will release more carbon dioxide, which will warm the climate even further. As a result, soil will grow drier, forest fires will occur more frequently, plant pests will thrive, and methane trapped in the world's seabeds will be released and will increase global warming much further—in effect, there will be a "runaway greenhouse effect." Leggett also hints at the possibility that polar ice caps will melt and raise sea levels by hundreds of feet.

Taking the opposing view, in "Warming Theories Need Warning Label," S. Fred Singer emphasizes the uncertainties in the projections of global warming and their dependence on the accuracy of the computer models that generate them, and he argues that improvements in the models have consistently shrunk the size of the predicted change. There will be no catastrophe, he argues, and money spent to ward off the climate warming would be better spent on "so many pressing—and real—problems in need of resources."

Global warming, says the UN Environment Programme, will do some $300 billion in damage each year to the world economy by 2050. In March 2001 President George W. Bush announced that the United States would not take steps to reduce greenhouse emissions—called for by the international treaty negotiated in 1997 in Kyoto, Japan—because such reductions would harm the American economy (the U.S. Senate has not ratified the Kyoto treaty). Since the Intergovernmental Panel on Climate Change (IPCC) had just released its third report saying that past forecasts were, in essence, too conservative, Bush's stance provoked immense outcry.

The analysis of data and computer simulations described by the IPCC in the following selection indicates that global warming is a genuine problem. According to the IPCC, climate warming is already apparent and will get worse than previous forecasts had suggested. Sea level will rise, ice cover will shrink, rainfall patterns will change, and human activities—particularly emissions of carbon dioxide—are to blame. The report excerpt reprinted here does not suggest that anything in particular should be done, but other writers, such as Stephen H. Schneider and Kristin Kuntz-Duriseti ("Facing Global Warming," *The World & I* [June 2001]), pull no punches: "Nearly all knowledgeable scientists agree that some global warming is inevitable, that major warming is quite possible, and that for the bulk of humanity the net effects are more likely to be negative than positive. This will hold true particularly if global warming is allowed to increase beyond a few degrees, which is likely to occur by the middle of this century if no policies are undertaken to mitigate emissions."

Kevin A. Shapiro is more optimistic. In the second selection, he argues that past global warming predictions have been wrong and that there is too much room for error in the data and computer simulations to support calls for immediate action to reduce emissions of carbon dioxide.

**Intergovernmental Panel on Climate Change**

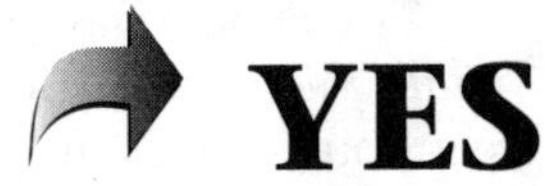


# Summary for Policymakers

The Third Assessment Report of Working Group I of the Intergovernmental Panel on Climate Change (IPCC) builds upon past assessments and incorporates new results from . . . five years of research on climate change. Many hundreds of scientists from many countries participated in its preparation and review.

This Summary for Policymakers (SPM), which was approved by IPCC member governments in Shanghai in January 2001, describes the current state of understanding of the climate system and provides estimates of its projected future evolution and their uncertainties. . . .

*An increasing body of observations gives a collective picture of a warming world and other changes in the climate system.*

Since the release of the Second Assessment Report (SAR), additional data from new studies of current and palaeoclimates, improved analysis of data sets, more rigorous evaluation of their quality, and comparisons among data from different sources have led to greater understanding of climate change.

*The global average surface temperature has increased over the 20th century by about 0.6°C.*

- The global average surface temperature (the average of near surface air temperature over land, and sea surface temperature) has increased since 1861. Over the 20th century the increase has been 0.6 ± 0.2°C. This value is about 0.15°C larger than that estimated by the SAR for the period up to 1994, owing to the relatively high temperatures of the additional years (1995 to 2000) and improved methods of processing the data. These numbers take into account various adjustments, including urban heat island effects. The record shows a great deal of variability; for example, most of the warming occurred during the 20th century, during two periods, 1910 to 1945 and 1976 to 2000.
- Globally, it is very likely that the 1990s was the warmest decade and 1998 the warmest year in the instrumental record, since 1861.

From Intergovernmental Panel on Climate Change, "Climate Change 2001: The Scientific Basis," A Report of Working Group I of the Intergovernmental Panel on Climate Change (2001).  Notes omitted.

- New analyses of proxy data for the Northern Hemisphere indicate that the increase in temperature in the 20th century is likely to have been the largest of any century during the past 1,000 years. It is also likely that, in the Northern Hemisphere, the 1990s was the warmest decade and 1998 the warmest year. Because less data are available, less is known about annual averages prior to 1,000 years before present and for conditions prevailing in most of the Southern Hemisphere prior to 1861.
- On average, between 1950 and 1993, night-time daily minimum air temperatures over land increased by about 0.2°C per decade. This is about twice the rate of increase in daytime daily maximum air temperatures (0.1°C per decade). This has lengthened the freeze-free season in many mid- and high latitude regions. The increase in sea surface temperature over this period is about half that of the mean land surface air temperature.

*Temperatures have risen during the past four decades in the lowest 8 kilometres of the atmosphere.*

- Since the late 1950s (the period of adequate observations from weather balloons), the overall global temperature increases in the lowest 8 kilometres of the atmosphere and in surface temperature have been similar at 0.1°C per decade.
- Since the start of the satellite record in 1979, both satellite and weather balloon measurements show that the global average temperature of the lowest 8 kilometres of the atmosphere has changed by +0.05 ± 0.10°C per decade, but the global average surface temperature has increased significantly by +0.15 ± 0.05°C per decade. The difference in the warming rates is statistically significant. This difference occurs primarily over the tropical and sub-tropical regions.
- The lowest 8 kilometres of the atmosphere and the surface are influenced differently by factors such as stratospheric ozone depletion, atmospheric aerosols, and the El Niño phenomenon. Hence, it is physically plausible to expect that over a short time period (e.g., 20 years) there may be differences in temperature trends. In addition, spatial sampling techniques can also explain some of the differences in trends, but these differences are not fully resolved.

*Snow cover and ice extent have decreased.*

- Satellite data show that there are very likely to have been decreases of about 10% in the extent of snow cover since the late 1960s, and ground-based observations show that there is very likely to have been a reduction of about two weeks in the annual duration of lake and river ice cover in the mid- and high latitudes of the Northern Hemisphere, over the 20th century.
- There has been a widespread retreat of mountain glaciers in non-polar regions during the 20th century.
- Northern Hemisphere spring and summer sea-ice extent has decreased by about 10 to 15% since the 1950s. It is likely that there

has been about a 40% decline in Arctic sea-ice thickness during late summer to early autumn in recent decades and a considerably slower decline in winter sea-ice thickness.

*Global average sea level has risen and ocean heat content has increased.*

- Tide gauge data show that global average sea level rose between 0.1 and 0.2 metres during the 20th century.
- Global ocean heat content has increased since the late 1950s, the period for which adequate observations of sub-surface ocean temperatures have been available.

*Changes have also occurred in other important aspects of climate.*

- It is very likely that precipitation has increased by 0.5 to 1% per decade in the 20th century over most mid- and high latitudes of the Northern Hemisphere continents, and it is likely that rainfall has increased by 0.2 to 0.3% per decade over the tropical (10°N to 10°S) land areas. Increases in the tropics are not evident over the past few decades. It is also likely that rainfall has decreased over much of the Northern Hemisphere sub-tropical (10°N to 30°N) land areas during the 20th century by about 0.3% per decade. In contrast to the Northern Hemisphere, no comparable systematic changes have been detected in broad latitudinal averages over the Southern Hemisphere. There are insufficient data to establish trends in precipitation over the oceans.
- In the mid- and high latitudes of the Northern Hemisphere over the latter half of the 20th century, it is likely that there has been a 2 to 4% increase in the frequency of heavy precipitation events. Increases in heavy precipitation events can arise from a number of causes, e.g., changes in atmospheric moisture, thunderstorm activity and large-scale storm activity.
- It is likely that there has been a 2% increase in cloud cover over mid- to high latitude land areas during the 20th century. In most areas the trends relate well to the observed decrease in daily temperature range.
- Since 1950 it is very likely that there has been a reduction in the frequency of extreme low temperatures, with a smaller increase in the frequency of extreme high temperatures.
- Warm episodes of the El Niño-Southern Oscillation (ENSO) phenomenon (which consistently affects regional variations of precipitation and temperature over much of the tropics, sub-tropics and some mid-latitude areas) have been more frequent, persistent and intense since the mid-1970s, compared with the previous 100 years.
- Over the 20th century (1900 to 1995), there were relatively small increases in global land areas experiencing severe drought or severe wetness. In many regions, these changes are dominated by inter-decadal and multi-decadal climate variability, such as the shift in ENSO towards more warm events.
- In some regions, such as parts of Asia and Africa, the frequency and intensity of droughts have been observed to increase in recent decades.

*Some important aspects of climate appear not to have changed.*

- A few areas of the globe have not warmed in recent decades, mainly over some parts of the Southern Hemisphere oceans and parts of Antarctica.
- No significant trends of Antarctic sea-ice extent are apparent since 1978, the period of reliable satellite measurements.
- Changes globally in tropical and extra-tropical storm intensity and frequency are dominated by inter-decadal to multi-decadal variations, with no significant trends evident over the 20th century. Conflicting analyses make it difficult to draw definitive conclusions about changes in storm activity, especially in the extra-tropics.
- No systematic changes in the frequency of tornadoes, thunder days, or hail events are evident in the limited areas analysed.

*Emissions of greenhouse gases and aerosols due to human activities continue to alter the atmosphere in ways that are expected to affect the climate.*

Changes in climate occur as a result of both internal variability within the climate system and external factors (both natural and anthropogenic). The influence of external factors on climate can be broadly compared using the concept of radiative forcing. A positive radiative forcing, such as that produced by increasing concentrations of greenhouse gases, tends to warm the surface. A negative radiative forcing, which can arise from an increase in some types of aerosols (microscopic airborne particles) tends to cool the surface. Natural factors, such as changes in solar output or explosive volcanic activity, can also cause radiative forcing. Characterisation of these climate forcing agents and their changes over time is required to understand past climate changes in the context of natural variations and to project what climate changes could lie ahead.

*Concentrations of atmospheric greenhouse gases and their radiative forcing have continued to increase as a result of human activities.*

- The atmospheric concentration of carbon dioxide ($CO_2$) has increased by 31% since 1750. The present $CO_2$ concentration has not been exceeded during the past 420,000 years and likely not during the past 20 million years. The current rate of increase is unprecedented during at least the past 20,000 years.
- About three-quarters of the anthropogenic emissions of $CO_2$ to the atmosphere during the past 20 years is due to fossil fuel burning. The rest is predominantly due to land-use change, especially deforestation.
- Currently the ocean and the land together are taking up about half of the anthropogenic $CO_2$ emissions. On land, the uptake of anthropogenic $CO_2$ very likely exceeded the release of $CO_2$ by deforestation during the 1990s.
- The rate of increase of atmospheric $CO_2$ concentration has been about 1.5 ppm (0.4%) per year over the past two decades. During the 1990s the year to year increase varied from 0.9 ppm (0.2%) to

2.8 ppm (0.8%). A large part of this variability is due to the effect of climate variability (e.g., El Niño events) on $CO_2$ uptake and release by land and oceans.

- The atmospheric concentration of methane ($CH_4$) has increased by 1060 ppb (151%) since 1750 and continues to increase. The present $CH_4$ concentration has not been exceeded during the past 420,000 years. The annual growth in $CH_4$ concentration slowed and became more variable in the 1990s, compared with the 1980s. Slightly more than half of current $CH_4$ emissions are anthropogenic (e.g., use of fossil fuels, cattle, rice agriculture and landfills). In addition, carbon monoxide (CO) emissions have recently been identified as a cause of increasing $CH_4$ concentration.
- The atmospheric concentration of nitrous oxide ($N_2O$) has increased by 46 ppb (17%) since 1750 and continues to increase. The present $N_2O$ concentration has not been exceeded during at least the past thousand years. About a third of current $N_2O$ emissions are anthropogenic (e.g., agricultural soils, cattle feed lots and chemical industry).
- Since 1995, the atmospheric concentrations of many of those halocarbon gases that are both ozone-depleting and greenhouse gases (e.g., $CFCl_3$ and $CF_2Cl_2$), are either increasing more slowly or decreasing, both in response to reduced emissions under the regulations of the Montreal Protocol and its Amendments. Their substitute compounds (e.g., $CHF_2Cl$ and $CF_3CH_2F$) and some other synthetic compounds (e.g., perfluorocarbons (PFCs) and sulphur hexafluoride ($SF_6$)) are also greenhouse gases, and their concentrations are currently increasing. . . .

*Confidence in the ability of models to project future climate has increased.*

Complex physically-based climate models are required to provide detailed estimates of feedbacks and of regional features. Such models cannot yet simulate all aspects of climate (e.g., they still cannot account fully for the observed trend in the surface-troposphere temperature difference since 1979) and there are particular uncertainties associated with clouds and their interaction with radiation and aerosols. Nevertheless, confidence in the ability of these models to provide useful projections of future climate has improved due to their demonstrated performance on a range of space and time-scales.

- Understanding of climate processes and their incorporation in climate models have improved, including water vapour, sea-ice dynamics, and ocean heat transport.
- Some recent models produce satisfactory simulations of current climate without the need for non-physical adjustments of heat and water fluxes at the ocean-atmosphere interface used in earlier models.
- Simulations that include estimates of natural and anthropogenic forcing reproduce the observed large-scale changes in surface temperature over the 20th century. However, contributions from some

additional processes and forcings may not have been included in the models. Nevertheless, the large-scale consistency between models and observations can be used to provide an independent check on projected warming rates over the next few decades under a given emissions scenario.
- Some aspects of model simulations of ENSO, monsoons and the North Atlantic Oscillation, as well as selected periods of past climate, have improved.

*There is new and stronger evidence that most of the warming observed over the last 50 years is attributable to human activities.*

The SAR concluded: "The balance of evidence suggests a discernible human influence on global climate". That report also noted that the anthropogenic signal was still emerging from the background of natural climate variability. Since the SAR, progress has been made in reducing uncertainty, particularly with respect to distinguishing and quantifying the magnitude of responses to different external influences. Although many of the sources of uncertainty identified in the SAR still remain to some degree, new evidence and improved understanding support an updated conclusion.

- There is a longer and more closely scrutinised temperature record and new model estimates of variability. The warming over the past 100 years is very unlikely to be due to internal variability alone, as estimated by current models. Reconstructions of climate data for the past 1,000 years also indicate that this warming was unusual and is unlikely to be entirely natural in origin.
- There are new estimates of the climate response to natural and anthropogenic forcing, and new detection techniques have been applied. Detection and attribution studies consistently find evidence for an anthropogenic signal in the climate record of the last 35 to 50 years.
- Simulations of the response to natural forcings alone (i.e., the response to variability in solar irradiance and volcanic eruptions) do not explain the warming in the second half of the 20th century. However, they indicate that natural forcings may have contributed to the observed warming in the first half of the 20th century.
- The warming over the last 50 years due to anthropogenic greenhouse gases can be identified despite uncertainties in forcing due to anthropogenic sulphate aerosol and natural factors (volcanoes and solar irradiance). The anthropogenic sulphate aerosol forcing, while uncertain, is negative over this period and therefore cannot explain the warming. Changes in natural forcing during most of this period are also estimated to be negative and are unlikely to explain the warming.
- Detection and attribution studies comparing model simulated changes with the observed record can now take into account uncertainty in the magnitude of modelled response to external forcing, in particular that due to uncertainty in climate sensitivity.
- Most of these studies find that, over the last 50 years, the estimated rate and magnitude of warming due to increasing concentrations of

greenhouse gases alone are comparable with, or larger than, the observed warming. Furthermore, most model estimates that take into account both greenhouse gases and sulphate aerosols are consistent with observations over this period.

- The best agreement between model simulations and observations over the last 140 years has been found when all the above anthropogenic and natural forcing factors are combined. These results show that the forcings included are sufficient to explain the observed changes, but do not exclude the possibility that other forcings may also have contributed.

In the light of new evidence and taking into account the remaining uncertainties, most of the observed warming over the last 50 years is likely to have been due to the increase in greenhouse gas concentrations.

Furthermore, it is very likely that the 20th century warming has contributed significantly to the observed sea level rise, through thermal expansion of sea water and widespread loss of land ice. Within present uncertainties, observations and models are both consistent with a lack of significant acceleration of sea level rise during the 20th century.

*Human influences will continue to change atmospheric composition throughout the 21st century.*

Models have been used to make projections of atmospheric concentrations of greenhouse gases and aerosols, and hence of future climate, based upon emissions scenarios from the IPCC Special Report on Emission Scenarios (SRES). These scenarios were developed to update the IS92 series, which were used in the SAR and are shown for comparison here in some cases.

## Greenhouse Gases

- Emissions of $CO_2$ due to fossil fuel burning are virtually certain to be the dominant influence on the trends in atmospheric $CO_2$ concentration during the 21st century.
- As the $CO_2$ concentration of the atmosphere increases, ocean and land will take up a decreasing fraction of anthropogenic $CO_2$ emissions. The net effect of land and ocean climate feedbacks as indicated by models is to further increase projected atmospheric $CO_2$ concentrations, by reducing both the ocean and land uptake of $CO_2$.
- By 2100, carbon cycle models project atmospheric $CO_2$ concentrations of 540 to 970 ppm for the illustrative SRES scenarios (90 to 250% above the concentration of 280 ppm in the year 1750). These projections include the land and ocean climate feedbacks. Uncertainties, especially about the magnitude of the climate feedback from the terrestrial biosphere, cause a variation of about −10 to +30% around each scenario. The total range is 490 to 1260 ppm (75 to 350% above the 1750 concentration).
- Changing land use could influence atmospheric $CO_2$ concentration. Hypothetically, if all of the carbon released by historical land-use changes could be restored to the terrestrial biosphere over

the course of the century (e.g., by reforestation), $CO_2$ concentration would be reduced by 40 to 70 ppm.

- Model calculations of the concentrations of the non-$CO_2$ greenhouse gases by 2100 vary considerably across the SRES illustrative scenarios, with $CH_4$ changing by −190 to +1,970 ppb (present concentration 1,760 ppb), $N_2O$ changing by +38 to +144 ppb (present concentration 316 ppb), total tropospheric $O_3$ changing by −12 to +62%, and a wide range of changes in concentrations of HFCs, PFCs and $SF_6$, all relative to the year 2000. In some scenarios, total tropospheric $O_3$ would become as important a radiative forcing agent as $CH_4$ and, over much of the Northern Hemisphere, would threaten the attainment of current air quality targets.
- Reductions in greenhouse gas emissions and the gases that control their concentration would be necessary to stabilise radiative forcing. For example, for the most important anthropogenic greenhouse gas, carbon cycle models indicate that stabilisation of atmospheric $CO_2$ concentrations at 450, 650 or 1,000 ppm would require global anthropogenic $CO_2$ emissions to drop below 1990 levels, within a few decades, about a century, or about two centuries, respectively, and continue to decrease steadily thereafter. Eventually $CO_2$ emissions would need to decline to a very small fraction of current emissions.

## Aerosols

The SRES scenarios include the possibility of either increases or decreases in anthropogenic aerosols (e.g., sulphate aerosols, biomass aerosols, black and organic carbon aerosols) depending on the extent of fossil fuel use and policies to abate polluting emissions. In addition, natural aerosols (e.g., sea salt, dust and emissions leading to the production of sulphate and carbon aerosols) are projected to increase as a result of changes in climate.

## Radiative Forcing over the 21st Century

For the SRES illustrative scenarios, relative to the year 2000, the global mean radiative forcing due to greenhouse gases continues to increase through the 21st century, with the fraction due to $CO_2$ projected to increase from slightly more than half to about three quarters. The change in the direct plus indirect aerosol radiative forcing is projected to be smaller in magnitude than that of $CO_2$.

*Global average temperature and sea level are projected to rise under all IPCC SRES scenarios.*

In order to make projections of future climate, models incorporate past, as well as future emissions of greenhouse gases and aerosols. Hence, they include estimates of warming to date and the commitment to future warming from past emissions.

## Temperature

- The globally averaged surface temperature is projected to increase by 1.4 to 5.8°C over the period 1990 to 2100. These results are for the full range of 35 SRES scenarios, based on a number of climate models.
- Temperature increases are projected to be greater than those in the SAR, which were about 1.0 to 3.5°C based on the six IS92 scenarios. The higher projected temperatures and the wider range are due primarily to the lower projected sulphur dioxide emissions in the SRES scenarios relative to the IS92 scenarios.
- The projected rate of warming is much larger than the observed changes during the 20th century and is very likely to be without precedent during at least the last 10,000 years, based on palaeoclimate data.
- By 2100, the range in the surface temperature response across the group of climate models run with a given scenario is comparable to the range obtained from a single model run with the different SRES scenarios.
- On timescales of a few decades, the current observed rate of warming can be used to constrain the projected response to a given emissions scenario despite uncertainty in climate sensitivity. This approach suggests that anthropogenic warming is likely to lie in the range of 0.1 to 0.2°C per decade over the next few decades under the IS92a scenario. . . .
- Based on recent global model simulations, it is very likely that nearly all land areas will warm more rapidly than the global average, particularly those at northern high latitudes in the cold season. Most notable of these is the warming in the northern regions of North America, and northern and central Asia, which exceeds global mean warming in each model by more than 40%. In contrast, the warming is less than the global mean change in south and southeast Asia in summer and in southern South America in winter.
- Recent trends for surface temperature to become more El Niño-like in the tropical Pacific, with the eastern tropical Pacific warming more than the western tropical Pacific, with a corresponding eastward shift of precipitation, are projected to continue in many models.

## Precipitation

Based on global model simulations and for a wide range of scenarios, global average water vapour concentration and precipitation are projected to increase during the 21st century. By the second half of the 21st century, it is likely that precipitation will have increased over northern mid- to high latitudes and Antarctica in winter. At low latitudes there are both regional increases and decreases over land areas. Larger year to year variations in precipitation are very likely over most areas where an increase in mean precipitation is projected. . . .

## El Niño

- Confidence in projections of changes in future frequency, amplitude, and spatial pattern of El Niño events in the tropical Pacific is tempered by some shortcomings in how well El Niño is simulated in complex models. Current projections show little change or a small increase in amplitude for El Niño events over the next 100 years.
- Even with little or no change in El Niño amplitude, global warming is likely to lead to greater extremes of drying and heavy rainfall and increase the risk of droughts and floods that occur with El Niño events in many different regions.

## Monsoons

It is likely that warming associated with increasing greenhouse gas concentrations will cause an increase of Asian summer monsoon precipitation variability. Changes in monsoon mean duration and strength depend on the details of the emission scenario. The confidence in such projections is also limited by how well the climate models simulate the detailed seasonal evolution of the monsoons.

## Thermohaline Circulation

Most models show weakening of the ocean thermohaline circulation which leads to a reduction of the heat transport into high latitudes of the Northern Hemisphere. However, even in models where the thermohaline circulation weakens, there is still a warming over Europe due to increased greenhouse gases. The current projections using climate models do not exhibit a complete shut-down of the thermohaline circulation by 2100. Beyond 2100, the thermohaline circulation could completely, and possibly irreversibly, shutdown in either hemisphere if the change in radiative forcing is large enough and applied long enough.

## Snow and Ice

- Northern Hemisphere snow cover and sea-ice extent are projected to decrease further.
- Glaciers and ice caps are projected to continue their widespread retreat during the 21st century.
- The Antarctic ice sheet is likely to gain mass because of greater precipitation, while the Greenland ice sheet is likely to lose mass because the increase in runoff will exceed the precipitation increase.
- Concerns have been expressed about the stability of the West Antarctic ice sheet because it is grounded below sea level. However, loss of grounded ice leading to substantial sea level rise from this source is now widely agreed to be very unlikely during the 21st century, although its dynamics are still inadequately understood, especially for projections on longer time-scales.

## Sea Level

Global mean sea level is projected to rise by 0.09 to 0.88 metres between 1990 and 2100, for the full range of SRES scenarios. This is due primarily to thermal expansion and loss of mass from glaciers and ice caps. The range of sea level rise presented in the SAR was 0.13 to 0.94 metres based on the IS92 scenarios. Despite the higher temperature change projections in this assessment, the sea level projections are slightly lower, primarily due to the use of improved models, which give a smaller contribution from glaciers and ice sheets.

*Anthropogenic climate change will persist for many centuries.*

- Emissions of long-lived greenhouse gases (i.e., $CO_2$, $N_2O$, PFCs, $SF_6$) have a lasting effect on atmospheric composition, radiative forcing and climate. For example, several centuries after $CO_2$ emissions occur, about a quarter of the increase in $CO_2$ concentration caused by these emissions is still present in the atmosphere.
- After greenhouse gas concentrations have stabilised, global average surface temperatures would rise at a rate of only a few tenths of a degree per century rather than several degrees per century as projected for the 21st century without stabilisation. The lower the level at which concentrations are stabilised, the smaller the total temperature change.
- Global mean surface temperature increases and rising sea level from thermal expansion of the ocean are projected to continue for hundreds of years after stabilisation of greenhouse gas concentrations (even at present levels), owing to the long timescales on which the deep ocean adjusts to climate change.
- Ice sheets will continue to react to climate warming and contribute to sea level rise for thousands of years after climate has been stabilised. Climate models indicate that the local warming over Greenland is likely to be one to three times the global average. Ice sheet models project that a local warming of larger than 3°C, if sustained for millennia, would lead to virtually a complete melting of the Greenland ice sheet with a resulting sea level rise of about 7 metres. A local warming of 5.5°C, if sustained for 1,000 years, would be likely to result in a contribution from Greenland of about 3 metres to sea level rise.
- Current ice dynamic models suggest that the West Antarctic ice sheet could contribute up to 3 metres to sea level rise over the next 1,000 years, but such results are strongly dependent on model assumptions regarding climate change scenarios, ice dynamics and other factors.

*Further action is required to address remaining gaps in information and understanding.*

Further research is required to improve the ability to detect, attribute and understand climate change, to reduce uncertainties and to project future climate changes. In particular, there is a need for additional systematic and sustained observations, modelling and process studies. A serious concern is the decline of observational networks. The following are high priority areas for action.

- Systematic observations and reconstructions:
  - Reverse the decline of observational networks in many parts of the world.
  - Sustain and expand the observational foundation for climate studies by providing accurate, long-term, consistent data including implementation of a strategy for integrated global observations.
  - Enhance the development of reconstructions of past climate periods.
  - Improve the observations of the spatial distribution of greenhouse gases and aerosols.

- Modelling and process studies:
  - Improve understanding of the mechanisms and factors leading to changes in radiative forcing.
  - Understand and characterise the important unresolved processes and feedbacks, both physical and biogeochemical, in the climate system.
  - Improve methods to quantify uncertainties of climate projections and scenarios, including long-term ensemble simulations using complex models.
  - Improve the integrated hierarchy of global and regional climate models with a focus on the simulation of climate variability, regional climate changes and extreme events.
  - Link more effectively models of the physical climate and the biogeochemical system, and in turn improve coupling with descriptions of human activities.
  - Cutting across these foci are crucial needs associated with strengthening international co-operation and co-ordination in order to better utilise scientific, computational and observational resources. This should also promote the free exchange of data among scientists. A special need is to increase the observational and research capacities in many regions, particularly in developing countries. Finally, as is the goal of this assessment, there is a continuing imperative to communicate research advances in terms that are relevant to decision making.

**Kevin A. Shapiro**

# NO

# Too Darn Hot?

Natives of Hawaii, inured by more than a thousand years of island life to the vagaries of the weather and the seas, have a somewhat elliptical saying: "the mists are those that know of a storm upon the water." It can be taken to mean that those nearest to something are the first to become aware of what is happening to it. Using similar reasoning, perhaps, many environmentalists today regard the small islands that dot the Pacific as a sort of planetary weathervane, outcrops of flora and fauna that are sensitive indicators of large-scale shifts in the ecological balance of the earth. If these islands are already beginning to buckle under the stresses imposed on the planet by human activity, it is a sign that we must act quickly lest catastrophe result.

An alarming presentation of this argument can be found in *Rising Waters: Global Warming and the Fate of the Pacific Islands,* an hour-long documentary that aired on PBS [in] April [2001] on Earth Day. *Rising Waters* paints a picture of island nations on the veritable brink of ruin: homes destroyed in the wake of storms or threatened by eroding shorelines, churchyards and crop-fields inundated by the rising sea, and shoals of once-vivid coral bleached by overheated waters. On camera, fishermen complain of poor hauls; a Samoan environmentalist laments the looming disappearance of his cultural heritage; Teburoro Tito, the president of tiny Kiribati, speaks glumly of the possibility that the entire populace of his cluster of atolls will have to be relocated.

What is causing this potentially immense disruption? *Rising Waters* mentions several factors, including seasonal weather fluctuations and over-development, but ultimately it places most of the blame on a long chain of processes at the end of which is: global warming. The nature of this menace is well known and has been widely discussed. Increases in the industrial emission of gases like carbon dioxide ($CO_2$), it is said, have caused the atmosphere to absorb infrared radiation that would otherwise be reflected back into outer space. The resulting "greenhouse effect" lifts the average temperature of the earth's surface. Among the many consequences are rising sea levels caused by the melting of the polar ice caps and increases in the frequency and intensity of storm activity.

Though *Rising Waters* offers the disclaimer that the earth's climate is a complex and somewhat unpredictable system—"we don't know how it behaves completely," says Fred MacKenzie, a professor of oceanography at the University of Hawaii—its overarching message is that unregulated $CO_2$ emissions have already begun to heat the planet to dangerous levels. To forestall further warming, we must cut those emissions globally by as much as 80 percent over the next several decades. Alas, as *Rising Waters* notes with a hint of impending doom, the prospects for such a cut are not auspicious.

On this last point, the documentary is certainly correct. Talks in the Hague on implementing the 1997 Kyoto Protocol, an international agreement aimed at reducing the $CO_2$ emissions of industrial nations to pre-1990 levels by the year 2012, collapsed in December, in the last month of Bill Clinton's presidency. By mid-March, the Bush administration had announced it would not seek to regulate the $CO_2$ emissions of power plants, provoking an outcry from environmentalists and angering European leaders who maintain (in the words of Dutch prime minister Wim Kok) that the United States is acting "irresponsibly." Two weeks later, President Bush declared that it made "no sense" for the United States to pursue implementation of the Kyoto Protocol. European governments, positively livid, dispatched an emergency delegation to Washington, but to no avail; they now plan to assemble an international coalition aimed at "shaming" the United States into reconsidering its stance. Another round of talks on Kyoto will be held in Bonn [in] July [2001], and the conflict over global warming is certain to deepen in the months and years ahead.

Against this backdrop, *Rising Waters* can only serve to underscore the now almost incessant warnings about the disaster that awaits us if we fail to change our profligate energy habits. Global warming has already been blamed for ecological hazards ranging in scale from disruptions in the migration patterns of butterflies and declining amphibian populations to extreme weather events, droughts, and food shortages in farflung portions of the globe. And the dangers that lie ahead are said to be far worse, if not horrific: famine brought on by widespread agricultural failure, an increase in epidemics of infectious disease, even mass extinctions of animal and human populations.

If anything remotely resembling this scenario is likely, it is not hard to see why so many Europeans, and with them many Americans, are apoplectic over President Bush's determination to scrap the Kyoto deal, the fruit of years of intense multinational discussions among lawmakers, economists, scientists, and environmentalists. Senator Joseph Lieberman has even promised a congressional investigation of the President's environmental decisions, declaring that they "ignore the public interest and defy common sense."

Is Lieberman right? There are indeed many things about the global-warming debate that "ignore the public interest and defy common sense." But the decision to abandon the Kyoto Protocol is not one of them.

In a sense, the decision was hardly even newsworthy. The agreement has been effectively dead—at least as far as the United States is concerned—since shortly after it was negotiated in 1997. For no sooner did Clinton's negotiators return from Japan than the Senate voted 95–0 to oppose ratification of any treaty that would impose significant burdens on our national economy and that lacked "specific scheduled commitments" for emissions reductions in what are now known as "developing" countries. As Kyoto has never been amended to address these concerns, it is perplexing that any policymaker could have continued to regard the accord as viable.

Indeed, far more inscrutable than President Bush's final rejection of Kyoto is the vast amount of rhetorical and diplomatic effort that has been and continues to be expended on the agreement's behalf. Even apart from the unanimous vote in the Senate, there are serious questions about whether the provisions of the treaty could ever be implemented and enforced, and therefore about whether it really represents a workable mechanism for managing climate change.

From its very inception, as the analyst David G. Victor shows in a new monograph, the Kyoto Protocol was a product of diplomatic wishful thinking. For one thing, the limits it called for on greenhouse gas emissions were draconian. Thus, by 2012 the United States would have been required to reduce $CO_2$ emissions to 7 percent below 1990 levels—a modest-sounding target until one considers that by the end of 1999, emissions were already 12 percent above 1990 levels and were continuing to rise. Compliance with Kyoto would therefore have required a likely cut of as much as 30 percent by the time the treaty took effect in 2008. Not only would this cost hundreds of billions of dollars in GDP [gross domestic product] but, because most greenhouse gases are released in the course of burning fossil fuels for energy, cutbacks on such a scale would deal a major blow to significant sectors of the U.S. economy—particularly electricity generation, which is already struggling mightily to keep pace with demand.

The agreement was also exceedingly inequitable. Russia, for example, would have been required only to freeze its emissions at 1990 levels; but because the Russian economy has contracted sharply since the collapse of the Soviet Union, its emissions are already far below target, and are unlikely to recover by 2008. Though it remains a significant industrial polluter, Moscow would thus be required to do absolutely nothing. South Korea and Mexico, now formally considered "developed" countries (as defined by membership in the Organization for Economic Cooperation and Development), have for their part also not agreed to curtail emissions.

At the same time, Kyoto sets no targets at all for the developing nations, though these countries will account for half the world's greenhouse gases by 2020. The two largest such nations, India and China, have refused outright to accept any limits on their emissions output.

---

In short, the Kyoto Protocol demands that the United States hobble its economy with drastic cuts in energy production, while Russia, India, China, and other nations enjoy the freedom to grow untrammeled. To deal with this gross imbalance, a number of observers have proposed amending the agreement. One proposal involves altering the way emissions are accounted for—for example, by permitting industrialized countries to earn "credits" if they maintain or create carbon sinks, i.e., forest and soil zones that absorb $CO_2$. Another alternative would be to allow trading, whereby industrialized countries could buy the right to emit carbon dioxide from those nations whose emissions are below targeted levels.

Both of these ideas have their attractions for the United States, but they also entail immense practical and political difficulties. On the positive side, the U.S. might offset its Kyoto obligations by counting carbon sinks that resulted from intentional changes in land-use policy. If, in addition, it were permissible to count those resulting from unintentional changes (like the spontaneous reforestation of abandoned agricultural lands), we might no longer be a net emitter. But an amendment of this sort would almost certainly prove unacceptable to Europe and Japan, which, unlike the U.S., have limited capacity to plant new forests. A more fundamental problem is that the Kyoto Protocol provides no standard definitions, methods, or data for quantifying the absorption of $CO_2$ by trees and soils, making it easy for nations to cheat by claiming credit for carbon sinks that are short-lived or even nonexistent.

Emissions trading is beset with its own difficulties. The present terms of the Kyoto Protocol would seem to award countries with low baselines—like Russia—a windfall in fictitious credits, the sale of which would result in no reduction in global emissions whatsoever. David Victor has correctly spelled out the political implications of any such arrangement: "No Western legislature will ratify a deal that merely enriches Russia and Ukraine while doing nothing to control emissions and slow global warming."

If the most widely discussed ways of amending the Kyoto agreement are infeasible, what then? Policy analysts like Victor continue to hold out hope that the Bush administration will develop a coherent approach to global warming—perhaps a modified trading system combined with international taxes on $CO_2$ emissions and supplemented by investments in new technology. As for the Bush administration, the President himself has spoken of global warming as a "serious problem," and the U.S. will be participating in the upcoming talks in Bonn with the hope of finding a workable alternative to Kyoto.

---

The operative assumption here, of course, is that man-made climate change is a real phenomenon, and that averting catastrophe requires doing something about it, and soon. As this assumption has increasingly come to be taken for granted, disputing it has become commensurately perilous, especially for politicians. According to a 1997 poll taken for the World Wildlife Federation, two-thirds of American voters regard global warming as a "serious threat" and support an international agreement to cut greenhouse-gas emissions, even if this comes at some economic cost. A full three-quarters endorse the view that "the only scientists who do not believe global warming is happening are paid by big oil, coal, and gas companies to find the results that will protect business interests." Only 15 percent accept the statement that "scientists disagree among themselves" about the extent of the coming danger.

Clearly, climate change is no longer an issue up for grabs. Even if the public could be persuaded that the Kyoto Protocol would be disastrous for the U.S. economy and is the result of junk diplomacy, it would be far harder for a politician to make the case that the research behind Kyoto is junk science, too. But much of it is.

Let us return for a moment to those Pacific islands. It is undeniable that they have been buffeted by a series of severe storms in the past decade, accompanied by unusually intense episodes of the El Niño-Southern Oscillation (ENSO) phenomenon, a periodic fluctuation in sea temperature in the tropical Pacific that has been observed since the last century. What is not clear is whether these have anything to do with global warming.

Storm activity in the Pacific varies from year to year; 1998 saw an above-average incidence of tropical storms, while 1997 was comparatively quiet. The cause of this variation remains unknown. The ENSO phenomenon is not well understood, and it is not predicted by any model of climate change. A United Nations body called the Intergovernmental Panel on Climate Change (IPCC) has rightly observed that while many small island states fear that "global warming will lead to changes in the character and pattern of tropical cyclones (i.e., hurricanes and typhoons)," this fear is not confirmed by the most recent research. Rather, "model projections suggest no clear trend, so it is not possible to state whether the frequency, intensity, or distribution of tropical storms and cyclones will change."

And what of rising waters? In 1980, climatologists predicted that global warming would melt the polar icecaps, causing sea levels to rise more than 25 feet over the course of the next century. Such an event would undoubtedly be disastrous not only for the Pacific islands but also for densely populated coastal regions in all parts of the world.

Fortunately for those of us in Boston, Miami, New York, and Los Angeles, the deluge failed even to begin to materialize. According to the latest data, the polar icecaps do not appear to be melting at all. The 2001 IPCC report discerns "no significant trends" in the extent of Antarctic sea-ice since 1978, when reliable satellite measurements began to be taken; nor, at the other pole, is there evidence from satellite records that the air above the Arctic has warmed substantially.

With the polar caps essentially intact, it does not come as a surprise that sea levels have risen only a paltry 2 millimeters per year in the mid-1990's—roughly the same rate observed over the past 100 years. Even the gloomiest doomsayers have been compelled to jettison the dire forecasts put forward in 1980. Under the *worst*-case scenario now envisioned by the IPCC, the oceans should rise no more than a foot over the next century, not nearly enough to pose a major threat. And this forecast is in turn based on the assumption that sea levels will increase by approximately 5 millimeters per year, *give or take* 3 millimeters—in other words, the rate of rise may not change at all.

As for the climate itself, despite the alarmed rhetoric from so many quarters, we do not know for certain that it is even changing in significant ways. It is an established fact that the earth's climate has warmed slightly over the past century. Average temperatures near the surface have risen since 1900 and are now probably higher than they have been at any time in the past 600 to 1,000 years. But that statement more or less exhausts the scientific consensus. On every other important question—what the major causes of global warming are, what its effects will be, whether we should try to prevent it and, if so, how—there is considerable uncertainty.

Most of what we "know" about the earth's future is derived from enormously sophisticated computer models that utilize millions of parameters to simulate the earth's climate. These models are still far from reliable. The editors of *Nature,* arguably the world's most prestigious scientific journal, pointed out on March 15 that "the accuracy of any model depends significantly on the quality of the underlying raw data." But the quality of the data being used for climate prediction, they go on to state, is "patchy." For example, it is not at all easy to measure the amount of sunlight absorbed by the atmosphere or reflected by its surface back into space—and yet this one key parameter alone might (or might not) account for six times the amount of energy that would be added to the climate system by the doubling of atmospheric $CO_2$. Similar uncertainties attend other crucial variables like the impact of differing degrees of cloud cover and water vapor.

Given the room for error, it should come as no surprise that climate-prediction models have racked up an exceedingly poor track record over the years. According to those models, the average global temperature should have increased by at least 1 degree centigrade since the beginning of the 20th century, when industrial emissions of greenhouse gases first began to rise. But the best available measurements indicate that the average global temperature has increased by only 0.5 degrees in 100 years, and much of that increase occurred before 1940—too early in the century, in other words, to have been caused by a growth in $CO_2$ levels.

Contrary to the simulations, moreover, the marginal uptick in surface temperatures in the years since 1970 has not been accompanied by warming of the lower atmosphere (as we know from satellite data). A pair of recent papers in the journal *Science* attempts to account for this discrepancy by locating the missing heat in the oceans, a "discovery" trumpeted by the media as yet another blow to those who remain skeptical of global warming. But this was not a discovery at all, and was not based on any finding that whatever warming may have occurred has been caused by human activity. Rather, it was merely the product of "improved" models, which have their own "improved" assumptions and their own set of poorly understood parameters.

---

In the face of such scientific shell-games, and in the face of the huge costs the United States has been asked to incur to combat a problem that may or may not exist, President Bush was certainly right to pull the plug on the Kyoto Protocol. But whether he will be able to stand firm against the torrent of criticism that has been unleashed against him remains an open question. According to the Natural Resources Defense Council (NRDC), the Bush administration's decision to abandon Kyoto "will have massively destructive consequences for the earth and its people." Although the IPCC has specifically rejected any direct linkage between today's local environmental perturbations and global warming, the Sierra Club is instructing its members that the apocalypse is upon us *now,* in the form of "heat waves, droughts, coastal flooding, and malaria outbreaks."

There are more narrowly partisan interests at play as well. "Democrats See Gold in Environment," ran the headline of a recent *New York Times* story describing how Bush's environmental decisions have galvanized activists in the Democratic party. Indeed, reports the *Times,* some party officials are positively "gleeful" at the political opportunities now opening up. One such official is evidently Senator Lieberman. Assuming Al Gore's mantle as the party's leading spokesman on matters environmental, Lieberman has called the decision to abandon Kyoto "flabbergasting," and is now invoking the specter of "sea levels [that] could swell up to 35 feet, potentially submerging millions of homes and coastal property."

That this is the same Joseph Lieberman who in 1997 joined 94 other Senators in voting to denounce the Kyoto Protocol suggests that when it comes to global warming we are indeed facing a rising tide—of hysteria, mixed with sheer political cynicism. As against these twin forces, it may seem hopelessly naïve to suggest that we would do better to focus on phasing out those greenhouse gases that can be eliminated at relatively low cost, like sulfur hexafluoride and perfluorocarbons, while adopting a wait-and-see attitude toward $CO_2$, secure in the knowledge that advances in technology and in the accuracy of prediction will allow us to address climate change more effectively and more cheaply in the future. Naïve it may be, but at present there is no basis in scientific evidence for more drastic action. All that is required is a politician tough enough and brave enough to say so.

# POSTSCRIPT

## Should Society Act Now to Halt Global Warming?

The United Nations Conference on Environment and Development in Rio de Janeiro, Brazil, took place in 1992. High on the agenda was the problem of global warming, but despite widespread concern and calls for reductions in carbon dioxide releases, the United States refused to consider rigid deadlines or set quotas. The uncertainties seemed too great, and some thought the economic costs of cutting back on carbon dioxide might be greater than the costs of letting the climate warm.

James Kasting of Pennsylvania State University and James Walker of the University of Michigan warn that if one looks a little further into the future than the next century, the prospects look much more frightening. They predict that by 2100 the amount of carbon dioxide in the atmosphere will reach double its preindustrial level. By the 2200s it could be 7.6 times the preindustrial level. With draconian restrictions, however, it could be held to 4 times the preindustrial level. Global warming may therefore turn out to be much worse in the long term than anyone is predicting for the next century, although it is difficult to be at all sure of such predictions. See David Schneider, "The Rising Seas," *Scientific American* (March 1997) and Thomas R. Karl, Neville Nicholls, and Jonathan Gregory, "The Coming Climate," *Scientific American* (May 1997). See also "Bangladesh: The Next Atlantis?" *Environment* (June 2003), which reports recent modeling studies warning that if the IPCC projections are correct, over half of Bangladesh could be under water for most of each year by 2100.

The nations that signed the UN Framework Convention on Climate Change in Rio de Janeiro in 1992 met again in Kyoto, Japan, in December 1997 to set carbon emissions limits for the industrial nations. The United States agreed to reduce its annual greenhouse gas emissions 7 percent below the 1990 level between 2008 and 2012. In November 1998 they met in Buenos Aires, Argentina, to work out practical details (see Christopher Flavin, "Last Tango in Buenos Aires," *World Watch* [November/December 1998]). Unfortunately, developing countries, where carbon emissions are growing most rapidly, face few restrictions, and political opposition in developed nations—especially in the United States—remains strong. Ross Gelbspan, in "Rx for a Planetary Fever," *American Prospect* (May 8, 2000), blames much of that opposition on "big oil and big coal [which] have relentlessly obstructed the best-faith efforts of government negotiators." Nor do some portions of the industry seem interested in acting on their own. In May 2003, Exxon Mobil rejected proposals that it address global warming and develop renewable energy. CEO Lee Raymond, who had previously denounced the Kyoto

Protocol, said the company does not "make social statements at the expense of shareholder return."

The opposition remains, despite the latest IPCC report. Critics stress uncertainties in the data and the potential economic impacts of attempting to reduce carbon dioxide emissions. See Richard A. Kerr, "Rising Global Temperature, Rising Uncertainty," *Science* (April 13, 2001). Some feel that climate change may well be less severe than expected and also beneficial overall to agriculture and human well-being. See Patrick J. Michaels and Robert C. Balling, Jr., *The Satanic Gases: Clearing the Air About Global Warming* (Cato Institute, 2000).

There is also opposition based on the view that the methods of reducing greenhouse gas emissions called for in the Kyoto treaty are, at root, unworkable. See Frank N. Laird, "Just Say No to Greenhouse Gas Emissions Targets," *Issues in Science and Technology* (Winter 2000–2001). However, researchers have proposed a number of innovative ways to keep from adding carbon dioxide to the atmosphere. See Howard Herzog, Baldue Eliasson, and Olav Kaarstad, "Capturing Greenhouse Gases," *Scientific American* (February 2000). Fred Krupp, President of Environmental Defense, "Global Warming and the USA," *Vital Speeches of the Day* (April 15, 2003), recommends a market-based approach to finding and developing innovative approaches. Thomas J. Wilbanks, Sally M. Kane, Paul N. Leiby, Robert D. Perlack, Chad Settle, Jason F. Shogren, and Joel B. Smith, "Possible Responses to Global Climate Change: Integrating Mitigation and Adaptation," *Environment* (June 2003), note that many mitigation techniques are under study around the world, but people will also have to adapt to a warming world.

In June 2002 the U.S. Environmental Protection Agency (EPA) issued its *U.S. Climate Action Report—2002* (available at `http://www.epa.gov/globalwarming/publications/car/index.html`) to the United Nations. In it, the EPA admits for the first time that global warming is real and that human activities are most likely to blame. President George W. Bush immediately dismissed the report as "put out by the bureaucracy" and said he still opposes the Kyoto Protocol. He insists more research is necessary before we can even begin to plan a proper response, which prompts Ian Frazier, "As the World Burns," *Mother Jones* (March/April 2003), tongue slightly in cheek, to call him "a man with a plan—about planning to plan." Seth Dunn, *Reading the Weathervane: Climate Policy from Rio to Johannesburg* (Worldwatch Paper 160, August 2002), urges swift implementation of the Kyoto Protocol as the best way to achieve global action on climate change.

# ISSUE 6

## Do Environmentalists Overstate Their Case?

**YES: Ronald Bailey,** from "Debunking Green Myths," *Reason* (February 2002)

**NO: David Pimentel,** from "Skeptical of the Skeptical Environmentalist," *Skeptic* (vol. 9, no. 2, 2002)

### ISSUE SUMMARY

**YES:** Environmental journalist Ronald Bailey argues that the natural environment is not in trouble, despite the arguments of many environmentalists that it is. He holds that the greatest danger facing the environment is not human activity but "ideological environmentalism, with its hostility to economic growth and technological progress."

**NO:** David Pimentel, a professor of insect ecology and agricultural sciences, argues that those who contend that the environment is not threatened are using data selectively and that the supply of basic resources to support human life is declining rapidly.

For over two centuries, seemingly everyone who has claimed to see environmental disaster in the offing has been challenged. In 1798, for example, English parson Thomas Malthus thought population must inevitably outstrip the ability of the environment to produce food. When the crisis he foretold did not come about, he was ridiculed; indeed, his failure has been held up ever since as a main reason why we need not be concerned about the consequences of population growth, urbanization, industrialization, and other human activities.

Yet the environmentalists have continued to find things to be concerned about. Rachel Carson (1907–1964) is famous for realizing the dangers of pesticides and other chemicals that we release to the environment, which she reported in her best-seller *Silent Spring* (Houghton Mifflin, 1962). Ecologists Paul Ehrlich and Garrett Hardin have reiterated Malthus's concern about population. A Massachusetts Institute of Technology team lead by Donella Meadows and Dennis Meadows used computer models to analyze population, development, and pollution trends and forecast a crisis of resource depletion and economic collapse before 2050 (see *The Limits to Growth* [Universe Books, 1972]). In 1992 the study was repeated with improved computer models, and even more pessimistic conclusions were reached (see *Beyond the Limits: Confronting Global Collapse, Envisioning a Sustainable Future* [Chelsea Green, 1992]). In 1980 the U.S. government published *The Global 2000 Report to the President,* which projected increased environmental degradation, loss of resources, and a widening gap between the rich and the poor.

No one likes such conclusions. Nor does anyone like the implications for what must be done: limit industrial development and population growth. Conservatives object to proposals to regulate industrial development, for only unchecked industry can generate the wealth needed to solve problems, and the free market can be trusted to produce solutions for all problems that truly need solutions. They also object to proposals to limit family size. Liberals object that restricting development will harm the poor much more than it will the rich. Some also object that the true problem is modern capitalism, which emphasizes short-term economic payoffs over longer-term benefits.

The growing sense that we do indeed face environmental crises lies behind the long series of international conferences arranged by the United Nations, from 1968's Biosphere Conference through 1972's Conference on the Human Environment and 1992's Earth Summit (or the Conference on Environment and Development) to 2002's World Summit on Sustainable Development. The concept of sustainable development became prominent after 1992 and has now taken center stage. Yet the debate is hardly over. Analysts such as Niles Eldredge (*Life in the Balance: Humanity and the Biodiversity Crisis* [Princeton University Press, 1998]) have argued that development in the traditional sense cannot be sustained in a world whose resources are finite; sustainable development must mean development without growth in industrial activity or population.

One prominent contrary voice was that of economist Julian L. Simon (1932–1998), who argued that environmental problems could only be short-term problems; increased population and the free market would ensure an ever-improving standard of living and an ever-healthier environment (see *The Ultimate Resource* [Princeton University Press, 1981]). In 1998 statistician and political scientist Bjorn Lomborg joined the fray with *The Skeptical Environmentalist: Measuring the Real State of the World* (Cambridge University Press, 2001). In it, he accuses environmentalists of distorting the truth in a litany of disaster. The truth, he says, is that "mankind's lot has actually improved in terms of practically every measurable indicator."

Is Lomborg right? The following selections represent two of the many reviews that have discussed this question. In the first selection, Ronald Bailey argues that Lomborg is indeed correct. Despite the claims of environmentalists, he contends, the natural environment is not in trouble from human activity but is, in fact, more threatened by ideological environmentalism. In the second selection, David Pimentel argues that Lomborg misrepresents the truth by selecting only data that support his case. He maintains that human activities do threaten the environment and that mankind's lot is at the mercy of a rapidly declining supply of basic resources.

**Ronald Bailey**

# Debunking Green Myths

Modern environmentalism, born of the radical movements of the 1960s, has often made recourse to science to press its claims that the world is going to hell in a handbasket. But this environmentalist has never really been a matter of objectively describing the world and calling for the particular social policies that the description implies.

Environmentalism is an ideology, very much like Marxism, which pretended to base its social critique on a "scientific" theory of economic relations. Like Marxists, environmentalists have had to force the facts to fit their theory. Environmentalism is an ideology in crisis: The massive, accumulating contradictions between its pretensions and the actual state of the world can no longer be easily explained away.

The publication of *The Skeptical Environmentalist,* a magnificent and important book by a former member of Greenpeace, deals a major blow to that ideology by superbly documenting a response to environmental doomsaying. The author, Bjorn Lomborg, is an associate professor of statistics at the University of Aarhus in Denmark. On a trip to the United States a few years ago, Lomborg picked up a copy of *Wired* that included an article about the late "doomslayer" Julian Simon.

Simon, a professor of business administration at the University of Maryland, claimed that by most measures, the lot of humanity is improving and the world's natural environment was not critically imperiled. Lomborg, thinking it would be an amusing and instructive exercise to debunk a "right-wing" anti-environmentalist American, assigned his students the project of finding the "real" data that would contradict Simon's outrageous claims.

Lomborg and his students discovered that Simon was essentially right, and that the most famous environmental alarmists (Stanford biologist Paul Ehrlich, Worldwatch Institute founder Lester Brown, former Vice President Al Gore, *Silent Spring* author Rachel Carson) and the leading environmentalist lobbying groups (Greenpeace, the World Wildlife Fund, Friends of the Earth) were wrong. It turns out that the natural environment is in good shape, and the prospects of humanity are actually quite good.

Lomborg beings with "the Litany" of environmentalist doom, writing: "We are all familiar with the Litany. . . . Our resources are running out. The population is ever growing, leaving less and less to eat. The air and water are becoming ever more polluted. The planet's species are becoming extinct in vast numbers. . . . The world's ecosystem is breaking down. . . . We all know the Litany and have heard it so often that yet another repetition is, well, almost reassuring." Lomborg notes that there is just one problem with the Litany: "It does not seem to be backed up by the available evidence."

Lomborg then proceeds to demolish the Litany. He shows how, time and again, ideological environmentalists misuse, distort, and ignore the vast reams of data that contradict their dour visions. In the course of *The Skeptical Environmentalist,* Lomborg demonstrates that the environmentalist lobby is just that, a collection of interest groups that must hype doom in order to survive monetarily and politically.

Lomborg notes, "As the industry and farming organizations have an obvious interest in portraying the environment as just-fine and no-need-to-do-anything, the environmental organizations also have a clear interest in telling us that the environment is in a bad state, and that we need to act now. And the worse they can make this state appear, the easier it is for them to convince us we need to spend more money on the environment rather than on hospitals, kindergartens, etc. Of course, if we were equally skeptical of both sorts of organization there would be less of a problem. But since we tend to treat environmental organizations with much less skepticism, this might cause a grave bias in our understanding of the state of the world." Lomborg's book amply shows that our understanding of the state of the world is indeed biased.

❧

So what is the real state of humanity and the planet?

Human life expectancy in the developing world has more than doubled in the past century, from 31 years to 65. Since 1960, the average amount of food per person in the developing countries has increased by 38 percent, and although world population has doubled, the percentage of malnourished poor people has fallen globally from 35 percent to 18 percent, and will likely fall further over the next decade, to 12 percent. In real terms, food costs a third of what it did in the 1960s. Lomborg points out that increasing food production trends show no sign of slackening in the future.

What about air pollution? Completely uncontroversial data show that concentrations of sulfur dioxide are down 80 percent in the U.S. since 1962, carbon monoxide levels are down 75 percent since 1970, nitrogen oxides are down 38 percent since 1975, and ground level ozone is down 30 percent since 1977. These trends are mirrored in all developed countries.

❧

Lomborg shows that claims of rapid deforestation are vastly exaggerated. One United Nations Food and Agriculture survey found that globally, forest cover has been reduced by a minuscule 0.44 percent since 1961. The World Wildlife Fund claims that two-thirds of the world's forests have been lost since the dawn of agriculture; the reality is that the world still has 80 percent of its forests. What about the Brazilian rainforests? Eighty-six percent remain uncut, and the rate of clearing is falling. Lomborg also debunks the widely circulated claim that the world will soon lose up to half of its species. In fact, the best evidence indicates that 0.7 percent of species might be lost in the next 50 years if nothing is done. And of course, it is unlikely that nothing will be done.

Finally, Lomborg shows that global warming caused by burning fossil fuels is unlikely to be a catastrophe. Why? First, because actual measured temperatures aren't increasing nearly as fast as the computer climate models say they should be—in fact, any increase is likely to be at the low end of the predictions, and no one thinks that would be a disaster. Second, even in the unlikely event that temperatures were to increase substantially, it will be far less costly and more environmentally sound to adapt to the changes rather than institute draconian cuts in fossil fuel use. The best calculations show that adapting to global warming would cost $5 trillion over the next century. By comparison, substantially cutting back on fossil fuel emissions in the manner suggested by the Kyoto Protocol would cost between $107 and $274 trillion over the same period. (Keep in mind that the current yearly U.S. gross domestic product is $10 trillion.) Such costs would mean that people living in developing countries would lose over 75 percent of their expected increases in income over the next century. That would be not only a human tragedy, but an environmental one as well, since poor people generally have little time for environmental concerns.

Where does Lomborg fall short? He clearly understands that increasing prosperity is the key to improving human and environmental health, but he often takes for granted the institutions of property and markets that make progress and prosperity possible. His analysis, as good as it is, fails to identify the chief cause of most environmental problems. In most cases, imperiled resources such as fisheries and airsheds are in open-access commons where the incentive is for people to take as much as possible of the resource before someone else beats them to it. Since they don't own the resource, they have no incentive to protect and conserve it.

Clearly, regulation has worked to improve the state of many open-access commons in developed countries such as the U.S. Our air and streams are much cleaner than they were 30 years ago, in large part due to things like installing catalytic converters on automobiles and building more municipal sewage treatment plants. Yet there is good evidence that assigning private property rights to these resources would have resulted in a faster and cheaper cleanup. Lomborg's analysis would have been even stronger had he more directly taken on ideological environmentalism's bias against markets. But perhaps that is asking for too much in an already superb book.

"Things are *better* now," writes Lomborg, "but they are still not *good* enough." He's right. Only continued economic growth will enable the

800 million people who are still malnourished to get the food they need; only continued economic growth will let the 1.2 billion who don't have access to clean water and sanitation obtain those amenities. It turns out that ideological environmentalism, with its hostility to economic growth and technological progress, is the biggest threat to the natural environment and to the hopes of the poorest people in the world for achieving better lives.

"The very message of the book," Lomborg concludes, is that "children born today—in both the industrialized world and the developing countries—will live longer and be healthier, they will get more food, a better education, a higher standard of living, more leisure time and far more possibilities—without the global environment being destroyed. And that is a beautiful world."

**David Pimentel**

# Skeptical of the Skeptical Environmentalist

Bjorn Lomborg discusses a wide range of topics in his book and implies, through his title, that he will inform readers exactly what the real state of world is. In this effort, he criticizes countless world economists, agriculturists, water specialists, and environmentalists, and furthermore, accuses them of misquoting and/or organizing published data to mislead the public concerning the status of world population, food supplies, malnutrition, disease, and pollution. Lomborg bases his optimistic opinion on his selective use of data. Some of Lomborg's assertions will be examined in this review, and where differing information is presented, extensive documentation will be provided.

Lomborg reports that "we now have more food per person than we used to." In contrast, the Food and Agricultural Organization (FAO) of the United Nations reports that food per capita has been declining since 1984, based on available cereal grains (Figure 1). Cereal grains make up about 80% of the world's food. Although grain yields per hectare (abbreviated ha) in both developed and developing countries are still increasing, these increases are slowing while the world population continues to escalate. Specifically from 1950 to 1980, U.S. grains yields increased at about 3% per year, but after 1980 the rate of increase for corn and other grains has declined to only about 1% (Figure 2).

Obviously fertile cropland is an essential resource for the production of foods but Lomborg has chosen not to address this subject directly. Currently, the U.S. has available nearly 0.5 ha of prime cropland per capita, but it will not have this much land if the population continues to grow at its current rapid rate. Worldwide the average cropland available for food production is only 0.25 ha per person. Each person added to the U.S. population requires nearly 0.4 ha (1 acre) of land for urbanization and transportation. One example of the impact of population growth and development is occurring in California where an average of 156,000 ha of agricultural land is being lost each year. At this rate it will not be long before California ceases to be the number one state in U.S. agricultural production.

In addition to the quantity of agricultural land, soil quality and fertility is vital for food production. The productivity of the soil is reduced when it is eroded by rainfall and wind. Soil erosion is not a problem, according to Lomborg, especially in the U.S. where soil erosion has declined during the

From "Skeptical of the Skeptical Environmentalist," *Skeptic,* vol. 9, no. 2 (2002).  Notes omitted.

*Figure 1*

**Cereal Grain Production per Capita in the World from 1961 to 1999**

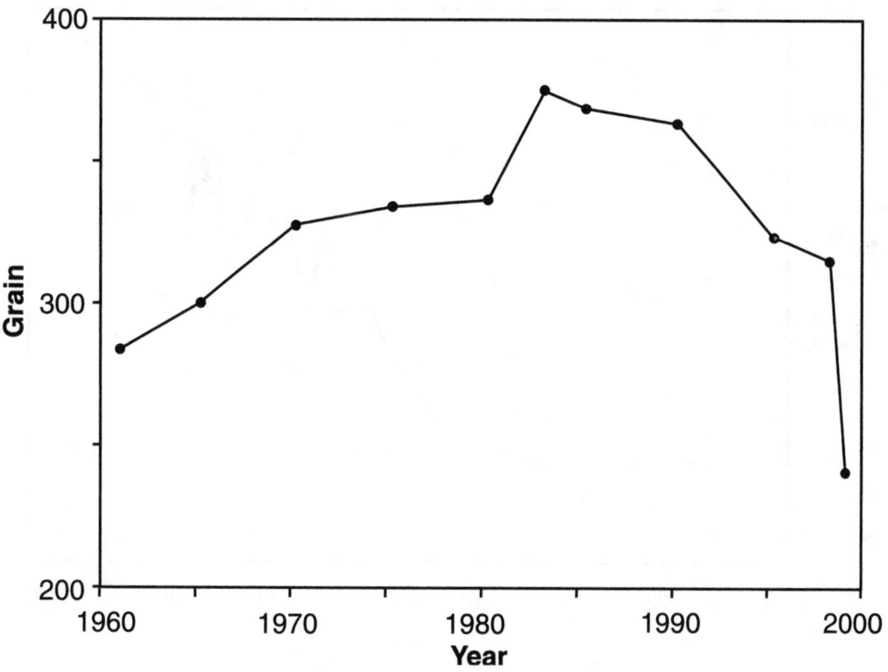


FAO, 1961 1999

past decade. Yes, as Lomborg states, instead of losing an average of 17 metric tons per hectare per year on cropland, the U.S. cropland is now losing an average of 13 t/ha/yr. However, this average loss is 13 times the sustainability rate of soil replacement. Exceptions occur, as during the 1995–96 winter in Kansas, when it was relatively dry and windy, and some agricultural lands lost as much as 65 t/ha of productive soil. This loss is 65 times the natural soil replacement in agriculture.

Worldwide soil erosion is more damaging than in the United States. For instance, the India soil is being lost at 30 to 40 times its sustainability. Rate of soil loss in Africa is increasing not only because of livestock overgrazing but also because of the burning of crop residues due to the shortages of wood fuel. During the summer of 2000, NASA published a satellite image of a cloud of soil from Africa being blown across the Atlantic Ocean, further attesting to the massive soil erosion problem in Africa. Worldwide evidence concerning soil loss is substantiated and it is difficult to ignore its effect on sustainable agricultural production.

Contrary to Lomborg's belief, crop yields cannot continue to increase in response to the increased applications of more fertilizers and pesticides. In fact, field tests have demonstrated that applying excessive amounts of

*Figure 2*

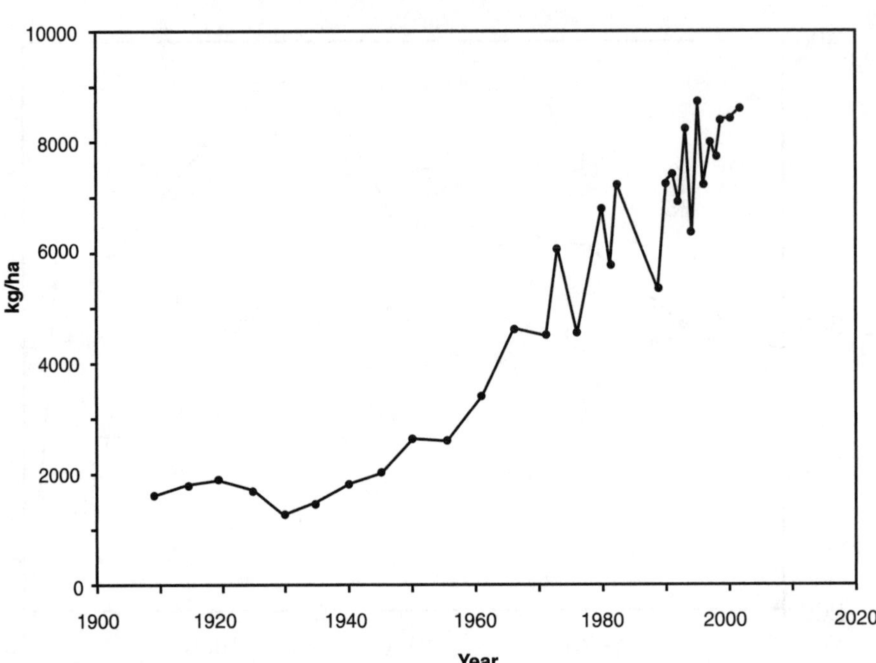


USDA, 1910–2000

nitrogen fertilizer stresses the crop plants, resulting in declining yields. The optimum amount of nitrogen for corn, one of the crops that require heavy use of nitrogen, is approximately 120 kg/ha.

Although U.S. farmers frequently apply significantly more nitrogen fertilizer than 120 kg/ha, the extra is a waste and pollutant. The corn crop can only utilize about one-third of the nitrogen applied, while the remainder leaches either into the ground or surface waters. This pollution of aquatic ecosystems in agricultural areas results in the high levels of nitrogen and pesticides occurring in many U.S. water bodies. For example, nitrogen fertilizer has found its way into 97% of the well-water supplies in some regions, like North Carolina. The concentrations of nitrate are above the U.S. Environmental Protection Agency drinking-water standard of 10 milligrams per liter (nitrogen) and are a toxic threat to young children and young livestock. In the last 30 years, the nitrate content has tripled in the Gulf of Mexico, where it is reducing the Gulf fishery.

In an undocumented statement Lomborg reports that pesticides cause very little cancer. Further, he provides no explanation as to why human and other nontarget species are not exposed to pesticides when crops are treated. There is abundant medical and scientific evidence that confirms that pesticides cause significant numbers of cancers in the U.S. and throughout the world. Lomborg also neglects to report that some herbicides stimulate the production of toxic chemicals in some plants, and that these toxicants can cause cancer.

In keeping with Lomborg's view that agriculture and the food supply are improving, he states that "fewer people are starving." Lomborg criticizes the validity of the two World Health Organization [WHO] reports that confirm more than 3 billion people are malnourished. This is the largest number and proportion of malnourished people ever in history! Apparently Lomborg rejects the WHO data because they do not support his basic thesis. Instead, Lomborg argues that only people who suffer from calorie shortages are malnourished, and ignores the fact that humans die from deficiencies of protein, iron, iodine, and vitamin A, B, C, and D.

Further confirming a decline in food supply, the FAO reports that there has been a three-fold decline in the consumption of fish in the human diet during the past seven years. This decline in fish per capita is caused by overfishing, pollution, and the impact of a rapidly growing world population that must share the diminishing fish supply.

In discussing the status of water supply and sanitation services, Lomborg is correct in stating that these services were improved in the developed world during the 19th century, but he ignores the available scientific data when he suggests that these trends have been "replicated in the developing world" during the 20th century. Countless reports confirm that developing countries discharge most of their untreated urban sewage directly into surface waters. For example, of India's 3,119 towns and cities, only eight have full waste water treatment facilities. Furthermore, 114 Indian cities dump untreated sewage and partially cremated bodies directly into the sacred Ganges River. Downstream the untreated water is used for drinking, bathing, and washing. In view of the poor sanitation, it is no wonder that water borne infectious diseases account for 80% of all infections worldwide and 90% of all infections in developing countries.

Contrary to Lomborg's view, most infectious diseases are increasing worldwide. The increase is due not only to population growth but also because of increasing environmental pollution. Food-borne infections are increasing rapidly worldwide and in the United States. For example, during 2000 in the U.S. there were 76 million human food-borne infections with 5,000 associated deaths. Many of these infections are associated with the increasing contamination of food and water by livestock wastes in the United States.

In addition, a large number of malnourished people are highly susceptible to infectious diseases, like tuberculosis (TB), malaria, schistosomiasis, and AIDS. For example, the number of people infected with tuberculosis in the U.S. and the world is escalating, in part because medicine has not kept up with the new forms of TB. Currently, according to the World Health Organization, more than 2 billion people in the world are infected with TB, with nearly 2 million people dying each year from it.

Consistent with Lomborg's thesis that world natural resources are abundant, he reports that the U.S. Energy Information Agency for the period 2000

***Figure 3***

**Number of Hectares in Forests Worldwide (x 1 million ha) from 1961 to 1994**

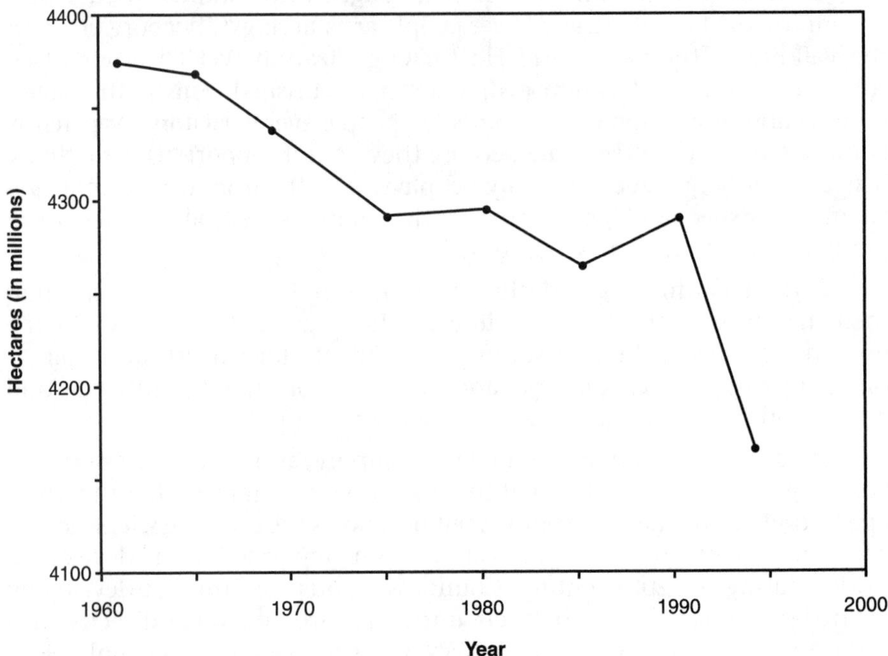


FAOSTAT Database, consulted September 3, 2001

to 2020 projects an almost steady oil price over the next two decades at about $22 per barrel. This optimistic projection was crossed late in 2000 when oil rose to $30 or more per barrel in the United States and the world. The best estimates today project that world oil reserves will last approximately 50 years, based on current production rates.

Lomborg takes the World Wildlife Fund (WWF) to task for their estimates on the loss of world forests during the past decade and their emphasis on resulting ecological impacts and loss of biodiversity. Whether the loss of forests is slow, as Lomborg suggests, or rapid as WWF reports, there is no question that forests are disappearing worldwide (Figure 3). Forests not only provide valuable products but they harbor a vast diversity of species of plants, animals and microbes. Progress in medicine, agriculture, genetic engineering, and environmental quality depend on maintaining the species diversity in the world.

This reviewer takes issue with Lomborg's underlying thesis that the size and growth of the human population is not a major problem. The difference between Lomborg's figure that 76 million humans were added to the world population in 2000, or the 80 million reported by the Population Reference Bureau, is not the issue, though the magnitude of both projections is of serious concern. Lomborg neglects to explain that the major problem with world population growth is the young age structure that now exists. Even if the world adopted a policy of only two children per couple tomorrow, the world population would continue to increase for more than 70 years before stabilizing at more than 12 billion people. As an agricultural scientist and ecologist, I wish I could share Lomborg's optimistic views, but my investigations and those of countless scientists lead me to a more conservative outlook. The supply of basic resources, like fertile cropland, water, energy, and an unpolluted atmosphere that support human life is declining rapidly, as nearly a quarter million people are daily added to the Earth. We all desire a high standard of living for each person on Earth, but with every person added, the supply of resources must be divided and shared. Current losses and degradation of natural resources suggest concern and a need for planning for future generations of humans. Based on our current understanding of the real state of the world and environment, there is need for conservation and protection of vital world resources.

# POSTSCRIPT

## Do Environmentalists Overstate Their Case?

One of the basic issues at work in the debate between "Malthusians" (who believe that the environment can only support a limited number of people and amount of industrial activity) and "cornucopians" (who believe that there are no such limits) is whether or not past trends can be extrapolated reliably into the future. Cornucopians see little problem in such extrapolation: If the per capita food supply has continued to increase for the last half century, it will continue to do so ad infinitum. Ecologists point out that natural environments have a finite supply of resources (water, soil nutrients, and so on). In nature, population growth follows an S-shaped curve with a steep rise phase followed by a leveling-off at what is known as the "carrying capacity." In "Anticipating Environmental 'Surprise,'" in Lester R. Brown et al., *State of the World 2000* (W. W. Norton, 2000), Chris Brown stresses that straight-line extrapolation cannot be trusted in the real world, because real-world trends are not linear; straight-line trends level off, and they may even peak and fall.

Bjorn Lomborg's *The Skeptical Environmentalist,* with its essentially optimistic message that conditions will continue to get better and better and that we do not need to worry about environmental issues, received very positive responses from the press. However, the scientific community reacted very differently. The January 2002 issue of *Scientific American,* for example, features a series of articles by leading scientists under the heading "Misleading Math About the Earth." Stephen Schneider deals with Lomborg's comments on global warming, John P. Holdren deals with energy, John Bongaarts addresses population, and Thomas Lovejoy discusses biodiversity. All four document the numerous ways in which they feel that Lomborg distorts the truth. Richard B. Norgaard, in "Optimists, Pessimists, and Science," *Bioscience* (March 2002), calls the *Scientific American* article series "devastating" and develops an explanation for Lomborg's approach in the very different ways that economics and science approach the world. Russ Baker, in "The Lomborg File: When the Press Is Lured by a Contrarian's Tale," *Columbia Journalism Review* (March/April 2002), bemoans the uncritical reaction of the nonscientific media, quoting Winston Churchill's famous remark "A lie gets halfway around the world before the truth has a chance to get its pants on."

In "The Skeptical Environmentalist Replies," *Scientific American* (May 2002), Lomborg rebuts his detractors. However, John Rennie, editor in chief of *Scientific American,* charges that Lomborg fails to address the scientists' points and continues to be selective about data.

On the other hand, a review in the May/June 2002 issue of *Foreign Affairs* calls the responses of the scientists "highly critical, even petulant" and says that Lomborg's own "occasionally tendentious examination of sources pales in comparison with the errors of Lomborg's targets." In "Green With Ideology," *Reason* (May 2002), Ronald Bailey argues that the scientists' responses amply demonstrate the truth of his point that environmentalism is an ideology. The debate between Lomborg and his opponents failed to affect planning for the Johannesburg World Summit on Sustainable Development, which is premised on the belief that humanity needs to adjust its behavior if it is to continue to thrive on earth.

Andrew C. Aulist, "Opportunity Lost: Error and Bias Undermine *The Skeptical Environmentalist*," *Quarterly Review of Biology* (March 2003), says that, "Lomborg's house of cards teeters on a shaky foundation of flawed statistical analysis and collapses under the weight of ill-formed conclusions. Not all of the book's information is misleading or erroneous, though. To the contrary, the volume is a curious and often frustrating mix of fact, reason, error, opinion, and hand-picked information, all cemented together with a heavy dose of skeptical bias, and a seemingly genuine concern for the environment. In the end, it is little more than a polemic and surely not the dispassionate analysis it purports to be." In January 2003, the Committees on Scientific Dishonesty of the Danish Research Agency (Denmark's equivalent of the U.S. National Academy of Sciences) declared that Lomborg's *Skeptical Environmentalist* fell "within the concept of scientific dishonesty" and "was clearly contrary to the standards of good scientific practice." See Bob Schildgen, "Book Busted," *Sierra* (March/April 2003). Social scientists promptly objected; see Alison Abbott, "Social Scientists Call for Abolition of Dishonesty Committee," *Nature* (February 13, 2003). Robert W. Kates, "Further Reflections on *The Skeptical Environmentalist*," *Environment* (March 2003), "would have preferred a finding that said *The Skeptical Environmentalist* does not meet the standards of science or policy analysis scholarship and therefore should be judged by standards of journalism or advocacy."

# ISSUE 7

## Will Hydrogen Replace Fossil Fuels for Cars?

**YES: Jeremy Rifkin,** from "Hydrogen: Empowering the People," *The Nation* (December 23, 2002)

**NO: Henry Payne and Diane Katz,** from "Gas and Gasbags . . . or, the Open Road and Its Enemies," *National Review* (March 25, 2002)

### ISSUE SUMMARY


**YES:** Social activist Jeremy Rifkin asserts that fossil fuels are approaching the end of their usefulness and that hydrogen fuel holds the potential not only to replace them but also to reshape society.

**NO:** Henry Payne and Diane Katz maintain that hydrogen can only be made widely available if society invests heavily in nuclear power. Market mechanisms will keep fossil fuels in play for years to come.


The 1973 "oil crisis" heightened awareness that the world—even if it was not yet running out of oil—was extraordinarily dependent on that fossil fuel (and therefore on supplier nations) for transportation, home heating, and electricity generation. Since the supply of oil and other fossil fuels was clearly finite, some people worried that there would come a time when demand could not be satisfied, and our dependence would leave us helpless. At the same time, we became acutely aware of the many unfortunate side effects of fossil fuels, notably air pollution.

The 1970s saw the modern environmental movement gain momentum. The first Earth Day was in 1970. Numerous government steps were taken to deal with air pollution, water pollution, and other environmental problems. In response to the oil crisis, a great deal of public money went into developing alternative energy supplies. The emphasis was on "renewable" energy, meaning conservation, wind, solar, and fuels such as hydrogen gas (which, when burned with pure oxygen, produces only water vapor as exhaust). However, when the crisis passed and oil supplies were once more ample (albeit it did cost more to fill a gasoline tank), most public funding for alternative-energy research and demonstration projects vanished. What work continued was at the hands of a few enthusiasts and those corporations that saw future opportunities. In 1991, Roger Billings, who had converted cars to run on hydrogen, developed the use of metal hydrides for hydrogen storage, founded corporations to develop and market hydrogen technology, and self-published *The Hydrogen World View* (a new edition appeared in 2000); his dream was a future when hydrogen would be the universal fuel, as widely employed for transportation and home heating (among other uses) as oil is today. That dream was not his alone. For instance, in 2001, the Worldwatch Institute published Seth Dunn's *Hydrogen Futures: Toward a Sustainable Energy System.* In 2002, MIT Press published Peter Hoffman's *Tomorrow's Energy: Hydrogen, Fuel Cells, and the Prospects for a Cleaner Planet.* On the corporate side, fossil fuel companies have long been major investors in alternative energy systems; in just the last few years, Shell, BP/Amoco, and ChevronTexaco have invested large amounts of money in renewables, hydrogen, photovoltaics, and fuel cells.

What drives the continuing interest in hydrogen and other alternative or renewable energy systems is the continuing problems associated with fossil fuels (and the discovery of new problems such as global warming), concern about dependence and potential political instability, and the growing realization that the availability of petroleum will peak in the near future. See Colin J. Campbell, "Depletion and Denial: The Final Years of Oil," *USA Today Magazine* (November 2000), and Charles C. Mann, "Getting Over Oil," *Technology Review* (January–February 2002).

Will that interest come to anything? There are, after all, a number of other ways to meet the need. Coal can be converted into oil and gasoline (though the air pollution and global warming problems remain). Cars can be made more efficient (and mileage efficiency is much greater than it was in the 1970s despite the popularity of SUVs). Cars can be designed to use natural gas or battery power; "hybrid" cars use combinations of gasoline and electricity, and some are already on the market. See Jennifer Hattam, "Righteous Road Trip," *Sierra* (May/June 2002).

The hydrogen enthusiasts remain. In the selections that follow, Jeremy Rifkin maintains that as oil supplies decline, hydrogen can fill the gap with many fewer side effects. In addition, because hydrogen can be produced by small-scale operations, it will take energy supplies out of the hands of major corporations and favor the development of a decentralized, environmentally benign economy. Henry Payne and Diane Katz do not agree that hydrogen can be produced locally; they contest that it can only be made widely available if society invests heavily in nuclear power. Oil and other fossil fuels will remain in use for years to come, with market mechanisms ensuring steady supply.

**Jeremy Rifkin** 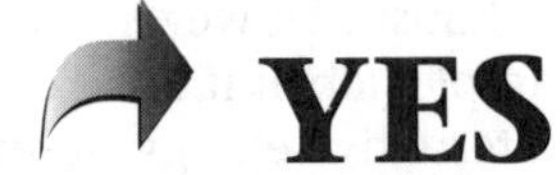

# Hydrogen: Empowering the People

While the fossil-fuel era enters its sunset years, a new energy regime is being born that has the potential to remake civilization along radically new lines—hydrogen. Hydrogen is the most basic and ubiquitous element in the universe. It never runs out and produces no harmful $CO_2$ emissions when burned; the only byproducts are heat and pure water. That is why it's been called "the forever fuel."

Hydrogen has the potential to end the world's reliance on oil. Switching to hydrogen and creating a decentralized power grid would also be the best assurance against terrorist attacks aimed at disrupting the national power grid and energy infrastructure. Moreover, hydrogen power will dramatically reduce carbon dioxide emissions and mitigate the effects of global warming. In the long run, the hydrogen-powered economy will fundamentally change the very nature of our market, political and social institutions, just as coal and steam power did at the beginning of the Industrial Revolution.

Hydrogen must be extracted from natural sources. Today, nearly half the hydrogen produced in the world is derived from natural gas via a steam-reforming process. The natural gas reacts with steam in a catalytic converter. The process strips away the hydrogen atoms, leaving carbon dioxide as the byproduct.

There is, however, another way to produce hydrogen without using fossil fuels in the process. Renewable sources of energy—wind, photovoltaic, hydro, geothermal and biomass—can be harnessed to produce electricity. The electricity, in turn, can be used, in a process called electrolysis, to split water into hydrogen and oxygen. The hydrogen can then be stored and used, when needed, in a fuel cell to generate electricity for power, heat and light.

Why generate electricity twice, first to produce electricity for the process of electrolysis and then to produce power, heat and light by way of a fuel cell? The reason is that electricity doesn't store. So, if the sun isn't shining or the wind isn't blowing or the water isn't flowing, electricity can't be generated and economic activity grinds to a halt. Hydrogen provides a way to store renewable sources of energy and insure an ongoing and continuous supply of power.

Hydrogen-powered fuel cells are just now being introduced into the market for home, office and industrial use. The major auto makers have spent more than $2 billion developing hydrogen-powered cars, buses and

Reprinted with permission from the December 23, 2002 issue of *The Nation* pp. 40–45. For subscription information, call 1-800-333-8536. Portions of each week's *Nation* magazine can be accessed at `http://www.thenation.com`.

trucks, and the first mass-produced vehicles are expected to be on the road in just a few years.

In a hydrogen economy the centralized, top-down flow of energy, controlled by global oil companies and utilities, would become obsolete. Instead, millions of end users would connect their fuel cells into local, regional and national hydrogen energy webs (HEWs), using the same design principles and smart technologies that made the World Wide Web possible. Automobiles with hydrogen cells would be power stations on wheels, each with a generating capacity of 20 kilowatts. Since the average car is parked most of the time, it can be plugged in, during nonuse hours, to the home, office or the main interactive electricity network. Thus, car owners could sell electricity back to the grid. If just 25 percent of all U.S. cars supplied energy to the grid, all the power plants in the country could be eliminated.

Once the HEW is set up, millions of local operators, generating electricity from fuel cells onsite, could produce more power more cheaply than can today's giant power plants. When the end users also become the producers of their energy, the only role remaining for existing electrical utilities is to become "virtual power plants" that manufacture and market fuel cells, bundle energy services and coordinate the flow of energy over the existing power grids.

To realize the promise of decentralized generation of energy, however, the energy grid will have to be redesigned. The problem with the existing power grid is that it was designed to insure a one-way flow of energy from a central source to all the end users. Before the HEW can be fully actualized, changes in the existing power grid will have to be made to facilitate both easy access to the web and a smooth flow of energy services over the web. Connecting thousands, and then millions, of fuel cells to main grids will require sophisticated dispatch and control mechanisms to route energy traffic during peak and nonpeak periods. A new technology developed by the Electric Power Research Institute called FACTS (flexible alternative current transmission system) gives transmission companies the capacity to "deliver measured quantities of power to specified areas of the grid."

Whether hydrogen becomes the people's energy depends, to a large extent, on how it is harnessed in the early stages of development. The global energy and utility companies will make every effort to control access to this new, decentralized energy network just as software, telecommunications and content companies like Microsoft and AOL Time Warner have attempted to control access to the World Wide Web. It is critical that public institutions and nonprofit organizations—local governments, cooperatives, community development corporations, credit unions and the like—become involved early on in establishing distributed-generation associations (DGAs) in every country. Again, the analogy to the World Wide Web is apt. In the new hydrogen energy era, millions of end users will generate their own "content" in the form of hydrogen and electricity. By organizing collectively to control the energy they produce—just as workers in the twentieth century organized into unions to control their labor power—end users can better dictate the terms with commercial suppliers of fuel cells for lease, purchase or other use arrangements and with virtual utility companies, which will manage the decentralized "smart" energy grids. Creating the appropriate partnership between commercial and noncommercial interests will be critical to establishing the legitimacy, effectiveness and long-term viability of the new energy regime.

I have been describing, thus far, the implementation of hydrogen power mainly in industrialized countries, but it could have an even greater impact on emerging nations. The per capita use of energy throughout the developing world is a mere one-fifteenth of the consumption enjoyed in the United States. The global average per capita energy use for all countries is only one-fifth the level of this country. Lack of access to energy, especially electricity, is a key factor in perpetuating poverty around the world. Conversely, access to energy means more economic opportunity. In South Africa, for example, for every 100 households electrified, ten to twenty new businesses are created. Making the shift to a hydrogen energy regime—using renewable resources and technologies to produce the hydrogen—and creating distributed generation energy webs that can connect communities all over the world could lift billions of people out of poverty. As the price of fuel cells and accompanying appliances continues to plummet with innovations and economies of scale, they will become far more broadly available, as was the case with transistor radios, computers and cellular phones. The goal ought to be to provide stationary fuel cells for every neighborhood and village in the developing world.

Renewable energy technologies—wind, photovoltaic, hydro, biomass, etc.—can be installed in villages, enabling them to produce their own electricity and then use it to separate hydrogen from water and store it for subsequent use in fuel cells. In rural areas, where commercial power lines have not yet been extended because they are too expensive, stand-alone fuel cells can provide energy quickly and cheaply.

After enough fuel cells have been leased or purchased, and installed, mini energy grids can connect urban neighborhoods as well as rural villages into expanding energy networks. The HEW can be built organically and spread as the distributed generation becomes more widely used. The larger hydrogen fuel cells have the additional advantage of producing pure drinking water as a byproduct, an important consideration in village communities around the world where access to clean water is often a critical concern.

Were all individuals and communities in the world to become the producers of their own energy, the result would be a dramatic shift in the configuration of power: no longer from the top down but from the bottom up. Local peoples would be less subject to the will of far-off centers of power. Communities would be able to produce many of their own goods and services and consume the fruits of their own labor locally. But, because they would also be connected via the worldwide communications and energy webs, they would be able to share their unique commercial skills, products and services with other communities around the planet. This kind of economic self-sufficiency becomes the starting point for global commercial interdependence, and is a far different economic reality from that of colonial regimes of the past, in which local peoples were made subservient to and dependent on powerful forces from the outside. By redistributing power broadly to everyone, it is possible to establish the conditions for a truly equitable sharing of the earth's bounty. This is the essence of reglobalization from the bottom up.

Two great forces have dominated human affairs over the course of the past two centuries. The American Revolution unleashed a new human aspiration to universalize the radical notion of political democracy. That force continues to gain momentum and will likely spread to the Middle East, China and every corner of the earth before the current century is half over.

A second force was unleashed on the eve of the American Revolution when James Watt patented his steam engine, inaugurating the beginning of the fossil-fuel era and an industrial way of life that fundamentally changed the way we work.

The problem is that these two powerful forces have been at odds with each other from the very beginning, making for a deep contradiction in the way we live our lives. While in the political arena we covet greater participation and equal representation, our economic life has been characterized by ever greater concentration of power in ever fewer institutional hands. In large part that is because of the very nature of the fossil-fuel energy regime that we rely on to maintain an industrialized society. Unevenly distributed, difficult to extract, costly to transport, complicated to refine and multifaceted in the forms in which they are used, fossil fuels, from the very beginning, required a highly centralized command-and-control structure to finance exploration and production, and coordinate the flow of energy to end users. The highly centralized fossil-fuel infrastructure inevitably gave rise to commercial enterprises organized along similar lines. Recall that small cottage industries gave way to large-scale factory production in the late nineteenth and early twentieth centuries to take advantage of the capital-intensive costs and economies of scale that went hand in hand with steam power, and later oil and electrification. In the discussion of the emergence of industrial capitalism, little attention has been paid to the fact that the energy regime that emerged determined, to a great extent, the nature of the commercial forms that took shape.

Now, on the cusp of the hydrogen era, we have at least the "possibility" of making energy available in every community of the world—hydrogen exists everywhere on earth—empowering the whole of the human race. By creating an energy regime that is decentralized and potentially universally accessible to everyone, we establish the technological framework for creating a more participatory and sustainable economic life—one that is compatible with the principle of democratic participation in our political life. Making the commercial and political arenas seamless, however, will require a human struggle of truly epic proportions in the coming decades. What is in doubt is not the technological know-how to make it happen but, rather, the collective human will, determination and resolve to transform the great hope of hydrogen into a democratic reality.

**Henry Payne and Diane Katz**

# Gas and Gasbags . . . Or, the Open Road and Its Enemies

Any crisis in the Middle East inevitably prompts Washington to scapegoat the automobile as a threat to national security. The dust had barely settled on lower Manhattan last fall before calls went forth—from pundits and pols across the spectrum—to relinquish our "gas-guzzlers" in the name of energy independence.

But just as the Cassandras will dominate media coverage of energy, so will Middle Eastern oil continue to fuel America's vehicles for the foreseeable future. Simple economics, geography, and consumer choice all demand it.

Since Sept. 11, Washington has mobilized to end our "dangerous addiction" to foreign energy sources. Sens. John Kerry and John McCain are proposing dramatic increases in federal fuel-economy standards. The energy package crafted by majority leader Tom Daschle advocates "biodiesels," and the Natural Resources Defense Council is insisting that we could cut gasoline consumption by 50 percent over ten years—if only the feds would mandate what and where we drove.

Even the "oil men" in the Bush administration have advocated doling out millions in research subsidies for hydrogen fuel cells that supposedly would replace the internal-combustion engine. The project, Energy Secretary Spencer Abraham announced in January, is "rooted in President Bush's call to reduce American reliance on foreign oil."

In fact, the price of oil has declined since Sept. 11, as it consistently has for decades, and with producers scattered all over the world, no single nation or region can stop the flow.

But supporters of a comprehensive energy policy seem undeterred by these realities. "Logic," Robert Samuelson writes in the *Washington Post,* "is no defense against instability. We need to make it harder for [Middle Easterners] to use the oil weapon and take steps to protect ourselves if it is used. Even if we avoid trouble now, the threat will remain."

Past efforts to attain a petroleum-free utopia, however, have largely failed. For example, despite three decades of federal fuel-economy standards, oil imports as a share of U.S. consumption have risen from 35 to 59 percent.

A market-based solution, such as a gas tax, is the most obvious approach to cutting consumption, but even environmentalists concede that proposing one would spell political suicide. Moreover, gas taxes are an expensive solution and come with no guarantee of energy independence. The European Union, for example, taxes gas up to $4 per gallon—and still imports over half its oil.

So instead of enraging consumers at the pump, Washington has largely relied on backdoor taxes.

The regulatory regime known as CAFE (Corporate Average Fuel Economy) was hatched in the wake of the oil-price shocks of the early 1970s, when sedans still made up most of the nation's fleet. Instead of the redesigned smaller, lighter, and less powerful vehicles, however, consumers flocked to minivans, small trucks, and sport utility vehicles, which are held to a lower CAFE standard (20.7 mpg versus the 27.5 mpg required for cars).

Today, both passenger cars and light trucks are more efficient than ever, having improved 114 percent and 56 percent, respectively, since 1974. But gasoline is so cheap, despite continuing Middle Eastern crises, that on average Americans are driving twice as many miles as in years past.

A recent study by H. Sterling Burnett of the National Center for Policy Analysis found that raising CAFE standards by 40 percent—as Kerry and others recommend—would not "reduce future U.S. dependence on foreign oil." CAFE's only function is to keep regulators busy calculating elaborate formulas for determining compliance in which manufacturers then look for loopholes. (CAFE requires that a manufacturer's trucks meet an *average* standard of 20.7 mpg. Thus DaimlerChrysler AG, for example, designates its popular PT Cruiser as a "truck" in order to offset the low mpg of its large SUVs, such as the Dodge Durango.)

Worse, stricter CAFE standards would surely undermine the very economic security that proponents vow to protect. The profits of U.S. automakers—and tens of thousands of UAW jobs—depend on sales of SUVs and light trucks. According to an analysis by Andrew N. Kleit, a professor at Pennsylvania State University, the Kerry CAFE proposal would reduce the profits of General Motors by $3.8 billion, of Ford by $3.4 billion, and of Daimler-Chrysler by $2 billion. Foreign manufacturers, which largely specialize in smaller vehicles, would see a profit *increase* of $4.4 billion.

Evidently hoping to shield automakers from a CAFE assault—and to win PR points for expanded domestic drilling—the Bush administration has embraced the latest alternative-fuel fad: the hydrogen fuel cell.

The Bush plan replaces the Partnership for a New Generation of Vehicles, Al Gore's vain attempt to produce an affordable, emissions-free family sedan capable of 80 mpg by 2004. Over eight years, Washington pumped more than $1.5 billion into the program—in addition to the $1.5 billion sunk into it by the Big Three. In its annual review of the project last August, the National Research Council judged the super-car goals to be inherently "unrealistic."

The Bush plan has drawn broad political support. Former Clinton chief of staff John Podesta cheers, "The next step is hydrogen-powered fuel-cell vehicles. But the only way to get these vehicles out of the lab and onto the road is with incentives and requirements aimed at producing 100,000 vehicles by 2010, 2.5 million by 2020."

But the 100-year dominance of conventional internal-combustion engines over alternatives is no accident. A quick primer on the complexities of hydrogen power helps explain why.

Hydrogen's status as the new darling of the sustainable-energy movement is understandable. Its promise lies first in its performance: Unlike ethanol, it supplies more energy per pound than gasoline. When used to power an automobile, its only emission is water—making it especially attractive to an industry already under pressure from clean-air and global-warming rules. And hydrogen is one of the most plentiful elements on the planet.

The trouble is, hydrogen always comes married to another element—as in methane gas or water.

Most fuel-cell technology today relies on hydrogen extracted from methane, in a process that emits large quantities of greenhouse gases. And as *Car and Driver* magazine's technical analyst, Patrick Bedard, explains, domestic sources of methane are "[t]oo limited to serve any significant demand for automobiles." A study by the Argonne National Laboratory concluded that the U.S. would have to look to foreign sources—primarily in Russia and Iran, and in other Middle East nations.

Goodbye, oil dependence. Hello, methane dependence.

Given these hurdles, attention is turning instead to electrolysis—the extraction of hydrogen from water, which is readily obtainable along America's ample coasts. Electrolysis is, however, the most energy-intensive process of any fuel alternative; studies differ on whether it would consume more carbon-based fuels than the use of hydrogen would save. What is certain, points out Stanford University professor John McCarthy, is that "the advantage of hydrogen, if you have to burn carbon fuels (coal, oil, or gas) to manufacture it, would be negligible."

In other words, McCarthy explains, the unspoken truth about hydrogen is that "it is a synonym for nuclear power."

Leading researchers in the field—including David Scott of the University of Victoria in Canada, Cesare Marchetti of the International Institute for Applied Systems Analysis, and Jesse Ausubel of Rockefeller University—say that the only way to produce liquid hydrogen in the mass quantities needed for transportation is with a major investment in nuclear power. Says Scott: "[A]pplying the most elementary numeracy, nuclear fission is the only realistic option."

Ironically, many of the political voices now embracing hydrogen fuel are the same ones that have prevented the construction of a single new U.S. nuclear plant in 25 years. Ausubel has written in *The Industrial Physicist* magazine that "understanding how to use nuclear power, and its acceptance, will take a century or more."

For now, the answer is still gasoline. Compared with the technical barriers to developing alternative fuels, there already exist numerous market mechanisms to mitigate potential oil shortages. As suggested by Donald Losman, a National Defense University economist, these include: stockpiling, futures contracts, diversifying the supplier base, and relaxing the restrictions that currently mandate some 13 different fuel blends in 30 cities.

Dramatic improvements in fuel efficiency also could be achieved if Washington allowed automakers to market diesel-powered vehicles. In Germany, for example, Volkswagen mass markets the 80-mpg Lupo, which is powered by a direct-injection diesel engine. But that's anathema to American greens who insist—without evidence—that diesel's particulate emissions are dangerous to public health.

All fuels require trade-offs, of course. But politically correct, misguided energy schemes will not make America more independent. Gasoline remains by far the best deal we have.

# POSTSCRIPT

## Will Hydrogen Replace Fossil Fuels for Cars?

Hydrogen as a fuel offers definite benefits. As Joan M. Ogden notes in "Hydrogen: The Fuel of the Future?" *Physics Today* (April 2002), the technology is available and compared to the alternatives, it "offers the greatest potential environmental and energy-supply benefits." To put hydrogen to use, however, will require massive investments in facilities for generating, storing, and transporting the gas, as well as manufacturing hydrogen-burning engines and fuel cells. Currently, large amounts of hydrogen can easily be generated by "reforming" natural gas or other hydrocarbons. Hydrolysis—splitting hydrogen from water molecules with electricity—is also possible, and in the future this may use electricity from renewable sources such as wind or from nuclear power. The basic technologies are available right now. See Thammy Evans, Peter Light, and Ty Cashman, "Hydrogen—A Little PR," *Whole Earth* (Winter 2001). Daniel Sperling notes in "Updating Automotive Research," *Issues in Science and Technology* (Spring 2002), that "Fuel cells and hydrogen show huge promise. They may indeed prove to be the Holy Grail, eventually taking vehicles out of the environmental equation," but making that happen will require research, government assistance in building a hydrogen distribution system, and incentives for both industry and car buyers. But there may be an unforeseen obstacle: Tracey K. Tromp, Run-Lie Shia, Mark Allen, John M. Eiler, and Y. L. Yung, "Potential Environmental Impact of a Hydrogen Economy on the Stratosphere," *Science* (June 13, 2003), calculate that the pipelines and other equipment of a full-fledged hydrogen economy would leak so much hydrogen that stratospheric ozone would be destroyed (worsening the ozone hole caused by chlorofluorocarbons). There could also be an increase in high-altitude clouds and a decrease in stratospheric temperature.

Is the hydrogen economy—if it happens—likely to be as decentralized as Jeremy Rifkin envisions? Jim Motavalli, "Hijacking Hydrogen," *E Magazine* (January–February 2003), worries that the fossil fuel and nuclear industries will dominate the hydrogen future. The former wish to use "reforming" to generate hydrogen from coal, and the latter see hydrolysis as creating demand for nuclear power. Nuclear power, he says, is particularly favored by the U.S. government's 2001 National Energy Policy.

In January 2003, President George W. Bush proposed $1.2 billion in funding for making hydrogen-powered cars an on-the-road reality. Gregg Easterbrook, "Why Bush's H-Car Is Just Hot Air," *New Republic* (February 24, 2003), thinks it would make much more sense to address fuel-economy standards; Bush should "leave futurism to the futurists." Peter Schwartz and

Doug Randall, "How Hydrogen Can Save America," *Wired* (April 2003), commend Bush's proposal but say the proposed funding is not enough. We need, they say, "an Apollo-scale commitment to hydrogen power. The fate of the republic depends on it." Toward that end, they list five steps essential to making the hydrogen future real.

1. Develop fuel tanks that can store hydrogen safely and in adequate quantity.
2. Encourage mass production of fuel cell vehicles.
3. Convert the fueling infrastructure to hydrogen.
4. Increase hydrogen production.
5. Mount a PR campaign.

But are fossil fuels as scarce as industry critics and hydrogen enthusiasts say? They are certainly finite, but it has become apparent that not all fossil fuels are included in most accountings of available supply. A major omission is methane hydrate, a form of natural gas locked into cage-like arrangements of water molecules and found as masses of white ice-like material on the seabed. There appear to be vast quantities of methane hydrate on the bottom of the world's seas. If they can be recovered—and there are major difficulties in doing so—they may provide huge amounts of additional fossil fuels. Once liberated, their methane may be burned directly or "reformed" to generate hydrogen, making the nuclear approach less necessary. However, the methane still poses global warming risks. Indeed, if methane hydrate deposits ever gave up their methane naturally, they could change world climate abruptly (just such releases may have been responsible for past global climate warmings). See Erwin Suess, Gerhard Bohrmann, Jens Greinert, and Erwin Lausch, "Flammable Ice," *Scientific American* (November 1999).

Will nuclear power be part of the hydrogen economy? Some scientists and even some environmentalists are now recognizing that properly designed and managed nuclear power plants may have fewer environmental side effects than fossil fuel power plants. See James A. Lake, Ralph G. Bennett, and John F. Kotek, "The Case for Nuclear Power," *Scientific American* (January 2002).

# On the Internet . . .

## Cell Phones and Cancer

At this site, John E. Moulder, professor of radiation oncology, radiology, and pharmacology/toxicology at the Medical College of Wisconsin, answers frequently asked questions about the relationship between cell phones and cancer. The site also links to two related FAQ sites—the relationship between power lines and cancer, and the relationship between static electromagnetic fields and cancer.

http://www.mcw.edu/gcrc/cop/cell-phone-health-FAQ/toc.html

## Vaccines and Autism

The Centers for Disease Control says, "The weight of currently available scientific evidence does not support the hypothesis that vaccines cause autism. We recognize there is considerable public interest in this issue, and therefore support additional research regarding this hypothesis. CDC is committed to maintaining the safest, most effective vaccine supply in history."

http://www.cdc.gov/nip/vacsafe/concerns/autism/

## Malaria Foundation International

The Malaria Foundation International seeks "to facilitate the development and implementation of solutions to the health, economic and social problems caused by malaria."

http://www.malaria.org/

## Risk Assessment: What It Is, What It Can (and Can't) Do

The Hampshire Research Institute maintains this site to explain the nature of environmental risk.

http://www.hampshire.org/risk01.htm

## National Institute of Environmental Health Sciences

The National Institute of Environmental Health Sciences studies the health risks of numerous environmental factors, many of which are associated with the use of technology.

http://www.niehs.nih.gov

# PART 3

## Health

*Many people are concerned about new technological and scientific discoveries because they fear their potential impacts on human health. In the past, fears have been expressed concerning nuclear bombs and power plants, irradiated food, the internal combustion engine, medications such as thalidomide and diethylstilbestrol, pesticides and other chemicals, and more. Today people worry about the possible health risks of cell phones and childhood vaccines, among other things. It is worth stressing that risks may be real (as they are with insecticides such as DDT) but there may be a trade-off for genuine health benefits.*

# ISSUE 8

## Do Cell Phones Cause Cancer?

**YES: George Carlo and Martin Schram,** from *Cell Phones: Invisible Hazards in the Wireless Age: An Insider's Alarming Discoveries About Cancer and Genetic Damage* (Carroll & Graf, 2001)

**NO: Tamar Nordenberg,** from "Cell Phones and Brain Cancer: No Clear Connection," *FDA Consumer* (November–December 2000)

### ISSUE SUMMARY

**YES:** Public health scientist George Carlo and journalist Martin Schram argue that there is a definite risk that the electromagnetic radiation generated by cell phone antennae can cause cancer and other health problems.

**NO:** Freelance journalist Tamar Nordenberg argues that although research is continuing, so far the evidence does not indicate that there is any clear connection between cell phones and cancer.

It seems inevitable that new technologies will alarm people. For example, in the late 1800s, when electricity was new, people feared the new wires that were strung overhead. See Joseph P. Sullivan, "Fearing Electricity: Overhead Wire Panic in New York City," *IEEE Technology and Society Magazine* (Fall 1995). More recently, electromagnetic fields (EMFs) have drawn attention. Now cell phones and other forms of wireless communications technology are the focus of controversy.

EMFs are emitted by any device that uses electricity. They weaken rapidly as one gets farther from the source, but they can be remarkably strong close to the source. Users of electric blankets (before the blankets were redesigned to minimize EMFs) and personal computers are thus subject to high exposures. Since EMF strength also depends on how much electricity is flowing through the source, people who live near power lines, especially high-tension, long-distance transmission lines, are also open to high EMF exposure.

Are EMFs dangerous? There have been numerous reports suggesting a link between EMF exposure and cancer, but inconsistency has been the curse of research in this area. In 1992 the Committee on Interagency Radiation Research and Policy Coordination, an arm of the White House's Office of Science and Technology Policy, released *Health Effects of Low Frequency Electric and Magnetic Fields,* a report that concluded, "There is no convincing [published] evidence . . . to support the contention that exposures to extremely low frequency electric and magnetic fields generated by sources such as household appliances, video terminals, and local powerlines are demonstrable health hazards." In 1996 Jon Palfreman, in "Apocalypse Not," *Technology Review* (April 1996), summarized the controversy and the evidence against any connection between cancer and EMFs. And in "Residential Exposure to Magnetic Fields and Acute Lymphoblastic Leukemia in Children," *The New England Journal of Medicine* (July 3, 1997), Martha S. Linet et al. report that they failed to find any support for such a connection.

Since cell phones are electrical devices, they emit EMFs. But they—or their antennae—also emit electromagnetic radiation in the form of radio signals. And after a few cell phone users developed brain cancer and sued the phone makers, people began to worry. See Gordon Bass, "Is Your Cell Phone Killing You?" *PC Computing* (December 1999). Now more lawsuits are being filed, and the research reports are coming in. Indeed, in 1999 Professor John Moulder and his colleagues published a review of the evidence in "Cell Phones and Cancer: What Is the Evidence for a Connection?" *Radiation Research* (May 1999). In it, they concluded, "Overall, the existing evidence for a causal relationship between RF radiation from cell phones and cancer is found to be weak to nonexistent."

As with EMFs, however, the reports do not agree with each other, and some researchers are being attacked for perceived conflicts of interest. For example, Jeffrey Silva, in "Litigation Frenzy Hits Wireless," *RCR News* (January 22, 2001), states, "Adding fuel to the controversy are two new studies: one conducted by German scientists who claimed a link between mobile phones and eye cancer and another performed by U.S. scientists that failed to find genetic damage from human blood exposed to mobile-phone radiation. One scientist who worked on the latter study, Dr. Joseph Roti Roti, has been paid in the past by Motorola to conduct cell phone–cancer experiments. Martin Meltz, another scientist on the same study, has been outspoken in claiming that cell phones are safe."

In the following selections, George Carlo and Martin Schram argue that there is a definite risk that the electromagnetic radiation generated by cell phone antennae can cause cancer and other health problems. Furthermore, wireless Internet devices also emit such radiation and may pose similar risks. Tamar Nordenberg argues that the evidence to date does not indicate any clear connection between cell phones and cancer, although she admits that the evidence is sufficient to justify further research.

George Carlo and Martin Schram 

# Cell Phones: Invisible Hazards in the Wireless Age

## Follow-the-Science: Piecing Together the Cancer Puzzle

Scientific findings are like pieces of a puzzle. Individually, they may not seem to show anything clearly. But by trying to fit the pieces together, it is possible to see if they form a big, coherent picture.

In the puzzle of cell phone radiation research, the pieces of scientific evidence we have now do fit together. Although many pieces are still missing, those that are in place indicate a big picture of cancer and health risk. The picture is alarming, because even if the risk eventually proves to be small, it will still be real—and that means millions of people around the world will develop cancer or other health problems due to using mobile phones.

Even more alarming, however, is that many in the industry, who are paid by the industry—and some who are paid by the public to oversee and regulate the industry—have persisted in talking publicly as if they cannot see the picture that is taking shape even as they speak.

In the study of public health, there is a well-known template that researchers use to put together individual scientific findings—like the pieces of a puzzle—to see if they show evidence of a public-health hazard. This template, known as the Koch-Henle Postulates, is a means of determining whether the findings indicate a true cause-and-effect process, from biological plausibility to exposure and dose-response. The postulates are:

1. If there is a biological explanation for the association derived from separate experiments that is consistent with what is known about the development of the disease, then the association is more likely to be causal. Scientists term this *biological plausibility.*
2. If several studies of people are showing the same finding while employing different methods and different investigators, the association that is being seen is more likely to be cause and effect, or causal. Scientists term this *consistency.*

3. If it is clear that the exposure precedes the development of the disease, then the association is more likely to be causal. Scientists term this *temporality*.
4. If the increase in risk is significant—more than a doubling in the risk or an increase that is statistically significant—the association is more likely to be causal. Scientists term this *significance*.
5. If the more severe the level of exposure, the higher the risk for the disease or the biological effect that is being studied, the association is more likely to be causal. Scientists term this *dose–response upward*.
6. If the absence of exposure corresponds to the absence of the disease, the more likely the association is to be causal. Scientists term this *dose–response downward*.
7. If there are similar findings in human, animal, and *in vitro* studies—in other words, if the same conclusions can be drawn from all—the more likely the association that is seen is causal. Scientists term this *concordance*.

Researchers use the Koch-Henle Postulates as a checklist. The greater the number of postulates that are met, the greater the likelihood that a hazard exists. For some of the more commonly recognized carcinogens, it has taken decades for the hazards to be judged as valid. For example, in the case of cigarette smoking, it took two decades of study and more than 100 years of consumer use to gather enough information that could be judged against the Koch-Henle standards to demonstrate the need for the U.S. Surgeon General's warning label on cigarette packs.

In the case of cellular telephones, consumers are fortunate that the health-hazard picture can be seen much sooner than that. Each of the red-flag findings about cell phone radiation provides a vital piece of information that fits into the overall cancer puzzle. A number of the other earlier studies, which on their own were inconclusive or seemed uninterpretable, now appear to fit into the puzzle as well. They clarify a troubling picture of cancer and health risk that is just now becoming clear.

Here is how the scientific pieces fit into the larger cancer puzzle:

**Human blood studies** These studies—by Drs. Ray Tice and Graham Hook, and most recently [corroborated by] Dr. Joseph Roti Roti—show genetic damage in the form of micronuclei in blood cells exposed to cell phone radiation. They provide evidence of the Koch-Henle postulate of *biological plausibility* for the development of the tumors following exposure to radio waves. Without some type of genetic damage, it is unlikely that radio waves would be able to cause cancer. Every direct mechanism that has been identified in the development of cancer involves genetic damage; the linkage is so strong that if an absence of genetic damage had been proven in these studies, scientists would have considered that to be reason enough to conclude that cancer is not caused by cell phones. (Indeed, that is what scientists were justified in saying prior to 1999.) Scientific literature has repeatedly confirmed that brain cancer is clearly linked to chromosome damage; brain tumors have consistently been shown to have a variety of chromosomal abnormalities.

The studies by Tice, Hook, and Roti Roti consistently showed chromosomal damage in blood exposed to wireless phone radio waves.

**Breakdown in the blood brain barrier** The findings of genetic damage by Tice, Hook, and Roti Roti now give new meaning and importance to Dr. Leif Salford's 1994 studies that showed a breakdown in the blood brain barrier of rats when they were exposed to radio waves. The blood brain barrier findings now fit into the overall cancer picture by providing a two-step explanation for how cancer could be caused by cell phone radiation. (The blood brain barrier filters the blood by not allowing dangerous chemicals to reach sensitive brain tissue.)

Step One: A breakdown in the blood brain barrier filter would provide an avenue for chemical carcinogens in the bloodstream (from tobacco, pesticides, or air pollution, for example) to leak into the brain and reach sensitive brain tissue that would otherwise be protected. Those chemicals, upon reaching sensitive brain tissue, could break the DNA in the brain or cause other harm to reach those cells.

Step Two: While a number of studies showed that cell phone radiation by itself does not appear to break DNA, the micronuclei findings of Tice, Hook, and Roti Roti suggest that DNA repair mechanisms in brain cells could be impaired by mobile phone radiation. (One reason micronuclei occur is that there has been a breakdown in the cell's ability to repair itself.) If the brain cells become unable to repair themselves, the process of chemically induced carcinogenesis—the creation of tumors—could begin.

This is further evidence of the Koch-Henle postulate of *biological plausibility* for cell phone radiation involvement in the development of brain cancer.

**Studies of tumors in people who use cell phones** There have been four studies of tumors in people who use cellular phones—Dr. Ken Rothman's study of deaths among cell phone users, Joshua Muscat's two studies of brain cancer and acoustic neuroma, and Dr. Lennart Hardell's study of brain tumors. All four epidemiological studies, done by different investigators who used different methods, show some evidence of an increased risk of tumors associated with the use of cellular phones. This is evidence of the Koch-Henle postulate of *consistency.*

All four epidemiological studies provide some assurance in the methods used by the investigators that the people studied had used cellular telephones before they were clinically diagnosed as having tumors. This is evidence of the Koch-Henle postulate of *temporality.*

All four epidemiological studies showed increases in risk of developing brain tumors. Muscat's study of cell phone users showed a doubling of the risk of developing neuro-epithelial tumors. (The result was statistically significant.) Hardell's study showed that among cell phone users, tumors were twice as likely to occur in areas of the brain at the side where the user normally held the phone. (This result was also statistically significant.) Rothman's study showed that users of handheld cell phones have more than twice the risk of dying from brain cancer than do car phone users—whose antennas are mounted on the body of the car, far removed from the users' heads. (That finding was not statistically significant.) Muscat's study of acoustic neuroma indicates that cell phone users have a 50-percent increase in risk of developing tumors of the auditory nerve. (This finding was statistically significant only when correlated with the years of cell phone usage by the patient.) These findings are evidence of the Koch-Henle postulate of *significance*.

**Studies of cell phone radiation dosage and response** In Dr. Michael Repacholi's study of mice, the risk of lymphoma increased significantly with the number of months that mice were exposed to the radio waves.

In the work by Tice, Hook, and Roti Roti, the risks of genetic damage as measured by the formation of micronuclei increased as the amount of radiation increased.

In the three epidemiological studies—two by Muscat and one by Hardell—that were able to estimate radiation exposure to specific parts of the brain, the risk of tumors was greater in the areas of the brain near where the cell phone was held.

These findings are all evidence of the Koch-Henle postulate known as *dose–response upward*. (In cell phones, minutes of phone usage are not a reliable indication of dosage, because the distance of the telephone from a base station during the call and any physical barriers to the signal are the most important factors in the amount of radiation the phone antenna emits during the call.)

The Hardell epidemiological study showed that patients with tumors in areas of the brain that could not be reached by radiation from a cell phone antenna were likely not to have been cell phone users. Similarly, in Muscat's study, when all brain-tumor patients were included in his analysis—those with tumors that were outside the range of radiation from the cellular phone antenna and those whose tumors were within that range—there was no increase in the risk of brain cancer. This is evidence of the Koch-Henle postulate that is called *dose–response downward*—which simply means that if there is no chance that cell phone radiation dosage could have been received, chances are the tumor was caused by something else.

**Agreement of findings from in vitro and in vivo studies** The test-tube studies by Tice and Hook; the mouse study by Repacholi; and the four epidemiological studies by Rothman, Muscat, and Hardell are all in agreement in that they suggest an increase in the risk of cancer among people who use mobile phones. This is evidence of the Koch-Henle postulate of *concordance*.

### *. . . And the Largest Piece of the Puzzle*

As the officials of the government, officials of the industry, and just plain unofficial people try to fit together jigsaw pieces to see whether mobile phones indeed pose a cancer risk, the cancer experts themselves have provided what is by far the biggest and most revealing piece of the puzzle.

Writing in the U.S. government's own *Journal of the National Cancer Institute,* and other prestigious professional publications, these experts have made it clear that, if there are findings that micronuclei develop in blood cells exposed to mobile phone radiation, that is in itself evidence of a cancer risk. The risk is so persuasive, the experts have written, that preventative treatment should be given in order to best protect those people whose levels of micronuclei have increased.

### The Big Picture

The pieces of the cell phone puzzle do indeed fit together to form the beginnings of a picture that researchers, regulators, and mobile phone users can all see for themselves. Many pieces are still missing. But enough pieces are already in place to see that there are legitimate reasons to be concerned about the health of people who use wireless phones.

Most alarming to public health scientists should be the fact that all seven of the Koch-Henle postulates have been met within the first decade of widespread mobile phone usage.

The big picture is becoming disturbingly clear: There is a definite risk that the radiation plume that emanates from a cell phone antenna can cause cancer and other health problems. It is a risk that affects hundreds of millions of people around the world. It is a risk that must be seen and understood by all who use cell phones so they can take all the appropriate and available steps to protect themselves—and especially to protect young children whose skulls are still growing and who are the most vulnerable to the risks of radiation.

## Safety First: Health Recommendations

As the big picture becomes clear and we see that radiation from mobile phones poses a real cancer and health risk, it also becomes clear that there are basic recommendations that now demand the urgent attention of all who use, make, research, or regulate cell phones.

Mobile telephones are a fact of life and a fixture in the lifestyles of more than half a billion people around the world. That only makes it all the more vital that we understand and follow the recommendations by which all who use mobile phones can minimize their health risk, and especially can protect our children. Here are some basic suggests for mobile phone users, manufacturers, and science and medical researchers.

### Recommendations for Consumers

To avoid radiation exposure and minimize health risks when using wireless phones:

1. The best advice is to keep the antenna away from your body by using a phone with a headset or earpiece. Another option is a phone with speakerphone capability.

2. If you must use your phone without a headset, be sure the antenna is fully extended during the phone's use. Radiation plumes are emitted mainly from the mid-length portion of the antenna; when the antenna is recessed inside the phone, the entire phone functions as the antenna—and the radiation is emitted from the entire phone into a much wider area of your head, jaw, and hand.
3. Children under the age of ten should not use wireless devices of any type; for children over the age of ten, pagers are preferable to wireless phones because pagers are not put up to the head and they can be used away from the body.
4. When the signal strength is low, do not use your phone. The reason: The lower the signal strength, the harder the instrument has to work to carry the call—and the greater the radiation that is emitted from the antenna.
5. Emerging studies, and common sense, make clear that handheld phones should not be used while driving a vehicle.

## A Few Words of Caution for Consumers

The public is bombarded with waves of claims that are made at times by individuals who are well-meaning but not well-informed—and at other times by special interests who really want to sell a product. For example, there is no scientific basis for recommendations that have been made by some groups to limit phone use as a means of minimizing the risk of health effects. It is not possible to determine scientifically the difference in radiation exposure from one ten-minute call and ten one-minute calls. The total number of minutes is the same, but the pattern and amount of radiation could be very different. Also, the amount of radiation emitted by a mobile phone depends on the distance of the phone from a base station; the further the distance, the harder the phone has to work and the greater the radiation. Finally, the greatest amount of radiation emitted by a phone is during dialing and ringing. People who keep their phones on their belts or in their pockets should move the phones away from their bodies when the phones are ringing. (The amounts of radiation in a single call can vary by factors of ten to 100 depending on all of these variables.)

Consumers also need to be cautious about unverified claims that seem to have scientific backing. For example: The media recently carried an account published in Britain's *Which?* magazine that said a group called the Consumers' Association (with which the magazine is affiliated) had shown in tests that some cell phone headsets actually cause more radiation to go to the brain than the phones themselves. But the claim is unsubstantiated by any scientific evidence, and has been refuted by a number of studies by recognized researchers using established scientific methods. The only conclusion that can be drawn from existing scientific evidence is that headsets are the best option for mobile phone users to minimize exposure to wireless phone radiation.

Also, a number of devices on the market claim to eliminate the effects of antenna radiation and are being marketed as alternatives to using headsets or speakerphones. These products need to be tested to see if they will really protect consumers—a caution expressed by Great Britain's Stewart Commission. They recommended that their government set in place "a national system which enables independent testing of shielding devices and hands-free kits . . . which enable clear information to be given about the effectiveness of such devices. A kite mark or equivalent should be introduced to demonstrate conformity with the testing standard." In the United States, the FDA has been silent on the matter.

## Recommendations for the Mobile Phone Industry

To enhance consumer protection:

1. Phones should be redesigned to minimize radiation exposure to consumers—antennas that extend out at an angle, away from the head, or that carry the radiation outward should be developed.
2. Headsets and other accessories that minimize radiation exposure should be redesigned so they are more durable and can be conveniently used.
3. Consumers should be given complete information about health risks and solutions through brochures, product inserts, and Internet postings so they can make their own decisions about how much of the risk inherent to mobile telephone use they wish to assume.
4. Emerging and advancing phone technologies need to be premarket tested for biological effects so dangerous products do not make it to the market.
5. Post-market surveillance is necessary for all phone users—surveys of analog and digital phone users to see if they experience any adverse health effects, and databases should be maintained where people can report any health effects they have experienced due to their phones.

## Recommendations for Scientific, Medical, and Public Health Officials

To help consumers:

1. Science, medicine, and government must move immediately and aggressively with the goal of minimizing the impact of radio waves on adults, children, and pregnant women.
2. One federal agency must be designated as the lead agency for protecting people who use wireless communications devices, rather than having the responsibility remain undefined and shared among multiple agencies including the FDA, FCC, EPA, and others.
3. A genuine safety standard needs to be established to serve as the basis for future regulatory decisions. Since the specific absorption rate alone does not measure biological effects on humans, it does not serve the safety needs of consumers. . . .

## Recommendations for Industry and Government Concerning the Wireless Internet

We need to recognize and learn from the mistakes we made when cellular phones were first introduced. The phones were sold to the public before there had been any premarket testing to determine whether they were safe or posed a potential health risk. Because the cell phones were not tested initially, by the time they were on the market, efforts to research the problem became intertwined with the forces of politics and profit. Consumer protection was not the highest priority.

As we enter the age of the wireless Internet, no one can say for sure whether or not the radio waves of the these new wireless products will prove harmless or harmful. But this much is known: The concern about mobile phones focuses on the near-field radiation that extends in a 2-to-3-inch plume from an antenna, and the radiation from the many wireless laptop and handheld computer products is just about the same. It would seem that these latter products should be safer because users don't hold their laptops and handheld computers against their heads. But no one has researched what the effect will be of a roomful of wireless products all being used simultaneously, with radio waves invisibly crisscrossing the space that is occupied by people. Will these passive occupants run a risk similar to nonsmokers in a room filled with smokers, who end up affected by passive smoke?

Thus, it is important that these new products must be formally testing under official regulatory control that includes specific premarket screening guidelines. There must also be post-market surveys of people who use the wireless Internet to see if health problems emerge that were not found in the premarket testing.

**Tamar Nordenberg**

# Cell Phones and Brain Cancer: No Clear Connection

Of the 100 million American cellular phone subscribers, some use their wireless phone only in a crisis—to call a friend or 911. They put their rap sessions on hold until arriving home, where phoning a friend costs no cents per minute.

For other wireless phone owners, it could be the fear of brain cancer, not an unwieldy wireless bill, that keeps them from using their cell phones for leisure chats.

Convinced that a nine-year cell phone habit led to his brain cancer, neurologist Chris Newman, M.D., has filed an $800 million lawsuit in Baltimore against his cell phone's maker and several other telecommunications companies. His suit comes five years after the dismissal, for lack of evidence, of a lawsuit filed in Florida by David Reynard, who alleged that a cell phone was responsible for his wife's fatal brain cancer.

In Newman's case, his lawyer has said, "it's really not a question at all" whether the cancer is cell phone-related. The evidence, she says: Newman's own doctors made the connection between his long-time cell phone use and his tumor, which is positioned in "the exact anatomical location where the radiation from the cell phone emitted into his skull."

Newman has been front and center in a renewed public focus . . . on whether the fear of brain cancer from wireless phones is well-founded or folly. For his part, epidemiologist Sam Milham, M.D., recently expressed a breakaway scientific viewpoint when he told the television audience of CNN's *Larry King Live* show that there is "plenty of reason for concern" about cell phones causing brain cancer.

Hold the phone. Is there really cause for concern? Do steps need to be taken, as Milham told Larry King, to avoid a brain cancer epidemic among the millions of cell phone users in this country and around the world?

No, current scientific evidence does not show any negative health effects from the low levels of electromagnetic energy emitted by mobile phones, says the Food and Drug Administration [FDA]. But some recent studies suggest a possible link between mobile phones and cancer and warrant follow-up, the agency says, to determine with more certainty whether cell phones are safe.

From the *FDA Consumer*, November–December 2000, pp. 19–23.

"We don't see a risk looking at currently available data," says David Feigal, M.D., director of FDA's Center for Devices and Radiological Health. "But we need more definite answers about the biological effects of cell phone radiation, and about the more complicated question of whether mobile phones might cause even a small increase in the risk of developing cancer."

## Radiation Without Risk?

Like televisions, alarm systems, computers, and all other electrical devices, mobile phones emit electromagnetic radiation. FDA can regulate these devices to ensure that the radiation doesn't pose a health hazard to users, but only once the existence of a public health hazard has been established.

In the United States, mobile phones operate in a frequency ranging from about 850 to 1900 megahertz (MHz). In that range, the radiation produced is in the form of *non-ionizing* radiofrequency (RF) energy. This RF energy is different than the *ionizing* radiation like that from a medical x-ray, which can present a health risk at certain doses.

At high enough levels, RF energy, too, can be harmful, because of its ability to heat living tissue to the point of causing biological damage. In a microwave oven, it's RF energy that cooks the food, but the heat generated by cell phones is small in comparison.

A mobile phone's main source of RF energy is its antenna, so the closer the antenna is to a phone user's head, the greater the person's expected exposure to RF energy.

Because RF energy from a cell phone falls off quickly as distance increases between a person and the radiation source, the safety of mobile phones with an antenna mounted away from the user—like on the outside of a car—has not been called into question. Also not in doubt is the safety of those so-called cordless phones that have a base unit attached to a home's telephone wiring and operate at much lower power levels than cell phones.

Many experts say that no matter how near the cell phone's antenna—even if it's right up against the skull—the six-tenths of a watt of power emitted couldn't possibly affect human health. They're probably right, says John E. Moulder, Ph.D., a cancer researcher and professor of radiation oncology at the Medical College of Wisconsin. It's true, he says, that from the physics standpoint, biological effects from mobile phones are "somewhere between impossible and implausible."

At the same time, Moulder supports further studies into the science of cell phone radiation. "Some people think the power emitted by the phones is so low, it's a silly thing to research. But I think it remains a legitimate area of study."

## Studies in Perspective

Some mobile phone users have been diagnosed with brain cancer, and many others who have not used mobile phones have gotten the disease, too. Each year in the United States, brain cancer occurs at a rate of about six new cases per 100,000 people. Among the 100 million Americans who own mobile phones, then, about 6,000 cases of brain cancer would be expected among them in a year, even if they had not used mobile phones.

Scientific studies have focused on the question of whether the statistical risk of getting brain cancer is increased in those who use mobile phones compared to non-users, leaving to the courts the judgment of whether Chris Newman or other individuals would have gotten the disease had they not used a cell phone.

Two types of studies are generally used to investigate suspected cancer causes: epidemiological studies, which look at the incidence of a disease in certain groups of people, and animal studies.

Epidemiological studies are sometimes difficult to carry out in a way that can determine whether a cause-and-effect relationship exists between a single variable in a person's life (in this case, cell phone use) and the person's disease (brain cancer). Some factors that complicate research into the asserted link between cell phones and brain cancer: Brain cancer can take years or even decades to develop, making possible long-term effects of mobile phone use difficult to study; mobile phone technology is ever-evolving; and so many lifestyle factors—even down to the precise position in which a person holds the phone, as well as his or her own anatomy—can affect the extent of radiation exposure.

Studies in animals are easier to control, but entail complications of their own. For example, how should results obtained in rats and mice be interpreted in terms of human health risks? And how can scientists account for the fact that these studies sometimes expose animals to RF almost continuously—up to 22 hours a day—and to whole-body radiation, unlike people's head-only exposure?

While studies generally have shown no link between cell phones and brain cancer, there is some conflicting scientific evidence that may be worth additional study, according to FDA. (See box.)

Based on the evidence so far and possible limitations in some studies' research methods, FDA is closely following ongoing research into whether there might be any association between cell phones and cancer, according to the agency's Feigal.

A long-term study by the government's National Cancer Institute is already under way to examine possible risk factors for brain cancer. It compares past usage of mobile phones (as well as other environmental, lifestyle, and genetic factors) by 800 people with brain tumors compared with 800 others who don't have tumors.

The study, the first part of which is expected to be published early next year, will provide a "snapshot" of what the risks from cell phones could be, says Peter Inskip, Sc.D., one of the study's principal investigators. But this research, he cautions, has its own limitations. For one thing, the study was started in 1994 and it considers radiation exposures from cell phones that occurred between the mid-1980s and 1998. That time frame in large part predates the explosion in the popularity of cell phones, as well as the introduction of digital phones that work on a fraction of the energy compared with older analog varieties.

## STUDIES SO FAR

Epidemiological and animal studies undertaken by the U.S. cell phone industry and others have yielded mixed results.

- In a study published in 1999, investigators at the Orebro Medical Centre in Sweden compared the past mobile phone use of 209 Swedish brain tumor patients and 425 healthy people. Conclusion: The study found no mobile phone/brain cancer link "in virtually all respects," cancer researcher John E. Moulder, PhD, says in the August 2000 issue of *IEEE Spectrum*, the official magazine of the Institute of Electrical and Electronics Engineers. Investigators did find that mobile phone users who got certain types of brain tumors tended to report using the phone on the side of the head where they developed the tumor. The study's limitations, according to Moulder, include a weak association between cell phone use and tumor development, as well as a possibility that the cancer patients' recollections were biased by already knowing on which side of their head the brain cancer developed.
- In a yet-unpublished study presented at a 1999 scientific meeting, researcher Joshua Muscat looked for an association between mobile phone use and a type of brain cancer called glioma. Muscat did not find evidence that cell phone use increased people's risk of this type of brain cancer generally. He did, however, observe an increase in one rare kind of glioma, which FDA scientists say might have occurred by chance. Interestingly, with increased hours of mobile phone use, the risk tended to decrease rather than increase as might be expected.
- A few animal studies have suggested that low levels of RF exposure could speed up development of cancer in laboratory animals. In one recent Australian study, for example, mice genetically altered to be predisposed to developing lymphoma got more than twice as many of these cancers when exposed to RF energy compared to mice not exposed to the radiation.
- A large number of laboratory tests have been conducted to assess RF's effects on genetic material, looking for mutations, chromosomal changes, DNA strand breaks, and structural changes in blood cells' genetic material. One kind of test, called a micronuculeus assay, showed structural changes in genetic material after exposure to simulated cell phone radiation. The changes occurred only after 24 hours of continuous exposure, which experts say raises questions about this test's sensitivity to heating effects and whether that sensitivity could be solely responsible for the results.

In one study of brain function and RF exposure, two groups of 18 people were given cognitive function tests while being exposed to simulated mobile phone signals. No changes were seen in the ability to recall words, numbers, or pictures, or in spatial memory, but among the 20 variables compared, there was one standout observation: The participants were actually able to make choices more quickly in one visual test when they were exposed to the signals.

—T.N.

Recently, FDA announced that it will collaborate with the Cellular Telecommunications Industry Association (CTIA) on additional laboratory and human studies of mobile phone safety. A "cooperative research and development agreement" signed in June [2000] provides for research to be conducted by third parties, with industry funding and FDA oversight to help ensure the studies' quality.

Specifically, FDA will identify the scientific questions that merit attention, propose research to address those questions, review study proposals from those interested in doing the research, make recommendations on the selection of researchers, and oversee the development of study design. Once research is begun, FDA will review the progress of ongoing studies, review the results of completed studies, and issue a report to the CTIA.

Beyond this planned research, according to the industry association, there are hundreds of scientific studies completed or in progress around the world to investigate RF's possible health effects, with half of them specifically addressing the frequencies used by wireless phones. FDA is a leading participant in the World Health Organization's International EMF (electric and magnetic fields) project to coordinate research and the harmonization of international radiation standards.

## Fear Factor

The new studies may bolster current scientific knowledge, but they will never be able to prove cell phones to be absolutely safe. Proving that cell phones *don't* cause cancer presents the insurmountable scientific obstacle of trying to prove a negative, Moulder explains. "The closest thing to proving that something is safe—that it doesn't cause cancer—is to try to prove that it does, and fail, and fail enough times and in enough different ways."

Even when scientists are convinced of the safety of a technology—be it the technology of cell phones or of televisions, radios, computers, or microwave ovens—it doesn't necessarily follow that public fears will be put to rest. Lay people interpret scientific evidence differently from scientists, according to risk experts, and the general public may be more likely to be frightened when preliminary research shows a mere possibility of harm.

Scientist Moulder is already confident that cell phone use doesn't increase a person's chance of getting brain cancer—so confident, in fact, that he sees nothing wrong with using a cell phone for even hours each day. "Go right ahead," the cancer researcher says, "but please-please-please don't use it while driving. *That's* dangerous."

# POSTSCRIPT

## Do Cell Phones Cause Cancer?

Is the cell phone cancer scare nothing more than media hype, as Sid Deutsch called the EMF cancer scare in "Electromagnetic Field Cancer Scares," *Skeptical Inquirer* (Winter 1994)? Or do cell phones pose a genuine hazard? Recent studies that were reported in the *Journal of the National Cancer Institute, The New England Journal of Medicine,* and *Journal of the American Medical Association* found no cancer risk. L. Hardell, A. Hallquist, K. Hansson Mild, M. Carlberg, A. Pahlson, and A. Lilja reported in "Cellular and Cordless Telephones and the Risk for Brain Tumours," *European Journal of Cancer Prevention* (August 2002), that long-term users of older, analog phones were more likely to suffer brain tumors. U.S. District Judge Catherine Blake, presiding over the most famous phone-cancer lawsuit, was not swayed. She declared that the claimant had provided "no sufficiently reliable and relevant scientific evidence" and said she intended to dismiss the case (Mark Parascandola, "Judge Rejects Cancer Data in Maryland Cell Phone Suit," *Science,* October 11, 2002).

Skeptics insist that the threat is real. However, if it is real, this is not yet clear beyond a doubt. Unfortunately, society cannot always wait for certainty. In connection with EMFs, Gordon L. Hester, in "Electric and Magnetic Fields: Managing an Uncertain Risk," *Environment* (January/February 1992), asserts that just the possibility of a health hazard is sufficient to justify more research into the problem. The guiding principle, says Hester, is "'prudent avoidance,' which was originally intended to mean that people should avoid fields 'when this can be done with modest amounts of money and trouble.'" The same guideline surely applies to cell phone radiation.

Is it possible to prove that cell phones do *not* cause cancer? Unfortunately, no, because small, sporadic effects might not be detected even in massive studies. Thus, for some people, the jury will forever be out.

What should society do in the face of weak, uncertain, and even contradictory data? Can we afford to conclude that there is no hazard? Or must we ban or redesign a useful technology with no justification other than our fear that there might be a real hazard? Many scientists and politicians argue that even if there is no genuine medical risk, there is a genuine impact in terms of public anxiety. See Gary Stix, "Closing the Book," *Scientific American* (March 1998). It is therefore appropriate, they say, to fund further research and to take whatever relatively inexpensive steps to minimize exposure are possible. Failure to do so increases public anxiety and distrust of government and science.

Some of those "relatively inexpensive steps" are pretty simple. As Carlo and Schram note, they include repositioning cell phone antennae and using headsets. As Nordenberg says, quoting Professor John Moulder, using a cell phone while driving is much more hazardous even than using a conventional high-radiation cell phone. By 2003, cell phones were being broadly indicted as hazards on the highway. See "Cell Phones Distract Drivers, Hands Down," *Science News* (February 8, 2003), and "New Studies Define Cell Phone Hazards," *Consumer Reports* (May 2003). The basic problem is that using a cell phone increases the mental workload on the driver, according to Roland Matthews, Stephen Legg, and Samuel Charlton, "The Effect of Cell Phone Type on Drivers' Subjective Workload During Concurrent Driving and Conversing," *Accident Analysis & Prevention* (July, 2003); they too recommend using a hands-free phone. As a result of such studies, several states have already banned handheld phones while driving, with good effect; see Anne T. McCartt, Elisa R. Braver, and Lori L. Geary, "Drivers' Use of Handheld Cell Phones Before and After New York State's Cell Phone Law," *Preventive Medicine* (May 2003).

# ISSUE 9

## Do Vaccines Cause Autism?

**YES: Marnie Ko,** from "Safe from What?" *Report/Newsmagazine* (National Edition) (September 23, 2002)

**NO: Roger Bernier,** from "Vaccine Safety and Autism," *Testimony before the House Committee on Government Reform* (June 19, 2002)

### ISSUE SUMMARY

**YES:** Investigative reporter Marnie Ko reports that vaccines, many of which use a mercury compound as a preservative, are associated with numerous cases of childhood autism and other conditions. Vaccines are not adequately tested for safety.

**NO:** Roger Bernier, Associate Director for Science, National Immunization Program, Centers for Disease Control and Prevention, U.S. Department of Health and Human Services, asserts that numerous studies fail to show that vaccines cause autism, and the mercury-containing preservative is no longer used for childhood vaccines in any event. Further research into vaccine safety is under way.

Autism is a condition featuring poor communication and language skills, abnormal movements such as head-banging, self-injury, and failure to make eye contact, among other symptoms. It tends to appear before age two, apparently because aspects of normal neural function fail to develop. Thirty years ago, it affected one child in 2,000. Today, the incidence of "autistic behaviors" is one in 300 and rising rapidly. See E. Fombonne, "The Prevalence of Autism," *Journal of the American Medical Association* (January 1, 2003). It is not surprising that people refer to an autism "epidemic" and want to know what is causing it.

When seeking causes, the natural tendency is to draw connections between events that occur close together. If there is fog on the highway and cars are crashing, perhaps the fog has something to do with the crashes! But not all events that occur close together are causally linked. People get married and then have babies, but it isn't getting married that causes the babies. If infants receive vaccines and some later develop autism, perhaps the vaccines cause the autism. Or perhaps not.

The question is how to tell. Epidemiologists look for correlations between what people are exposed to (such as tobacco) and diseases (such as lung cancer). Strong correlations are taken to mean a causative link. Weak correlations are treated more cautiously. With vaccines and autism, the correlation is not strong—although almost all children are vaccinated, most children by far do not develop autism. If there is a link, it must depend on the state of the children's immune systems, other environmental factors, or genetic factors.

Given a weak correlation, what should we do about it, besides conduct further research? In environmental science, decision-making is often guided by the "precautionary principle," which says that "lack of full scientific certainty shall not be used as a reason for postponing cost-effective measures to prevent" damage. The mercury-containing preservative thimerosal has been removed from childhood vaccines as just such a cost-effective precaution. Some parents would like to keep their children from being vaccinated, but the law often requires vaccinations before children can enter school (with provision for religious and some other exemptions). And passing up vaccinations poses its own risks: Vaccines are popular because they protect against childhood diseases that used to kill thousands of children every year.

Should vaccine makers be given protection from lawsuits filed by those injured by vaccines? After September 11, 2001, and the ensuing anthrax scare, vaccines became a national security issue, not just a child health issue. Fears mounted that smallpox could be deliberately spread, and a vaccination program was begun. Homeland Security legislation included a provision that broadened liability protection for vaccine makers, and the parents of children whose autism might have been caused by vaccines or thimerosal immediately protested. See Kathleen Schuckel, "A Shot in the Dark," *Indianapolis Monthly* (May 2003). Legislators immediately promised to remove the protection. See Carol Kohn and C. W. Henderson, "Vaccine Makers' Protection Will Be Eliminated, Republicans Say," *Bioterrorism Week* (February 3, 2003).

In the following selections, investigative reporter Marnie Ko reports on growing concerns that vaccines, many of which use a mercury compound as a preservative, are associated with numerous cases of childhood autism and other conditions and must be tested more carefully for safety. Roger Bernier, Associate Director for Science, National Immunization Program, Centers for Disease Control and Prevention, U.S. Department of Health and Human Services, maintains that numerous studies fail to show that vaccines cause autism, and the mercury-containing preservative is no longer used for childhood vaccines in any event. Further research into vaccine safety is under way.

**Marnie Ko**

# YES

# Safe from What?

It is not surprising that Dr. Michael Palmer's new medical thriller, Fatal, is flying off bookstore shelves across North America. The author is a nine-time *New York Times* best-selling author, medical doctor and former emergency-room physician, and the book is an engrossing novel about corrupt and dirty dealings by pharmaceutical companies that manufacture childhood vaccinations and sell them with little scientific study on their safety. But while the book may be fiction, the 59-year-old Massachusetts medic's concern about vaccinations is quite real.

When Dr. Palmer's son Luke was born in 1990, the boy received the standard vaccinations. "I didn't think about it. I'm a doctor. I vaccinated, no questions asked," says Dr. Palmer ruefully. By eight months of age, Luke began to suffer ear infections, which continued relentlessly until he was 19 months. He then needed an operation to have tubes put in. Then, by the time Luke was three, he was diagnosed with a form of autism, Asperger's syndrome, known as "right brain autism." Dr. Palmer took him to a variety of treatment centres and met dozens of other parents with developmentally delayed children.

"The similarities from case to case were striking," he recalls. Often, chronic ear infections developed soon after immunizations, and soon after that an onset of autistic symptoms. "Healthy, normal children suddenly developed autism after childhood shots."

For parents whose healthy child has received a vaccine and regressed in development or stopped responding altogether, there are too many "what-ifs." During research for his book, Dr. Palmer met parents across the U.S. who believed vaccines were directly responsible for their children's autism because the shots contained thimerosal, a mercury derivative used since the 1930s as a preservative and anti-biological agent. Mercury is one of the most toxic elements on earth, a heavy metal and neurotoxin known to have devastating effects on humans, including neurological damage, according to some medical experts.

The problems are not limited to American children, either. Vaccine-related lawsuits around the world have alleged mercury causes immune-system, sensory, neurological, motor and behavioural dysfunction, especially involving the central nervous system, in children and adults. Mercury has

 Marnie Ko is a national investigative reporter who lives in Canada.

been linked to autism, learning disabilities, multiple sclerosis, lupus, arthritis and other diseases. The number of children affected by autism has skyrocketed in the last five years. According to a study released by the Ontario government earlier this year, almost 800 children aged six and under were diagnosed with autism in 1998—a 53% increase over two years.

On May 9, a group of Canadian parents launched a historic lawsuit against Aventis Pasteur, Merck Frosst Canada and GlaxoSmithKline Inc., all large Canadian pharmaceutical companies. The suit alleges that the drug manufacturers knowingly used mercury preservatives in childhood vaccines, causing neurological damage and resulting in autism in about 100 infants. (Aventis Pasteur, the main target of the suit, used thimerosal as a preservative in diphtheria-pertussis-tetanus [DPT] combination vaccine in the '80s, and up to about 1994 in some provinces, according to company officials. Company spokesman Nancy Simpson says the firm's infant vaccinations no longer contain thimerosal.)

The lawsuit, launched in the Ontario Supreme Court and representing families from Alberta, Saskatchewan, Manitoba and Ontario, is the first of its kind in this country, but similar suits have been filed in the United Kingdom, the U.S. and New Zealand. In the course of legal action, one U.S. law firm obtained a confidential report authored by the U.S. Centers for Disease Control. The report studied whether mercury in shots could result in autism or neurological injury. The official version of the report released to the public claimed the study was inconclusive. However, the confidential version of the study obtained by lawyers concluded that an infant exposed to more than 62.5 micrograms of mercury—an amount contained in some combinations of vaccines within three months of birth would be two-and-a-half times more likely to develop autism. (U.S. courts have generally ruled that a relative increased risk of 2.0 or higher is sufficient to prove exposure to a substance causes the disease.)

That is not to say the Canadian parents will have an easy time winning. Aventis Pasteur manufactures one billion vaccine doses for about 400 million people worldwide each year. The firm also owns Connaught Laboratories, which manufactured most Canadian vaccines until the '90s and also produced the "hot lot" under scrutiny in Baby Alan Yurko's death in Florida. Shortly after the class-action lawsuit was filed, company spokeswoman Shirley Ernstberger told reporters the company would "vigorously defend" against the lawsuit. "All products produced by the company and marketed in Canada were approved by Health Canada at all times," she said.

The suit demands $1 billion in compensation and $250 million in punitive damages on behalf of about 100 families, alleging the drug company "continued to sell the vaccines in Canada when it knew or ought to have known that the thimerosal in the vaccines is hazardous to the health of infants." It will be early next year before the court decides whether it will accept the class-action lawsuit. If it does not, David Klein of Vancouver, lawyer for the parents, plans to file individual suits across the country.

Audra East and her son Keean, now nine, of Fort Fraser, Ont., are the representative claimants in the class-action lawsuit, which claims that all the victims were born healthy and developed normally until receiving DPT or hepatitis B (hep B) shots as part of routine vaccine programs, at which time they developed serious illnesses and neurological damage. For example, Keean was a healthy, well-adjusted two-year-old until he received his third DPT shot. Almost overnight, his parents allege, he became withdrawn and unresponsive. He stopped making eye contact and began hurting himself, banging his head and biting his hands—all classic symptoms of autism.

Cindy Stark, a Vancouver mother, also had a frightening experience after having her son vaccinated. He received his shots at the recommended times, including hep B and haemophilus influenzae type b (Hib), both of which contained thimerosal. After each shot, the baby was screaming and arching his back, and either could not sleep at all or slept excessively. Each time, doctors assured Mrs. Stark this was "a normal reaction."

By nine months, the baby had little comprehension and stopped making eye contact. By 20 months, he was diagnosed with autism. "He started spinning, and stopped looking and responding to us," says Mrs. Stark. She is still deciding whether to join the class-action lawsuit or launch her own against the vaccine manufacturer. Her son, now four, has severe allergies, especially to red dye, and has to wear gloves at preschool just to paint. He is still in diapers and uses a bottle. "In some ways, he's like a one-year-old," she says. He was tested by a U.S. doctor, who found abnormally high levels of mercury in his bloodstream. "We blame the vaccines. Where else is he going to get mercury at this level?"

The medical community has voiced concerns over the toxicity of mercury to humans for more than 50 years. By 1996, the U.S. Food and Drug Administration (FDA) took steps to stop the sale and use of over-the-counter mercurial topical ointments, including those that contained thimerosal. A 1998 FDA review concluded that children receiving the full set of recommended shots could be exposed to 30 to 50 times more mercury than recommended by the U.S. Environmental Protection Agency. But it was not until July 1999 that the American Academy of Pediatrics issued a warning that vaccines containing thimerosal should not be given to children. The same year, the FDA announced that an infant receiving just one combination vaccine (a vaccine for more than one disease) could be exposed to 100 times the safe level of mercury for humans. Even then, the agency requested only that vaccine manufacturers voluntarily phase out thimerosal from their products. However, many clinics are still believed to maintain older stocks of vaccines containing thimerosal that have not yet been used up.

So far, at least one vaccine lawsuit has been successful. In May 2001, a French court upheld an earlier, lower court ruling accepting the existence of a connection between the hepatitis B vaccine, made by GlaxoSmithKline, and multiple sclerosis. Two women launched the suit after developing MS following hep B shots. The court did not demand proof of a direct link, but ordered the firm to compensate the women financially. But Nancy Pekarek, spokeswoman for GlaxoSmithKline, told reporters, "There's no scientific evidence that there is any harm caused by thimerosal-containing vaccines. Vaccines have done an incredible job of preventing disease. It would just be terrible if people used something like this to stop vaccinating." Meanwhile in the U.S., about 10 law firms in 25 states are involved in a national thimerosal class-action lawsuit, with dozens of individual lawsuits also in progress.

Ever since 1986, when the U.S. Congress set up a national no-fault vaccine injury compensation fund, American doctors have been legally required to report suspected cases of vaccine damage to VAERS (Vaccine Adverse Event Reporting System). Still, FDA officials say 90% of doctors do not report reactions to the shots. Some doctors refuse to believe a child's injury is related to the vaccine, despite the parents' insistence that their child was healthy before being vaccinated. Still, 12,000 to 14,000 reactions to vaccines are reported to VAERS annually, and these include hospitalizations, irreversible brain damage and hundreds of deaths.

If only 10% of adverse reactions are reported, that would place the real number as high as 140,000 vaccine-induced injuries to infants each year. But David Kesler, former head of the FDA, told reporters a mere 1% of serious adverse drug reactions are reported. If he is correct, the number of infants damaged after a vaccination may be in the millions.

A surtax on each vaccine is earmarked for the compensation fund. If a child dies after a vaccination, the family is awarded $250,000 out of the fund. When a child is brain-damaged or otherwise seriously harmed, the awards are much more substantial, compensating for pain, suffering and lifelong medical bills. VAERS has already paid out more than $1 billion in compensation, with thousands of cases pending. Some cases have also led to private settlements with the drug companies. The VAERS system is fast, with most hearings completed within two days and claims adjudicated within a year. However, the program has a downside. Lawyers' fees may or may not be covered, and legal representation is recommended because procedures are complicated. All cases are heard in the U.S. Court of Federal Claims in Washington, and only lawyers admitted to practise in that court can appear. But if a child received a vaccine and subsequently developed a condition listed on the vaccine injury table (such as seizures, brain damage or paralysis), compensation is awarded and the family does not have to prove vaccines were the culprit.

If not for the VAERS chart, few families would be successful in obtaining compensation for their vaccine-damaged children. "No human studies have proved that mercury from amalgams or from the preservative causes autism in children," said Boyd Haley, chairman of the University of Kentucky chemistry department and a mercury toxicity expert. Nonetheless, he told U.S. reporters this comes down to "common sense." "Thimerosal is the best suspect for the huge increase in autism, and maybe other neurological disorders," he said.

In contrast, Dr. Liana Nolan, medical officer of health for Waterloo, Ont., told reporters recently thimerosal in vaccines has been linked to autism only by allegations, and there is "no satisfactory evidence of a link." The thimerosal in the Canadian hepatitis B vaccine, for example, "is a trace amount," she said.

Dr. Nolan's reassurances offer cold comfort to Christine Colebeck, a Kitchener, Ont., mother. She qualifies to join the Canadian vaccine lawsuit on behalf of her youngest son Carter, age six. He was vaccinated as a baby. The injection site became swollen and red, and he cried uncontrollably after the shots. Doctors assured the family his reaction was normal. But by age three, he was not behaving like a normal child. "He didn't play with toys. He lined them up and classified them." He had little short-term memory, and developed behaviour problems.

Carter was eventually diagnosed with Asperger's syndrome, obsessive-compulsive disorder and verbal tics. Despite his afflictions, he is brilliant with mathematical problems, and is considered an "autistic savant," meaning he has exceptional but narrow abilities. (At one time, individuals who had talents in one area with an overall cognitive impairment, or even mental retardation, were known as "idiot savants," from a French term referring to unlearned skill. Savant abilities can include mathematical calculations, amazing memory feats and artistic and musical aptitude.) But while Carter can perform complicated multiplication problems in his head and count higher than most adults, he is emotionally and socially inept. He licks people, hugs strangers and currently says the word "ass" more than his parents would like. He has trouble making friends and does not behave appropriately in social situations. Mrs. Colebeck, a nurse who left the profession to home-school her children, blames her son's neuro-immunological dysfunction on childhood shots. He received various vaccines, including diptheria and tetanus, polio and Hib. Since then, he has regressed gradually but continuously.

It is the second such tragedy for the Colebeck family. In 1986, the couple's daughter Laura died at three months, several hours after receiving her first vaccination. While doctors attributed her demise to SIDS (sudden infant death syndrome), Mrs. Colebeck now blames the pertussis vaccine, which contained live disease.

Mrs. Colebeck is working with other parents to force the Canadian government to start a federal injury-compensation program like the one in the U.S. "My daughter's life will not be lost for nothing," says the mother. The family has decided to hire a lawyer and pursue legal action on behalf of Carter.

Meanwhile, vaccine programs across the country are moving ahead at full throttle. In May, Alberta announced it would make the pneumococcal conjugate vaccine part of routine shots offered to infants. It will cost $14 million a year, beginning in this fall. Even though pneumococcal disease results in an average of just 15 deaths a year in Alberta children under five, out of about 40,000 infants born, health officials believe the vaccine is worthwhile.

But according to Dr. Palmer, there are far too many unanswered questions about vaccines. The medical profession, he says, is "not studying the long-range complications of vaccinations. Many researchers stop looking at these vaccines the moment they are approved. What if there is something wrong? What if vaccines do have a role in autism, MS, asthma or diabetes?

"What most struck me was how little people question, whether they are parents, scientists or doctors. Everyone is willing to discard science. Nobody has done carefully designed, double-blind studies when it comes to vaccines. The moment there is a new one, people want it in circulation. They don't want to spend 10 years evaluating its effectiveness and safety." . . .

**NO** 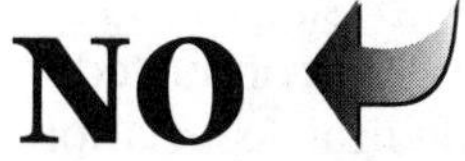

**Roger Bernier**

# Vaccine Safety and Autism

## Autism and Vaccines

Autism spectrum disorders (ASD) are a group of life-long developmental disabilities caused by an abnormality of the brain. The most recent data suggests that between 2 and 6 children per 1,000 have ASD. The impact on families of children diagnosed with autism spectrum disorders is tremendous. We recognize that there is considerable public interest and concern on this issue and we are committed to addressing concerns of parents and families. The Department of Health and Human Services (HHS) is dedicated to finding the answer to what causes autism and how it can be prevented. There is a great deal of ongoing research throughout the various public health agencies. While my focus today is on vaccine safety related issues, it should be noted that HHS has implemented an Interagency Autism Coordinating Committee (IACC). . . .

Some parents, researchers and others have expressed concerns about a potential link between autism and vaccines currently being used in the United States, focusing primarily on thimerosal, a preservative in some vaccines, and secondly, on measles, mumps, and rubella (MMR) vaccine.

In mid-1999, the United States Public Health Service agencies, including NIH, FDA, HRSA, and CDC took action, working collaboratively with the American Academy of Pediatrics, the American Academy of Family Physicians and the vaccine manufacturers, to begin removing thimerosal preservative from the vaccine supply. While the risk of harm was only theoretical, the decision was made as a precautionary measure in order to reduce overall mercury exposure of infants. As a result of this action, all manufacturers are now producing only vaccines that are free of thimerosal as a preservative for routine infant immunization.

The suggestion that MMR vaccine, which has never contained thimerosal, triggers autism was initially based on some reports of cases of autism in which parents noted the onset of autistic behaviors shortly after MMR vaccination. Over the last few years, a number of studies have been performed in countries around the world to address this issue. Systematic scientific reviews by some of the most prestigious medical bodies around the world including the Medical Research Council in the United Kingdom, the American Academy of Pediatrics, and the Institute of Medicine of the National Academy of

From Testimony before the House Committee on Government Reform, June 19, 2002.

Sciences have unanimously concluded that evidence does not support a relationship between MMR and autism. The most recent review was conducted in the United Kingdom and commissioned by the British Medical Association. British experts reviewed five decades of research on the MMR vaccine and concluded that there is no link to autism or bowel disease. However, despite these findings and because of continued public concerns, CDC is committed to further scientific research on this issue as detailed in this testimony.

## CDC's Commitment to Vaccine Safety

CDC is actively involved in detecting and investigating vaccine safety concerns and supporting a wide range of vaccine safety research to address safety questions.

In order to enhance the understanding of rare adverse effects of vaccines, CDC developed the Vaccine Safety Datalink (VSD) project in 1990. This project is a collaborative effort, which utilizes the databases of eight large health maintenance organizations (HMOs). The database contains comprehensive medical and immunization histories of approximately 7.5 million children and adults. The VSD enables vaccine safety research studies comparing incidence of health problems between unvaccinated and vaccinated people. Over the past decade, the VSD has been used to answer many vaccine-related questions, and has been used to support policy changes that have reduced adverse effects from vaccines.

CDC recognizes the importance of data sharing when questions are raised regarding a particular study's design and methodology. Therefore, CDC has been actively engaged with the participating HMOs to determine how their clients' personal medical records can be maintained confidentially and the proprietary interests of the HMOs protected, while still allowing for external researchers to reanalyze the data from studies which have been conducted through the Vaccine Safety Datalink. As a result, CDC has developed a data sharing process designed to allow an independent researcher to replicate or conduct a modified analysis of a previous VSD study, while maintaining the confidential nature of the data.

Another critical part of our vaccine safety effort is the objective, scientific evaluation of safety concerns by independent experts. In collaboration with NIH and other U.S. Public Health Service agencies, CDC requested the Institute of Medicine (IOM) to conduct independent reviews by independent scientific experts to determine: 1) whether the available scientific information favors, or does not favor, vaccines playing a role in causation, 2) the level of public health priority the concern should receive, and 3) recommendations for research. The IOM Immunization Safety Review Committee has released reports on MMR Vaccine and Autism, Thimerosal and Neurodevelopmental Disorders, Hepatitis B and Neurological Disorders and the Multiple Immunizations and Immune Dysfunction. The IOM was asked to review the available scientific information on these issues. CDC has initiated a broad range of studies to address recommendations made by the IOM Immunization Safety Review Committee.

## MMR and Autism Studies

In its report regarding the association between the MMR vaccine and autism spectrum disorder (ASD) in April 2001, the IOM concluded "the evidence favors rejection of a causal relationship at the population level between MMR vaccine and autism spectrum disorder." The IOM made several recommendations regarding future research including the following epidemiological studies:

1. Explore whether exposure to MMR vaccine is a risk factor for ASD in a small number of children;
2. Develop targeted investigations of whether or not measles vaccine-strain virus is present in the intestines of some children with ASD;
3. Study the possible effects of different MMR immunization exposures; and
4. Conduct further clinical and epidemiological studies of sufficient rigor to identify risk factors and biological markers of ASD in order to better understand genetic or environmental causes.

CDC takes this issue very seriously and therefore, is currently funding five research studies that address the above four recommendations from the IOM:

The first study, the Metropolitan Atlanta Developmental Disabilities Surveillance Program (MADDSP) MMR/Autism Study, is a large case-control study. The autism cases for the study were identified through MADDSP. The control subjects were selected from the same or similar schools in the Atlanta area and matched to cases based on age and gender. The study is assessing the relationship between the timing of receipt of the first MMR vaccine and risk for developing autism. The analyses for this study and a manuscript should be completed by early fall 2002.

The second study, the MMR/Regression Autism Study funded by CDC and the National Institutes of Child Health and Human Development (NICHD) is also a large case-control study that is using a sample of autism cases identified as part of the NICHD and the National Institute on Deafness and other Communication Disorders (NIDCD) 10 Collaborative Programs of Excellence in Autism (CPEA). This study is specifically designed to examine the association between regression autism and the timing of first receipt of the MMR vaccine. The study is being carried out over a three-year period and results from this study are expected in the spring of 2004.

The third study, the Denmark MMR/Autism Study, is a recent study that was carried out in Denmark in collaboration with CDC. The study was designed to follow-up on approximately 537,000 children born in Denmark during the period from January 1, 1991 to December 31, 1998. Of these, 82% received MMR vaccine. The cohort was generated based on data obtained from the Danish Civil Registration System and subsequently linked with other national registries. This manuscript has been submitted for publication this year.

The fourth study is a large epidemiological study to identify risk factors and biological markers of ASD to better understand genetic or environmental causes. The study is being planned in the four Centers for Autism and

Developmental Disabilities Research and Epidemiology (CADDRE), which are being supported by CDC.

Additionally, CDC is in the early stages of planning a study to investigate whether or not measles vaccine-strain virus is present in the intestines of some children with ASD.

There have been a limited number of laboratory reports of the finding of measles virus sequences in intestinal tissue and white blood cells of children with ASD; therefore, there has been speculation that MMR vaccine either precipitates or aggravates ASD. However, other epidemiologic and laboratory studies do not support this observation. To resolve differences in results from previous studies that may have occurred due to differences in study design, sampling biases, and differences in laboratory [testing] procedures and their sensitivity, an independent, multicenter study is being designed. The study plan is to determine the prevalence of measles virus vaccine strain gene sequences in bowel biopsy tissue from children with gastrointestinal tract complaints with and without ASD. The study will be designed to ensure use of standardized clinical and laboratory protocols, appropriate enrollment of controls, blinding of specimens, use of standardized laboratory reagents and assays, and appropriate statistical evaluation.

## Thimerosal and Neurodevelopmental Delay Studies

In October 2001, the IOM Immunization Safety Review Committee published a report on the possible association between thimerosal-containing vaccines and neurodevelopmental disorders. In this report, the IOM concluded "that the evidence is inadequate to accept or reject a causal relationship between exposure to thimerosal from childhood vaccines and the neurodevelopmental disorders of autism, ADHD (attention deficit hyperactivitity disorder), and speech or language delay." The IOM made several recommendations regarding future research studies including several epidemiological studies. They recommended:

A. Case-control studies examining the potential link between neurodevelopmental disorders and thimerosal-containing vaccines;
B. Further analysis of neurodevelopmental outcomes in several cohorts of children outside the U.S. who participated in a clinical trial of DTaP vaccine; and,
C. Conducting epidemiological studies that compare the incidence and prevalence of neurodevelopmental disorders before and after the removal of thimerosal from vaccines.

While there have been no vaccines being produced for routine childhood immunization for over a year that contain thimerosal as a preservative, CDC takes this issue very seriously and therefore, has undertaken several studies that address the above IOM recommendations:

The first study, the Thimerosal Screening Analysis in the Vaccine Safety Datalink (VSD) project, was started in the fall of 1999. The VSD, described earlier, was used to screen for possible associations between exposure to thimerosal-containing vaccines and a variety of renal, neurologic and developmental problems. In the first phase of this study, the CDC used data from the 2 VSD HMOs with automated outpatient data (where more subtle effects of mercury toxicity might be seen). The CDC and VSD researchers found statistically significant associations between thimerosal and neurodevelopmental disorders, such as language and speech delays, ADHD, stuttering, and tics. No association was shown with autism. However, the associations were weak and were not consistent between the two HMOs. In the second phase of the investigation, CDC investigators examined data from a third HMO with similar available automated vaccination and outpatient databases to see if these findings could be replicated. Analyses of these data using the same methods as the first study did not confirm results seen in the first phase. A statistically significant relationship between autism and thimerosal was not found in either the preliminary study or the later, larger analysis. Due to the methodological limitations of the screening analysis using automated data and the difference between the preliminary study and the later analyses, the results required further examination.

CDC and VSD researchers are committed to clarifying the results encountered during the VSD Screening Analysis; therefore, a Thimerosal Follow-Up Study will be conducted. This second study will be designed to assess whether preliminary results from automated data used in the Thimerosal Screening Analysis can be confirmed using objective neuropsychological testing. The study will focus on the conditions found in the first screening analyses, including language and speech delays and ADHD. The design of the new study will address the main drawback of the Thimerosal Screening Analysis, which was that children were not objectively assessed on the neurodevelopmental disorders of interest. The various VSD HMOs categorize neurodevelopmental disabilities in different ways, provide different services for these disorders, and often refer children out of the health care network when they are identified with these particular disorders.

The Thimerosal Follow-Up Study is planned to examine approximately 1200 children between the ages of 7 and 9 years of age randomly selected from four VSD HMOs based on thimerosal exposure during the first 3 months of life. All 1200 children will be brought into their respective HMOs and will be assessed using a standardized set of neuropsychological test batteries. The preliminary proposal for this study was presented to a panel of external consultants including a consumer representative in March of 2001. In September of 2001, CDC awarded a contract to Abt Associates Inc. to carry out the planning phase of the study. The panel of external consultants continues to provide individual input into the study design and the planning phase should be completed by June 2002. Data collection is expected to begin in the latter half of 2002. Abt Associates Inc. is expected to present the results of the study by the end of 2003.

Several additional studies are being planned to address additional issues raised by the IOM. These include:

The Thimerosal/Autism Study will be a case-control study to be conducted simultaneously with the Thimerosal Follow-up Study. Autism cases identified through review of automated medical records will be assessed objectively by using a standardized autism assessment tool. Controls will be selected from the Thimerosal Follow-up Study and matched to cases by age and sex.

CDC has developed a proposal for a pilot study to conduct further analyses of a group of Italian children who had participated in a prior DTaP trial in which thimerosal exposure was randomly allocated. CDC is pursuing this to determine the feasibility of recruiting these participates for a follow-up study of neurodevelopmental outcomes.

Two other studies being planned will examine changes over time in the diagnosis of neurodevelopmental delays including autism. These studies will use inpatient and outpatient discharge diagnoses to compare rates of these conditions over time with changes in levels of thimerosal in recommended childhood vaccines. Because recommendations for the removal of thimerosal from vaccines did not occur until 1999, several years of data following the removal of thimerosal will be necessary before these comparisons can be made. Thus, results will not be available until 2005 or later.

## Benefits of Vaccines

We remain vigilant to assure the safety of vaccines. We must also remember that vaccines benefit the public by protecting persons from the consequences of infectious diseases. Continued high U.S. vaccination rates are crucial to prevent the spread of diseases such as measles, pertussis (whooping cough) and rubella among U.S. children. Current measles coverage is approximately 91% in children 19–35 months old and about 97% at school entry, and only about 100 cases of measles have been reported per year; many of the cases are imported; and ongoing indigenous transmission of measles no longer occurs. From 1989–91, a measles epidemic in the United States led to more than 55,000 cases of measles and more than 11,000 hospitalizations, with 123 deaths in three years. Before this epidemic, vaccination coverage was estimated at 61–66% nationally and at 51–79% in 15 major cities. These outbreaks stopped only when vaccination coverage increased. Thus, if pre-school coverage dropped by 25–30% below the current level, large measles outbreaks are likely to occur once again. Additionally, pertussis has continued to be a public health threat. For example, in 1999, there were 7297 cases of pertussis in the United States, with 15 reported deaths.

Vaccines are cited as one of the greatest achievements of biomedical science and public health in the 20th century. We can point to the remarkable success we have had in controlling numerous infectious diseases which used to be widely prevalent in the United States, including polio, measles, and pertussis. In fact, several of these vaccine-preventable infectious diseases are known to cause developmental disabilities, including Haemophilus influenzae type b (Hib) and congenital rubella syndrome (CRS), one of the few known causes of autism. Rubella vaccine, by preventing CRS, thus prevents some cases of autism. Prior to routine immunization with Hib vaccine, of young children who developed Hib meningitis, 5 percent died and another 15 to 30 percent were left with residual brain damage leading to language disorders and mental retardation.

While we have made great progress to reduce the number of cases of vaccine-preventable diseases, the threats posed by vaccine-preventable diseases are known and real. The viruses and bacteria that cause vaccine-preventable diseases still circulate in the U.S. and around the world. Maintaining vaccination coverage and high levels of immunity are crucial to protect the U.S. population and to continue progress toward elimination of diseases that, at one time, caused millions of infections in the U.S. each year and that globally remain the leading causes of death and of preventable birth defects.

## Conclusion

CDC remains committed to collecting accurate data on prevalence of autism and conducting studies on vaccine safety. Research is already underway, and more is planned, to look at the relationship between the MMR vaccine and autism. We want each child to be born healthy and to grow and develop normally, so that they are able to lead productive lives. Vaccines are one of our most valuable weapons against disease and have afforded us one of our proudest achievements in public health.

# POSTSCRIPT

## Do Vaccines Cause Autism?

Late in 2002, a Danish study of autism and the measles-mumps-rubella (MMR) vaccine found no link; see Kreesten Meldgaard Madsen, Anders Hviid, Mogens Vestergaard, Diana Schendel, Jan Wohlfahrt, Poul Thorsen, Jørn Olsen, and Mads Melbye, "A Population Based Study of Measles, Mumps, and Rubella Vaccination and Autism," *The New England Journal of Medicine* (November 7, 2002). Activists promptly objected that the study did not address other vaccines, thimerosal, or interactions with thimerosal-containing vaccines. See "Denmark Study on Vaccine Link to Autism Is Inconclusive, Advocacy Group Reports," *Virus Weekly* (December 10, 2002).

According to the *Harvard Medical Health Letter* (April 2003), "A popular suspect in autism is the measles-mumps-rubella (MMR) vaccine, which came into widespread use around 1990. Children are given the vaccine, which contains viruses that could theoretically infect the brain, at about 15 months of age. . . . To the relief of public health officials and parents concerned about contagious diseases, it is becoming increasingly clear that immunization is not the source of the problem." Another suspect is thimerosal, the mercury-containing preservative used until recently in vaccines, but "blood levels of mercury did not become unusually high in children who received thimerosal-containing vaccines for diphtheria, tetanus, whooping cough, hepatitis B, and influenza at 2, 4, and 6 months of age. They were compared with controls who took the same vaccines packaged without the preservative. Mercury levels were the same in both groups and well below the amount considered dangerous to health." A similar conclusion is reached by Karin B. Nelson and Margaret L. Bauman, "Thimerosal and Autism?" *Pediatrics* (March 2003), who conclude that, "On the basis of current evidence, we consider it improbable that thimerosal and autism are linked." Katherine Hobson, "The Vaccine Conundrum," *U.S. News & World Report* (March 17, 2003), notes that "It's possible that some vaccines produce very rare, but harmful, allergic responses in some people—that's why the government has a fund to compensate victims of those reactions. . . . But vaccines are studied in tens of thousands of people before they're licensed. And the risk of allowing these diseases to gain hold again is far greater than any risk from the vaccines. . . . [T]he very small risk of injury must be weighed against the public-health benefits."

Some scholars see a risk in the way issues such as vaccine safety are covered by the media. C. J. Clements and S. Ratzan, "Misled and Confused? Telling the Public about MMR Vaccine Safety," *Journal of Medical Ethics* (February 2003), say that, "Vaccines are as safe as humans can presently make them. Yet as in any health intervention, some level of uncertainty will always remain. It is not easy to present this concept accurately and ethically to the public without giving them the impression that vaccination should be avoided. . . . Ultimately the public must decide whether to follow the lead of the antivaccine lobby and the media that encourages rejection of government vaccination policy, or to follow the official voice that encourages vaccination. But if confidence falters, vaccine coverage dips, and an outbreak of measles, mumps, or rubella ensues, with cases and deaths from measles, or babies born with congenital rubella syndrome. . . ."

# ISSUE 10

## Should DDT Be Banned Worldwide?

**YES: Anne Platt McGinn,** from "Malaria, Mosquitoes, and DDT," *World Watch* (May/June 2002)

**NO: Roger Bate,** from "A Case of the DDTs," *National Review* (May 14, 2001)

### ISSUE SUMMARY

**YES:** Anne Platt McGinn, a senior researcher at the Worldwatch Institute, argues that although DDT is still used to fight malaria, there are other, more effective and less environmentally harmful methods. She maintains that DDT should be banned or reserved for emergency use.

**NO:** Roger Bate, director of Africa Fighting Malaria, asserts that DDT is the cheapest and most effective way to combat malaria and that it should remain available for use.

DDT is a crucial element in the story of environmentalism. The chemical was first synthesized in 1874. Swiss entomologist Paul Mueller was the first to notice that DDT has insecticidal properties, which, it was quickly realized, implied that the chemical could save human lives. It had long been known that more soldiers died during wars because of disease than because of enemy fire. During World War I, for example, some 5 million lives were lost to typhus, a disease carried by body lice. DDT was first deployed during World War II to halt a typhus epidemic in Naples, Italy. It was a dramatic success, and DDT was soon used routinely as a dust for soldiers and civilians. During and after the war, DDT was also deployed successfully against the mosquitoes that carry malaria and other diseases. In the United States cases of malaria fell from 120,000 in 1934 to 72 in 1960, and cases of yellow fever dropped from 100,000 in 1878 to none. In 1948 Mueller received the Nobel Prize for medicine and physiology because DDT had saved so many civilian lives.

DDT was by no means the first pesticide. But its predecessors—arsenic, strychnine, cyanide, copper sulfate, and nicotine—were all markedly toxic to humans. DDT was not only more effective as an insecticide, it was also less hazardous to users. It is therefore not surprising that DDT was seen as a beneficial substance. It was soon applied routinely to agricultural crops and used to control mosquito populations in American suburbs. However, insects quickly became resistant to the insecticide. (In any population of insects, some will be more resistant than others; when the insecticide kills the more vulnerable members of the population, the resistant ones are left to breed and multiply. This is an example of natural selection.) In *Silent Spring* (Houghton Mifflin, 1962), marine scientist Rachel Carson demonstrated that DDT was concentrated in the food chain and affected the reproduction of predators such as hawks and eagles. In 1972 the U.S. Environmental Protection Agency banned almost all uses of DDT (it could still be used to protect public health). Other developed countries soon banned it as well, but developing nations, especially those in the tropics, saw it as an essential tool for fighting diseases such as malaria.

It soon became apparent that DDT is by no means the only pesticide or organic toxin with environmental effects. As a result, on May 24, 2001, the United States joined 90 other nations in signing the Stockholm Convention on Persistent Organic Pollutants (POPs). This treaty aims to eliminate from use the entire class of chemicals to which DDT belongs, beginning with the pesticides DDT, aldrin, dieldrin, endrin, chlordane, heptachlor, mirex, and toxaphene, and the industrial chemicals polychlorinated biphenyls (PCBs), hexachlorobenzene (HCB), dioxins, and furans. Fifty more countries signed during the next year, but according to the Pesticide Action Network North America (`http://panna.igc.org`), only eight (not including the United States) have formally ratified the treaty.

In the following selection, Anne Platt McGinn, granting that malaria remains a serious problem in the developing nations of the tropics, especially Africa, contends that although DDT is still used to fight malaria in these nations, it is far less effective than it used to be. She argues that the environmental effects are also serious concerns and that DDT should be banned or reserved for emergency use. In the second selection, Roger Bate argues that DDT remains the cheapest and most effective way to combat malaria and that it should remain available for use.

**Anne Platt McGinn**  **YES**

# Malaria, Mosquitoes, and DDT

This year, like every other year within the past couple of decades, uncountable trillions of mosquitoes will inject malaria parasites into human blood streams billions of times. Some 300 to 500 million full-blown cases of malaria will result, and between 1 and 3 million people will die, most of them pregnant women and children. That's the official figure, anyway, but it's likely to be a substantial underestimate, since most malaria deaths are not formally registered, and many are likely to have escaped the estimators. Very roughly, the malaria death toll rivals that of AIDS, which now kills about 3 million people annually.

But unlike AIDS, malaria is a low-priority killer. Despite the deaths, and the fact that roughly 2.5 billion people (40 percent of the world's population) are at risk of contracting the disease, malaria is a relatively low public health priority on the international scene. Malaria rarely makes the news. And international funding for malaria research currently comes to a mere $150 million annually. Just by way of comparison, that's only about 5 percent of the $2.8 billion that the U.S. government alone is considering for AIDS research in fiscal year 2003.

The low priority assigned to malaria would be at least easier to understand, though no less mistaken, if the threat were static. Unfortunately it is not. It is true that the geographic range of the disease has contracted substantially since the mid-20th century, but over the past couple of decades, malaria has been gathering strength. Virtually all areas where the disease is endemic have seen drug-resistant strains of the parasites emerge—a development that is almost certainly boosting death rates. In countries as various as Armenia, Afghanistan, and Sierra Leone, the lack or deterioration of basic infrastructure has created a wealth of new breeding sites for the mosquitoes that spread the disease. The rapidly expanding slums of many tropical cities also lack such infrastructure; poor sanitation and crowding have primed these places as well for outbreaks—even though malaria has up to now been regarded as predominantly a rural disease.

What has current policy to offer in the face of these threats? The medical arsenal is limited; there are only about a dozen antimalarial drugs commonly in use, and there is significant malaria resistance to most of them. In the absence of a reliable way to kill the parasites, policy has tended to focus on killing the mosquitoes that bear them. And that has led to an abundant use of synthetic pesticides, including one of the oldest and most dangerous: dichlorodiphenyl trichloroethane, or DDT.

DDT is no longer used or manufactured in most of the world, but because it does not break down readily, it is still one of the most commonly detected pesticides in the milk of nursing mothers. DDT is also one of the "dirty dozen" chemicals included in the 2001 Stockholm Convention on Persistent Organic Pollutants [POPs]. The signatories to the "POPs Treaty" essentially agreed to ban all uses of DDT except as a last resort against disease-bearing mosquitoes. Unfortunately, however, DDT is still a routine option in 19 countries, most of them in Africa. (Only 11 of these countries have thus far signed the treaty.) Among the signatory countries, 31—slightly fewer than one-third—have given notice that they are reserving the right to use DDT against malaria. On the face of it, such use may seem unavoidable, but there are good reasons for thinking that progress against the disease is compatible with *reductions* in DDT use.

Malaria is caused by four protozoan parasite species in the genus *Plasmodium.* These parasites are spread exclusively by certain mosquitoes in the genus *Anopheles.* An infection begins when a parasite-laden female mosquito settles onto someone's skin and pierces a capillary to take her blood meal. The parasite, in a form called the *sporozoite,* moves with the mosquito's saliva into the human bloodstream. About 10 percent of the mosquito's lode of sporozoites is likely to be injected during a meal, leaving plenty for the next bite. Unless the victim has some immunity to malaria—normally as a result of previous exposure—most sporozoites are likely to evade the body's immune system and make their way to the liver, a process that takes less than an hour. There they invade the liver cells and multiply asexually for about two weeks. By this time, the original several dozen sporozoites have become millions of *merozoites*—the form the parasite takes when it emerges from the liver and moves back into the blood to invade the body's red blood cells. Within the red blood cells, the merozoites go through another cycle of asexual reproduction, after which the cells burst and release millions of additional merozoites, which invade yet more red blood cells. The high fever and chills associated with malaria are the result of this stage, which tends to occur in pulses. If enough red blood cells are destroyed in one of these pulses, the result is convulsions, difficulty in breathing, coma, and death.

As the parasite multiplies inside the red blood cells, it produces not just more merozoites, but also *gametocytes,* which are capable of sexual reproduction. This occurs when the parasite moves back into the mosquitoes; even as they inject sporozoites, biting mosquitoes may ingest gametocytes if they are feeding on a person who is already infected. The gametocytes reproduce in the insect's gut and the resulting eggs move into the gut cells. Eventually, more sporozoites emerge from the gut and penetrate the mosquito's salivary glands, where they await a chance to enter another human bloodstream, to begin the cycle again.

Of the roughly 380 mosquito species in the genus *Anopheles,* about 60 are able to transmit malaria to people. These malaria vectors are widespread throughout the tropics and warm temperate zones, and they are very efficient at spreading the disease. Malaria is highly contagious, as is apparent from a measurement that epidemiologists call the "basic reproduction number," or BRN. The BRN indicates, on average, how many new cases a single infected person is likely to cause. For example, among the nonvectored diseases (those in which the pathogen travels directly from person to person without an intermediary like a mosquito), measles is one of the most contagious. The BRN for measles is 12 to 14, meaning that someone with measles is likely to infect 12 to 14 other people. (Luckily, there's an inherent limit in this process: as a pathogen spreads through any particular area, it will encounter fewer and fewer susceptible people who aren't already sick, and the outbreak will eventually subside.) HIV/AIDS is on the other end of the scale: it's deadly, but it burns through a population slowly. Its BRN is just above 1, the minimum necessary for the pathogen's survival. With malaria, the BRN varies considerably, depending on such factors as which mosquito species are present in an area and what the temperatures are. (Warmer is worse, since the parasites mature more quickly.) But malaria can have a BRN in excess of 100: over an adult life that may last about a week, a single, malaria-laden mosquito could conceivably infect more than 100 people.

## Seven Years, Seven Months

"Malaria" comes from the Italian "mal'aria." For centuries, European physicians had attributed the disease to "bad air." Apart from a tradition of associating bad air with swamps—a useful prejudice, given the amount of mosquito habitat in swamps—early medicine was largely ineffective against the disease. It wasn't until 1897 that the British physician Ronald Ross proved that mosquitoes carry malaria.

The practical implications of Ross's discovery did not go unnoticed. For example, the U.S. administration of Theodore Roosevelt recognized malaria and yellow fever (another mosquito-vectored disease) as perhaps the most serious obstacles to the construction of the Panama Canal. This was hardly a surprising conclusion, since the earlier and unsuccessful French attempt to build the canal—an effort that predated Ross's discovery—is thought to have lost between 10,000 and 20,000 workers to disease. So the American workers draped their water supplies and living quarters with mosquito netting, attempted to fill in or drain swamps, installed sewers, poured oil into standing water, and conducted mosquito-swatting campaigns. And it worked: the incidence of malaria declined. In 1906, 80 percent of the workers had the disease; by 1913, a year before the Canal was completed, only 7 percent did. Malaria could be suppressed, it seemed, with a great deal of mosquito netting, and by eliminating as much mosquito habitat as possible. But the labor involved in that effort could be enormous.

That is why DDT proved so appealing. In 1939, the Swiss chemist Paul Müller discovered that this chemical was a potent pesticide. DDT was first used during World War II, as a delousing agent. Later on, areas in southern Europe, North Africa, and Asia were fogged with DDT, to clear malaria-laden mosquitoes from the paths of invading Allied troops. DDT was cheap and it seemed to be harmless to anything other than insects. It was also long-lasting: most other insecticides lost their potency in a few days, but in the early years of its use, the effects of a single dose of DDT could last for up to six months. In 1948, Müller won a Nobel Prize for his work and DDT was hailed as a chemical miracle.

A decade later, DDT had inspired another kind of war—a general assault on malaria. The "Global Malaria Eradication Program," launched in 1955, became one of the first major undertakings of the newly created World Health Organization [WHO]. Some 65 nations enlisted in the cause. Funding for DDT factories was donated to poor countries and production of the insecticide climbed.

The malaria eradication strategy was not to kill every single mosquito, but to suppress their populations and shorten the lifespans of any survivors, so that the parasite would not have time to develop within them. If the mosquitoes could be kept down long enough, the parasites would eventually disappear from the human population. In any particular area, the process was expected to take three years—time enough for all infected people either to recover or die. After that, a resurgence of mosquitoes would be merely an annoyance, rather than a threat. And initially, the strategy seemed to be working. It proved especially effective on islands—relatively small areas insulated from reinfestation. Taiwan, Jamaica, and Sardinia were soon declared malaria-free and have remained so to this day. By 1961, arguably the year at which the program had peak momentum, malaria had been eliminated or dramatically reduced in 37 countries.

One year later, Rachel Carson published *Silent Spring,* her landmark study of the ecological damage caused by the widespread use of DDT and other pesticides. Like other organochlorine pesticides, DDT bioaccumulates. It's fat soluble, so when an animal ingests it—by browsing contaminated vegetation, for example—the chemical tends to concentrate in its fat, instead of being excreted. When another animal eats that animal, it is likely to absorb the prey's burden of DDT. This process leads to an increasing concentration of DDT in the higher links of the food chain. And since DDT has a high chronic toxicity—that is, long-term exposure is likely to cause various physiological abnormalities—this bioaccumulation has profound implications for both ecological and human health.

With the miseries of malaria in full view, the managers of the eradication campaign didn't worry much about the toxicity of DDT, but they were greatly concerned about another aspect of the pesticide's effects: resistance. Continual exposure to an insecticide tends to "breed" insect populations that are at least partially immune to the poison. Resistance to DDT had been reported as early as 1946. The campaign managers knew that in mosquitoes, regular exposure to DDT tended to produce widespread resistance in four to seven years. Since it took three years to clear malaria from a human population, that didn't leave a lot of leeway for the eradication effort. As it turned out, the logistics simply couldn't be made to work in large, heavily infested areas with high human populations, poor housing and roads, and generally minimal infrastructure. In 1969, the campaign was abandoned. Today, DDT resistance is widespread in *Anopheles,* as is resistance to many more recent pesticides.

Undoubtedly, the campaign saved millions of lives, and it did clear malaria from some areas. But its broadest legacy has been of much more dubious value. It engendered the idea of DDT as a first resort against mosquitoes and it established the unstable dynamic of DDT resistance in *Anopheles* populations. In mosquitoes, the genetic mechanism that confers resistance to DDT does not usually come at any great competitive "cost"—that is, when no DDT is being sprayed, the resistant mosquitoes may do just about as well as nonresistant mosquitoes. So once a population acquires resistance, the trait is not likely to disappear even if DDT isn't used for years. If DDT is reapplied to such a population, widespread resistance will reappear very rapidly. The rule of thumb among entomologists is that you may get seven years of resistance-free use the first time around, but you only get about seven months the second time. Even that limited respite, however, is enough to make the chemical an attractive option as an emergency measure—or to keep it in the arsenals of bureaucracies committed to its use.

## Malaria Taxes

In December 2000, the POPs Treaty negotiators convened in Johannesburg, South Africa, even though, by an unfortunate coincidence, South Africa had suffered a potentially embarrassing setback earlier that year in its own POPs policies. In 1996, South Africa had switched its mosquito control programs from DDT to a less persistent group of pesticides known as pyrethroids. The move seemed solid and supportable at the time, since years of DDT use had greatly reduced *Anopheles* populations and largely eliminated one of the most troublesome local vectors, the appropriately named *A. funestus* ("funestus" means deadly). South Africa seemed to have beaten the DDT habit: the chemical had been used to achieve a worthwhile objective; it had then been discarded. And the plan worked—until a year before the POPs summit, when malaria infections rose to 61,000 cases, a level not seen in decades. *A. funestus* reappeared as well, in KwaZulu-Natal, and in a form resistant to pyrethroids. In early 2000, DDT was reintroduced, in an indoor spraying program. (This is now a standard way of using DDT for mosquito control; the pesticide is usually applied only to walls, where mosquitoes alight to rest.) By the middle of the year, the number of infections had dropped by half.

Initially, the spraying program was criticized, but what reasonable alternative was there? This is said to be the African predicament, and yet the South African situation is hardly representative of sub-Saharan Africa as a whole.

Malaria is considered endemic in 105 countries throughout the tropics and warm temperate zones, but by far the worst region for the disease is sub-Saharan Africa. The deadliest of the four parasite species, *Plasmodium falciparum,* is widespread throughout this region, as is one of the world's most effective malaria vectors, *Anopheles gambiae.* Nearly half the population of sub-Saharan Africa is at risk of infection, and in much of eastern and central Africa, and pockets of west Africa, it would be difficult to find anyone who has not been exposed to the parasites. Some 90 percent of the world's malaria infections and deaths occur in sub-Saharan Africa, and the disease now accounts for 30 percent of African childhood mortality. It is true that malaria is a grave problem in many parts of the world, but the African experience is misery on a very different order of magnitude. The average Tanzanian suffers more infective bites each *night* than the average Thai or Vietnamese does in a year.

As a broad social burden, malaria is thought to cost Africa between $3 billion and $12 billion annually. According to one economic analysis, if the disease had been eradicated in 1965, Africa's GDP would now be 35 percent higher than it currently is. Africa was also the gaping hole in the global eradication program: the WHO planners thought there was little they could do on the continent and limited efforts to Ethiopia, Zimbabwe, and South Africa, where eradication was thought to be feasible.

But even though the campaign largely passed Africa by, DDT has not. Many African countries have used DDT for mosquito control in indoor spraying programs, but the primary use of DDT on the continent has been as an agricultural insecticide. Consequently, in parts of west Africa especially, DDT resistance is now widespread in *A. gambiae.* But even if *A. gambiae* were not resistant, a full-bore campaign to suppress it would probably accomplish little, because this mosquito is so efficient at transmitting malaria. Unlike most *Anopheles* species, *A. gambiae* specializes in human blood, so even a small population would keep the disease in circulation. One way to get a sense for this problem is to consider the "transmission index"—the threshold number of mosquito bites necessary to perpetuate the disease. In Africa, the index overall is 1 bite per person per month. That's all that's necessary to keep malaria in circulation. In India, by comparison, the TI is 10 bites per person per month.

And yet Africa is not a lost cause—it's simply that the key to progress does not lie in the general suppression of mosquito populations. Instead of spraying, the most promising African programs rely primarily on "bednets"—mosquito netting that is treated with an insecticide, usually a pyrethroid, and that is suspended over a person's bed. Bednets can't eliminate malaria, but they can "deflect" much of the burden. Because *Anopheles* species generally feed in the evening and at night, a bednet can radically reduce the number of infective bites a person receives. Such a person would probably still be infected from time to time, but would usually be able to lead a normal life.

In effect, therefore, bednets can substantially reduce the disease. Trials in the use of bednets for children have shown a decline in malaria-induced mortality by 25 to 40 percent. Infection levels and the incidence of severe anemia also declined. In Kenya, a recent study has shown that pregnant women who use bednets tend to give birth to healthier babies. In parts of Chad, Mali, Burkina Faso, and Senegal, bednets are becoming standard household items. In the tiny west African nation of The Gambia, somewhere between 50 and 80 percent of the population has bednets.

Bednets are hardly a panacea. They have to be used properly and retreated with insecticide occasionally. And there is still the problem of insecticide resistance, although the nets themselves are hardly likely to be the main cause of it. (Pyrethroids are used extensively in agriculture as well.) Nevertheless, bednets can help transform malaria from a chronic disaster to a manageable public health problem—something a healthcare system can cope with.

So it's unfortunate that in much of central and southern Africa, the nets are a rarity. It's even more unfortunate that, in 28 African countries, they're taxed or subject to import tariffs. Most of the people in these countries would have trouble paying for a net even without the tax. This problem was addressed in the May 2000 "Abuja Declaration," a summit agreement on infectious diseases signed by 44 African countries. The Declaration included a pledge to do away with "malaria taxes." At last count, 13 countries have actually acted on the pledge, although in some cases only by reducing rather than eliminating the taxes. Since the Declaration was signed, an estimated 2 to 5 million Africans have died from malaria.

This failure to follow through with the Abuja Declaration casts the interest in DDT in a rather poor light. Of the 31 POPs treaty signatories that have reserved the right to use DDT, 21 are in Africa. Of those 21, 10 are apparently still taxing or imposing tariffs on bednets. (Among the African countries that have *not* signed the POPs treaty, some are almost certainly both using DDT and taxing bednets, but the exact number is difficult to ascertain because the status of DDT use is not always clear.) It is true that a case can be made for the use of DDT in situations like the one in South Africa in 1999—an infrequent flare-up in a context that lends itself to control. But the routine use of DDT against malaria is an exercise in toxic futility, especially when it's pursued at the expense of a superior and far more benign technology.

## Learning to Live with the Mosquitoes

A group of French researchers recently announced some very encouraging results for a new anti-malarial drug known as G25. The drug was given to infected aotus monkeys, and it appears to have cleared the parasites from their systems. Although extensive testing will be necessary before it is known whether the drug can be safely given to people, these results have raised the hope of a cure for the disease.

Of course, it would be wonderful if G25, or some other new drug, lives up to that promise. But even in the absence of a cure, there are opportunities for progress that may one day make the current incidence of malaria look like some dark age horror. Many of these opportunities have been incorporated into an initiative that began in 1998, called the Roll Back Malaria (RBM) campaign, a collaborative effort between WHO, the World Bank, UNICEF, and the UNDP [United Nations Development Programme]. In contrast to the earlier WHO eradication program, RBM grew out of joint efforts between WHO and various African governments specifically to address African malaria. RBM focuses on household- and community-level intervention and it emphasizes apparently modest changes that could yield major progress. Below are four "operating principles" that are, in one way or another, implicit in RBM or likely to reinforce its progress.

1. Do away with all taxes and tariffs on bednets, on pesticides intended for treating bednets, and on antimalarial drugs. Failure to act on this front certainly undercuts claims for the necessity of DDT; it may also undercut claims for antimalaria foreign aid.

2. Emphasize appropriate technologies. Where, for example, the need for mud to replaster walls is creating lots of pothole sized cavities near houses—cavities that fill with water and then with mosquito larvae—it makes more sense to help people improve their housing maintenance than it does to set up a program for squirting pesticide into every pothole. To be "appropriate," a technology has to be both affordable and culturally acceptable. Improving home maintenance should pass this test; so should bednets. And of course there are many other possibilities. In Kenya, for example, a research institution called the International Center for Insect Physiology and Ecology has identified at least a dozen native east African plants that repel *Anopheles gambiae* in lab tests. Some of these plants could be important additions to household gardens.

3. Use existing networks whenever possible, instead of building new ones. In Tanzania, for example, an established healthcare program (UNICEF's Integrated Management of Childhood Illness Program) now dispenses antimalarial drugs—and instruction on how to use them. The UNICEF program was already operating, so it was simple and cheap to add the malaria component. Reported instances of severe malaria and anemia in infants have declined, apparently as a result. In Zambia, the government is planning to use health and prenatal clinics as the network for a coupon system that subsidizes bednets for the poor. Qualifying patients would pick up coupons at the clinics and redeem them at stores for the nets.

4. Assume that sound policy will involve action on many fronts. Malaria is not just a health problem—it's a social problem, an economic problem, an environmental problem, an agricultural problem, an urban planning problem. Health officials alone cannot possibly just make it go away. When the disease flares up, there is a strong and understandable temptation to strap on the spray equipment and douse the mosquitoes. But if this approach actually worked, we wouldn't be in this situation today. Arguably the biggest opportunity for progress against the disease lies, not in our capacity for chemical innovation, but in our capacity for *organizational innovation*—in our ability to build an awareness of the threat across a broad range of policy activities. For example, when government officials are considering loans to irrigation projects, they should be asking: has the potential for malaria been addressed? When foreign donors are designing antipoverty programs, they should be asking: do people need bednets? Routine inquiries of this sort could go a vast distance to reducing the disease.

Where is the DDT in all of this? There isn't any, and that's the point. We now have half a century of evidence that routine use of DDT simply will not prevail against the mosquitoes. Most countries have already absorbed this lesson, and banned the chemical or relegated it to emergency only status. Now the RBM campaign and associated efforts are showing that the frequency and intensity of those emergencies can be reduced through systematic attention to the chronic aspects of the disease. There is less and less justification for DDT, and the futility of using it as a matter of routine is becoming increasingly apparent: in order to control a disease, why should we poison our soils, our waters, and ourselves?

# NO 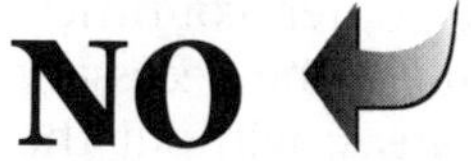

**Roger Bate**

# A Case of the DDTs

Militants from Greenpeace have been mounting protests in an effort to close down the only major DDT-production facility in the world, located in Cochin, India. The protesters won't be getting any support from Jocchonia Gumede, a domestic servant in Johannesburg, South Africa: In the past two years, six of Jocchonia's close relatives have died from malaria. His family lives in northern KwaZulu Natal, where malaria has always been endemic—Jocchonia himself contracted it twice while growing up—and DDT is simply the cheapest and most effective way to combat this dread disease.

Malaria is now on the increase, not just in Africa but in all tropical regions of the planet. It afflicted well over 300 million people last year, and killed over 1 million. Prof. Wen Kilama of the African Malaria Vaccine Testing Network in Tanzania characterizes the death toll as "equivalent to crashing seven jumbo jets filled with children every day."

That's a devastating human cost. And it has far-reaching consequences, beyond even the sad plight of the sufferers and the huge burden the disease imposes on health resources. In many countries, the disease is also clouding the long-term economic future: When people are unable to work effectively because of illness, productivity suffers—and this, in turn, scares away investors. Professor Jeffrey Sachs of the Harvard Center for International Development estimates that every year, malaria destroys around 1 percent of the wealth—not just income, but *total wealth*—of Africa.

Given such devastating human and economic costs, one might expect the "international community" to be fighting malaria with all its might. But the chief effort of the world's politicians has been to try force developing countries to abandon their best weapon in the fight against malaria—the pesticide dichlorodiphenyl-trichloroethane, known commonly as DDT. The United Nations is actually promoting a treaty that might ban the use of DDT globally—and on April 18 [2001], President Bush agreed to sign the treaty.

This is absurd, because DDT is the proven solution to malaria. Today malaria is a tropical disease, but until the 1920s it was endemic all over Europe and America. Epidemics were found as far north as Archangel in the Russian Arctic Circle, and occurred regularly in Holland and England. After World War II, Europe and North America eradicated it with DDT. The pesticide saved countless millions of lives by killing the malarial mosquito, but it never had complete success in some of the world's poorer countries, because their governments lacked the capacity to implement the necessary spraying programs and removal of mosquito breeding areas; without the appropriate medical and organizational ability, even the best sprays won't be effective in eradicating a disease. Then, in the late 1960s, environmentalists started to complain about DDT, and it was removed from the malaria-control program in many countries; some 20 countries—most in Africa—continued to use it.

According to Donald Roberts, a professor of tropical public health at the Uniformed Services University of the Health Sciences, the huge drop in the number of houses sprayed with DDT has had severe consequences: From the mid 1980s to the mid 1990s, Latin America experienced an annual increase of more than 1.8 million malaria cases (more than 4.8 per 1,000 people)—and the rate has continued to grow since 1996. Ecuador, however, continued to use DDT, and its malaria rate *fell* over the period 1988–97.

Other mosquito-borne diseases are also on the rise. Until the 1970s, DDT was used to eradicate the *Aedes aegypti* mosquito from most tropical regions of the Americas. A new invasion of *Aedes aegypti* has since brought devastating outbreaks of dengue fever and a renewed threat of urban yellow fever. Roberts says the international anti-DDT groups, with what he calls their "high-pressure tactics," bear some responsibility for this public-health disaster.

About 40 years ago, suspicions about DDT—inspired by Rachel Carson's book *Silent Spring*—sparked the first green crusade. When it was used in vast quantities in agriculture, DDT probably did harm reproduction in birds of prey. (This harm subsequently proved reversible.) But after decades of research, there is not one replicated study that shows any harm to human beings at all. Furthermore, DDT is now only sprayed inside houses. Dr. Amir Attaran, a researcher at Harvard's Center for International Development, estimates that the amount of DDT used to spray a few acres of cotton in America in the early 1960s would be enough to spray all the homes in Guyana of those at risk of malaria. Such indoor spraying, he concludes, would have "negligible impacts on the environment." Even Green presidential nominee Ralph Nader has come out in favor of DDT use.

Undeterred, Greenpeace continues to try to shut down the Indian DDT factory—and, in effect, to prevent some of the world's poorest countries from using the least expensive method of eradicating malaria. [Recently], the Indian government gave an assurance to Greenpeace that production would cease in 2005—but officials of that country's anti-malaria program, which has used DDT since 1953, objected to this commitment; the government may make an embarrassing but felicitous U-turn. (There is precedent for such a switch. In 1996, South Africa stopped using DDT, and the death rate from malaria rose by around 1,000 percent. In desperation, the country has returned to using the pesticide.)

There are other pesticides that work against malaria, but they are at least twice—and sometimes up to 20 times—as expensive, and none is as effective a repellent. These substitutes are less persistent than DDT—they don't linger in the environment as long—and this is what makes them so attractive to the greens. But when you are using pesticides indoors, a persistent material is better: It means you might have to spray only once a year—and to a poor country, this kind of cost consideration could make all the difference.

Despite these basic facts of science and economics, international-pesticide-treaty negotiators decided . . . to restrict the use of DDT. Their decision is not final; they will meet again in Sweden . . . , when environmental ministers are expected to sign a final text. It may get worse between now and then; the negotiators may yet decide to replace the restrictions with an outright ban. But even the restrictions demanded under the existing draft will be onerous for the poorest countries, some of which have health budgets of less than $5 per person per year (rich countries spend well over 400 times this amount on health care). Even worse, many countries have been coming under pressure from international health and environment agencies to give up DDT or face losing aid grants: Belize and Bolivia are on record admitting they gave in to pressure on this issue from the U.S. Agency for International Development.

South Africa has asked for an exemption from the DDT restrictions. Jocchonia Gumede reports that the number of mosquitoes is down since DDT was reintroduced in February 2000. He is cautiously optimistic that the situation will improve, but his quick smile belies the anguish that he feels. Jocchonia was not aware of the reason for the removal of DDT, nor is he aware of the debate surrounding whether to ban the substance outright. He is simply one of countless millions around the world whose health and prosperity depend, ominously, on sensible decision-making by global bureaucrats.

# POSTSCRIPT

## Should DDT Be Banned Worldwide?

Over and over again, the debates over environmental issues come down to which we should do first: Should we meet human needs regardless of whether or not species die and air and water are contaminated? Or should we protect species, air, water, and other aspects of the environment even if some human needs must go unmet? What if this means endangering the lives of children? In the debate over DDT, the human needs are clear, for insect-borne diseases have killed and continue to kill a great many people. Yet the environmental needs are also clear. The question is one of choosing priorities and balancing risks. See John Danley, "Balancing Risks: Mosquitoes, Malaria, Morality, and DDT," *Business and Society Review* (Spring 2002).

Mosquitoes can be controlled in various ways: Swamps can be drained (which carries its own environmental price), and other breeding opportunities can be eliminated. Fish can be introduced to eat mosquito larvae. And mosquito nets can be used to keep the insects away from people. But these (and other) alternatives do not mean that there does not remain a place for chemical pesticides. In "Pesticides and Public Health: Integrated Methods of Mosquito Management," *Emerging Infectious Diseases* (January–February 2001), Robert I. Rose, an arthropod biotechnologist with the Animal and Plant Health Inspection Service of the U.S. Department of Agriculture, says, "Pesticides have a role in public health as part of sustainable integrated mosquito management. Other components of such management include surveillance, source reduction or prevention, biological control, repellents, traps, and pesticide-resistance management."

Gordon S. Jones, "The Destructive Legacy of Rachel Carson," *Human Events* (August 26, 2002), blames Carson for millions of deaths from malaria that could have been stopped with DDT. Alexander Gourevitch, "Better Living through Chemistry," *Washington Monthly* (March 2003) covered the conflict between malaria-fighters and environmentalists well, noting that "African governments know what they need to do to control malaria—they just need the money." In May 2003, U.S. President George W. Bush signed an aid package giving $15 billion to fight disease in Africa. The package included aid for antimalaria programs but did not explicitly authorize the use of DDT. Critics immediately objected, saying that it is unfair to apply Western environmental standards and withhold support for something that works as well as DDT. See Nicole Itano, "Push to Fund DDT in Fight Against Malaria in Africa," *Christian Science Monitor* (May 29, 2003). *The Economist* ("Africa's Other Plague," May 3, 2003) noted that $1.5–$2.5 billion in aid per year could cut the death toll in half by 2010.

Researchers have long sought a vaccine against malaria, but the parasite has demonstrated a persistent talent for evading all attempts to arm the immune system against it. The difficulties are covered by Thomas L. Richie and Allan Saul in "Progress and Challenges for Malaria Vaccines," *Nature* (February 7, 2002). Early in 2003, a new vaccine for humans was looking good; see David Lawrence, "Combination Malaria Vaccine Shows Early Promise in Human Trials," *Lancet (Elsevier)* (May 2003). A newer approach is to develop genetically engineered (transgenic) mosquitoes that either cannot support the malaria parasite or cannot infect humans with it; see Jane Bradbury, "Transgenic Mosquitoes Bring Malarial Control Closer," *The Lancet* (May 25, 2002).

It is worth stressing that malaria is only one of several mosquito-borne diseases that pose threats to public health. Two others are yellow fever and dengue. A recent arrival to the United States is West Nile virus, which mosquitoes can transfer from birds to humans. However, West Nile virus is far less fatal than malaria, yellow fever, or dengue, and a vaccine is in development. See Dwight G. Smith, "A New Disease in the New World," *The World & I* (February 2002) and Peter Jaret, "West Nile," *Reader's Digest* (June 2003). According to Howard Shapiro and Sandra Micucci, fighting West Nile could require pesticides, just as does fighting malaria; see "Pesticide Use for West Nile Virus," *CMAJ: Canadian Medical Association Journal* (May 27, 2003).

It is also worth stressing that global warming means climate changes that may increase the geographic range of disease-carrying mosquitoes. Many climate researchers are concerned that malaria, yellow fever, and other now mostly tropical and subtropical diseases may return to temperate-zone nations and even spread into areas where they have never been known. See P. R. Hunter, "Climate Change and Waterborne and Vector-Borne Diseases," *Journal of Applied Microbiology* (May 2003 Supplement).

# On the Internet . . .

## National Aeronautics and Space Administration

At this site, you can find out the latest information on the International Space Shuttle, space exploration, and other space-related news.

http://www.nasa.gov

## Mars Exploration

This NASA Web site provides a host of links related to Mars exploration and colonization.

http://nssdc.gsfc.nasa.gov/planetary/mars_colonize_terraform.html

## SETI Institute

The SETI Institute serves as a home for scientific research in the general field of life in the universe, with an emphasis on the search for extraterrestrial intelligence (SETI).

http://www.seti-inst.edu

## SETI League

The SETI League, Inc., is dedicated to the electromagnetic (radio) search for extraterrestrial intelligence.

http://seti1.setileague.org

## Near-Earth Objects

This site provides a list of upcoming close approaches to Earth.

http://neo.jpl.nasa.gov/

## Space News

For the very latest in what's happening . . .

http://spacedaily.com/

# PART 4

## Space

*Many interesting controversies arise in connection with technologies that are so new that they often sound more like science fiction than fact. Some examples are technologies that allow the exploration of outer space, the search for extraterrestrial intelligence, and genetic engineering. Such advances offer capabilities undreamed of in earlier ages, and they raise genuine, important questions about what it is to be a human being, the limits on human freedom in a technological age, and the place of humanity in the broader universe. They also raise questions of how we should respond: Should we accept the new devices and abilities offered by scientists and engineers? Or should we reject them? Should we use them to make human life safer and more secure? Or should we remain at the mercy of the heavens?*

- Should We Expand Efforts to Find Near-Earth Objects?
- Is the Search for Extraterrestrial Life Doomed to Fail?
- Should NASA Continue to Pursue Manned Space Exploration?

# ISSUE 11

## Should We Expand Efforts to Find Near-Earth Objects?

**YES: Joseph Burns,** from *Statement (for the National Research Council) before House Committee on Science* (October 3, 2002)

**NO: Edward Weiler,** from *Statement before House Committee on Science* (October 3, 2002)

### ISSUE SUMMARY

**YES:** Professor of Engineering and Astronomy Joseph Burns contests that the hazards posed to life on Earth by near-Earth objects (NEOs) are great enough to justify increased efforts to detect and catalog NEOs. Scientific benefits may also be expected.

**NO:** Edward Weiler asserts that NASA's present efforts to detect the larger and more hazardous NEOs are adequate. It is premature to expand the program.

Thomas Jefferson once said that he would rather think scientists were crazy than believe that rocks could fall from the sky. Since then, we have recognized that rocks do indeed fall from the sky. Most are quite small and do no more than make pretty streaks across the sky as they burn up in the atmosphere; they are known as meteors. Some—known as meteorites—are large enough to reach the ground and even to do damage. Every once in a while, the news reports one that crashed through a car or house roof. Very rarely, a meteorite is big enough to make a crater in the Earth's surface, much like the ones that mark the face of the Moon. An example is Meteor Crater in Arizona, almost a mile across, created some 20,000 to 50,000 years ago by a meteorite 80 feet in diameter. (The Meteor Crater Web site, `http://www.meteorcrater.com/`, includes an animation of the impact.) A more impressive impact is the one that occurred 65 million years ago; the scar has been found at Chicxulub, Mexico: The results included the extinction of the dinosaurs (as well as a great many other species). Chicxulub-scale events are very rare; a hundred million years may pass between them. Meteor Crater–scale events may occur every thousand years, releasing as much energy as a

100-megaton nuclear bomb and destroying an area the size of a city. And it has been calculated that a human being is more likely to die as the result of such an event than in an airplane crash.

It's not just Hollywood sci-fi, *Deep Impact* and *Armageddon*. Some people think we really should be worried. We should be doing our best to identify meteoroids (as they are called before they become meteors or meteorites) in space, plot their trajectories, tell when they are coming our way, and even develop ways of deflecting them before they cause enormous loss of life. In 1984, Thomas Gehrels, a University of Arizona astronomer, initiated the Spacewatch project, which aimed to identify space rocks that cross Earth's orbit. In the early 1990s, NASA workshops considered the hazards of these rocks. NASA now funds the international Spaceguard Survey, which finds about 25 new near-Earth Asteroids every month, and has identified more than 600 over 1 kilometer in diameter (1000 meters; 1.6 km equals 1 mile); none seem likely to strike Earth in the next century. See Peter Tyson, "Comet Busters," *Technology Review* (February/March 1995), Duncan Steel, *Target Earth: How Rogue Asteroids and Doomsday Comets Threaten our Planet* (Reader's Digest Association, 2000), and David Morrison, "Target Earth," *Astronomy* (February 2002). However, the news periodically issues alarming reports; David Whitehouse, "Space Rock 'On Collision Course,'" BBC News Online (July 24, 2002), noted the discovery of a 2-kilometer-wide asteroid on a course that could strike Earth in 2019 (the initial projection did not pan out). Leon Jaroff, "A Near Miss from Outer Space," *Time* (January 21, 2002), described a thousand-foot rock that missed Earth by only 500,000 miles (just a whisker in astronomical terms). Other news items have noted the discovery of asteroids only as they recede from Earth after a near-miss.

Professor of engineering and astronomy Joseph Burns argues that the hazards posed to life on Earth by near-Earth objects (NEOs) are large. NEOs less than 300 meters (about 1,000 feet) in diameter can cause enormous numbers of deaths, and there is about a 1 percent chance of such a disaster in every century. Increased efforts to detect and catalog NEOs are justified. The same efforts would increase scientific knowledge of the solar system. Edward Weiler argues that only larger objects, over 1 kilometer in diameter, pose truly serious, global risks. NASA's present efforts have focused on those objects and are adequate. It is premature to expand the program before public discussion settles the question of where to set the cutoff point between NEOs "big enough" and "too small" to worry about.

**Joseph Burns**

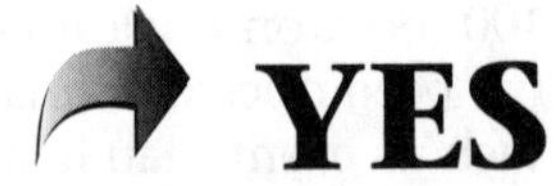


# The Threat of Near-Earth Asteroids, October 2002

## Statement of Joseph Burns (for the National Research Council)

. . . [T]he Astronomy and Astrophysics community has a long history of creating, through the National Research Council (NRC), decadal surveys of their field. These surveys lay out the community's research goals for the next decade, identify key questions that need to be answered, and propose new facilities with which to conduct this fundamental research.

In April 2001, NASA Associate Administrator for Space Science Edward Weiler asked the NRC to conduct a similar survey for planetary exploration. Our report, New Frontiers in the Solar System, is the result of that activity. The Solar System Exploration Survey was conducted by an ad hoc committee of the Space Studies Board (SSB), overseen by COMPLEX. This committee was comprised of some 50 scientists, drawn from a diverse set of institutions, research areas, and backgrounds; it also received input from more than 300 colleagues. The SSE Survey had four subpanels which focused on issues pertaining to different types of solar system bodies (Inner Planets, Giant Planets, Large Satellites, and Primitive Bodies) and received direct input from COMPLEX on Mars issues and from the Committee on the Origins and Evolution of Life on issues pertaining to Astrobiology.

New Frontiers in the Solar System (the Executive Summary is appended to this statement) recommends a scientific and exploration strategy for NASA's Office of Space Science that will both enable dramatic new discoveries in this decade and position the agency to continue to make such discoveries well into the future. Your invitation indicated that I should focus on the conclusions that the SSE Survey reached in the area of Near-Earth Objects (NEOs).

### Near-Earth Objects

The SSE Survey's charge from NASA included a request to summarize the extent of our current understanding of the solar system. This task was delegated to the subpanels, which in the particular case of NEOs was handled by the Primitive Bodies Panel.

From a Statement before the House Committee on Science, October 3, 2002.

Scientifically, the history of impacts on the Earth is vital for understanding how the planet evolved and how life arose. For example, it has been suggested that a majority of the water on this planet was delivered by comet impacts. A better known example of the role of impacts is the Cretaceous-Tertiary event that led to global mass extinctions, including that of the dinosaurs. Another case is the 20 megaton (MT) equivalent-energy explosion that devastated 2000 square-kilometers of pine forest in the Siberian tundra in 1908. The SSE Survey identifies the exploration of the terrestrial space environment with regards to potential hazards as a new goal for the nation's solar system exploration enterprise.

Current surveys have identified an estimated 50 percent of NEOs that have a diameter of 1 kilometer or greater and approximately 10–15 percent of objects between 0.5 and 1 km. The vast majority of these latter objects have yet to be discovered, but a statistical analysis indicates a 1% probability of impact by a 300-m body in the next century. Such an object would deliver 1000 MT of energy, cause regional devastation, and (assuming an average of 10 people per square-kilometer on Earth) result in 100,000 fatalities. The damage caused by an impact near a city or into a coastal ocean would be orders of magnitude higher. As of a year ago, 340 objects larger than a kilometer had been catalogued as Potentially Hazardous Asteroids. In addition, the number of undiscovered comets with impact potential is large and unknown.

The Primitive Bodies panel went on to state: "Important scientific goals are associated with the NEO populations, including their origin, fragmentation and dynamical histories, and compositions and differentiation. These and other scientific issues are also vital to the mitigation of the impact hazard (emphasis added), as methods of deflection of objects potentially on course for an impact with Earth are explored. Information especially relevant to hazard mitigation includes knowledge of the internal structures of near-Earth asteroids and comets, their degree of fracture and the presence of large core pieces, the fractal dimensions of their structures, and their degree of cohesion or friction."

While almost all of the SSE Survey's recommendations involved NASA flight missions, the Primitive Bodies subpanel recommended that ground-based telescopes be used to do a majority of the study of NEOs, supplemented by airborne and orbital telescopes.

A survey for NEOs demands an exacting observational strategy. To locate NEOs as small as 300 m requires a survey down to 24th magnitude (16 million times fainter than the feeblest stars that are visible to the naked eye). If images are to be taken every 10 sec to allow the sky to be studied often, the necessary capability is almost 100 times better than that of existing survey telescopes. NEOs spend only a fraction of each orbit in Earth's neighborhood, where they are most easily seen. Repeated observations over a decade would be required to explore the full volume of space populated by these objects. Such a survey would identify several hundred NEOs per night and obtain astrometric (positional) measurements on the much larger (and growing) number of NEOs that it had already discovered. Precise astrometry is needed to determine the orbital parameters of the NEOs and to assign a hazard assessment to each object. Astrometry at monthly intervals would ensure against losing track of these fast-moving objects in the months and years after discovery.

**Large-Aperture Synoptic Survey Telescope** In its most recent decadal survey, the Astronomy and Astrophysics community selected the proposed Large-aperture Synoptic Survey Telescope (LSST) as their third major ground-based priority. In addition, our SSE Survey chose LSST to be its top-ranked ground-based facility. Telescopes like HST and Keck peer at selected, very localized regions of the sky or study individual sources with high sensitivity. However, another type of telescope is needed to survey the entire sky relatively quickly, so that periodic maps can be constructed that will reveal not only the positions of target sources, but their time variability as well. The Large-aperture Synoptic Survey Telescope is a 6.5-m-effective-diameter, very wide field (~3 deg) telescope that will produce a digital map of the visible sky every week. For this type of survey observation, the LSST will be a hundred times more powerful than the Keck telescopes, the world's largest at present. Not only will LSST carry out an optical survey of the sky far deeper than any previous survey, but also—just as importantly—it will also add the new dimension of time and thereby open up a new realm of discovery. By surveying the sky each month for over a decade, LSST would revolutionize our understanding of various topics in astronomy concerning objects whose brightnesses vary on time scales of days to years. NEOs, which drift across a largely unchanging sky, are easily identified. The LSST could locate 90 percent of all near-Earth objects down to 300 m in size, enable computations of their orbits, and permit assessment of their threat to Earth. In addition, this facility could be used to discover and track objects in the Kuiper Belt, a largely unexplored, primordial component of our solar system. It would discover and monitor a wide variety of variable objects, such as the optical afterglows of gamma-ray bursts. In addition, it would find approximately 100,000 supernovae per year, and be useful for many other cosmological observations.

The detectors of choice for the temporal monitoring tasks would be thinned charge-coupled devices (CCDs); the requisite extrapolation from existing systems should constitute only a small technological risk. An infrared capability of a comparably wide field would be considerably more challenging but could evolve as the second phase of the telescope's operation. Instrumentation for LSST would be an ideal way to involve independent observatories with this basically public facility.

## NASA/NSF Cooperation

Historically, the National Science Foundation (NSF) has built and operated ground-based telescopes, whereas NASA has done the same for space-based observatories. Although the Astronomy and Astrophysics Survey was noncommittal on who should build the LSST, the SSE Survey included a recommendation that NASA share equally with NSF in the telescope's construction and operations costs.

Such an arrangement has precedent. The SSE Survey noted that "NASA continues to play a major role in supporting the use of Earth-based optical telescopes for planetary studies. It funds the complete operations of the IRTF (InfraRed Telescope Facility), a 3-m diameter telescope located on Hawaii's Mauna Kea. In return for access to 50 percent of the observing time for non-solar-system observations, the NSF supports the development of IRTF's instrumentation. This telescope has provided vital data in support of flight missions and will continue to do so. As another example, NASA currently buys one-sixth of the observing time on the privately operated Keck 10-m telescopes. This time was purchased to test interferometric techniques in support of future spaceflight missions such as SIM (Space Interferometry Mission) and TPF (Terrestrial Planet Finder)."

The solar system exploration community is concerned that the NSF is often unwilling to fund solar system research. This is particularly unfortunate given NSF's charter to support the best science and its leadership role in other aspects of ground-based astronomy.

The shared responsibility between NASA and the NSF that we recommend is also endorsed by the more general findings last year of the NRC's Committee on the Organization and Management of Research in Astronomy and Astrophysics (COMRAA), chaired by Norman Augustine. COMRAA's report recommended that NASA continue to "support critical ground-based facilities and scientifically enabling precursor and follow-up observations that are essential to the success of space missions." COMRAA also noted that in 1980 the NSF provided most of the research grants in astronomy and astrophysics, but today NASA is the major supporter of such research.

The roles of the agencies also affect the ability of scientists to conduct a census of Near-Earth Objects. The SSE Survey commented that:

"interestingly enough, NASA has no systematic survey-capability to discover the population distribution of the solar-system bodies. To do this, NASA relies on research grants to individual observers who must gain access to their own facilities. The large NEOs are being efficiently discovered using small telescopes for which NASA provides instrumentation funding, but all the other solar system populations—e.g., comets, Centaurs, satellites of the outer planets, and Kuiper Belt Objects—are being characterized almost entirely using non-NASA facilities. This is a major deficiency . . ."

The construction of the LSST would provide a central, federally sponsored location for such research.

**LSST Costs and Survey Below 300 Meters** The costs of the LSST are projected by the 2001 Astronomy and Astrophysics Survey as being $83 million for capital construction and $42 million for data processing and distribution for 5 years of operation, for a total cost of $125 million. Routine operating costs, including a technical and support staff of 20 people, are estimated at approximately $3 million per year. The LSST will be able to routinely discover and characterize NEOs down to 300 m in diameter. Increasing the sensitivity of the survey to 100 m would mean increasing the sensitivity of the telescope by a factor of ten. This may represent a "beyond the state-of-the-art" challenge to telescope builder, and certainly a much larger telescope—3 times the LSST and probably 10 to 100 times the cost unless innovative designs are found. The number of discovered objects would correspondingly increase substantially; this large data set may challenge current capabilities.

**Concluding Thoughts** By way of summary, let me place the LSST into the context of a robust scientific program. Systematically building an inventory of the Near-Earth Objects is crucial to an improved understanding of Earth's environment, especially to the prediction of future hazards posed to our species. It is also a necessary first step towards a rational program of NASA's exploration of these bodies with spacecraft: many of the most interesting targets may remain, as yet, undiscovered. The ability to create and play a "motion picture" of the night sky will also provide new insights in a wide variety of disciplines from cosmology to astrophysics to solar system exploration. A suitable analog might be the deepened knowledge that is obtained from dynamic movies of swirling clouds and weather patterns, as compared to an occasional static photo.

The immense volume of data from the LSST would provide a reservoir of information for numerous graduate students and researchers, as well as established scientists. Further, LSST will support flight missions—for example, identifying possible fly-by targets for a spacecraft mission to explore the Kuiper Belt. All in all, the SSE Survey committee believes that broad areas of planetary science, particularly NEO studies, would benefit very substantially from the construction of the LSST for a relatively small investment. . . .

NO 

**Edward Weiler**

# The Threat of Near-Earth Asteroids, October 2002

## Statement of Edward Weiler

NASA's NEO Program makes ground-based observations with the goal of identifying 90 percent of those NEOs that are 1 km or larger and characterizing a sample of them. This is a ten-year program, which began in 1998 and should be completed in 2008. (It should be noted that NASA had begun searching for NEOs many years before this program officially started.)

The threshold size for an asteroid striking the Earth to produce a global catastrophe is 1 km in diameter. NASA has an active program to detect such objects that could potentially strike the Earth and to identify their orbits. The best current estimates are that the total population of NEOs with diameters larger than 1 km is about 1000. The 1-km diameter limit for an NEO was set after extensive discussions within the scientific community to determine the size of an object that would likely threaten civilization. This community consensus is codified in the Spaceguard Report and in the Shoemaker Report. For comparison, the object that likely caused the extinction of the dinosaurs was in the 5–10 km range. The current survey of NEOs in that range is considered complete.

### Status: NASA's NEO Search Program

As of the end of September, NASA has detected 619 NEOs with diameters larger than 1 km. We are currently discovering about 100 per year. At the present time, we have six groups which are funded by NASA's Near Earth Objects program to conduct this type of research. These groups, selected though peer review, have ten telescopes among them searching for NEOs. One of these groups just completed (and another one is about to complete) major upgrades to its facility; therefore, we expect this pace of discovery to continue, if not increase. In some cases, the search programs are not able to obtain the number of observations required to determine the orbit elements of certain objects to sufficient accuracy to fully characterize the orbital parameters. These objects require additional astrometric observations, commonly called "follow-up observations." We have also funded four investigations to obtain

From a Statement before the House Committee on Science, October 3, 2002.

astrometric follow-up observations of those objects that cannot be easily followed by the primary search programs.

Now, how well are we doing? I am happy to report that we are doing quite well; in fact, we are even a bit ahead of schedule.

There have been various reports to the effect that NASA would not reach its metric—90 percent of all the NEOs with diameters larger than 1 km—until many years after the end of 2008. However, these analyses have been based on the performance of individual search efforts, and they have tended not to use the current performance of the NEO search effort as a whole. As with most things, experience increases proficiency; therefore, we expect the rate of detection to increase. Even if we were to stay at our current rate, however, we are more than halfway to our goal of 90 percent by the end of 2008.

That does not mean we will grow complacent; we intend to continue to vigorously pursue detection of NEOs. In fact, we anticipate even better results due to technological developments such as better detector arrays, migration of existing search efforts to larger telescopes, and additional telescopes dedicated to the search program. In short, we are working to achieve both our goal and our metric and expect to be successful at both. One unanticipated result of the NEO search will be a list of over 1,000 potential candidates for future space science missions.

## NASA's Future Role with Respect to NEOs

Next I would like to turn to another question. What should NASA's role be in the future? NASA is a space agency. While we are proud of our success in implementing the Congress's direction to us with regard to the search for NEOs, we do not feel that we should play a role in any follow-on search and cataloging effort unless that effort needs to be specifically space-based in nature. There are other agencies with far more expertise in ground-based observations that would be more suitable candidates to lead that portion of a future NEO endeavor.

NASA does, however, continue to have a large role to play in the scientific space exploration of asteroids. The frequent access to space for small missions offered by NASA's Discovery Program has benefited the study of asteroids and comets as no other program to date. The first in-depth study of an NEO, Eros, was performed by the NEAR-Shoemaker mission. The body of data returned by NEAR-Shoemaker was so large, and the quality of the data so high, that NEAR's database will require years of analysis. Just this year, we initiated funding for the first 17 investigations of that data. NEAR-Shoemaker's exploration of Eros will be followed by detailed exploration of two other asteroids, Vesta and Ceres, by the upcoming DAWN mission, currently scheduled to launch in 2006. There is no reason to expect that science-driven exploration of the asteroids, and of course NEOs, will not continue through the Discovery program. We believe that the critical measurements required for developing potential mitigation efforts are substantially the same as those required to achieve the pure scientific goals identified for these objects. We must be able to understand and characterize these objects before any mitigation efforts are even considered.

In addition to NEAR and DAWN, NASA has several other missions dedicated to studying comets and asteroids, such as Deep Impact and Stardust. Our total investment in understanding these bodies, both in the past and in our current FY 2003 budget run-out, is approximately $1.6 billion. That does not even take into account those spacecraft that have provided "bonus" information, such as Galileo, which found a moon orbiting asteroid Ida, and Deep Space 1, a technology demonstration mission that performed a close-up fly-by of comet Borelly. NASA deeply regrets not having the potential discoveries from the recently failed CONTOUR mission, which was to have studied Comets Encke and Schwassmann-Wachmann 3.

NASA's bold new technology initiatives, the In-Space Propulsion (ISP) Initiative and the Nuclear Systems Initiative (NSI), together offer new opportunities to enable capable new missions to NEOs early in the next decade. Improvements in solar-electric propulsion and development of solar sails are examples of new capabilities that might allow a spacecraft like NEAR-Shoemaker to visit many NEOs during a single mission rather than just one (and at the cost of a Discovery mission). If we are ever faced with the requirement to modify the motion of an NEO over time to ensure that the object will not come close to the Earth, nuclear propulsion may very well be the answer. The Nuclear Systems Initiative could address two elements in understanding the potential hazards of NEOs by: (1) providing technologies that could significantly increase our ability to identify and track NEOs, and (2) to possibly—in the future—provide sufficient power to move an Earth-intersecting object. The NSI could enable power and propulsion for an extended survey (in one mission) of multiple NEOs to determine their composition, which is a critical factor in understanding how to mitigate the risk of an Earth-intersecting object. In the future, the technologies under development by the NSI could provide us with the means to redirect the path of an Earth-intersecting asteroid, once we understand the orbital mechanics of these objects sufficiently to understand how to do this. These programs are being developed to serve a wide range of needs across NASA, but they will most certainly prove beneficial for space missions that help us to better understand and characterize NEOs.

## What Should the Nation Be Doing beyond the Current Goal?

I feel that it is premature to consider an extension of our current national program to include a complete search for smaller-sized NEOs. There are several reasons for this belief. The first is that we need to have a better understanding of the true size of the population down to at least 100 m. How will we get the improved data we need on this population? We will obtain the necessary data from the existing NASA search effort for NEOs. The search program now finds about two NEOs with diameters less than 1 km for every large one (diameter greater than 1 km) that we find. In addition, we are supporting a search program which is optimized to detect smaller NEOs. We expect by the end of this decade to have a much better picture of the true size of the population, and hence, what will be required to detect all of them.

The second issue is how such a search could be most efficiently and cost-effectively implemented. Two groups that wish to build large survey systems have argued that the search goal should be extended to 300 m. NASA has at least two concerns with this proposition. First, we do not possess a non-advocate trade study to tell us how best to do such a search. For example, one issue to be addressed is whether it would be better to build one large 8-m class telescope or 2 4-m search telescopes. At these sizes, is a space-based system an option? Second, why 300m? The present limiting diameter of 1 km was the product of a broad public discussion. When we have another broad public discussion, the answer could be: "Leave the present limiting diameter as it stands." Or, perhaps the result of broad national debate on this issue would be: "Catalog the population down to 100 m." We at NASA don't know the answers to these questions, and we believe that further commitments to extend the search are simply premature at this point.

Within the Office of Space Science, the Solar System Exploration Division Director has appointed a small Science Definition Team (SDT) to consider the technical issues related to extending the search for NEOs to smaller sizes. The goal of the SDT is to evaluate what is technologically possible today. The scope of the SDT does not include consideration of any change to our present NEO search goal.

## Conclusion

NASA has made impressive strides in achieving its goal of cataloging 90 percent of all Near-Earth Objects with diameters of more than 1 km and characterizing a sample of them. We are currently ahead of schedule with respect to having this effort completed in the 2008 time frame. While NASA certainly agrees that because these objects pose a potential threat to the Earth, they should be studied and understood, we respectfully defend our position that any expansion of NASA's current NEO effort is premature. Before any further effort is undertaken, we would want input from the scientific community as to how this subject should be approached, and if indeed NASA is even the proper agency to lead this type of an undertaking. . . .

# POSTSCRIPT

## Should We Expand Efforts to Find Near-Earth Objects?

In the debate over the risks of NEO impacts on Earth, there are a few certainties: They have happened before, they will happen again, and they come in various sizes. Many past craters mark the Earth, even though many more have been erased by plate tectonics and erosion. See Timothy Ferris, "Killer Rocks from Outer Space," *Reader's Digest* (October 2002). Ivan Semeniuk, "Asteroid Impact," *Mercury* (November/December 2002), says that, "If there is one question that best sums up the current state of thinking about the impact hazard, it is this: At what size do we need to act? In the shooting gallery that is our solar system, everyone agrees we are the target of both cannonballs and BBs. The hard part is deciding where to draw the line that separates them. For practical reasons, that line is now set at 1 kilometer. Not only are objects of this diameter a global threat (no matter where they hit, we're all affected to some degree), they are also the easiest to spot. Under a mid-1990s congressional mandate, NASA currently funds search efforts to the tune of about $3.5 million per year . . . 'The existing commitment to 1 kilometer and larger is to retire the risk,' says Tom Morgan, who heads NASA's NEO group. 'By the end of this decade we'll be able to tell you if any of these objects presents a threat in the foreseeable future.'"

And if one of these objects does present a threat? In September 2002, NASA held a workshop on *Scientific Requirements for Mitigation of Hazardous Comets and Asteroids*, which concluded "that the prime impediment to further advances in this field is the lack of any assigned responsibility to any national or international governmental organization to prepare for a disruptive collision and the absence of any authority to act in preparation for some future collision mitigation attempt" and urged that "NASA be assigned the responsibility to advance this field" and "a new and adequately funded program be instituted at NASA to create, through space missions and allied research, the specialized knowledge base needed to respond to a future threat of a collision from an asteroid or comet nucleus." The results of the workshop were to appear as *Mitigation of Hazardous Impacts due to Asteroids and Comets* (Cambridge University Press, 2003).

The Organization for Economic Cooperation and Development (OECD) Global Science Forum held a "Workshop on Near Earth Objects: Risks, Policies and Actions" in January 2003. See `http://impact.arc.nasa.gov/index.html` for the report. It too concluded that more work is needed.

Given political will and funding, what could be done if a threat were identified? There have been numerous proposals, from launching nuclear missiles to pulverize approaching space rocks to sending astronauts (or robots) to install rocket engines and deflect the rocks onto safe paths (perhaps into the sun to forestall future hazards). Some possibilities are mentioned by Leon Jaroff and Dan Cray, "Whew!" *Time* (March 23, 1998). All require a stronger space program than any nation now has. Lacking such a program, knowing that a major rock is on the way would surely be little comfort. However, given sufficient notice—on the order of decades—a space program could be mobilized to deal with the threat.

# ISSUE 12

## Is the Search for Extraterrestrial Life Doomed to Fail?

**YES: Stephen Webb,** from *Where Is Everybody? Fifty Solutions to the Fermi Paradox and the Problem of Extraterrestrial Life* (Copernicus Books, 2002)

**NO: Seth Shostak,** from "SETI's Prospects Are Bright," *Mercury* (September/October 2002)

### ISSUE SUMMARY

**YES:** Physicist Stephen Webb argues that "the one gleaming, hard fact in the whole debate [is] that we have not been visited by" extraterrestrial intelligences. The only way to reconcile this fact with everything else we know is to conclude that we are the only intelligent species around.

**NO:** Radio astronomer and SETI researcher Seth Shostak is more optimistic. He contends that the only way to find extraterrestrial intelligence is to keep looking.

In the 1960s and early 1970s, the business of listening to the radio whispers of the stars and hoping to pick up signals emanating from some alien civilization was still new. Few scientists held visions equal to Frank Drake, one of the pioneers of the search for extraterrestrial intelligence (SETI) field. Drake and scientists like him utilize radio telescopes—large, dish-like radio receiver–antenna combinations—to scan radio frequencies (channels) for signal patterns that would indicate that the signal was transmitted by an intelligent being. In his early days, Drake worked with relatively small and weak telescopes out of listening posts that he had established in Green Bank, West Virginia, and Arecibo, Puerto Rico. See Carl Sagan and Frank Drake, "The Search for Extraterrestrial Intelligence," *Scientific American* (May 1975) and Frank Drake and Dava Sobel, *Is Anyone Out There? The Scientific Search for Extraterrestrial Intelligence* (Delacorte Press, 1992).

There have been more than 50 searches for extraterrestrial radio signals since 1960. The earliest ones were very limited. Later searches have been more ambitious, culminating in the 10-year program known as the High Resolution Microwave Survey (HRMS). The HRMS, which began on Columbus Day of 1992, uses several radio telescopes and massive computers to scan 15 million radio frequencies per second. New technologies and techniques continue to make the search more efficient. See Seth Shostak et al., "The Future of SETI," *Sky & Telescope* (April 2001).

At the outset, many people thought—and many still think—that SETI has about as much scientific relevance as searches for Loch Ness Monsters and Abominable Snowmen. However, to Drake and his colleagues, it seems inevitable that with so many stars in the sky, there must be other worlds with life upon them, and some of that life must be intelligent and have a suitable technology and the desire to search for alien life too.

Writing about SETI in the September–October 1991 issue of *The Humanist,* physicist Shawn Carlson compares visiting the National Shrine of the Immaculate Conception in Washington, D.C., to looking up at the stars and "wondering if, in all [the] vastness [of the starry sky], there is anybody out there looking in our direction. . . . [A]re there planets like ours peopled with creatures like us staring into their skies and wondering about the possibilities of life on other worlds, perhaps even trying to contact it?" That is, SETI arouses in its devotees an almost religious sense of mystery and awe, a craving for contact with the *other.* Success would open up a universe of possibilities, add immensely to human knowledge, and perhaps even provide solutions to problems that our interstellar neighbors have already defeated.

SETI also arouses strong objections, partly because it challenges human uniqueness. Many scientists have objected that life-bearing worlds such as Earth must be exceedingly rare because the conditions that make them suitable for life as we know it—composition and temperature—are so narrowly defined. Others have objected that there is no reason whatsoever to expect that evolution would produce intelligence more than once or that, if it did, the species would be similar enough to humans to allow communication. Still others say that even if intelligent life is common, technology may not be so common. Richard C. Teske, for example, in "Is This the E.T. to Whom I Am Speaking?" *Discover* (May 1993), argues that the geological processes that have supplied humans with the raw materials of technology—metals—are too unlikely to have been repeated elsewhere. A similar criticism is that technology may occupy such a brief period in the life of an intelligent species that there is virtually no chance that it would coincide with Earth scientists' current search. Whatever their reasons, SETI detractors agree that listening for extraterrestrial signals is futile.

In the selections that follow, physicist Stephen Webb represents the objections of skeptical scientists, arguing that because we have not been visited by extraterrestrials, there are probably very few ET civilizations. In fact, he says, we are probably alone. Seth Shostak defends SETI, arguing that "Thousands of communicating civilizations could populate our galaxy. And there are plenty of reasons why none of them have visited Earth." New tools make it ever more likely that the effort will succeed. We must maintain the search.

**Stephen Webb**

# Where Is Everybody? Fifty Solutions to the Fermi Paradox and the Problem of Extraterrestrial Life

[Enrico] Fermi was at Los Alamos in the summer of 1950. One day, he was chatting to Edward Teller and Herbert York as they walked over to Fuller Lodge for lunch. . . . Emil Konopinski joined them . . . [and] there followed a serious discussion about whether flying saucers could exceed the speed of light. Fermi asked Teller what he thought the probability might be of obtaining evidence for superluminal travel by 1960. Fermi said that Teller's estimate of one-in-a-million was too low; Fermi thought it was more like one-in-ten.

The four of them sat down to lunch, and the discussion turned to more mundane topics. Then, in the middle of the conversation and out of the clear blue, Fermi asked: "Where *is* everybody?" His lunch partners Teller, York and Konopinski immediately understood that he was talking about extraterrestrial visitors. And since this was Fermi, perhaps they realized that it was a more troubling and profound question than it first appears. York recalls that Fermi made a series of rapid calculations and concluded that we should have been visited long ago and many times over. . . .

. . . So why do we not hear from some of them? In fact, why are they not already here? If some of the civilizations are extremely long-lived, then we might expect them to colonize the Galaxy—and have done so before multicellular life even developed on Earth. The Galaxy should be swarming with extraterrestrial civilizations. Yet we see no sign of them. We should already know of their existence, but we do not. Where is everybody? *Where are they?* This is the Fermi paradox. . . .

. . . [It] was a 1975 paper by Michael Hart in the *Quarterly Journal of the Royal Astronomical Society* that sparked an explosion of interest in the paradox. Hart demanded an explanation for one key fact: there are no intelligent beings from outer space on Earth at the present time. He argued that there are four categories of explanation for this fact. First, "physical explanations," which are based on some difficulty that makes space travel unfeasible. Second, "sociological explanations," which in essence suppose that extraterrestrials have chosen not to visit Earth. Third, "temporal explanations," which suggest that ETCs [extraterrestrial civilizations] have not had time to reach us. Fourth, there are explanations arguing that perhaps they *have* been on Earth, but we do not see them now. These categories were meant to exhaust the possibilities. Hart then forcefully showed how none of these four categories provide a convincing account of the key fact, which led him to offer his own explanation: *we are the first civilization in our Galaxy.*

Hart's paper led to a vigorous debate, much of it appearing in the pages of the *Quarterly Journal*. It was a debate that anyone could enter—one of the earliest contributions came from the House of Lords at Westminster! Perhaps the most controversial offering came from Frank Tipler, in a paper with the uncompromising title "Extraterrestrial Intelligent Beings Do Not Exist." Tipler reasoned that advanced ETCs could use self-replicating probes to explore or colonize the Galaxy cheaply and in a relatively short time. The abstract to Tipler's paper sums it up: "It is argued that if extraterrestrial intelligent beings exist, then their spaceships must already be present in our Solar System." Tipler contended that the SETI program had no chance of success, and was therefore a waste of time and money. His argument poured oil on the fires of the debate and led to a further round of argument. The coolest and best summary of the arguments came from David Brin, who called the paradox the "great silence."

In 1979, Ben Zuckerman and Michael Hart organized a conference to discuss the Fermi paradox. The proceedings were published in book form, and although the volume contains a variety of views it is difficult to read it without concluding that ETCs have the means, motive and opportunity to colonize the Galaxy. The means: interstellar travel seems to be possible, if not easy. The motive: Zuckerman showed how some ETCs would be forced into interstellar travel by the death of their star, and in any case it seems a wise idea for a species to expand into space to guard against the possibility of planetary disaster. The opportunity: the Galaxy is 13 billion years old, but colonization can take place over a period of only a few million years. Yet we do not see them. If this were a murder mystery, we would have a suspect but no body.

Not everyone was struck by the force of the argument. A recent book by the mathematician Amir Aczel makes the case for the probability of extraterrestrial life being 1. The physicist Lee Smolin wrote that "the argument for the non-existence of intelligent life is one of the most curious I have ever encountered; it seems a bit like a ten-year-old child deciding that sex is a myth because he has yet to encounter it." The late Stephen Jay Gould, referring to Tipler's contention that ETCs would deploy probe technology to colonize the Galaxy, wrote that "I must confess that I simply don't know how to react to such arguments. I have enough trouble predicting the plans and reactions of people closest to me. I am usually baffled by the thoughts and accomplishments of humans in different cultures. I'll be damned if I can state with certainty what some extraterrestrial source of intelligence might do." . . .

Nevertheless, surely Hart's key fact *does* require an explanation. We have been searching for ETCs for more than 40 years. And the continuing silence, despite intensive searches, is beginning to worry even some of the most enthusiastic proponents of SETI. We observe a natural universe when we could so easily observe an artificial universe. Why? Where *is* everybody? Fermi's question still demands an answer. . . .

There is just one gleaming, hard fact in the whole debate: we have not been visited by ETCs, nor have we heard from them. So far, the Universe remains silent to us. . . .

. . . [With] just one piece of evidence to play with, our biases will come to the fore. My own biases, such as I can identify them, include optimism about our future. I like to think our scientific knowledge will continue to expand and our technology to improve; I like to think mankind will one day reach the stars—first by sending messages and then later, perhaps, by sending ships. I like to think something akin to the Galaxy-spanning civilization described by Asimov in his classic *Foundation* stories might one day come to pass. But these biases collide with the Fermi paradox: if *we* are going to colonize the Galaxy, why have *they* not already done so? They have had the means, the motive and the opportunity to establish colonies, yet they appear not to have done so. Why? . . .

[The] only position that is consistent with the observed absence of extraterrestrials and that at the same time supports my prejudices—the only resolution of the Fermi paradox that makes sense to me—is that we are alone.

If you look up at the sky on a clear moonless night and gaze with the naked eye at the myriads of stars and the vastness of space, it is difficult to believe we might be alone. We are too small and the Universe is too big for this to make sense. But appearances can be deceptive: even under ideal observing conditions you are unlikely to see more than about 3000 stars, and few of those would provide conditions hospitable to our form of life. The gut reaction we perhaps all feel when we look at the night sky—that there *must* be intelligent life somewhere out there—is not a good guide. We have to be guided by reason, not gut reaction, when discussing this matter. Well . . . reason tells us there are a few hundred billion stars in our Galaxy alone, and perhaps a hundred billion galaxies in the Universe. Just one sentient species when there is such an immense number of places life might get started? Come *on* . . . surely I cannot be serious?

When discussing some of the different types of paradox [earlier in the book], I noted Rapoport's observation that the shock of a paradox may compel us to discard an old (perhaps comfortable) conceptual framework. I believe the Fermi paradox provides a shock that forces us to examine the widespread notion that the vast number of planets in existence is sufficient to guarantee the existence of extraterrestrial intelligent life. In fact, we need not be too surprised. The Drake equation is a product of several terms. If one of those terms is zero, then the product of the Drake equation will be zero; if several of the terms are small, then the product of the Drake equation will be very small. We will be alone. . . .

It is usual at this point to pick some numbers favorable to one's position, plug them into the Drake equation, and then put forward the required result. I would prefer to present here a more pictorial approach.

When I was a schoolboy, I was fascinated by the Sieve of Eratosthenes. Eratosthenes was a Greek astronomer and mathematician, famed for being head of the Library at Alexandria and for being the first to provide an accurate measurement of Earth's circumference. He also developed a technique—his "sieve"—for finding all prime numbers less than some given number *N*. Primes—numbers evenly divisible only by themselves and 1—are extremely important in mathematics; they are like atoms, from which we can compose all other numbers through multiplication. If you are given a number at random, it can be difficult to know whether it is composite or prime. The Sieve of Eratosthenes is a technique for sifting out the composite numbers and leaving only the prime numbers standing.

Suppose you are a Greek mathematician who wants to find all primes less than or equal to 100. First, you take a sheet of papyrus and write down the numbers from 1 to 100. The number 1 is special, so ignore it. The number 2 is prime so leave it; but go through the list and cross out all its multiples: 4, 6, 8, . . . 100. Repeat the process, using the next smallest remaining number, 3; leave it because it is prime, but cross out its multiples all the way up to 99. Continue until you reach the end of the list. Remarkably quickly, you find all the numbers up to 100 have been deleted—except for the 25 prime numbers, which are still standing. Even for a computer, the Sieve of Eratosthenes is the quickest way of finding all primes less than about $10^8$.

As a schoolboy, I was intrigued by the way the Sieve caught more and more of the large numbers. The technique was inexorable: on large grids I found myself chopping down number after number. Since the distribution of primes thins out quickly the higher you count, there are long stretches where all the numbers have been crossed out—numbers that have failed to make it through the Sieve.

I picture something similar happening with the Fermi paradox. Imagine writing down a grid of numbers, from 1 to 1000,000,000,000, with each number representing an individual planet in the Galaxy. (I arrive at this number by multiplying the number of stars in the Galaxy, which is about $10^{11}$, with an assumed average of 10 planets per star. In fact, the number of stars is probably greater than this, with some estimates suggesting that our Galaxy contains as many as 400 billion stars. On the other hand, the average number of planets per star is likely to be less than 10. So although a figure of $10^{12}$ planets is a rough guess, it may not be too wrong—and anyway, this hardly matters when all the other numbers in the problem are so vague.) We assign Earth the number 1, since the Earth is special: it is the only planet on which we *know* intelligent life exists. Now start applying a sieve—let us call it the Sieve of Fermi. (The process I describe here is not meant to be the *only* way of working the numbers. You may prefer different numerical values for the quantities I describe, but the process shows why we should not be surprised if we discover that we are alone.)

*Step 1.* [Earlier] we briefly discussed the notion of a galactic habitable zone (GHZ) in which a star must reside before it can give rise to a viable planetary system. A recent suggestion is that the GHZ contains only 20% of the stars in the Galaxy. So cross out those numbers corresponding to planets not orbiting a star in the GHZ: with 10 planets per star, $2 \times 10^{10}$ planets remain. Now make a second application of the Sieve.

*Step 2.* The bright O and B stars die too quickly for life to evolve around them; the dull K and M stars are too miserly with their energy for life to prosper. For life *as we know it,* we need consider only stars like the Sun. . . . ([This] assumption may be an expression of chauvinism—or a failure of scientific imagination. But I think it is the best assumption we can make at this time.) Only about 5% of stars in our Galaxy are like the Sun; cross out numbers corresponding to planets not orbiting a Sun-like star, and $10^8$ planets remain.

*Step 3.* Life as we know it requires a terrestrial planet to remain in the continuously habitable zone (CHZ) for billions of years. . . . My own guess is that only 1% of planets will be both suitable for life and remain in a CHZ for billions of years. You may think a different figure is in order here (and one could argue for higher or lower figures), but 1% seems reasonable to me. So cross out numbers corresponding to planets that do not remain in a CHZ: $10^6$ planets remain.

*Step 4.* Of the million planets that orbit in the CHZ of a Sun-like star that is itself in the GHZ, how many are home to life? If you believe the genesis of life is exceptionally rare . . . , then the answer is: none. If you believe a special set of circumstances is required, such as life originating on a planet like Mars and then being transported via impact ejecta to an Earth-like planet . . . , then the answer is: not many. I prefer to believe that life is a probable occurrence: that if conditions are suitable, then there is a good chance of cells evolving. Let us say that the chance is 0.5. Cross out numbers corresponding to planets on which life does not arise, and $5 \times 10^5$ planets remain. Half a million planets with life!

*Step 5.* The Universe is a dangerous place. . . . On many planets, life may be snuffed out—or at least prevented from evolving into complex life-forms—by some disaster. My guess is that as many as 20% of planets may suffer such a fate. (This *is* just a guess, and it may be an overestimate.) So cross out numbers corresponding to planets on which disaster strikes: $10^5$ planets remain.

*Step 6.* . . . Earth's system of plate tectonics was important in the development of life . . . and . . . the Moon [played] a role. . . . If both these factors are *necessary* for the evolution of complex life, then the number of planets with the sentient species we are searching for may be small. However, although I believe these phenomena *are* important in some ways, I have no feel for the numbers involved. So I will ignore these factors, and at this stage of the sifting process all the planets make it through: $10^5$ planets still remain.

*Step 7.* Cross out numbers corresponding to planets where life never evolves beyond the prokaryotic grade. . . . The development of the modern eukaryotic cell took aeons on Earth, which perhaps indicates that this step is far from inevitable. No one knows what fraction of planets with prokaryotes will go on to host complex multicellular life-forms; my own estimate of one in ten may be *very* generous. We are left with $10^4$ numbers—ten thousand planets possessing complex multicellular life. Does that mean the Galaxy contains ten thousand ETCs? Unfortunately not, because we must make several further applications of the Sieve before we arrive at the number of species *with whom we can communicate*. Let us combine all these into one last pass through the sifting process.

*Step 8.* Cross out numbers corresponding to planets on which advanced life-forms do not develop tool use and the ability to continuously improve their technology. . . . Cross out numbers corresponding to planets on which advanced life-forms do not develop the type of abstract high-level intelligence we are familiar with. . . . Finally, and to my mind crucially, cross out numbers corresponding to planets on which advanced life-forms do not develop complex, grammatical language. . . . How many planets remain? Of course, no one knows; it is impossible to assign accurate probabilities to these matters. My feeling is that many of these developments were far from inevitable. The feeling arises because, of the 50 billion speciation events in the history of our planet, only one led to language—and language is the key that enabled all our other achievements to take place. My own guess, then, is that none of the planets make it through this final sifting process.

After applying the Sieve of Fermi I believe that *all* grid numbers will be crossed out, except the number 1. Only Earth remains. We are alone.

I believe that the Fermi paradox tells us mankind is the only sapient, sentient species in the Galaxy. (We are probably also unique in our Local Group of galaxies, since many Local Group galaxies are unlikely to possess a GHZ. Perhaps we are even unique in the whole Universe—although the finite speed of light means ETCs could now exist in very distant galaxies without us yet being aware of them.) Yet the Galaxy need not be sterile. The picture I have is of a Galaxy in which simple life is not uncommon; complex, multicellular life is much rarer, but not vanishingly rare. There may be tens of thousands of exceptionally interesting biospheres out there in the Galaxy. But only *one* planet—Earth—has intelligent life-forms.

Such a picture is often criticized as violating the Principle of Mediocrity. The picture seems to suggest that Earth, and mankind, is special. Is this not the height of arrogance?

Paradoxically, at least to my mind, the expectation that other sentient species *must* be out there itself smacks of arrogance. Or rather, it achieves the tricky feat of being both self-important and self-effacing at the same time. At the core of this expectation is the belief that *human* adaptations, attributes such as creativity, and general intelligence, that we think important, are qualities to which other Earth organisms aspire and alien creatures may possess in even more abundance. Allow us a few more million years, so the logic seems to go, and we might evolve into the cognitively, technologically and spiritually superior beings that already exist out there. But the converse of this position is surely false. Give chimps another few million years, so the reasoning goes, and they too will be as intelligent and creative as us. But why should they be? Chimpanzees are good at being chimpanzees; dolphins are good at being dolphins; elephants are good at being elephants. . . . Rather than patronizing these species for not exhibiting *human* characteristics, we should respect them on their own terms for earning a living in a harsh world that cares not whether they live or die.

On the other hand it is undeniable that mankind *is* profoundly different from every other species on Earth. We alone have language, a high level of self-consciousness, and a moral sense. We *are* special. But surely our uniqueness could not have arisen by mere chance, by the blind and random groping of evolution, could it? Well, why not?

As Stephen Jay Gould pointed out in a delightful analogy, we can account for any growth in the complexity of living organisms through a drunkard's walk effect. Imagine a drunk leaning against a wall. A few meters to his right is a gutter. If the drunk takes random equal-sized steps to his left or to his right, then he *inevitably* ends up in the gutter. No force propels him to his right; he moves randomly, and at any time he is as likely to move to his left as to his right. But the wall eventually stops his leftward motion; over time, there is only one direction in which to move. Eventually, completely by chance, the drunk stumbles into the gutter. The same effect can explain any advance we might observe in the complexity of organisms. At one end we have a wall of minimum complexity that organisms can possess and still be alive. This wall is where life began, and where most life on Earth remains. Over time, evolution tinkers with more advanced organisms; when life itself was young, that was the only available possibility—evolution could not try out simpler designs, because its path was blocked by the wall of minimum complexity. Some of the new designs worked, in the sense that the organisms were adapted well enough in their immediate environments to survive long enough to reproduce. And so evolution staggered on, like a blind drunk, tentatively producing organisms of greater complexity. After almost 4 billion years of random tinkering, we end up with the living world we see today. But there was nothing *inevitable* about the process; the purpose of evolution was not to produce us. Play the tape of history again, and there is no reason to suppose *Homo sapiens*—or any equivalent sentient species—would play any role at all.

Many eminent scientists argue that Mind is in some way predestined in this Universe. That far from being the outcome of chance, Mind is an inevitable outcome of deep laws of self-complexity. They argue that, over aeons, organisms will inevitably self-complexify and form a "ladder of progress": prokaryote to eukaryote to plants to animals to intelligent species like us. It is a comforting idea, but I know of no definite evidence in its favor, and I believe the silence of the Universe argues against it.

The famous French biologist Jacques Monod wrote that "evolution is chance caught on the wing." Even more evocatively, he wrote that "Man at last knows he is alone in the unfeeling immensity of the Universe, out of which he has emerged only by chance." It is a melancholy thought. I can think of only one thing sadder: if the only animals with self-consciousness, the only species that can light up the Universe with acts of love and humor and compassion, were to extinguish themselves through acts of stupidity. If we survive, we have a Galaxy to explore and make our own. If we destroy ourselves, if we ruin Earth before we are ready to leave our home planet . . . well, it could be a long, long time before a creature from another species looks up at its planet's night sky and asks: "Where *is* everybody?"

**Seth Shostak**

# SETI's Prospects Are Bright

Is there intelligence elsewhere in the Galaxy? Are there other beings who not only can see the stars, but who can also understand where they are and how they work? That's the question today's SETI experiments try to address. A single signal from the cosmos—a sudden burst of photons or a soft radio squeal—would immediately provide an answer.

It is now four decades since the first modern SETI experiment, and we still have not detected and confirmed such a signal. This is reason for some astronomers, including my distinguished opponent Ben Zuckerman, to question the premises of SETI, or simply the likelihood that it will ever succeed. To my mind, this is as if the crew aboard *The Resolution,* Captain James Cook's ship—having sailed for months in search of Terra Australis Incognita—opted to set up debating clubs to argue the possibility that they would ever stumble across the postulated southern continent. In fact, debate would have been far less useful than continuing to sail. Cook's repeated probes into uncharted southern latitudes both constrained the search space and indirectly told his successors where to look next. In 1820, nearly a half century after Cook's forays, Thaddeus von Bellinghausen finally sighted Antarctica. In other words, experiment is better than debate, and that's why SETI researchers continue to deploy their telescopes.

Frankly, it's possible that tomorrow, next week, or next year, SETI will receive a signal that renders all argument about the likelihood of success obsolete and quaint. I personally believe that the telescopes and techniques currently being developed—instruments that will increase by three orders of magnitude the number of star systems scrutinized for cosmic company—are likely to result in the detection of someone else's technology. But that's my opinion. Meanwhile, and in the spirit of interesting pugilistic polemics, I will take issue with some of the rationale Ben Zuckerman has offered in support of his assertion that SETI will fail. After all, he's not only telling us it will fail, he's telling us why.

## Planet-Sniffing Telescopes

Ben's fundamental insight is that all advanced civilizations will build telescopes able to detect small planets, and possibly even indications of biological activity, at distances out to a few hundred light-years. To Ben, this fact is obvious, given that we will soon have this capability ourselves. Indeed, having made this point, Ben then advises the SETI community to skip over nearby star systems and direct its scrutiny to more distant arenas. After all, he argues, why waste time investigating local stars until we know if they have Earth-size planets? Even better, he notes that in a decade or two, telescopes such as NASA's Terrestrial Planet Finder (TPF) will be able to sort out the best of these Earth-size worlds by spectroscopically analyzing their atmospheres for gases (e.g., oxygen and methane) that would betray the presence of life.

In other words, if you're going to look for extraterrestrials, it helps to know the territory, and by waiting a few decades, SETI researchers will have a list of all the Earth-like worlds around nearby stars. Stars without such planets can be skipped.

But this advice, although apparently reasonable, is not terribly helpful and will soon be irrelevant. While it's true that learning that, for example, a planet around the relatively nearby star 55 Cancri has oxygen in its atmosphere would surely improve its attractiveness for SETI, it hardly stamps it as a gold-plated SETI target. Earth's atmosphere has had an oxygen signature for 2 billion years, and nearly all that time our planet was devoid of sophisticated life. Even if advanced societies survive for tens of millions of years, only 1 in 100 life-bearing planets is likely to sport intelligent aliens right now. This already argues for extending the search beyond the nearest star systems, and in fact, this is being done. New detectors suitable for conducting SETI at optical wavelengths, as well as the extraordinary capabilities of the Allen Telescope Array . . . and its likely successor, the Square Kilometer Array, will shortly swell the list of SETI targets to hundreds of thousands of star systems, and, within a few decades, millions. The overwhelming majority will lie far beyond the "nearby stars" that Ben says waste SETI's time.

## If Aliens Are There, They'd Be Here

Having warned against using precious telescope time to investigate nearby stars now, Ben then takes the stance that all star systems out to a distance of a few hundred light-years are guaranteed to be alien-free. His reasoning is as follows: Any advanced extraterrestrials around these stars, wielding planet-sniffing telescopes, will discover Earth and its telltale, biogenic atmosphere. They will fire up their SETI telescopes but will fail to detect a signal because *Homo sapiens* has yet to arrive on the scene. At this point, they will face a quandary of curiosity: The relative motion of stars in the Galaxy ensures that the Sun and its planetary retinue will move out of their local neighborhood within a few million years. Rather than let an intriguing world slip their grasp, these aliens will come to visit. They'll do this in person, as exploration by robots is ultimately unsatisfying. The aliens will want to study our "redwood trees, dinosaurs, and whales" (although it's more likely they will only find our bacteria). Once these visitors arrive on the terrestrial scene, they will not return to whence they came, but lodge permanently on Earth. Because we don't see these alien squatters today, this means they didn't visit in the past, and consequently they're not within manageable traveling range—a distance Ben estimates to be hundreds of light-years.

This line of reasoning is merely a modification of an argument well known in SETI circles: the Fermi Paradox. If aliens can manage interstellar travel (and, after all, such travel does not violate the laws of physics), then at least some of them should have colonized the Galaxy by now. The fact that we don't see any evidence of these supercivilizations is taken by skeptics as proof that no extraterrestrials exist. Ben's logic is simply a truncated version of Fermi's Paradox. He assumes that technological societies will build their own TPFs and then visit those interesting places (including Earth) that they discover situated within a few hundred light-years.

Even if you buy into this, it still fails to rule out the possibility of finding an ET signal. Suppose that Ben is right: advanced aliens will colonize all biologically interesting worlds within, say, 500 light-years of their home, carving out a "sphere of influence" that's 1,000 light-years across. If 30,000 civilizations are randomly sprinkled throughout the Milky Way's voluminous star fields, then our galaxy will be fully stuffed with such spheres of influence. But if there are fewer than 30,000, there will be areas of the Galaxy that are untouched by the aliens. Frank Drake has frequently suggested that the number of contemporary alien societies in the Galaxy (the N in his famous equation) is about 10,000. If so, and if expansion reaches out hundreds of light-years as Ben has postulated, then the majority of the Milky Way's stars fall in the cracks—in the empty spaces between these inhabited zones—and would be free of curious, colonizing aliens. In this case, there's no reason to assume that, simply because extraterrestrials aren't walking the streets of your neighborhood, they're also absent from star systems that lie more than several hundred light-years away.

## Going All the Way

But let's do something Ben has not done, and extend his argument to more than a first generation of interstellar expansion. Suppose the first civilization to build atmosphere-analyzing telescopes spawns colonists that quickly reach out a few hundred light-years. Let's also assume that their descendants do the same. First, they build planet-sniffing hardware of their own and then they venture out a few hundred light-years beyond their colonized homes. Repeat this scenario a few hundred times. Within a few tens of millions of years, the colonizers will be ensconced on every attractive world in the Galaxy.

If this scenario were realistic, SETI supporters really would have a problem. The aliens or their mechanical proxies should be everywhere. This is, of course, the usual form of the Fermi Paradox, and it has been addressed in a substantial body of literature by folks who have been remarkably inventive in formulating scenarios that explain why such saturation colonization wouldn't take place. It would be both tedious and redundant to many readers to list all of these scenarios here, but they generally fall into three categories: (1) technical, (2) sociological, and (3) radical.

Among the technical explanations, an oft-cited suggestion is that interstellar travel is not as easy as Ben assumes. Aside from the enormous energy costs required to send a single craft to another star at 1% the velocity of light (3,000 kilometers per second), there's also the danger of interstellar material slamming into the nose of the spaceship at this blistering speed. In addition, one should be aware of the magnitude of the effort if large numbers of stars have habitable worlds. Within 500 light-years of us we can find about a million star systems! Ben might argue that only a small percentage of these will have decent planets, but if the number is small, then the probability of worlds with intelligent beings is smaller still. In this case, his whole argument falls apart because the chances that any potential colonizers have sprouted up within a few hundred light-years of us is negligible, even in the past 2 billion years when Earth has had an oxygenated atmosphere. In other words, if this is the case, then the reason we haven't yet detected extraterrestrials has nothing to do with their lack of presence on Earth, but is simply due to the fact that such societies are sparse. That could be the case. Indeed, it's the obvious rationale for increasing SETI's range of reconnaissance.

Among the sociological scenarios for the Paradox we can cite is the historical fact that colonization efforts on Earth have been much more limited than one would expect based on travel times or interest in distant lands. What stopped the Romans (or the Polynesians, etc.) from colonizing every temperate continent? Not travel time, and not a lack of appealing destinations. Competition, overextensions, or simply a decline in motivation brought a halt to all such efforts. It's also possible that long-lived extraterrestrial civilizations are passive. On Earth, the development of rocketry occurred in roughly the same epoch as the invention of nuclear weapons. Aggressive societies may self-destruct before colonization begins, suggesting that only the less adventurous societies survive. According to this line of reasoning, the oldest alien cultures have managed to rid themselves of aggression and are disinterested in colonization.

It's also worth noting that humans are not uniformly distributed over Earth, but are concentrated in relatively small cities and suburbs. Perhaps the aliens, too, are urbanized, clustered around objects where matter and energy are highly abundant. Our solar system may be an uninteresting desert, relatively speaking, in the vast landscape of the Galaxy.

It is difficult to evaluate the validity of these efforts to explain how the Galaxy could be semi-packed with aliens while still allowing for a bit of empty space (which we inhabit). Ben has apparently given thumbs up to option (3) and chosen one of the two radical explanations for Fermi's Paradox: We are alone. (The other radical explanation, that the aliens are here on Earth, is popular with much of the public, but not with many scientists.) Ben insists that because they're not here, they're not there. This is like deciding that the world doesn't host large animals because (1) despite the fact that big animals could roam the world in short order, (2) you still don't see any in your backyard.

## Bottom Line

My opponent has presented SETI scientists with two caveats. First, he argues that there's little point in observing nearby star systems now, because we will soon be able to learn which of these stellar habitats have Earth-like worlds. Second, the fact that Earth has not been settled by aliens indicates that none of the stars out to a distance of hundreds of light-years sports advanced societies.

The first point is moot, as SETI researchers are already extending their reconnaissance to greater distances. The second point is merely a special edition of the Fermi Paradox, in which it's assumed that only one generation of colonization will take place. But this argument also becomes less interesting as new telescopes push the radius of SETI searches farther into space. My opponent's arguments could be extended to the more general Fermi Paradox, which envisions a spread of civilization to every galactic nook and cranny. But there are many possible impediments to a thorough colonization of the Milky Way, and to summarily decide that our world has been left alone because there's no one anywhere else in the Galaxy is not logic, but merely conviction.

In short, while it is interesting and edifying to debate the likelihood that we will uncover evidence of thinking beings elsewhere, it is hubris to think that we can decide this issue based on the activities of our own society or the situation of our immediate neighborhood. Cook's sailors might just as well have concluded that Antarctica couldn't exist because there was ice-free water around their ship. It makes more sense to sail on.

# POSTSCRIPT

## Is the Search for Extraterrestrial Life Doomed to Fail?

If the universe is full of intelligent species, why haven't they shown up yet? As both Stephen Webb and Seth Shostak note, this is the Fermi Paradox. The idea is that at least some of those species should have been around for quite a long time, and they have had plenty of time to spread.

So why haven't they shown up? Are we in fact alone? Or first? Are the conditions that lead to life and intelligence rare? Are there aliens living in disguise amongst us? Or are we quarantined? Reservationed? Zooed? Or maybe there's nobody there at all—not even us! (Sure, that could be it—if we are just simulations in some cosmic computer.) In his book, Webb describes Fermi and his paradox in more detail and offers a variety of answers that have been suggested—most seriously, some a bit tongue-in-cheek—for why the search has not succeeded. His own opinion is on the pessimistic side.

The SETI community, however, remains convinced that their effort is worthwhile. *SETI 2020: A Roadmap for the Search for Extraterrestrial Intelligence* (SETI Press, SETI Institute, 2002) is the report of the Search for Extraterrestrial Intelligence (SETI) Science and Technology Working Group, which between 1997 and 1999 developed a plan for the SETI effort through 2020, which will center on multi-antenna arrays, improved multi-channel scanning, and initial efforts to look for infrared and optical signals. The book provides plentiful details, as well as a brief survey of SETI history, the science that backs up the idea that SETI is worth attempting, and the technology that makes SETI even remotely possible.

Naomi Lubick, "An Ear to the Stars," *Scientific American* (November 2002), describes the SETI career of Jill Tarter and discusses new technology being developed for the search. The Terrestrial Planet Finder is discussed by Ray Jayawardhana, "Searching for Alien Earths," *Astronomy* (June 2003).

What if SETI succeeds? Frank Drake noted in *Is Anyone Out There? The Scientific Search for Extraterrestrial Intelligence* (Delacorte Press, 1992) that positive results would have to be reported to everyone, at once, in order to prevent attempts to suppress or monopolize the discovery. Albert A. Harrison, "Confirmation of ETI: Initial Organizational Response," *Acta Astronautica* (August 2003), focuses on the need for a response to success but he is skeptical that an effective response is possible; he says, "Foresight and advance preparation are among the steps that organizations may take to prepare for contact, but conservative values, skepticism towards SETI, and competing organizational priorities make serious preparation unlikely." Should our response include sending an answer back to the source of whatever radio signals we detect? H. Paul Schuch, "The Search for Extraterrestrial Intelligence," *Futurist* (May/June 2003), suggests that there may be dangers in such a move.

Want to help? Look into the SETI@Home project (`http://www.setiathome.ssl.berkeley.edu`). Data collected from radio telescopes are distributed to home computers (4.5 million at last count) for analysis by software that runs in the background. See David P. Anderson, Jeff Cobb, Eric Korpela, Matt Lebofsky, and Dan Werthimer, "SETI@Home," *Communications of the ACM* (November 2002). SETI@Home and other efforts have turned up a few "tantalizing signals"; T. Joseph W. Lazio and Robert Naeye discuss them in "Hello? Are You Still There?" *Mercury* (May/June 2003).

# ISSUE 13

## Should NASA Continue to Pursue Manned Space Exploration?

**YES: John Derbyshire,** from "After *Columbia,*" *National Review* (February 24, 2003)

**NO: John Merchant,** from "Expanded and Updated from: A New Direction in Space," *IEEE Technology and Society* (Winter 1994)

### ISSUE SUMMARY

**YES:** Conservative writer John Derbyshire contests that although manned space flight is expensive, it is a romantic enterprise with a place in the American spirit.

**NO:** John Merchant, a retired staff engineer at Loral Infrared and Imaging Systems, argues that it will be much cheaper to develop electronic senses and remotely operated machines humans can use to explore other worlds.

The dream of conquering space has a long history. The pioneers of rocketry—the Russian Konstantin Tsiolkovsky (1857–1935) and the American Robert H. Goddard (1882–1945)—both dreamed of exploring other worlds, although neither lived long enough to see the first artificial satellite, the Soviet *Sputnik*, go up in 1957. That success sparked a race between America and the Soviet Union to be the first to achieve each step in the progression of space exploration. The next steps were to put dogs (the Soviet Laika was the first), monkeys, chimps, and finally human beings into orbit. Communications, weather, and spy satellites were designed and launched. And on July 20, 1969, the U.S. Project Apollo program landed the first men on the moon.

There were a few more *Apollo* landings, but not many. The United States had achieved its main political goal of beating the Soviets to the moon and, in the minds of the government, demonstrating American superiority. Thereafter, the United States was content to send automated spacecraft (computer-operated robots) to observe Venus, Mars, and the rings of Saturn; to land on Mars and study its soil; and even to carry recordings of Earth's sights and sounds past the distant edge of the solar system, perhaps to be retrieved in the distant future by intelligent life from some other world. (Those recordings are attached to the *Voyager* spacecraft, launched in 1977; published as a combination of CD, CD-ROM, and book, *Murmurs of Earth: The Voyager Interstellar Record,* it is now long out of print.) Humans have not left near-Earth orbit for two decades, even though space technology has continued to develop. The results of this development include communications satellites, space shuttles, space stations, and independent robotic explorers such as the *Mariners* and *Vikings* and—landing on Mars on July 4, 1997—the *Pathfinder* craft (now the Sagan Memorial Station) and its tiny robot rover, *Sojourner*. More robotic spacecraft and landers are planned. (For future missions, visit `http://www.nasa.gov/missions/future/index.html`.)

Why has human space exploration gone no further? One reason is that robots are now extremely capable. Although some robot spacecraft have failed partially or completely, there have been many grand successes that have added enormously to humanity's knowledge of Earth and other planets. Another is money: Lifting robotic explorers into space is expensive, but lifting people into space—along with all the food, water, air, and other supplies necessary to keep them alive for the duration of a mission—is much more expensive. And there are many people in government and elsewhere who cry that there are many better ways to spend the money on Earth.

Still another reason for the reduction in human space travel seems to be the fear that astronauts will die in space. This point was emphasized by the explosion on takeoff of the space shuttle *Challenger* in January 1986, which killed seven astronauts and froze the entire shuttle program for over two and a half years, and reinforced by the breakup of *Columbia* on entry February 1, 2003. After the latter event, the public reaction included many calls for an end to such risky, expensive enterprises. See Jerry Grey, "*Columbia*—Aftermath of a Tragedy," *Aerospace America* (March 2003); John Byron, "Is Manned Space Flight Worth It?" *Proceedings* (of the U.S. Naval Institute) (March 2003) (and Richard H. Truly's response in the May issue); and "Manned or Unmanned into Space?" *USA Today* (February 26, 2003), among many others.

Aerospace engineer John Merchant asserts that although the rocket technology of the twentieth century put humans into space, it is the information technology of the twenty-first century that will permanently and affordably establish human presence in space. Rather than send *either* people *or* independent robots into space, we can use modern computer technology to send people's eyes, ears, and hands in electronic (or virtual) form. His essay brings up-to-date his earlier "A New Direction in Space," *IEEE Technology and Society Magazine* (Winter 1994).

**John Derbyshire**

# After *Columbia*

But I, remembering, pitied well
And loved them, who, with lonely light,
In empty infinite spaces dwell,
Disconsolate. For, all the night,
I heard the thin gnat-voices cry,
Star to faint star, across the sky.

Rupert Brooke was speaking of the stars themselves, as seen from a country lane in Cambridgeshire on a crisp fall evening 95 years ago. It is hard not to feel, though, that he had some premonition of there one day being real human voices squeaking disconsolately to one another, "star to faint star," across the lonely sky. At any rate, whenever I catch a TV news clip showing astronauts on board an orbiting shuttle, and hear their distorted voices, it is Brooke's lines that come to my mind.

Those news clips are few and far between nowadays. Other than as brief "filler" items in a slow news season, manned space travel is not interesting to the TV-watching public, except when something ghastly happens. The heroic days of the *Apollo* program are an entire generation behind us. In all likelihood, NASA prefers things this way. The nation's manned space effort is a quiet program, chugging away behind the scenes, doing . . . what? Best not to inquire.

I did inquire. To be precise, I went to the Internet and pulled off the NASA press kit for Shuttle Mission STS-107—the one that ended so horribly on February 1 [2003]. Let us see. In the shuttle's payload bay we have: an experiment that will "examine bone formation . . . and bacterial and yeast cell responses to the stresses of spaceflight" . . . a German project to measure "the development of the gravity-sensing organs of fish in the absence of gravity" . . . the "Mediterranean Israeli Dust Experiment" . . . "the Critical Viscosity of Xenon-2" . . .

I do not doubt that these are very worthy experiments. But unfortunately, everything in this world must be paid for, and the price of carrying out these investigations aboard the shuttle is extraordinarily high—around $10,000 per pound of payload. Presumably the scientists looking into the critical viscosity of xenon-2 are happy to have their experiment aboard the shuttle. My guess, though, is that if they were told that no more shuttle flights were available, and that they would have to find some other way to spend their $10,000 per pound, they would not be inconsolable.

Contrariwise, there are many scientists whom the shuttle program makes very unhappy indeed. Take those involved with the Pluto-Kuiper Express [PKE] mission, for instance. This was a proposal to send a small, unmanned spacecraft to fly by the planet Pluto, at the outermost edge of the solar system. Pluto is the only planet not yet visited by a spacecraft. Its importance lies in the fact that it is not, strictly speaking, a planet at all, but just the largest member of the Kuiper Belt, a zone of billions of icy objects left over from the solar system's formation. It is thought that these objects are occasionally dislodged from their orbits by tiny gravitational changes arising from their mutual interactions, and from the sun's passage among the stars. They then fall in to the inner solar system, adding to the chances of a civilization-destroying impact with our own planet. It would be nice to understand more about the Kuiper Belt, and about Pluto, which at present is known to us only as a fuzzy blob. Unfortunately, the PKE mission was canceled in September 2000 due to cost overruns. A scaled-down version has since been approved, with an absolute cost cap of $500 million, but it has been a long and hard-fought struggle.

By way of comparison, three years ago the General Accounting Office estimated the cost of a single shuttle launch at $512 million. The shuttle budget is a cuckoo in the nest of the space budget as a whole, grabbing all funds for itself from the limited amount Congress is willing to appropriate for non-military space flight. For less than the cost of putting seven people into orbit for two weeks and acquiring some incremental understanding of things like "yeast cell responses to the stresses of spaceflight," we could map Pluto and get a better fix on our odds for survival as a species.

These are the tradeoffs that space scientists are forced to engage in on account of the shuttle, and the political pressures to keep it flying. The situation has been made worse by the promotion of the International Space Station, a techno-diplomatic extravaganza of no practical value whose cost, name notwithstanding, falls mainly on the U.S. taxpayer.

As well as being expensive, the shuttle fleet is old. NASA should be spending much more than it does on planning a replacement. Over the past few years, Congress has in fact appropriated nearly $5 billion to such a replacement, but nothing has come of it. Everyone who knows the realities of the shuttle program—everyone, that is, other than the big aerospace contractors who milk it—is bitter and angry about these things. Here, for example, is spaceflight journalist Carlton Meyer, writing on the "Spacedaily" website late last year:

> Perhaps NASA should build a "Sea Station" 1000 feet below the sea and use submarines to take foreigners and other salaried government tourists on "missions" to conduct "experiments" and set "endurance records" while "improving international relations." This idea may seem crazy, but it would be much cheaper than the shuttle program and accomplish just as much.

Meyer predicted another catastrophic accident, but this did not require any special foresight on his part. The design of the shuttle—1970s technology, compromised by chronic funding uncertainties and severe budget constraints, and overseen by government bureaucrats—virtually guarantees regular failures. The clamor to fix whatever it was that caused *Columbia* to disintegrate will at best have the result of reducing by one the hundreds of things that can go wrong on a shuttle flight. Ten launches later—or 20, or 50—another seven astronauts will be killed by some different malfunction.

The shuttle is, in fact, extraordinarily dangerous. Now, space flight will never be an anxiety-free enterprise. The only practicable way to get human beings into space is by dint of a colossal controlled explosion. Having once got them into space, their velocity relative to the surface of the earth being then at least 17,000 miles per hour, getting them back—reducing that velocity to zero—needs either an equivalent explosion (in which case the explosive must be taken aloft with them) or else the use of air resistance for braking. Only the latter is realistic, and it means subjecting the reentry vehicle to extreme heat and stress at altitudes far beyond the reach of emergency help.

Barring some sensational discovery in fundamental physics—something equivalent to the gravity-shielding "Cavorite" that took H. G. Wells's astronauts aloft in *The First Men in the Moon*—we are stuck with these fiery realities of combustion and friction. There are good reasons to think, though, that the perils of manned space flight could be reduced by an order of magnitude. Just look at the record: The shuttle mission that ended in catastrophe on February 1 was the 113th. Of that 113, two ended in disaster, with the loss of all hands. This means that for an astronaut sitting in a shuttle waiting for ignition, his odds of being killed during the mission are, on present evidence (and there are people who will tell you we have been lucky), around 2 percent. Those are simply terrible odds. It is difficult to think of any human activity other than battlefield combat that is equally dangerous. The equivalent risk for an Air Force test pilot taking off is hundreds of times smaller. For a civilian starting up his car or boarding a plane, it is *tens of thousands* of times smaller. Forty years into the era of manned space flight, we can surely do much better than 2 percent.

For I do believe that manned space flight is worthwhile. Practical arguments aside, we *ought* to be taking slow, tentative, and sensibly funded steps into space. Those lines of Rupert Brooke's hint at an important feature of a manned space program: It is a romantic enterprise. It has an appeal to our deeper selves, most especially to those aspects of our consciousness that other national endeavors cannot reach—aspects concerned with our relationship to the larger cosmos, the future of our species, the fragility of our civilization, and the divine purpose in providing us with such inconceivably vast empty spaces to roam in, so innumerably many barren worlds of rock, ice, and frozen vapor to examine.

This romance is not a negligible consideration, not for Americans. For a coldly utilitarian people—the ancient Romans, say, or the modern Chinese—it might be. For us, as Calvin Coolidge noted a lifetime ago: "The things of the spirit come first." There is a respectable case to be made that, at this point in human development, there is no need for human beings to be in space at all. I doubt Americans can be persuaded by that case. Popular sentiment is in favor of a manned space program, and the nation ought to have one; but not, surely, one in which spiders and yeast cells are hoisted aloft at $500 million a throw, with 2 percent odds on fiery destruction. Let us do a little rethinking about what we want from manned space flight, and how best we can get it.

**John Merchant**  **NO**

# A New Direction in Space

The human exploration of space touches a deep chord within us. For centuries we have dreamed of going to other planets, not knowing (just as the early terrestrial explorers did not) exactly what we might find or do there, or what might be gained. Then, in the middle of the last century, we finally broke free from the iron grip of Earth's gravity. The space age had begun. Neil Armstrong took that famous "One small step for man, one giant leap for mankind." Humankind's first great adventure, the exploration and development of the mother Earth, being essentially complete, it seemed then that our *next* great adventure, the human exploration and development of space, was about to begin. Sadly, that has not happened.

Thirty-four years after the triumph of the moon landings instead of going on to Mars (as many had hoped) we find ourselves back at a controversial space station in low Earth orbit, without any compelling rationale for humans in space. In contrast, *thirty-four* years after Lindbergh's pioneering flight across the Atlantic, luxury intercontinental jet travel had become available to all and was transforming the world into the global village that it has now become. We are on the wrong path in space, spending a lot of money on manned programs without any significant practical benefit.

Following the loss of Columbia, Congress will review our space program. If the manned space program is continued, substantially more funds will be needed to assure safety and to upgrade the ageing shuttle fleet. Yet this would not solve the underlying problem that the manned space program lacks a clear and compelling rationale. It would alienate the scientific community which feels that very expensive manned space programs have little practical value yet drain precious resources from important unmanned missions of scientific investigation. On the other hand, terminating the manned space program would alienate those who passionately believe in manned missions and could sound the death knell for NASA. The human exploration and development of space is the very heart and soul of the space program, and indeed the reason for NASA's existence.

This is the seemingly irreconcilable dilemma that any review of space exploration inevitably encounters. Manned missions are prohibitively expensive, dangerous, and have limited practical benefit, while unmanned missions do not satisfy the long-standing, deeply felt, and legitimate desire to extend humankind to space.

The manned equivalent mission is a third option that can resolve this seemingly intractable dilemma. By mid-century it could allow humans to be there *permanently* on Mars, moons, asteroids, and other space locations—not just exploring but most importantly generating great wealth from these environments, just as we have derived great wealth through the ages from our own planet. Migrating from our primal origin millions of years ago we have now explored and developed almost all of planet Earth. Along the way we have created the enormous wealth of modern civilization—out of nothing but the raw substance of the Earth. The manned equivalent mission would enable the continuation of this same process in space, thereby providing an immensely compelling and inspirational rationale for the human exploration and development of space in this century, and for centuries to come. There is no possibility whatsoever of this happening with manned missions.

Manned missions are not undertaken just to locate a human body in space, but for what can be accomplished, subjectively and objectively, by a human in space. The manned equivalent mission achieves the same result, but without locating the body in space.

Manned equivalent mission technology would have enormously important applications on Earth. At the end of the nineteenth century the invention of the telephone totally transformed human life by allowing humans to *communicate* over large distances without going there. By the middle of the $21^{st}$ century the development of manned equivalent mission technology would again transform human life, both on Earth and in space, by allowing humans to *perform physical work* over large distances without going there. One example, already under development, is to enable the special skill of surgeons to be instantly deployed wherever it may be needed anywhere over the world.

## The Problem Is a Deeply Imbedded Primeval Myth

Amazingly, the problem with our space program is not in our technology but in ourselves! We have been led into a dead-end path by a deeply imbedded primeval myth, comparable to the flat-Earth myth of antiquity. To explore and develop space, humans must certainly be-there in space. The origin of the great space dilemma is our erroneous belief that being-there means locating the body there. It does not!

### Being-There

Our entire species experience has been that the only way to be-there has been to locate the body there. Being-there without locating the body there appears to be an absurd contradiction in terms. For an inanimate object, being-there does indeed mean being-located there. A car is there in a parking lot only if it is actually located there. However being-there has an entirely different meaning for a human person. Suppose that someone travels to a neighboring city, but expires on arrival. That person's body is there, but the person can obviously not be said to be-there. This shows that for a human person "being-there" does not mean "locating the body there." Being-there means interacting normally with the environment there. Locating the body there is simply a means of doing that. A person who is interacting normally with an environment is there in that environment wherever his or her body may be located.

Locating the body in space, by a *manned mission*, is simply *one* way of interacting normally with the environment there—that is, of being there. Modern information technology can provide another. It is possible for a person to be-there in space, *without* going-there, by a *manned-equivalent mission*.

The telephone provides, in a very limited way, an indication of the great practical importance of being-there without locating the body there. The world as we know it today simply could not exist without the telephone. The manned equivalent mission and the telephone both relay human sensing and neuromuscular action over a distance. The human functions relayed by the manned equivalent mission are much more powerful than those relayed by the telephone. Manned equivalent mission technology, although conceived for space application, will therefore have enormously important *terrestrial* applications.

The sensing and neuromuscular functions relayed by the manned equivalent mission are not only more powerful, but also correspondingly very much more difficult to relay, particularly over interplanetary distances, than those relayed by the telephone. However, the information technology of the 21$^{st}$ century, that will be applied to implement the manned equivalent mission, is vastly superior to that harnessed by Alexander Graham Bell to create the telephone and is already transforming life in this century in ways that Bell could never have imagined. Consider the modern interactive web site. The web surfer may be sitting in Boston while the site is hosted on a server in Dallas or Los Angeles. The surfer clicks buttons and fills in blanks to initiate downloads or order merchandise. Some sites include such things as web cams, which in effect move the surfer's viewpoint to wherever the web cams are. Sometimes the surfer can click buttons, send messages, or even operate manual controls to make things happen at that distant location. A rapidly developing example is telesurgery, whereby a surgeon operates distant equipment to perform surgery. The surgeon's body may not be beside the patient, but in a very real sense the surgeon is!

## Types of Human Interaction

To be-there means to be interacting normally with the environment there. The manned equivalent mission is a space mission that allows an Earth-based explorer to interact normally with a space environment, as if he or she were located in that environment.

There are only three ways by which humans interact with any environment:

- Physical Interaction. (Exchange of physical substances between a person and the environment, e.g. eating and breathing).

- Social Interaction. (Interaction with other humans).
- Human Action. (Human action, also known as the Stimulus-Cognition-Response (SCR) paradigm, is the three-step process by which all of the world's work is done, whether on Earth or in space. A very simple example of human action is seeing an object, deciding to move it, and then moving it by neuromuscular (generally manual) action).

Physical interaction is not possible in space because the space environment is lethal for the human body. In the present context, social interaction will not occur in space.[1] Human action is the only type of human interaction that must be relayed to space by a manned equivalent mission.

Human action is an exchange of information between the person and the environment. A person effecting human action with an environment: (1) *receives* information about the current state of that environment via his or her senses (primarily vision); (2) *processes* this information to derive desired changes to the environment; and then (3) effects *these changes* on the environment by neuromuscular (primarily manual) action. The neuromuscular action is accomplished by transmitting nerve signals (information) to the muscles. Information is thereby, in effect, transmitted back to the environment to change the state, or information content, of the environment.

Human action is a centrally important concept. Everything that we have ever done, or ever will do, whether on Earth or in space, is by the three step process of human action.

The only way by which an astronaut on Mars (for example) can interact with the Martian environment is by effecting normal human action there. That is, by sensing the environment by the visual sense and by exerting action upon it by neuromuscular (mostly manual) action. Thus to explore and develop space, as we already have the Earth, we need to effect normal human action there. Locating the body there is one way of doing that. However human action is an information-exchange process, and information can be transmitted or projected over long distances. It follows that, in principle, there is indeed another way of being-there. We can be-there in space by the *remote projection* of normal human action. The *remote projection* of human action to space is implemented by the manned equivalent mission.

The manned-equivalent mission is a space mission that provides an Earth-based explorer with exactly the same subjective *visual-experience* (visual information) of Mars (over a full 360-degree field of view) and exactly the same objective *action capability* to get things done on Mars as an astronaut who was actually placed on Mars by a manned mission. Since visual-sensing and manual-action are the only ways by which an astronaut can interact with Mars, the Earth based explorer in the manned equivalent mission interacts with the Martian environment in exactly the same way as the astronaut.[2] The Earth-based explorer *is* there on Mars, even though his or her body is not. Locating the explorer's body on Mars by a manned mission would add nothing to the subjective experience, or objective capability, of the explorer.

(The manned equivalent mission is fundamentally different from unmanned robotic missions, as they are currently understood. Unmanned missions do not enable their Earth based controller to be there on Mars, and do not aspire to have that capability. They are precursors to manned missions. That is, they are based upon the myth that the only way a human can be-there is that his or her body be located there. The justification for the substantial effort required to upgrade unmanned robotic mission to manned equivalence would necessarily therefore never exist.)

## It Has Already Been Done

In principle at least, it is possible to be-there, without going there, by the remote projection of human action. But can this be implemented in actual practice? In one very limited, but extremely important way it already has—by the telephone.

The sense of hearing and the neuromuscular action of speech comprise a special and very important type of human action. The same three information-steps of human action are involved: (1) information is *received* from the environment by the sense of hearing; (2) this information is *processed* to derive desired changes to the environment, namely sound waves to be propagated though the air; (3) these *changes are then effected* by the neuromuscular action of the vocal chords. This particular type of human action is the means by which much of the communication between human beings is effected. Before the invention of the telephone (in 1876) it was necessary to be within a few feet of another person in order to communicate verbally. The telephone now allows this to be done over long distances, with incalculable economic advantage, by the remote projection of the particular type of human action involved in verbal communication. In the $21^{st}$ century the manned equivalent mission can allow humans to do physical work there (in space or on Earth) without being located there. This will be done by the remote projection of the human action required to do that work.

## Remote Projection of Human Action over Interplanetary Distances

To allow a person to communicate by telephone, equivalent to talking directly face-to-face, it is necessary to project only the subset of human action involved in verbal communication. Similarly, to allow a person on Earth to explore space, equivalent to direct exploration by an astronaut in space, it is necessary to project only those sensory and neuromuscular functions that the astronaut would be able, and would need, to deploy to explore and develop. The fidelity of the projection should be sufficient to allow the Earth-based explorer to experience the space environment and function there as effectively as a space-suited astronaut.

The device that is actually transported to the remote space location in a manned equivalent mission is not a robot but a Remote Projection Unit (RPU). The RPU relays, or projects, the full visual sensing and action capabilities of the Earth-based human explorer to the space location. The term robot is very specifically not used because that would imply that the device is an inanimate independent being, like R2D2. It is not. It is a projection of the Earth-based human explorer, with all of the intelligence, judgment and capability of the human explorer. The corresponding unit on Earth is a Local Projection Unit (LPU), to which the Earth-based explorer is interfaced.

Vision and manual action are the only components of human action needed to explore and develop space.

To allow the Earth based explorer to see the Martian scene (for example) over his or her full visual field, in spite of the limited data-link bandwidth and the long transmission delay, video imagery will be transmitted back to create (off-line) in the LPU a 3-D computer model of the essentially static Martian scene in the vicinity of the RPU. An Earth-based computer will create (in real-time) a continuous sequence of panoramic views of this computer model of the Martian scene from the positions and directions as currently specified by the Earth-based explorer. These dynamic views will then be instantly displayed to the explorer on a very wide-angle screen covering his or her entire visual field. The Earth-based controller does not see the raw video relayed back from Mars, but a computer reconstruction of that video data. (It is interesting to note that in normal direct vision, the subjective visual sensation is a similar *reconstruction* by the brain of the raw data sensed by the retina, not the raw data from the retina itself. Thus, for example, we are not aware of the blind spot near the center of the visual field where the optic nerve connects with the retina.)

To effect mechanical action in spite of the transmission delay, the equipment on Mars must be capable of autonomous operation over periods of the order of the transmission delay, which is about 30 minutes for Mars. The human explorer, back on Earth, will function in a supervisory mode sending high level commands—for example "move over there," "pick up that rock" (designating these items on a dynamic panoramic display of the Martian scene)—and then letting the autonomous system on Mars carry out these directives during the transmission delay time. The Earth based explorer does not directly control the mechanical effectors of the RPU. The effector-commands are derived by a computer within the RPU, based upon real time video data of the scene currently being acted upon and the high level commands received from the Earth-based controller. The explorer, operating in this *supervisory* mode, should have the same capability to get things done on Mars as if he were located there on Mars as a space-suited astronaut working *directly* on the task. (Again, it is interesting to note that in normal direct human action we function in a similar supervisory mode, although over a much shorter time period. For example, a conscious high-level decision to stand up is implemented autonomously, below the conscious level, by innumerable sensing and neuromuscular actions.)

The beginnings of the technology required to implement the manned equivalent mission have already been successfully demonstrated in the Pathfinder mission to Mars. Earth-based controllers issued high-level directives (go "there," do "that") and the rover then autonomously performed these tasks during the transmission delay period. A 3-D computer model of the landing site was constructed from the video data received from Mars. Fly-over video sequences derived from this model were released to the TV networks by NASA. These sequences provided the visual effect of being-there and moving around at will.

The development of the manned equivalent mission will be a major undertaking. However, as previously noted, the manned equivalent mission is not an entirely new system concept but a development (albeit a very major one) from existing (e.g., Pathfinder) technology.

The manned equivalent mission should be identified now as a candidate means for the human exploration and development of space. This very important first step would, for the first time, establish a clear and rational direction for a program that has been drifting for many years.

## Intangibles

Manned missions inspire great admiration for the courage and adventurous sprit of the human space explorer. A manned equivalent mission would not. Lindbergh's first flight across the Atlantic was immensely inspirational and he rightly got a ticker tape parade. But today if someone wishes to go to Europe they fly in jumbo-jet luxury. No ticker tape parade for this traveler! Lindbergh pioneered aviation, and thanks to him and many other early aviators, aviation is now part of the rich fabric of our civilization. Similarly, brave astronauts and cosmonauts have pioneered space. But it is the manned equivalent mission that will make space useful, practical and profitable.

Emotionally, we might prefer to explore, as we always have, by the old familiar way of brave men and women going down to ships at the harbor, casting off, and setting sail for unknown lands. But now that space has become potentially open to us, exploration has taken on an entirely new dimension. In life generally, we revere the past but must always move forward. Faced with the daunting challenge of space we should not abandon our dreams, but seize the great opportunity it presents. We should set a goal for humans to be-there permanently and affordably on Mars, moons and asteroids, etc. by manned equivalent missions—not just for scientific exploration, but most importantly to derive great wealth from space as we already have over the ages from planet Earth.

## Notes

1. In a manned equivalent mission with multiple Earth-based explorers, the explorers would interact normally with each other on Earth. A combined manned and manned equivalent mission is logically inconsistent—the manned equivalent mission is undertaken because the manned mission cannot be. A manned mission only is outside the present context.
2. There are other components of human action such as speech and hearing. In the highly unlikely event that any of these should be applicable in a particular scenario, they could be readily implemented.

# POSTSCRIPT

## Should NASA Continue to Pursue Manned Space Exploration?

As a result of the *Columbia* tragedy, the United States shuttle fleet is down to three: the *Endeavour, Atlantis,* and *Discovery*. All are younger than *Columbia* was—and thus presumably less prone to failure in the near future—but all are grounded until the investigation into the *Columbia* failure is complete. Meanwhile, travel to and from the International Space Station must be on Russian spacecraft. Stephen L. Petuanch, "No More Shuttles, Please," *Discover* (May 2003), denounces the space shuttle program as too expensive and unsafe, but the next generation of shuttles is far from ready; see Bill Sweetman, "Space Shuttle: The Next Generation," *Popular Science* (May 2003), and Mark Alpert, "Rethinking the Shuttle," *Scientific American* (April 2003). There are also efforts to develop an affordable spacecraft capable of many safe trips to and from orbit; see Michael A. Dornheim, "Affordable Spaceship," *Aviation Week & Space Technology* (April 21, 2003).

Do we need to send people—real or virtual—into space? Won't robots do? The question is timely because in 1997—two decades after the two *Viking* landers extensively mapped and characterized the Red Planet—scientists returned to Mars with the *Pathfinder* lander and its accompanying *Sojourner* rover. The Mars *Global Surveyor* arrived in September to photograph the planet from orbit, inventory rock types, and map future landing sites. Further robotic missions to Mars were scheduled for launch in 2003; Europe launched the *Beagle 2* lander on June 2, 2003, and the U.S. was scheduled to launch additional missions later in the year. It seems likely that as long as the robots continue to succeed in their missions, manned missions will continue to be put off because funding shortages will probably continue. Funding for space exploration remains low largely because problems on Earth (environmental and other) seem to need money more urgently than space exploration projects do. The prospects for manned space expeditions to the moon, Mars, or other worlds seem very dim, although Paul D. Spudis, "Harvest the Moon," *Astronomy* (June 2003), asserts that there are four good reasons for putting people at least on the Moon: "The first motivation to revisit the Moon is that its rocks hold the early history of our own planet and the solar system. Next, its unique environment and properties make it an ideal vantage point for observing the universe. The Moon is also a natural space station where we can learn how to live off-planet. And finally, it gives us an extraterrestrial filling station, with resources to use both locally and in near-Earth space." Alex Ellery, "Humans versus Robots for Space Exploration and Development," *Space Policy* (May 2003), maintains that although "robotics and artificial intelligence are becoming more sophisticated, they will not be able to deal with 'thinking-on-one's-feet' tasks that require generalisations from past experience. . . . [T]here will be a critical role for humans in space for the foreseeable future."

Few nations have the wealth and industrial infrastructure to contemplate mounting manned space expeditions. The Russians remain capable of supplying the International Space Station but seem to have no plans for other efforts. In the past, astronauts from Europe and other parts of the world have ridden U.S. space shuttles into space. Europe has no current plans for its own manned space program. China reported in January 2003 that it is going ahead with plans to put astronauts in orbit and is considering a lunar exploration program. For current news, see `http://www.spacedaily.com/`.

# On the Internet . . .

## Center for Democracy & Technology

The Center for Democracy & Technology works to promote democratic values and constitutional liberties in the digital age.

http://www.cdt.org/

## Electronic Frontier Foundation

The Electronic Frontier Foundation is concerned with protecting individual freedoms and rights such as privacy as new communications technologies emerge.

http://www.eff.org

## Banned Books Week

The American Library Association's Banned Books Week Web site shows that the issue of censorship is by no means restricted to the Internet.

http://www.ala.org/content/NavigationMenu/Our_association/offices/Intellectual_Freedom3/Banned_books_week/Banned_books_week.htm

## Project Gutenberg

Project Gutenberg is an ongoing project to convert the classics of literature into digital format.

http://www.gutenberg.net

## Pew Internet & American Life Project

The Pew Internet & American Life Project explores the impact of the Internet on children, families, communities, the work place, schools, health care, and civic/political life.

http://www.pewinternet.org/

# PART 5

## The Computer Revolution

*Fans of computers are sure that the electronic wonders offer untold benefits to society. When the first personal computers appeared in the early 1970s, they immediately brought unheard-of capabilities to their users. Ever since, those capabilities have been increasing. Today children command more sheer computing power than major corporations did in the 1950s and 1960s. Computer users are in direct contact with their fellow users around the world. Information is instantly available and infinitely malleable.*

*Some observers wonder about the purported untold benefits of computers. Specifically, will such benefits be outweighed by threats to children (by free access to pornography), civil order (by free access to sites that advocate racism and violence), traditional institutions (will books, for example, become an endangered species?), or to human pride (a computer has already outplayed the human world chess champion)? And does all that time we spend online weaken our connections to our fellow human being?*

- Does the Internet Strengthen Community?
- Does the War on Terrorism Threaten Privacy?
- Will Screens Replace Pages?

# ISSUE 14

## Does the Internet Strengthen Community?

**YES: John B. Horrigan,** from "Online Communities: Networks that Nurture Long-Distance Relationships and Local Ties," Pew Internet & American Life Project (October 2001)

**NO: Jonathon N. Cummings, Brian Butler, and Robert Kraut,** from "The Quality of Online Social Relationships," *Communications of the ACM* (July 2002)

### ISSUE SUMMARY

**YES:** John B. Horrigan asserts that when people go online, they form both relationships with distant others who share their interests and strengthen their involvement with their local communities.

**NO:** Jonathon N. Cummings, Brian Butler, and Robert Kraut maintain that online communication is less valuable for building strong social relationships than more traditional face-to-face and telephone communication.

It is a truism to say that technologies have social impact, and that that impact can be both far-reaching and unforeseen. Thus the Gutenberg printing press, whose first product was the Bible, wound up contributing to the Protestant Reformation, making public schools essential, creating the scientific and industrial revolutions, and spreading the idea of human rights and thus leading to the American, French, and other revolutions. It also quite shattered what used to be thought of as "community" when most people lived and died within a mile of their birthplace and took the shape of their lives from a single unquestionable religious or civil authority.

Whether these effects were for good or ill depends very much on whom you ask. Most citizens of the modern developed world—the products and beneficiaries of those changes—would surely say they were for good. Some are more skeptical.

When the Internet was new, its partisans promised that it would bring a new age of public participation in political decision-making and link together far-flung people to create a "global village" far more real than anything forecast for television by Marshall McLuhan. However, some people feared that it would be harmful to society. Clifford Stoll claimed the Internet would weaken commitment to and enjoyment of real friendships (*Silicon Snake Oil,* Doubleday, 1995). David Paletz wrote that "the new information technology . . . can inspire populism, but one based on ignorance; it can facilitate the expression of public opinion, but one inspired by demagoguery; it can engender community, but of ethnic, religious, and single-issue groups" ("Advanced Information Technology and Political Communication," *Social Science Computer Review,* Spring 1996). Sherry Turkle feared the Internet would lead to the destruction of meaningful community ("Virtuality and Its Discontents: Searching for Community in Cyberspace," *American Prospect,* Winter 1996). Robert Kraut et al. reported that new Internet users became less socially involved and more depressed ("Internet Paradox: A Social Technology that Reduces Social Involvement and Psychological Well-Being?" *American Psychologist,* 53[9], 1998). Andrew L. Shapiro admitted that the Internet's potential for fostering personal growth and social progress seemed limitless but worried that "customizing our lives to the hilt could undermine the strength and cohesion of local communities . . . shared experience is an indisputable essential ingredient" ("The Net that Binds," *Nation,* June 21, 1999). At least one critic criticizes the Internet because it fosters "voluntary" communities based on mutual interests and argues that "learning to make the best of circumstances one has not chosen is part of what it means to be a good citizen and a mature human being. We should not organize our lives around the fantasy that entrance and exit can always be cost-free: On-line groups can fulfill important emotional and utilitarian needs. But they must not be taken as comprehensive models of a future society" (William A. Galston, "Does the Internet Strengthen Community?" *National Civic Review,* October 2000).

Since then, the Internet has grown tremendously. By late 2002, over a tenth of the world population (634 million people) had Internet access. The social impact of online communication is thus increasingly a matter of global concern. Does it strengthen society by helping people make and keep friends, form "virtual" communities stretching around the globe, and exchange information? Or does it weaken society by drawing people away from face-to-face interactions and local community groups, substituting weak friendships for strong ones, and interfering with the development of mature, good citizens?

John B. Horrigan, a senior researcher with the Pew Internet & American Life Project, reports the results of a survey showing that Internet users strengthen their connections to others, expand their social worlds, and increase their involvement with communities, both local and virtual, in a process called "glocalization." Jonathon N. Cummings, Brian Butler, and Robert Kraut maintain that online communication is less valuable for building strong social relationships than more traditional face-to-face and telephone communication. The overall effect depends on whether online communication replaces or supplements traditional communication.

**John B. Horrigan** 

# Online Communities: Networks that Nurture Long-Distance Relationships and Local Ties

## Summary of Findings

### The Vibrant Social Universe Online

In recent years, there has been concern about the social impact of the Internet on several levels. One major worry was that use of the Internet would prompt people to withdraw from social engagement and become isolated, depressed, and alienated. A related fear was that Internet users might abandon contact with their local communities as they discovered how easy it is to go online to communicate with those in other parts of the world and get information from every point on the planet.

We surveyed 1,697 Internet users in January and February [2001] to explore the breadth and depth of community online. Our findings suggest that the online world is a vibrant social universe where many Internet users enjoy serious and satisfying contact with online communities. These online groups are made up of those who share passions, beliefs, hobbies, or lifestyles. Tens of millions of Americans have joined communities after discovering them online. And many are using the Internet to join and participate in longstanding, traditional groups such as professional and trade associations. All in all, 84% of Internet users have at one time or another contacted an online group.

The pull of online communities in the aftermath of the September 11 attacks shows how Americans have integrated online communities into their lives. In the days following the attacks, 33% of American Internet users read or posted material in chat rooms, bulletin boards, or other online forums. Although many early posts reflected outrage at the events, online discussions soon migrated to grieving, discussion and debate on how to respond, and information queries about the suspects and those who sponsored them. With the dramatic displays of community spirit around the country following September 11, there are hopes that Americans' repulsion and shock [from] the attacks might have sparked a renewal of civic spirit in the United States. The existing vibrancy of online communities profiled in this report suggests that Internet groups can play a supporting role in any enduring boon to community life in the aftermath of the attacks.

Our winter survey also showed that many Americans are using the Internet to intensify their connection to their local community. They employ email to plan church meetings, arrange neighborhood gatherings, and petition local politicians. They use the Web to find out about local merchants, get community news, and check out area fraternal organizations. Moreover, there is evidence that this kind of community engagement is particularly appealing to young adults.

Sociologist Barry Wellman argues that many new social arrangements are being formed through "glocalization"—the capacity of the Internet to expand users' social worlds to faraway people and simultaneously to bind them more deeply to the place where they live. This report illustrates how widely "glocalization" is occurring. The Internet helps many people find others who share their interests no matter how distant they are, and it also helps them increase their contact with groups and people they already know and it helps them feel more connected to them.

## 90 Million Americans Have Participated in Online Groups

- 84% of Internet users, or about 90 million Americans, say they have used the Internet to contact or get information from a group. We call them "Cyber Groupies."
- 79% of Cyber Groupies identify at least one particular group with which they stay in regular contact.
- 49% of Cyber Groupies say the Internet has helped them connect with groups or people who share their interests.
- Cyber Groupies try out different groups; the average Cyber Groupie has contacted four online groups at one time or another.

Use of the Internet often prompts Americans to join groups. More than half of Cyber Groupies (56%) say they joined an online group *after* they began communicating with it over the Internet. This includes those who joined traditional groups whose existence predated the Internet, such as professional or fraternal groups. In other words, Internet access is helping people join all kinds of communities, including those that are not exclusively virtual communities.

- 40% of Cyber Groupies say the Internet has helped them become more involved with groups to which they already belong.

## 28 Million Have Used the Internet to Deepen Their Ties to Their Local Communities

In addition to helping users participate in communities of interest that often have no geographical boundaries the Internet is a tool for those who are involved with local groups, particularly church groups.

- 26% of Internet users have employed the Internet to contact or get information about local groups. That comes to 28 million people.

## Virtual Third Places

In the face of widespread worries that community activity is ebbing in the United States, these findings demonstrate that the Internet, while not necessarily turning the tide, has become an important new tool to connect people with shared interests globally and locally. In some ways, online communities have become *virtual third places* for people because they are different places from home and work. These places allow people either to hang out with others or more actively engage with professional associations, hobby groups, religious organizations, or sports leagues.

## Online Communities Foster Chatter and Connection

These groups are lively online communities. People exchange emails, hash out issues, find out about group activities, and meet face-to-face as a result of online communities. Approximately 23 million Americans are *very* active in online communities, meaning that they email their principle online group several times a week.

- 60% of Cyber Groupies say they use email to communicate with the group; of these emailers 43% email the group several times a week.
- 33% of the 28 million Local Groupies who use email send email to their main local organization several times a week.

## More Contact with Different People

Many Cyber Groupies and Local Groupies say that online communities have spurred connections to strangers and to people of different racial, ethnic, and economic backgrounds.

- 50% of Cyber Groupies say that participation in an online community has helped them get to know people they otherwise would not have met.
- 35% of Local Groupies say that participation in an online community has helped them get to know people they otherwise would not have met. This lower number relative to Cyber Groupies may be due to the fact that Local Groupies probably were acquainted already with members of the online group.
- 37% of Cyber Groupies say the Internet has helped them connect with people of different ages or generations.
- 27% of Cyber Groupies say the Internet has helped them connect with people from different racial, ethnic, or economic backgrounds.

The types of connections people establish depend on the kind of group to which they belong. Members of some cyber groups go to their groups to establish personal relationships, while others just want to keep up with group news and activities.

- Members of belief groups, ethnic online groups, and especially online groups oriented to lifestyle issues are most interested in using the Internet to establish personal relationships.

- Members of entertainment, professional, and sports online groups tend to use email in group activities less often than those who belong to other kinds. They focus their online activities on getting information about popular culture.
- Men tend to be drawn to online groups involving professional activities, politics, and sports.
- Women tend to be drawn to online medical support groups, local community associations that are online, and cyber groups relating to entertainment.

## Joiners of Online Groups Differ from Those Who Belonged to the Group Prior to Participating in It via the Internet

There are differences between those who have used the Internet to join a group and those who use the Internet to participate in groups to which they already belong. Many who join online groups are relative newcomers to the Internet. They tend to be urban dwellers, young adults, and less well-educated than the typical Internet user. As a cohort they are more ethnically diverse than other Internet users, and more likely to be interested in online groups relating to fun activities.

The 56% of Cyber Groupies who joined a group after having first contacted it through the Internet have very different tastes in online groups than the "Long-timers" who belonged to the group before engaging with it online. Joiners of Cyber Groups identify hobby groups as the online community that they contact most, followed closely by trade or professional associations. A significant number of joiners also say they contact online fan groups of an entertainer or TV show. In contrast, Long-timers are most likely to say they are most closely in touch with trade or professional groups online.

At the local level, Long-timers are anchored in faith-based and community groups, while the joiners—who make up 20% of the Local Groupie population—show a greater tendency toward groups devoted to sports or with an explicitly social orientation.

Net Joiners of local groups are demographically diverse. They also tend to be highly experienced Internet users. This suggests that the Internet use is drawing new and different kinds of people to local groups. Once people have found local groups online and joined them, they report high levels of community involvement.

## Civic Involvement by the Young

These differences among Joiners—particularly their relative youth, newness to the Internet, and racial diversity—suggests that the Internet may be drawing a segment of the population to community engagement who have not been very tied to civic activities. Political scientist Robert Putnam has argued that one major reason for the decline in civic engagement in the United States is the reluctance among younger people to participate in community groups. Our findings indicate that many young people are turning to the Internet as an outlet for community activity. Although young people tend to focus on online groups that involve hobbies, they also are much more likely than other users to report that the Internet has helped them become more involved organizations in their community and connect with people of different generations, economic backgrounds, and ethnic groups. In other words, the primary draw to online communities for young people appears to be hobby groups; however, a secondary outcome, as young people surf to other online communities, is to connect many to groups that help foster civic engagement.

## The Internet's Role in Local Engagement

At the local level, people use the Internet mainly as an information utility to find out about local merchants and community activities. The Internet's role in public deliberation is modest. Public access to the Internet is only moderately available throughout the United States.

- 41% Internet users say that they "often" or "sometimes" go online to seek out information about local stores or merchants.
- 35% of Internet users "often" or "sometimes" go online for news about their local community or to find out about community events.
- 30% go online "often" or "sometimes" for information about local government.
- 24% go online "often" or "sometimes" to get information about local schools.
- 13% of Internet users say that they "often" or "sometimes" email public officials. This low rate may be because only half of all Internet users say their town has a Web site, and few Internet users find the town's Web site very useful.
- 11% of Internet users say that they are aware of at least one local issue in which the Internet played a role in organizing citizens to communicate with public officials. However, this percentage doubles to 22% for Internet users who are active members of online communities.
- 51% percent of all Americans know of a place in their community where the Internet is publicly available. Overwhelmingly, these places are public libraries. African-Americans are the most likely to say that their community lacks public access to the Internet; 42% of African-Americans say their community does not have publicly available Internet terminals somewhere, compared with 29% of whites and 33% of Hispanics.

# Main Report

## Part 1: Background

When ARPANET, the Internet's precursor, came online in 1969, it did not have a foundational moment like the telephone's, where Alexander Graham Bell ordered his associate Thomas Watson: "Mr. Watson, come here, I want you." That sentence signaled an era of person-to-person communication over distance. In contrast, ARPANET connected a community. In its earliest days, it was a community of computer researchers at major U.S. universities working on similar problems. Since then, the Internet's capability of allowing many-to-many communications has fostered communities of various sizes and sorts.

In this report, we assess the scope of online communities in the United States and the impact they are having on people's lives. We examine two kinds of communities—those that are primarily cyber-based with no inherently geographic aspect (i.e., online communities) and those in which people use the Internet to connect with groups based in the community in which they live (i.e., communities online). We call members of the former group "Cyber Groupies." We define people who belong to any group having to do with their community as "Local Groupies" and analyze how they use the Internet to stay in touch with local affairs.

Our survey suggests that going online to connect with a group is a central part of Americans' Internet experience. More people have used the Internet to contact an online group than have done extremely popular activities, such as getting news online, health information, or financial information. More people participate in online groups than have bought things online. Fully 84% of all Internet users have contacted an online group at one time or another. We call them Cyber Groupies and there are about 90 million of them. Some 79% of Cyber Groupies identify a particular group with which they remain in contact. Additionally, Cyber Groupies often surf to more than one online group; the average Cyber Groupie has gone to about four different online groups at one time or another. Finally, a quarter of Internet users (26%) say they have used email and the Web to contact or get information about groups and organizations in their communities. These Local Groupies number more than 28 million.

The demographics of the Cyber Groupie population are fairly close to the overall Internet population. Where differences do emerge, the pattern suggests that early adopters of the Internet are more likely to have contacted online groups. This means that Cyber Groupies are more likely to be men and to have college educations or better. Cyber Groupies also tend to be younger than non-groupies. This no doubt is linked to the fact that online groups play a minor role in the lives of people over the age of 55.

The broad appeal of online groups and the youthful tilt of the Cyber Groupie population—especially among those active in online groups and those who have recently joined them—suggests that the Internet is providing an important place for associational activity for some of the most enthusiastic online Americans. This is occurring in the context of widespread worry that Americans are less and less willing to get involved in community affairs and group activities. It is too soon to say that use of the Internet is reversing that trend. But the findings from this survey indicate that group activity is flourishing online and it is a place that attracts Internet users to new group activity.

## Part 2: The Internet, Communities, and the Virtual "Third Place"

Social scientists cite any number of indicators to illustrate that Americans' level of civic engagement is on the decline. Membership in organizations whose health may be seen as an indicator of strong community involvement—such as the Parent-Teachers Association (PTA)—has declined steadily over the past several decades. The share of Americans voting in presidential elections has fallen since the 1960s, with voting rates in some local elections no higher than 10%. There has been some evidence of growth in certain kinds of organization called "tertiary associations," but that has not been encouraging to those who worry about the decline of community in America. Tertiary organizations have members spread throughout the country, rarely have local chapters, and usually ask members only for a membership check in exchange for an occasional newsletter. These organizations expect little of their members besides their financial contributions.

While concurring that community involvement is on the wane, many activists believe that the Internet might be able to reverse the trend. Since the early days of the Web, activists have argued that "community networks" could bind increasingly fragmented communities together and provide a voice for segments of society that have been traditionally ignored. Such electronic communities can lower the barriers to democratic participation. Advocates hope lower barriers, coupled with deliberate activities that bring all segments of a town or city into the planning process for building community networks, can help revive the community spirit in America. These advocates do not argue that it is inevitable that the Internet will create community involvement, but rather that the Internet presents an opportunity to build community at a time when the need is great.

Though often focused on the opportunities the Internet presents for a renaissance of local places, technology activists also recognize that virtual communities (i.e., online groups that connect people with common interests without any concern about distance) can play an important role in users' lives. One of the earliest proponents of virtual communities, Howard Rheingold, argues that "people anywhere . . . inevitably build virtual communities" as "informal public spaces disappear from our real lives." Rheingold holds out hope that virtual communities can revive democratic participation, in part by increasing the diversity of sources of information and by sparking public debate that is not mediated by large corporations or special interests.

The hopes for the Internet and community are tempered by the acknowledgement that it is a technology that has the potential to undermine community. As author Andrew Shapiro points out, the Internet's potential to give people more control also allows them to restrict the flow of information they receive. By giving people a choice to block out information that somehow does not "fit" with a community's beliefs or norms, the Internet could exacerbate existing trends toward community fragmentation. Nothing about this is inevitable, but Shapiro notes that the evidence on online communities suggests that some degree of face-to-face interaction is necessary for an online community to be sustainable. As Katie Hafner points out in her new account of the pioneering online community "The Well," this cyber group really gained vitality once members, most of whom lived in the San Francisco Bay Area, had met face-to-face.

The findings of the Pew Internet & American Life Project survey indicate that something positive is afoot with respect to the Internet and community life in the United States. People's use of the Internet to participate in organizations is not necessarily evidence of a revival of civic engagement, but it has clearly stimulated new associational activity. And, because they have been both physical and virtual, these group interactions are richer than those found in "tertiary associations." This type of activity might be likened to what sociologist Ray Oldenburg calls the "third place"—the corner bar, café, or bookstore where people hang out to talk about things that are going on in their lives and neighborhood.

Although Oldenburg very clearly has physical interaction in mind in talking about third places, the Internet has spurred in cyberspace the types of conversations that Oldenburg describes in third places. Our survey suggests that significant numbers of Cyber Groupies are enjoying new relationships because of their use of the Internet. One-quarter (27%) of Cyber Groupies say the Net has helped them connect with people of different economic and ethnic backgrounds and 37% say it has helped them connect with people of different generations. Whether through cyber groups or online groups grounded in local communities, the Internet's "virtual third places" appear to be building bridges among their participants. . . .

**Jonathon N. Cummings, Brian Butler, and Robert Kraut**

# NO

# The Quality of Online Social Relationships

People use the Internet intensely for interpersonal communication, sending and receiving email, contacting friends and family via instant messaging services, visiting chat rooms, or subscribing to distribution lists, among other activities. The evidence is clear that interpersonal communication is an important use of the Internet, if not its *most* important use. For example, both self-report surveys and computer monitoring studies indicate that email is the most popular online application.

Claims regarding the Internet's usefulness for developing social relationships, however, remain controversial. Both personal testimonials and systematically collected data document the deep and meaningful social relationships people can cultivate online.

This evidence, however, conflicts with data comparing the value that people place on their online relationships with offline relationships and with data comparing social relationships among heavy and light Internet users. For example, Parks and Roberts surveyed users of multiplayer environments called MOOs. Ninety-three percent of the users had made friends online, but when asked to compare their online friendships with those offline, respondents rated offline ones higher. Respondents to Nie's national survey reported spending less time with friends and family since going online, with the decline greatest among the most frequent Internet users. And Kraut et al. presented longitudinal evidence to demonstrate that among new Internet users, online time diminished social involvement and psychological well being.

Understanding the impact of the Internet on human social relationships requires two types of evidence. First, we need to know how computer-mediated communication affects the quality of particular social interactions and relationships. Are the online ones better, the same, or worse than those sustained by other means? Second, we need to know how computer-mediated communication affects one's mix of social interactions and relationships. The impact of the Internet is likely to be very different if it supplements communication with existing friends and family, or if instead it substitutes for more traditional communication and social ties.

From *Communications of the ACM,* vol. 45, no. 7, July 2002, pp. 103–108. 

This article addresses the first question by explicitly comparing online and offline social interaction. We briefly summarize evidence from several empirical studies, all of which suggest that computer-mediated communication, and in particular email, is less valuable for building and sustaining close social relationships than face-to-face contact and telephone conversations. These studies include the following surveys:

- International bank employees who describe the value of particular communication sessions for work relationships;
- College students, using the same methodology, but focusing on personal relationships;
- A longitudinal study of new Internet users; and
- Examination of behavior on email-based listservs.

## Comparing Communication over Different Media

One way to evaluate the usefulness of the Internet for developing and maintaining social ties is to ask people to compare particular communication sessions on relevant outcomes. One can then relate the outcomes to features of the communication session (for example, who it was with, the duration, and the modality over which it occurred). This technique has been used to uncover features of conversation that lead to the development of social relationships in face-to-face settings. We apply it to email, telephone, and face-to-face communication among bank employees and university students.

In our 1991 study, 979 employees of a multinational bank reported on their most recent communication conducted over different media. About 81% used email in their jobs, sending an average of 15 messages per week. Respondents evaluated the usefulness of communication episodes using criteria related to the success of work groups, including usefulness for getting work done and for developing or sustaining a work relationship, utilizing a 3-point scale, where 1 meant not very useful and 3 meant very useful. We report data on 5,205 communication episodes that occurred in person, by telephone, or by email. . . .

Respondents reported communication by email to be reliably worse than communication conducted face-to-face or by telephone, both for getting work done and for sustaining work relationships. However, the disadvantages of email were significantly greater for maintaining relationships than for getting work done. These differences among the media remain even when one statistically controls for relevant variables, including respondents' gender, age, job title, daily volume of communication, and experience with email.

One might object that this data comes from the early years of email, although employees in this firm had been using email since the mid-1970s. In addition, one might also object that personal relationships are not central to work activity, although many studies stress their importance for getting work done. To counter these objections, we replicated the original study in 1999 among students at an eastern university. These students used email extensively, estimating a mean of 11 messages per day, and were in a stage in life that stressed the importance of developing personal relationships. Some 39 students completed a diary, recording information about each of 259 communication episodes in which they had participated during a four-hour block—late afternoon to early evening. Students recorded their relationship with their communication partner (relative, friend, acquaintance, or other), its duration, the topic of conversation (schoolwork, personal, or other), and the modality over which it occurred. Respondents evaluated each communication for its usefulness in getting work done, exchanging information, and developing or maintaining a personal relationship. They made their evaluations on 5-point scale.

Like the banking study, students evaluated email communication sessions as an inferior means to maintaining personal relationships compared to those conducted in person ($p < 0.05$) and by telephone ($p < 0.05$), these latter being equal. The students, however, found email to be as good as the telephone and in-person communication for completing schoolwork ($p > 0.10$), and even better for the exchange of information ($p < 0.05$).

Students also estimated the frequency of communication over the different modalities and the strength of their relationship with each of the 148 partners. We created an index of relationship strength by averaging their answers to two questions: "How close do you feel to this person?" and "How often do you get favors or advice from this person" (alpha = 0.92). We used linear regression to predict the strength of the relationship from frequency of communication with that partner over the different modalities: email, in-person, and telephone. Frequency of communication across all three modalities was significantly related to the strength of relationship, both directly and once the partner's gender, nature of the relations, length of the relationship, and geographic distance between the parties were controlled statistically. However, communicating in person (Beta s = 0.36) and by telephone (Beta = 0.27) were both significantly better predictors of a strong relationship than was communication by email (Beta = 0.15).

## Comparing Internet Versus NonInternet Social Partners

In these studies, respondents selected communication episodes and partners based on the recency of the communication session. This procedure has the advantage of sampling all potential conversations, but may over-represent social relationships not important to the respondents, but are frequent simply because the partners are nearby. Here, we compare the value of using computer-mediated and noncomputer-mediated communication to keep up with partners with whom the respondents have a substantial amount of communication. The data comes from the HomeNet project, a field trial that tracked Internet usage and communication behavior among a sample of 93 households in Pittsburgh during their first year or two online.

Participants answered a series of questions about two individuals with whom they had frequent communication. The first, whom we refer to as the "Internet partner," was the individual outside of their household to whom they sent the most email, as recorded in computer-generated usage logs collected as part of the project. Some 111 respondents answered questions about an Internet partner. The second, whom we refer to as the "nonInternet partner," was the person outside of their household with whom respondents claimed to have the most frequent communication in any modality. Some 125 respondents answered questions about a nonInternet partner. To allow for comparisons between relationships conducted by email and those conducted primarily over other modalities, we limit our analyses here to the 99 respondents who answered questions both about an Internet and a non-Internet partner, and for whom these partners were different individuals.

Respondents indicated each partner's gender and age, duration of acquaintance, role relation (for example, family, friend, co-worker), and geographic proximity (for example, neighborhood, city, state). Participants then rated their frequency of email, face-to-face, and telephone communication: (5-daily, 4-weekly, 3-monthly, 2-less often, 1-never). A 5-point scale indicated psychological closeness with the partner: "I feel very close," "I could freely confide in this person," "This person is important to me," and "I understand this person fully" (alpha = 0.90).

We were interested in three questions: Do people differ in the overall volume of communication they have with the people they keep up with using different modalities? Do they differ in how close they feel toward them? Is communication with a partner over different modalities predictive of differing degrees of psychological closeness?

The number of respondents' communication sessions per month, broken and summed over all modalities, indicate that participants communicated less frequently with their Internet partner (5.2 times/month) than their nonInternet partner (7.2 times/month, $p < 0.001$). . . . Although respondents communicated more by email with their Internet partner ($p < 0.001$), they communicated less using the other modalities ($p < 0.001$ for face-to-face and $p < 0.001$ for telephone). Respondents also reported feeling less close to their Internet partner than to their nonInternet partner ($p < 0.001$).

Using a least squares regression analysis, we predicted psychological closeness from frequency of communication for the nonInternet partner and Internet partner, controlling for sex, age, role relation, duration of acquaintance, and physical proximity. Most notably, frequency of communication was a critical predictor of psychological closeness with the nonInternet partner (Beta = 0.40), but not with the Internet partner (Beta = –0.08). The difference is statistically significant ($p < 0.001$). The weaker association of communication with closeness for the Internet sample is analogous to findings from the student sample.

Social relationships offline involve more communication than those developed online, and thus predicted psychological closeness. Given our cross-sectional data, we cannot tell if communication does not lead to closeness when people are communicating electronically, or if people are exchanging email with people to whom they do not feel close. In either case, they are not getting as much social benefit from email as they do from their other communication activity.

## Online Social Groups

The research we described so far concentrates on dyadic relationships between individuals in their online and offline lives. Yet one of the prominent features of the Internet is the presence of larger social collectives, which researchers have called "electronic groups" or "communities." Even before the advent of the Web, the Internet provided an infrastructure for online group-level social behavior, through USENET and email-based distribution lists. In descriptions of social life on the Internet, these electronic or virtual communities are often described as groups where relationships form, and whose members provide each other with companionship, information, and social support.

While existing studies and stories of electronic groups provide insight into the types of social activity that can occur in electronic collectives, the anecdotal nature of this research leaves open the question of what typically happens. Are active, tightly knit electronic groups, in which people form personal relationships and develop a sense of belonging, the norm or are the cases reported in the literature interesting exceptions? To examine this question, we collected data from a sample of 204 Internet listservs. The data shows that, on average, listservs are much more like loosely knit, voluntary organizations than the tightly knit social communities highlighted in prior case studies.

The sample consisted of 204 unmanaged and unmoderated email-based listservs, drawn from a population of approximately 70,000 listservs. An initial random sample of 1,066 was stratified by topic type (work-related, personal, and mixed) to ensure it included a range of topics and member populations. Listservs were dropped from the initial sample if the list owner declined to participate in the study (21%); the listserv was defunct (16%); it had closed membership, generally as part of an organization, course, or task force (15%); or it could not provide membership data in an automated fashion. The final sample consisted of lists evenly divided among those oriented around professional, personal, and academic topics. Based on descriptions of the lists, we were able to classify them as purely electronic or as hybrid, combining both electronic and traditional communications, especially conventional face-to-face meetings. For example, a national list for youth hockey was judged as purely electronic, while the mailing list for a city-specific country dancers' group was judged as hybrid.

For a 130-day period we collected data on each listserv's membership and communication activity. During the observation period, membership was characterized in terms of size (number of members), growth (members entering as a percentage of initial size), loss (members leaving as a percentage of initial size), and net change in size (as a percentage of initial size). Communication activity was measured in terms of volume (number of messages per day) and interactivity (length of discussion threads). In addition, measures of member participation (percentage of members contributing messages and the concentration of message contributions among the active participants) were created for each listserv. . . .

Unlike traditional small groups, listservs have large, fluctuating memberships in which a small core of active participants generates relatively low levels of sporadic communication, whose messages rarely receive a response. Small groups, as described in the social psychological research literature, have between 3 and 15 members, with relatively low turnover. By comparison, the listservs were much larger (median of 64 members), with high churn (22% of original members dropping out annually and double this number joining). In contrast to highly interactive conversation involving almost all group members (typical of small groups), listservs exhibit little communication, with a full 33% exhibiting no communication during the 130-day observation period. Of those that did, the median listserv accrued 0.28 messages per day (or less than 0.0004 messages per subscriber per day). Over 50% of members contributed no messages over the 130-day observation period, and a small number generated most of the messages. Conversation was not interactive. On average, fewer than one message out of three received any response.

The hybrid groups differed little from the purely electronic groups. Though they were significantly smaller, probably reflecting the more limited geographic area from which they could attract members, both types of groups had similar high turnover, low volume of messages, low level of interactivity, and domination by a small proportion of their membership. Regardless of how the hybrid groups acted when they met face-to-face, online they acted like typical weak-tie collectives.

In terms of membership size and change, communication volume and structure, and participation levels, Internet listservs do not appear to be intimate social groups. These findings highlight a bias in prior research on online social activity. While the goal of describing the existence of true social behaviors in online environments has been well served by focusing on highly active and interactive examples of electronic collectives, these cases are not representative of what typically happens. For example, interactivity is a common theme in many descriptions of online social activity. However, our results imply that while interactivity can occur in these contexts, it is the exception, not the rule, when it occurs.

It was not the case that all listservs in this sample had impoverished social behavior, although this was the norm. Nor is it necessarily the case that all types of electronic collectives will look like listservs in terms of the quality of their social behavior. MUDs, MOOs, and Internet Relay Chat are highly interactive, at least among those who actively participate. As is the case with asynchronous media, however, research studying these phenomena has focused on interesting cases (that is, active ones). As a result, we know little about typical behavior in synchronic electronic collectives.

Clearly, there are cases of both synchronous and asynchronous electronic collectives that support the formation of substantial personal relationships and the development of group identity. On the other hand, these types of social activities seem unlikely to occur regularly in the typical listserv, where turnover is high and communication activities is low, noninteractive, and the result of contributions by a small percentage of the membership.

This suggests that social places on the Internet where close personal relationships are formed and maintained are rare.

## Conclusion

Using the Internet to build social relationships results in social interaction that is wanting, at least when it is explicitly compared to the standards of face-to-face and telephone communication, to social relationships that are primarily conducted offline, and to traditional small groups. We do not assert that online social interaction has little value. Surveys of the general public continually reveal that most people using the Internet value email and other forms of online social interaction. Even in the age of the Web and e-commerce, online social interaction is still the most important use of the Internet. However, in one-to-one comparisons, an email message is not as useful as a phone call or a face-to-face meeting for developing and sustaining social relationships. Listservs are not as valuable as small groups for establishing a sense of identity and belonging and for gaining social support. Relationships sustained primarily over the Internet are not as close as those sustained by other means.

Should these observations be a source of concern? To answer this question, we need additional information not yet available. Our data suggests the Internet is less effective than other means of forming and sustaining strong social relationships. The consequences of using the Internet for social relations, however, depend not only on the quality of the relationships sustained using it, but on opportunity costs as well. Do less-effective email messages substitute for or supplement telephone conversations and personal visits? Do weak social relationships formed online add to one's total stock of social relations or substitute for a more valuable partner? Does the time people spend reading listservs and participating in MUDs add to their social interaction, or substitute for time they would have spent in real-world groups? Only by examining people's full set of social behavior and examining their full inventory of social ties can we assess the net social impact of online social relationships.

# POSTSCRIPT

## Does the Internet Strengthen Community?

The debate over the social impact of the Internet is by no means over, although the opponents do tend to be less polarized today, perhaps because online communication clearly has benefits. For instance, in the first 48 hours after the September 11, 2001, destruction of the World Trade Towers in New York City, 4 million people used e-mail to check on friends and family (see Bruce Bower, "The Social Net," *Science News*, May 4, 2002). It has also become apparent that the initial effects of going online are not the same as later effects. Robert Kraut et al. reported that new Internet users became less socially involved and more depressed ("Internet Paradox: A Social Technology that Reduces Social Involvement and Psychological Well-Being?" *American Psychologist*, 53[9], 1998), but in a later study Robert Kraut, Sara Kiesler, Konka Boneva, Jonathon Cummings, Vicki Hegelson, and Anne Crawford conclude that the earlier negative effects largely dissipated with continued use of the Internet; they also note in a separate study of new computer and television purchasers that the outcome is clearly better for extraverts and those with more social support ("Internet Paradox Revisited," *Journal of Social Issues*, vol. 58, No. 1, 2002).

In February 2000, the Stanford Institute for the Quantitative Study of Society released a study by Norman Nie of Stanford and Lutz Erbring of the Free University of Berlin that found that "the more hours people use the Internet, the less time they spend in contact with real human beings," with a quarter of regular Internet users saying it has reduced their in-person or phone time "with friends and family or attending events outside the home." Since time online increases with the number of years one has had Internet access, Nie and Erbring see a potential problem in personal isolation and reduced community participation. James E. Katz, Ronald E. Rice, and Philip Aspden, on the other hand, used telephone surveys from 1995 to 2000 to conclude that Internet users typically have more social contacts and are more involved in their community and in politics ("The Internet, 1995–2000: Access, Civic Involvement, and Social Interaction," *American Behavioral Scientist*, November 2001). Janis Wolak, Kimberly J. Mitchell, and David Finkelhor, "Escaping or Connecting? Characteristics of Youth Who Form Close Online Relationships," *Journal of Adolescence* (February 2003), note that at least with younger people, "girls who had high levels of conflict with parents or were highly troubled were more likely than other girls to have close online relationships, as were boys who had low levels of communication with parents or were highly troubled, compared to other boys." Examining college students, Katie Bonebrake, "College Students' Internet Use,

Relationship Formation, and Personality Correlates," *CyberPsychology & Behavior* (December 2002), did not see such differences.

Paul DiMaggio, Eszter Hargittai, W. Russell Neuman, and John P. Robinson say that most of the research on the social impacts of the Internet is flawed, having been performed by nonacademic survey organizations and focused too much on individuals rather than the organizational structure of the Internet itself; more research by academic sociologists is needed. Still, they call the Internet "a potentially transformative technology," note that it "tends to complement rather than displace existing media and patterns of behavior," and call attention to the University of Maryland's "Scientific Research on the Internet" site at `http://www.webuse.umd.edu/` (see "Social Implications of the Internet," *Annual Review of Sociology*, 2001).

# ISSUE 15

## Does the War on Terrorism Threaten Privacy?

**YES: J. Michael Waller,** from "Fears Mount over 'Total' Spy System," *Insight on the News* (December 24, 2002)

**NO: Stuart Taylor, Jr.,** from "How Civil-Libertarian Hysteria May Endanger Us All," *National Journal* (February 22, 2003)

### ISSUE SUMMARY

**YES:** Writer J. Michael Waller describes objections to the Defense Department's proposed effort to search through government and commercial databases in search of patterns of behavior that can identify terrorists ("Total Information Awareness") and argues that it indeed threatens a severe invasion of privacy.

**NO:** Stuart Taylor, Jr., contests that the objectors have their priorities wrong: curbing "government powers in the name of civil liberties [exacts] too high a price in terms of endangered lives."

The Fourth Amendment to the U.S. Constitution established the right of private citizens to be secure against unreasonable searches and seizures. "Unreasonable" has come to mean "without a search warrant" for physical searches of homes and offices, and "without a court order" for interceptions of mail and wiretappings of phone conversations.

Private citizens who—for whatever reason—do not wish to have their communications with others shared with law enforcement and security agencies have long sought ways to preserve their privacy. They therefore welcomed changes in communications technology, from easily tappable copper wires to fiber optics, from analog (which mimics voice vibrations) to digital (which encodes them). But the U.S. Department of Justice sought legislation to require that the makers and providers of communications products and services ensure that their products remain tappable, and in September 1992, the Clinton Administration submitted to Congress the Digital Telephony Act, a piece of legislation designed to prevent advancing technology from limiting the government's ability legally to intercept communications. For a defense of this measure, see Dorothy Denning, "To Tap or Not to Tap," *Communications of the ACM* (March 1993).

Yet people fear the Internet because it makes a huge variety of information available to everyone with very little accountability. Even children can find sites dedicated to pornography, violence, and hate. Marketers can build detailed profiles. Fraud, identity theft, invasion of privacy, and terrorism have taken new forms. Criminals can use encryption (secret codes) to make their email messages and transmitted documents unreadable to anyone (such as law-enforcement personnel with the digital equivalent of wiretap warrants).

In response, the Department of Justice developed an Internet wiretapping system called Carnivore. It is a computer program designed to run on an Internet service provider's (ISP's) computers, sifting through the email messages and other Internet traffic of that ISP's clients, as well as all those messages that are relayed through that ISP's computers. Supposedly, Carnivore searches for activity only by certain persons (as specified by a court order) and ignores all other activity. Many people, however, are disturbed by Carnivore's invisibility; they see a potential for abuse in its ability to search Internet traffic without a court order and to search for any keywords its operators desire. They would be much happier if the objects of surveillance were told they were being watched or even if the objects of surveillance were able to monitor the surveillance itself. For a fertile discussion of the balance between surveillance and accountability, see David Brin, *The Transparent Society* (Perseus, 1999).

After September 11, 2001, the objections to Carnivore vanished almost entirely. The War on Terrorism had begun, and every tool that promised to help identify terrorists before or catch them after they committed their dreadful acts was seen as desirable. However, when the Department of Defense's Defense Advanced Research Projects Agency proposed a massive computer system capable of sifting through purchases, tax data, court records, and other information from government and commercial databases to seek suspicious patterns of behavior, the objections returned in force. In the following selections, J. Michael Waller describes the proposed "Total Information Awareness" (TIA) program and the objections, arguing that TIA indeed threatens a severe invasion of privacy. Stuart Taylor, Jr., argues that the objectors have their priorities wrong: curbing "government powers in the name of civil liberties [exacts] too high a price in terms of endangered lives."

J. Michael Waller

# Fears Mount Over 'Total' Spy System

The Pentagon has blundered into another self-made public-relations disaster, allowing critics for the second time in a year to fan flames of hysteria over development of high-tech means to wage the war on terrorism. Called Total Information Awareness (TIA), it is a small experimental program in its infancy deep within the Pentagon research unit that developed the Internet. TIA is designed to test whether terrorist attacks can be detected and stopped before they occur by combining massive amounts of electronic data already available on commercial and government databases.

Critics leaked, apparently falsely, that TIA would build electronic dossiers on the personal lives of all Americans. And while few would argue that it raises powerful concerns about civil liberties and the abuse of government power, the most inflammatory and paranoid allegations took on a life of their own when critics pointed to the official running TIA: retired Rear Adm. John Poindexter.

As national-security adviser to President Ronald Reagan, Poindexter took responsibility for the so-called Iran-Contra scandal, in which the White House had planned to rescue American hostages in the Middle East in exchange for selling weapons to Iran. The proceeds would be used to circumvent congressional restrictions—imposed by lawmakers sympathetic to Marxist-Leninist revolutionaries in Central America—and fund the military needs of the anti-communist Nicaraguan resistance fighters, known as "contras."

Poindexter took the political and legal bullet for President Reagan, and was convicted on five felony counts of lying to Congress and related charges. A higher court overturned the convictions. While legally exonerated, Poindexter remained a political hot potato with plenty of political enemies in Congress and the media. Even some of his fans agree off-the-record that it was unwise to place a political lightning rod in charge of a program that raised so many civil-liberties questions.

And so, the real purpose of TIA was lost amid the controversy. Insight has put together the pieces to explain what TIA is all about.

The Bush administration is building a layered defense against terrorists: First, destroy terrorist cells and capture or kill individual terrorists and their

From *Insight on the News,* December 24, 2002. 

sponsors abroad. Second, neutralize their bases of operation in other countries. Third, erect a security barrier to prevent their entry into the United States. Fourth, deny sanctuary to those who either have entered the United States or have been recruited here. Fifth, monitor, infiltrate and disrupt their domestic-support networks. Finally, move in on the terrorists themselves before they strike.

Federal antiterrorist investigators tell Insight that they severely lack the human resources—agents, officers and citizen volunteers—to make a dent in the terrorist-support infrastructure in the United States. While making some headway in such hot areas as Dearborn, Mich.—where a large, ethnic-Arab/Muslim community serves as a proverbial sea in which the terrorist fish swim—the FBI and other agencies say they have a long way to go to shut down terrorist networks already on U.S. soil.

Law enforcement continues to suffer from the 1970s campaigns against the federal security and intelligence agencies, and the since-abolished intelligence units of state and local police. With the loss of literally thousands of trained personnel and their painstakingly built support networks, authorities at all levels sometimes are waging the domestic antiterrorism war without eyes or ears. They say they need to use new information technologies to help close the gap.

The federal government, to say nothing of the legal system and political culture, is only starting to get used to the idea that it is responsible for defending the American people against terrorist attacks before they occur. This post-9/11 perspective throws previous custom and practice out of the window. FBI Director Robert Mueller is battling the bureau to change from a reactive investigative force that busts bad guys only after they maim and kill to a proactive force that stops the terrorists before they attack. That's a huge cultural shift for the by-the-book G-men, and it means changing the very essence of what the FBI has been since its inception, to say nothing of the mind-set and legal practice of federal prosecutors, defense lawyers and the judges who issue warrants and hear criminal cases. With revolutionary information technologies offering a possible solution to the human-intelligence shortage, new controversies have arisen.

Now, a combination of left-wing activists, Islamist sympathizers of terrorist groups, civil libertarians, gun-rights advocates and mainline conservatives are up in arms about the latest proposals to prevent terrorists from killing more Americans. They fear, for different reasons, that the Bush administration and Congress are vastly increasing and centralizing the power of the federal government over the American population in the name of fighting terrorism.

The existence of TIA became public information when the Defense Advanced Research Projects Agency (DARPA), the Pentagon's central research-and-development organization, solicited proposals last March for private companies to bid on developing the program. But it received little attention until Congress was passing the Homeland Security bill in November and conservative New York Times columnist William Safire attacked it as George Orwell's 1984 come to life. "To this computerized dossier on your private life from commercial sources, add every piece of information that government has about you—passport application, driver's license and bridge-toll records, judicial and divorce records, complaints from nosy neighbors to the FBI, your lifetime paper trail plus the latest hidden-camera surveillance—and you have the supersnoop's dream: 'Total Information Awareness' about every U.S. citizen" Safire wrote.

Framed in terms of the government keeping dossiers on every citizen, press commentary on TIA since has wobbled between paranoia and prudence. For once The Nation, long the keeper of the party line of the pro-Soviet left, and the happily unreconstructed McCarthyites of National Review sounded the same alarm: Big Brother is here. "Fighting terror by terrifying U.S. citizens," the panicked San Francisco Chronicle called it. "Orwellian," editorialized the Washington Post. A screaming page-one banner headline in the Washington Times cribbed Safire's line: "A supersnoop's dream." Popular Washington news-talk host Chris Core of WMAL radio likened TIA to the Soviet KGB and the Nazi Gestapo.

TIA was all the more dangerous, critics said, because the man running the alleged program was Poindexter. National Review called him a "pipesmoking Reagan capo." Sen. Charles Schumer (D-N.Y.) grandstanded on television, demanding that Defense Secretary Donald Rumsfeld fire the scholarly admiral. Rumsfeld ignored him.

"Take a nice deep, deep breath" Rumsfeld chided reporters. "It's a case of 'Ready. Shoot. Aim.' The hyped and alarmed approach [in the media] is a disservice to the public," he said. "Nothing terrible is going to happen."

Oddly, some of the most reasoned commentary came from foreign news organizations—and not all of them friendly to the United States. Khilafah.com, an Islamic revolutionary news organization devoted to promoting the re-establishment of the caliphate, tagged TIA not as a spy system to snoop on U.S. citizens but an "information matrix to track movements of America's enemies."

The American Civil Liberties Union (ACLU), which led the successful fight in the 1970s to cripple the FBI and CIA and abolish local police-intelligence units that monitored terrorist and subversive groups, launched a new campaign against TIA. The DARPA project, it says, is "a computer system that would provide government officials with the ability to snoop into all aspects of our private lives without a search warrant or proof of criminal wrongdoing." According to the ACLU, "Under this program, our entire lives would be catalogued and available to government officials." Poindexter, the ACLU alleges, "has been quietly promoting the idea of creating 'a virtual centralized database' that would have the 'data-mining' power to pry into the most minute and intimate details of our private lives."

The Pentagon says TIA is simply "an experimental prototype in the works that will determine the feasibility of searching vast quantities of data to determine links and patterns indicating terrorist activity." DARPA conceived of the terrorist-prediction data-crunching system with the benefit of the 20/20 hindsight from studies of past major terrorist attacks. "In all cases, terrorists have left detectable clues that are generally found after an attack," according to a DARPA fact sheet on the issue. If in the course of investigation federal authorities could identify and act upon clues that would let them wrap up terrorist cells, TIA developers reasoned, they could pre-empt the terrorism and save lives.

Administration officials working on TIA and related initiatives agree that a domestic-security matter should not be under the purview of the Pentagon. "If DARPA didn't support it when we needed to give it a try, what other agency would have?" asks a counterterrorism official. "The fact is, there was no one else. We're in a war, Poindexter had an idea worth testing and DARPA stepped up to the plate."

Given those considerations, the Bush administration planned from the beginning to move such projects from out of the purview of the Pentagon and DARPA and designed a new Security Advanced Projects Research Agency (SARPA) under the new Department of Homeland Security.

Undersecretary of Defense Pete Aldridge, under whose authority DARPA falls, says that TIA's mission consists of three parts: to research technologies that would allow rapid language translation, to discover connections between current activities and future events, and to develop "collaborative reasoning and decisionmaking tools to allow interagency communications and analysis"—just the tools needed to keep one agency informed of the intelligence produced by another agency.

Critics have cited the lack of communication between U.S. agencies as one of the main reasons several of the Sept. 11 terrorists were able to enter the country. The CIA reportedly tracked some of the future hijackers from the Philippines and Malaysia as they entered the United States, but the FBI apparently neither received nor followed up on the reports, thus allowing the terrorists to organize and launch their attacks undetected. Recent investigative reports have found that the State Department issued visas to several of the 9/11 hijackers even though the applications contained unacceptably incomplete and even demonstrably false information, and that alleged Washington Beltway sniper John Muhammad actually procured a U.S. passport with a birth certificate that a U.S. consular official suspected was forged, but which her superior apparently instructed her to ignore.

Some of those problems could be solved with bureaucratic restructuring, improved training and discipline, and changes of mission—all problems being addressed. Others require vastly improved information technologies to collect, analyze and synthesize ever-increasing quantities of data for human analysts and policymakers who already are overloaded with information.

"Even if we could find these clues faster and more easily, our counterterrorism defenses are spread throughout many different agencies and organizations at the national, state and local levels," notes DARPA's Information Awareness Office (IAO), which supervises TIA development. "To fight terrorism, we need to create a new intelligence infrastructure to allow these agencies to share information and collaborate effectively, and new information technology aimed at exposing terrorists and their activities and support systems. This is a tremendously difficult problem because terrorists understand how vulnerable they are and seek to hide their specific plans and capabilities. The key to fighting terrorism is information. Elements of the solution include gathering a much broader array of data than we do currently, discovering information from elements of the data, creating models of hypotheses and analyzing these models in a collaborative environment to determine the most probable current or future scenario."

According to the IAO, "The goal of the TIA program is to revolutionize the ability of the United States to detect, classify and identify foreign terrorists and decipher their plans—and thereby enable the U.S. to take timely action to successfully pre-empt and defeat terrorist acts. To that end, the TIA objective is to create a counterterrorism information system that: (1) increases information coverage by an order of magnitude and affords easy future scaling; (2) provides focused warnings within an hour after a triggering event occurs or an evidence threshold is passed; (3) can automatically queue analysts based on partial pattern matches and has patterns that cover 90 percent of all previously known foreign terrorist attacks; and (4) supports collaboration, analytical reasoning and information-sharing so that analysts can hypothesize, test and propose theories and mitigating strategies about possible futures so decisionmakers can effectively evaluate the impact of current or future policies and prospective courses of action."

The $10 million program is only an "experiment," explains Aldridge. "In order to preserve the sanctity of individual privacy, we're designing this system to ensure complete anonymity of uninvolved citizens, thus focusing the efforts of law-enforcement officials on terrorist investigations." By collecting applications for passports, visas, driver's licenses, airline-ticket purchases and rental-car reservations, as well as purchases of firearms and precursor chemicals for explosives, medical data and credit- and debit-card purchases, flying lessons, arrests and reports of suspicious activities, proponents say they hope TIA will develop a product able to single out factors indicating preparations for a possible terrorist attack. But the idea is for the information to be anonymous until such time that a warrant is needed for surveillance, arrest or detention.

And given the nature of so slippery an invasion of privacy, how can Americans be sure of that? "The data are subject to the same Privacy Act restrictions that currently govern law enforcement and government," says Aldridge. To investigate further requires government agencies to go through the same processes of procuring judge-issued warrants and other legal hoops to protect individual rights, he says.

Civil libertarians, privacy advocates, gun-rights groups and others worry that even experimenting with such a system risks transfer of unprecedented power to an unaccountable—and often incompetent—central government. Poindexter says that the TIA system is being built with safeguards embedded in the software, with audit trails and the protection of individual identities, and that his shop is only creating the experimental technology. How that technology would be used, he states, would be up to the executive branch, Congress and the courts, with all the necessary safeguards. He recognizes that the project will go nowhere without public support. Though his office now says he is not taking press interviews, he told the Washington Post, "We can develop the best technology in the world and, unless there is public acceptance and understanding of the necessity, it will never be implemented."

NO 

**Stuart Taylor, Jr.**

# How Civil-Libertarian Hysteria May Endanger Us All

Someday Americans may die because of Congress's decision earlier this month to cripple a Defense Department program designed to catch future Mohamed Attas before they strike. That's not a prediction. But it is a fear.

The program seeks to develop software to make intelligence-sharing more effective by making it instantaneous, the better to learn more about suspected terrorists and identify people who might be terrorists. It would link computerized government data-bases to one another and to some non-government databases to which investigators already have legal access. If feasible, it would also fish through billions of transactions for patterns of activities in which terrorists might engage.

But now these goals are all in jeopardy, because of a stunningly irresponsible congressional rush to hobble the Pentagon program in ways that are far from necessary to protect privacy. This is not to deny that, absent stringent safeguards and oversight, the ineptly named "Total Information Awareness" [TIA] program might present serious threats to privacy. It might, for example, subject thousands of innocent citizens and noncitizens alike to unwelcome scrutiny, and might even expose political dissenters to harassment by rogue officials.

But some curbs on potentially dangerous (and potentially life-saving) government powers in the name of civil liberties are not necessary to protect privacy and exact too high a price in terms of endangered lives. Congress's rush to strangle TIA in its infancy is such a case. It makes little more sense than would a flat ban on any and all wire-tapping of phones that might be used by U.S. citizens. Like TIA, wiretapping poses grave risks to privacy if not carefully restricted. So we restrict it. We don't ban it.

The problem with the near-ban on TIA—sponsored by Sens. Ron Wyden, D-Ore., and Charles Grassley, R-Iowa, and known as the Wyden amendment—is that rather than weighing the hoped-for security benefits against the feared privacy costs, and devising ways to minimize those costs, Congress was stampeded by civil-libertarian hysteria into adopting severe and unwarranted restrictions. The Bush administration shares the blame because the person it put in charge of TIA research is Adm. John M. Poindexter, whose record of lying to Congress about the Iran-Contra affair does not inspire trust.

"There are risks to TIA, but in the end I think the risks of not trying TIA are greater, and we should at least try to construct systems for [minimizing] abuse before we discard all potential benefits from technological innovation," says Paul Rosenzweig, a legal analyst at the Heritage Foundation who has co-authored a thoughtful 25-page analysis of the TIA program, including a list of muscular safeguards that Congress could adopt to protect privacy and prevent abuses. Instead of weighing such factors, Rosenzweig says, Congress has "deliberately and without much thought decided to discard the greatest advantage we have over our foes—our technological superiority."

The Wyden amendment seems reasonable enough at first blush. That may be why all 100 senators and the House conferees voted to attach it to the omnibus spending bill that cleared Congress on February 13. The amendment allows pure TIA *research* to continue, if the administration files a detailed report within 90 days or the president invokes national security needs. And the amendment's restrictions on TIA *deployment* have been sold as a temporary move to allow time for congressional oversight.

But such measures, once adopted, are a good bet to become permanent in today's habitually gridlocked Congress, where determined minorities have great power to block any change in the status quo. And the Wyden amendment's impact is likely to be far broader than advertised. It flatly bars *any* deployment of TIA-derived technology, by any agency, with exceptions only for military operations outside the U.S. and "lawful foreign intelligence activities conducted *wholly* [my emphasis] against non-United States persons" (defined to mean nonresident aliens).

The scope of the latter exception is ambiguous. But Rosenzweig fears that it will be read narrowly, and that the Wyden amendment will be read broadly—especially by officials fearful of congressional wrath—as barring virtually *all* uses of TIA technology, even to search the government's own databases for suspected foreign terrorists. This is because virtually all large databases are "mixed": They contain information about U.S. citizens, resident aliens, and nonresident aliens alike.

In any event, the Wyden amendment quite clearly prohibits any use of TIA technology to pursue the unknown but apparently substantial number of U.S. citizens and resident aliens who may be loyal to Al Qaeda, such as suspected dirty-bomb plotter Jose Padilla and the six suspected Yemeni-American "sleepers" arrested in Lackawanna, N.Y., last year. As a technical matter, the FBI, the CIA, and the Department of Homeland Security remain free to develop and deploy similar technology on their own. But they will hesitate to risk charges of evading Congress's will. Not to mention the wastefulness of barring these agencies from building on the TIA technology already developed by the Pentagon.

How did TIA become such a dreaded symbol of Big Brotherism? Part of the reason was well-founded concern that unless strictly controlled, the more exotic uses of TIA, such as surveying billions of transactions involving hundreds of millions of people for patterns deemed indicative of possible terrorist activities, could subject huge numbers of innocent Americans to scrutiny as potential terrorists. But Rosenzweig and others who share these concerns, including officials of the TIA program itself, have already been crafting safeguards. Among them are software designs and legal rules that would block human agents from learning the identities of people whose transactions are being "data-mined" by TIA computers unless the agents can obtain judicial warrants by showing something analogous to the "probable cause" that the law requires to justify a wiretap.

It was largely misinformation and over-heated rhetoric from civil-libertarian zealots—on both the left and the right—that pushed the Wyden amendment through Congress. The misinformation included the false claim that Poindexter would preside over a domestic spying apparatus, and the false suggestion that TIA was poised to rummage through the most private of databases to compile dossiers on millions of Americans' credit card, banking, business, travel, educational, and medical records and e-mails.

To the contrary, Poindexter's job is limited to developing software. And even without the Wyden amendment, TIA would give investigators access only to databases and records—government and nongovernment—that they already have a right to access. Its most basic function would be simply to expedite the kinds of intelligence-sharing that might have thwarted the September 11 attacks, by linking the government's own databases with one another and with any legally accessible private databases. The goal is to enable investigators to amass in minutes clues that now could take weeks or months to collect.

Here's a hypothetical example (adapted from Rosenzweig's analysis) of how as-yet-non-existent TIA technology might help stop terrorists—and how the Wyden amendment might prevent that.

Say the government learns from a reliable informant that the precursor elements of Sarin gas have been smuggled into the United States by unidentified Qaeda operatives via flights from Germany during the month of February. Its first investigative step might be a TIA-based "query" of foreign databases that might help generate a list of possible terrorists. (But the Wyden amendment would bar a TIA-based query for the names of any who might be Americans. And it could be construed as putting entirely off-limits *any* "mixed database" that includes Americans.)

A second step might be a pattern-based query to U.S. government databases to produce a list of all passengers, or perhaps all nonresident aliens, entering the U.S. on flights from Germany during February. (But the Wyden amendment would bar a query for all passengers, and would again pose the mixed-database problem.)

A third query might seek to find which of these passengers' names are also in government databases of known or suspected terrorists. (But the Wyden amendment would pose the same obstacles.)

Fourth, with a list of subjects for further investigation based on these queries, TIA could be used—perhaps after obtaining a judicial warrant—to link to any legally accessible commercial databases to find out whether any of these subjects has bought canisters suitable for deployment of Sarin gas, or rented airplanes suitable for dispersing it, or stayed in the same motels as other subjects of investigation. And so on. (But for the Wyden amendment, that is.)

It is not yet clear whether it is even possible to develop technology powerful enough to do all of this. But it might be possible. Shouldn't we be racing to find out?

# POSTSCRIPT

## Does the War on Terrorism Threaten Privacy?

The basic shape of the debate is simple: government insists that private citizens do not have the right to act in such a way that they cannot be watched, supervised, and punished if government deems it necessary. The Electronic Frontier Foundation (EFF), the Electronic Privacy Information Center (EPIC), and numerous other groups and individuals insist equally strenuously that the right to privacy must come first. Those who wish to read more about how the growing use of computers permits both government and private interests to intrude on individual privacy should see Marie A. Wright and John S. Kakalik, "The Erosion of Privacy?" *Computers and Society* (December 1997). For EPIC's site, see `http://www.epic.org/privacy/profiling/tia/`.

First Carnivore and now Total Information Awareness (TIA) reflect many fears about the Net—that it is a place where evil lurks, where technically skilled criminals use their skills to fleece the unsuspecting public, where terrorists plot unseen, and where technology lends immunity to detection, apprehension, and prosecution. Law enforcement has long wished to compensate for the advantages enjoyed here by evil-doers. Carnivore was a milestone attempt to maintain the upper hand. Echelon, an international and until recently top-secret version of Carnivore that searches emails, faxes, and phone calls, is operated by the U.S.'s National Security Agency in partnership with Canada, Australia, New Zealand, and Britain; see Daniel Schorr, "Europe's Wary Eye on America's 'Big Ear'," *Christian Science Monitor* (June 8, 2001), and Jim Wilson, "Spying on Us," *Popular Mechanics* (April 2001). According to Naomi Schaefer in "The Coming Internet Privacy Scrum," *American Enterprise* (January/February 2001), the debates have only begun. The TIA program is ample confirmation of her point. See Nat Hentoff, "1984 Is Here," *Free Inquiry* (Spring 2003), John Foley, "Data Debate," *InformationWeek* (May 19, 2003) and Wayne Madsen, "US Insight—The Secrets of DARPA's TIA: The US Government's Electronic Intelligence Snooping Machine," *Computer Fraud & Security* (May 2003).

Stuart Taylor, Jr., also objected to the critics earlier in "Big Brother and Another Overblown Privacy Scare," *National Journal* (December 7, 2002). In January 2003, the Data-Mining Moratorium Act was proposed by Senators Russ Feingold, Jon Corzine, and Ron Wyden; the bill would freeze domestic data-mining projects that lack explicit governmental approval and stop some of the scariest TIA provisions. "While TIA is still a huge threat to your civil liberties, this measure is an important step in its defeat," says the EFF as it urges people to support the Act. On the conservative side, the Cato Institute's Gene Healy, "Beware of Total Information Awareness" (`http://www.cato.org`;

see the Archives for January 20, 2003), is very aware of government abuse of surveillance powers. His colleague Clyde Wayne Crews, Jr. "The Poindexter Awareness Office: Turning the Tables on Mr. Supersnoop" (Cato, January 15, 2003) warns that modern surveillance technology works in both directions. At the Heritage Foundation, Paul Rosenzweig, "Congress Should not Prematurely Short-Circuit the Total Information Awareness Program" (`http://www.heritage.org/Research/HomelandDefense/em853.cfm`, January 28, 2003), urges that Congress not impose excessive limits.

By May 2003, TIA had been renamed to soothe public reactions; DARPA's *Report to Congress Regarding the Terrorism Information Awareness Program* (May 20, 2003) described TIA as no more than a prototype, experimental system. Safeguards would be built in to protect privacy. For DARPA's own description of the program, see the Information Awareness Office website at `http://www.darpa.mil/iao/TIASystems.htm`. Mark Fiore's "Terrorism Information Awareness: Big Brother Is Back . . . But in a Nice Way," *The Village Voice* (May 29, 2003) (see `http://www.villagevoice.com/fiore/`), comments caustically in an animated editorial cartoon.

Note that TIA is not the only computerized government threat to privacy. There is also the Transportation Security Administration's Computer-Assisted Passenger Prescreening System II (CAPPS II), which "is designed to scan multiple public and private databases for information on individuals traveling into and out of the United States. The system will feed the results to an analysis application that mathematically ranks travelers' potential as security threats." See Eliot Borin, "Private Info Becoming Plane Truth," *Wired News* (September 16, 2002). Critics fear that database data may not be accurate, "function creep" is inevitable, and government has a record of abusing its surveillance powers. But "U.S. Agencies Defend Data-Mining Plans," says Grant Gross, *Computerworld* (May 12, 2003).

And then there's DARPA's LifeLog project, which would construct computerized diaries tracking every move of volunteers (at first), again with an eye to spotting terrorists in time to stop them. See Noah Schachtman, "A Spy Machine of DARPA's Dreams," *Wired News* (May 20, 2003): "The Pentagon is about to embark on a stunningly ambitious research project designed to gather every conceivable bit of information about a person's life, index all the information and make it searchable. . . . The embryonic LifeLog program would dump everything an individual does into a giant database: every e-mail sent or received, every picture taken, every Web page surfed, every phone call made, every TV show watched, every magazine read. All of this—and more—would combine with information gleaned from a variety of sources: a GPS transmitter to keep tabs on where that person went, audio-visual sensors to capture what he or she sees or says, and biomedical monitors to keep track of the individual's health. This gigantic amalgamation of personal information could then be used to 'trace the "threads" of an individual's life,' to see exactly how a relationship or events developed."

# ISSUE 16

## Will Screens Replace Pages?

**YES: Steve Ditlea,** from "The Real E-Books," *Technology Review* (July/August 2000)

**NO: Stephen Sottong,** from "E-Book Technology: Waiting for the 'False Pretender,'" *Information Technology & Libraries* (June 2001)

**ISSUE SUMMARY**

**YES:** Writer Steve Ditlea argues that computers can simplify publishing, improve access to readers, and enhance the reading experience and that e-books are becoming both practical and popular.

**NO:** Librarian Stephen Sottong argues that e-books are not cheap, readable, or durable enough to replace paper books and that they pose special problems for libraries.

When personal computers first came on the market in the 1970s, they were considered useful tools, but their memory was limited to only a few thousand bytes, hard drives were expensive add-ons, and the Internet was a distant dream (though something similar was already connecting university and government mainframe computers). By the 1980s some people had begun to realize that computer disks could hold as much information as a book, were smaller, took less postage to mail, and could be recycled. By this time Project Gutenberg, founded in 1971 by Michael Hart at the University of Illinois, had already been converting works of classic literature into digital form and making them available on disk for a number of years. By 1990 several small companies—including Soft Press, Serendipity Systems, and High Mesa Publishing—were trying to turn this insight into profitable businesses. All are now gone.

The approach failed partly because people seemed to find paper books more congenial for reading than computer screens. But then the Internet came along, and the early 1990s saw an explosion of activity exploiting this new ability to put information of all kinds—including poetry, fiction, and nonfiction of precisely the sort one used to find only on paper—onto "Web pages" that Internet users could access for free. Digital publishing boomed, and companies such as Alexandria Digital Literature (`http://www.alexlit.com`),

Fictionwise (`http://www.fictionwise.com`), and Embiid Publishing (`http://www.embiid.net`) now sell their wares to be downloaded via the Internet. This is not the first time that the nature of publishing has changed. Five centuries ago the printing press greatly increased the availability of books, including Bibles, and contributed to the Protestant Reformation and the American and French Revolutions. See Rudi Volti, *Society and Technological Change*, 4th ed. (St. Martin's Press, 2001), chapter 11. The printing press also utterly destroyed the primacy of the scroll and delivered the first hard blow to literacy as a distinguishing characteristic of the social elite. There were, of course, protests aimed at the way this new technology was threatening handwritten text and undermining the social order.

Now major publishers are making books available in both paper and digital form, and e-books can be downloaded from online booksellers such as Barnes & Noble.com (`http://www.barnesandnoble.com`) and Amazon.com (`http://www.amazon.com`). At the same time, magazines and newspapers are insisting that contributors sign away electronic publishing rights (usually for no additional payment), while the same rights are becoming major negotiating points in book contracts. Also, a wide variety of e-book readers are now available (see Ronaleen R. Roha and Courtney McGrath, "Better Than Books?" *Kiplinger's Personal Finance Magazine* [July 2001]), and the National Book Awards are now open to e-books. Reviews of e-books now appear in major magazines. And Bill Gates is trumpeting the virtues of e-books—he expects their sales to rival those of paper books within a decade—from the parapets of Microsoft. See Bill Gates and Lora Haberer, "E-Books," *Executive Excellence* (April 2001).

In the following selections, Steve Ditlea argues that, at least so far, electronic publishing is no threat to conventional, paper publishing, but because computers can simplify publishing, improve access to readers, and enhance the reading experience, e-books are bound to become more and more familiar to readers. Stephen Sottong asserts that e-books are not cheap, readable, or durable enough to replace paper books. Nor is the technology mature or stable enough for libraries to trust for long-term storage. Libraries must be cautious about adopting the technology.

**Steve Ditlea**

# The Real E-Books

It took a contemporary master of macabre thrillers to awaken the media and public to the existence of e-books. [Recently], with great fanfare, Simon & Schuster brought out a novella by Stephen King called *Riding the Bullet*—the first work by a best-selling author released exclusively for electronic publication, to be read only on computerized screens, not paper. King's stunt made headlines and magazine covers, and the tsunami of demand for downloads of this e-book crashed Web sites and traditional publishing assumptions.

But the future of e-books may have less to do with Stephen King than with Eric Rowe and other less well-known authors. Rowe is a British potter who lives in the South of France, drawn there by the region's clays and minerals, which have been mined for stoneware since Roman times. To help ceramists in other areas unearth their own raw materials, he wrote *A Potter's Geology*. But he couldn't find a book publisher in England for his manuscript. This was just too specialized a topic for a publisher in any one country. Still, Rowe was certain that there would be interest in his book from potters everywhere.

Half a world away, in Medicine Hat, Alberta, Tony Hansen read about *A Potter's Geology* from a posting by Rowe in a ceramists' online discussion group. Hansen owns Digitalfire, a company specializing in software for calculations in ceramic chemistry. Hansen offered to publish Rowe's book electronically, selling the text on the Web as digital files in the Portable Document Format (PDF). PDF files are displayable on any Windows, DOS, Mac or Unix computer screen (and easily printed out) using the Acrobat reader software, downloadable free from Adobe Systems.

"I said I'd rather have my manuscript printed first," Rowe recalls. But Hansen won him over by pointing out that e-publication would produce immediate worldwide distribution. Now the book can be downloaded from the Web and viewed on any personal computer. Readers of the e-book can search the entire book and zoom in on high-resolution photos—even contact the author via an online hyperlink. The economics look good too: E-books require no printing, binding, inventory or shipping costs, allowing these savings to be passed on to the author in the form of higher royalties. *A Potter's Geology* has sold only a few dozen copies, but Rowe is optimistic:

"It won't be something that sells fast, but over a long time. It's not a subject that will go out of date. Even so, in digital format it's easy to update or improve."

Thanks to Digitalfire and other budding digital publishing enterprises, authors like Rowe are being empowered to write about esoteric, highly personal topics and still find a worldwide audience—transcending the antiquated economics of shipping ink on wood pulp and bypassing the gatekeepers to traditional publishing. Just a little searching on the Web finds a growing e-book industry: more than 150 e-book-only publishers, e-only bookstores, e-book trade publications online, even e-book best-seller lists. The new e-publishers are testing a variety of business models for digital book distribution, while opening the way for a broader range of authors and works to be published on old-fashioned bound paper.

The great wonder is that this hasn't happened any sooner. The first digital books date back to 1971 when Michael Hart was given a virtually unlimited account of computer time on the mainframe at the Materials Research Lab at the University of Illinois and decided that widely disseminating the contents of libraries was the greatest value computers could create. He typed in the text of the Declaration of Independence and so began Project Gutenberg, which now includes more than 2000 classic works online, all free. To date, these are all plain text files—lacking the typeset-quality formatting that makes books eminently readable, somewhat compromising the reading experience. "When we started," Hart recalls, "there was *only* uppercase—how about *that* for a compromise?" Because Project Gutenberg's books were no longer under copyright, the original e-books required no copy protection schemes. Hart explains: "We encourage everyone to repost our books in whatever formats they want. The most books to the most people—that's our only real goal."

In 1990, Voyager Co. introduced the first e-books meant to be read on personal computers. But these diskette-borne works, including *Jurassic Park* and *Alice in Wonderland,* were never offered by other publishers. Meanwhile, attempts to publish books on CD-ROM proved a dead end for all but encyclopedia and database publishers. The advent of the Web brought both opportunity and distraction for e-books. As the first universal publishing medium, the Web could make e-books easily accessible, with its Hypertext Markup Language (HTML) even retaining some print-style formatting. But HTML's orientation toward short documents was hardly optimized for book-length texts.

In the last year or so, the term "e-book" has been appropriated by companies selling portable gadgets whose sole purpose is to display electronic texts. . . . At the moment the number of these dedicated e-book readers—about 20,000—is dwarfed by the 6 million Palm Pilots and other Palm OS devices in use, making this versatile hardware the handheld reader of choice. "Single-purpose devices like handheld readers are never going to have as big an installed base as general-purpose ones," insists Mark Reichelt, CEO of Peanut Press, the Maynard, Mass., company that pioneered commercial e-book publishing on the Palm Pilot.

## Rubber and Glue

The most general-purpose hardware boxes of all are personal computers. Yet despite hundreds of millions of PCs in use around the world, only a few hundred thousand of their users have downloaded e-books. The slow start is partly due to the perception that an e-book doesn't fully replicate the book-reading experience. More importantly, the download culture—first evident with browser plug-ins, then with software upgrades and MP3 music files—has only taken hold recently with the non-geek public.

Ads by Microsoft would have us believe that what the e-book world has been waiting for is the company's Reader program, which will be given away with every new copy of Windows. Microsoft Reader features ClearType software that evens out type edges on the screen. The reality is, however, that ClearType is warmed-over technology that failed to save handheld Windows CE devices from oblivion. To people accustomed to reading text on a computer for hours at a time, e-book screen clarity is a nonissue. Microsoft Reader also provides copy protection for authors and booksellers. But while e-books rights management may be important to intellectual property holders, it could be a futile quest. Any PC-based copy protection scheme can be cracked, as happened within two days of Stephen King's first e-publication.

With more than 100 million Acrobat readers already downloaded onto computers, PDF is the de facto standard for e-book publication. PDF was specifically designed for preserving professional-quality documents across computer platforms and printers. And PDF technology offers a ready solution for those reluctant to read off a screen; simply print out the files. To counter Microsoft Reader, Adobe has recently beefed up its offerings with e-commerce encryption software called PDF Merchant, allowing rights to an electronic copy of a book to be assigned to a single computer. In addition, Adobe has challenged Microsoft's ClearType with screen-enhancement routines of its own, which it calls CoolType; the competing technologies are similar enough in performance to make screen clarity even less of a concern. . . . PDF will face a worthy challenger in the e-book format battle, as a consortium of e-book hardware makers, traditional publishers, and Microsoft push the new Open eBook (OEB) standard.

The difference between OEB and PDF is like the child's rhyme that begins: "I'm rubber, you're glue." PDF is glue, locking in a book's formatting so it can be preserved intact across output devices; once created, it is not meant to be modified in any way. This can be a drawback if an author or publisher wants to access parts of the text for excerpting or reconfiguring for a customized e-book, or for sampling or sale in smaller increments than book length. OEB is rubber: It allows an e-book's content to be reformatted on the fly, using a markup language that is essentially an extension of HTML. OEB also makes it easy for dedicated reading devices to reformat text to fit their proprietary display configurations.

The first published spec for OEB addresses neither security nor e-commerce protocols, leaving it to individual vendors to come up with their own approaches. This omission raises the possibility that the proposed standard could splinter into a variety of incompatible implementations. Ultimately, both OEB *and* PDF could survive, with the rival formats used for different output stages of the same e-book—OEB in the intermediate stages of massaging editorial content, and PDF for final versions. (For all the flexibility of digital books, scholarship will probably demand that different editions of a work remain available in permanent form.)

## Rewriting Business Models

E-books are shaking up publishing business models that have remained unchanged since the days of Dickens, much as MP3 compression technology has rocked the music industry. For the moment, even the most forward-looking print publishers are pricing their initial e-book offerings almost identically with paper editions, as if there were no difference in their underlying atoms versus bits economics. At St. Martin's Press, the first major publisher to simultaneously issue a hardcover and e-book edition of the same title (*Monica's Story* in March 1999), senior vice president for finance administration Steve Cohen explains: "Our prices on new titles are at the hardcover level because there's a high start-up cost for e-book editions." Kate Tentler, publisher of Simon & Schuster Online, was responsible for Web distribution of Stephen King's *Riding the Bullet* (priced at $2.50, the 66 pages of the e-novella averaged out to the retail per-page cost of a King hardcover novel). Says Tentler, "We think of an e-book as just another book."

As a few traditional publishers defensively convert to digital files for downloads, the independent e-publishing industry has seen countless business models bloom. On the same March day that the Stephen King brand name sold 400,000 paperless copies of *Riding the Bullet*, Frank Weyer received a grand total of two requests for his serialized e-mystery, *MIT Can Be Murder*, on his own site (e-bookpress.com). Despite such paltry numbers, efforts by Weyer and other e-book authors are already undermining the influence of blockbuster-minded agents and trend-driven book editors. Weyer, for example, had sent the manuscript for his first murder mystery to 10 literary agents, all of whom declined to submit it to book publishers. "They said the mystery field is difficult for a newcomer," Weyer recalls. "But how do you become a published mystery author if you can't get published?"

Self-publishing on paper, a solution for some, seemed prohibitive for this patent and trademark attorney and small-scale Internet entrepreneur (he holds exclusive right to sell Web domain names registered in the nation of Moldova—ending in .md—to doctors in California and New York). Rather than letting his manuscript molder in a drawer, Weyer decided to publish it via e-mail. The first four chapters of the whodunnit, inspired by the year he spent at MIT studying for a PhD in ocean engineering, were offered first to 3,000 MIT alumni, and then to 15,000 names on other university alumni lists. He released the rest of the 210-page book in 12 monthly installments. Some 1,400 readers have downloaded the entire e-novel.

Weyer's novel-by-subscription might seem like an innovation made possible by the digital era. In fact, it is a throwback to the early days of

19th-century book publishing, when books were sold by subscription before publication, to raise revenue to pay the printing costs up front. With no printing to worry about, the frictionless economy lets Weyer distribute his work for free. Now that he has successfully bypassed print publishers to get his words read, he has begun subscription-publishing the work of other writers. The first addition is *The Butcher's Cleaver*, a spy thriller by W. Patrick Lang. Soon Weyer plans to generate income by selling print-on-demand versions of both his and Lang's books. Nonetheless, he would like *MIT Can Be Murder* to be picked up by a mainstream publisher. "I just wanted to build word of mouth," he says of his e-book. "I would like to see it in as many forms as possible."

Giving away complete works to help an author build a following is still anathema to most traditional publishers, who must absorb the cost to produce, store and ship the physical books. But giving away paperless e-books is a no-brainer, following the time-tested freeware and shareware models in computer software. Independently published e-books may not be as polished or as slick as store-bought commercial offerings, but they can hold their own in user appreciation. And Frank Weyer's writing is certainly on par with that in much of today's mass-produced paperback fiction.

Traditional publishers' understandable fear that e-books may cannibalize sales of print editions seems to be overblown, at least judging from the experience of one of their more adventurous colleagues. [In] September [1999], veteran science-fiction publisher Jim Baen initiated what he calls eWebScriptions; for $10 a month, visitors to Baen.com may download quarter-of-a-book-sized installments of four titles about to appear in print. Even after receiving the full text in HTML, "more of our subscribers buy the finished book than don't buy it," says Baen. By March, the added promotion had already helped propel one of the earliest eWebScriptions titles, *Ashes of Victory* by David Weber, onto hardcover best-seller lists.

In addition to alternative marketing strategies, e-publishers can tap into income streams legally denied to traditional publishers. For instance, the U.S. Postal Service disallows low book-mailing rates for printed material that contains advertising. No such restriction inhibits the sales of ads for e-books. Bartleby.com, for example, offers free, ad-supported classics and reference works online. At BiblioBytes.com, books can be read on ad banner-sponsored Web pages, with some popular titles downloadable for a fee; authors get a cut of the ad revenue. Abroad, the alternatives are just as dramatic; in France, pioneer e-publisher Zero Hour is able to offer less-expensive editions of current books because digital files cannot be taxed as print books are.

## Embracing the E

The power of e-books as a promotional medium has probably best been demonstrated by Melisse Shapiro, who writes under the nom de plume M.J. Rose. Her first novel, *Lip Service*, an erotically charged thriller, was rejected by a dozen book publishers for being too steamy for the chain bookstores. She opted to publish from her own Web site, offering digital downloads for $10 or photocopies of the manuscript for $20.

Even when the password for her e-book was stolen and posted online, resulting in 1,000 pirated downloads, she managed to receive 150 paid orders for e-books and 500 orders for photocopies. She invested in printing 3,000 copies to help create buzz; at one point, it was the 123rd best-selling title on Amazon.com. Following her online blitz, Doubleday Direct picked up *Lip Service* for its mail-order book clubs and soon after, Pocket Books signed up print rights in hardcover and paperback. Building on her success, Shapiro has become a leading advocate of e-books, with her frequent reports to Wired News online providing the most comprehensive ongoing coverage of e-publishing. "Everything in my life would be different if not for e-books," she says.

On the same day in March that Stephen King generated 400,000 orders, Leta Childers' comic romance e-novel, *The Best Laid Plans*, was downloaded 200 times from her publisher's Web site, DiskUspublishing.com. Childers is King's peer in one respect: Hers is the best-selling work released to date among digital-format-only publishers, according to the best-seller list compiled by eBook Connections. With some 20,000 copies of her e-book issued (at $3.50 for a downloaded copy, $6.50 on diskette), the rural South Dakota-based Childers has helped establish DiskUs Publishing of Albany, Ind., as one of the most successful digital-only publishers. In the still largely New York-based traditional publishing world, Childers says, "submission envelopes with Midwest return addresses are easy to ignore." Then in a familiar refrain for e-book authors, she adds: "I would love to be traditionally published."

DiskUs is a publisher in the traditional sense of having editors who help prepare manuscripts for publication. Other e-publishers disseminate authors' works for a fee, without exercising editorial control. Such "vanity presses" have long been the Rodney Dangerfields of publishing, but vanity e-publishers are proving attractive to mainstream book firms exploring new publishing paradigms. Following a recent investment by Random House, Xlibris.com now provides a no-fee, no-frills e-publishing package. Barnes & Noble is backing iUniverse.com, which offers new authors a basic $99 e-publishing service; it reserves free publication for authors submitting out-of-print works, a program originally developed with The Authors Guild.

For authors who've already been in print, one of the greatest benefits that e-books can offer is the resurrection of their old hard-to-find titles. As publishing companies have consolidated, worthy works have been relegated to the limbo of out-of-print. E-publishing provides an inexpensive way to restore the availability of these lapsed works. Among the most innovative of e-publishers, Alexandria Digital Literature has revived hundreds of out-of-print stories and poems, typically priced from 30 cents to $1.25. Buyers are asked to send in their ratings; when enough ratings accumulate, they can be compared to others' ratings and other reading recommendations are offered.

Also being revived are questions about traditional publishers' exclusivity over their authors' works. When Simon & Schuster made Stephen King's *Riding the Bullet* available through online booksellers and e-book hardware and software firms, one site was pointedly excluded: Fatbrain.com. Since last fall, Fatbrain has been posting works it brands as "eMatter": original fiction and nonfiction ranging from 10 to 100 pages (lengths that many people will be willing to print out). Subsequently designating the site for such pieces MightyWords.com, Fatbrain has targeted a segment of publishing that falls between magazines and books, where the modern economics of print have all but shut out a once-thriving sector of short stories and novellas. Simon & Schuster saw Fatbrain as a rival.

Fatbrain's brief history shows how quickly e-book business plans and branding can change. A mere six months after launching the eMatter trademark and drawing attention to the similarly named Web site, Fatbrain decided to let its trademark lapse. "MightyWords was a name that could ring through to our professional audience, while eMatter is a generic term for the range of electronic documents we are publishing," explains Judy Kirkpatrick, executive vice president and general manager of MightyWords. Already the eMatter 10-to-100-page category encompasses many of e-book publishing's early milestones, including King's *Riding the Bullet*. Simon & Schuster may not like it, but Fatbrain's publication of an eMatter essay by science fiction author Arthur C. Clarke was the inspiration for King to test the digital publishing waters. Also fitting the eMatter designation: Eric Rowe's 91-page *A Potter's Geology*.

King and Rowe have something else in common: an abiding belief in the importance of traditional books. King has been widely quoted as stating: "I don't think anything will replace the printed word and the bound book. Not in my lifetime, at least." For Rowe, too, it's not a question of digital books supplanting analog ones. "For some kinds of book," he says, "the aesthetic pleasure of having the object in the hand will be difficult to replace."

It should come as no surprise that proponents of e-books are not out to eliminate paper publishing. After all, most e-books attempt to replicate traditional books' content and appearance. For the most part, e-books can be printed out with only minimal loss of information (primarily broken hypertext links). And for all their seeming differences, print and electronic publishers are putting out similar content. Eventually, digital downloads seem destined to become just one more format for readers, one more step on the convenience/cost continuum from hardcover to paperback to e-book.

At some point in the future, however, e-books and print are bound to diverge. Lurking amidst e-publishing today is the notion of multimedia books that seamlessly incorporate hypertext, sound and animation. A hypertext branching narrative in a novel or a history book, for instance, would be impossible to reproduce in a book.

A glimmer of tomorrow's multimedia books, or m-books, may be discerned in a dark-horse contender among e-publishing file formats called TK3. Introduced by Night Kitchen—a New York startup headed by Voyager Co. co-founder Bob Stein—TK3 is the basis for a sophisticated literary software environment. The Night Kitchen TK3 Reader offers the most booklike reading experience on a desktop or laptop computer screen—complete with highlighting, corner-folding bookmarks, even Post-it-like "stickie notes." And TK3's easy-to-use multimedia authoring tools are meant, according to

Stein, "to empower a new generation of authors who want to express themselves in the new media." Using this hyperlink-sound-and-motion superset of traditional books to express themselves, such a new generation of authors would hasten Stein's prediction that "the locus of intellectual discourse will shift from the print medium to the electronic medium."

For now, the advent of e-books means not replacing print, but supplementing it—redefining publishing economics and opening the way for authors whose work has been kept from appearing between book covers. If e-books do nothing more, regardless of the success or lack thereof of new gadgetry to display them, this technology will have a profound effect on what we read and what we think.

**Stephen Sottong**

# E-Book Technology: Waiting for the "False Pretender"

Technology is one of the foundations of today's library. Our catalogs have become databases while the venerable cards are shipped to the recycler or used as scratch paper. We process and deliver interlibrary loans via the Web along with an increasing number of journals and indexes. This transition forces libraries to make decisions about a plethora of new technologies on a daily basis. As an electronic engineer until 1993, I am especially interested in the relationship of technology to my new profession.

A model of the life cycle of a technology was proposed by Raymond Kurzweil in 1992. This model can help libraries determine whether a technology is appropriate to adopt. In this article, I will amplify Kurzweil's technology life cycle model and apply this improved model to determine the current state of e-books within Kurzweil's framework.

## Background

Raymond Kurzweil, noted inventor and futurist, wrote "The Futurecast" column for *Library Journal* in the early 1990s. A three-part series in this column titled "The Future of Libraries" appeared from January through March of 1992. The first part of this series, "The Technology of the Book," listed seven stages in the life cycle of a technology:

1. Precursor
2. Invention
3. Development
4. Maturity
5. False Pretenders
6. Obsolescence
7. Antiquity

In the precursor stage, ideas about a new technology exist, but have not been implemented (e.g., DaVinci's helicopter). Invention gives the ideas concrete form. Development hones the technology into a practical form (e.g., automobile technology at the turn of the last century). Finally the technology reaches maturity and is practical and useful. Maturity can last for years, decades, or centuries depending on how well the technology meets the need for which it was invented.

As the mature technology ages, newer technologies arise to challenge it. If the newer technologies have some superior features but are not yet comparable in all facets, they may become false pretenders. Kurzweil defined this stage: "Here an upstart threatens to eclipse the older technology. Its enthusiasts prematurely predict victory. While providing some distinct benefits, the newer technology is found on reflection to be missing some key element of functionality or quality". The false pretenders may coexist with the mature technology, but they will not supplant the mature technology.

A newer technology can supplant the mature technology only when most or all of its features are comparable, and it has some improved feature to compensate the user for the trouble and expense of switching technologies. When a newer technology supplants a mature technology, the older mature technology enters obsolescence, in which it coexists with the newer technology for approximately 5 percent to 10 percent of its mature lifespan. Finally a supplanted technology reaches antiquity and ceases to be produced or used.

Kurzweil's stages provide a useful framework for evaluating current and proposed technology. Investment in the precursor, invention, and development stages of a technology is not worthwhile because of their instability and lack of features. A false pretender, on the other hand, may have a long lifespan and be worth some investment. For example, audio cassette technology is a false pretender that has remained popular for thirty years. The majority of library investments, however, will be in mature technologies with proven quality and functionality.

## Criteria

Kurzweil did not provide criteria for determining which stage a particular technology had reached. After examining his examples in "The Future of Libraries" articles, I developed a set of eight criteria for determining how mature and newer technologies compare with each other.

With respect to the mature technology, the newer technology must have comparable:

1. quality
2. durability
3. initial cost
4. continuing cost
5. ease of use
6. features

In addition, the new technology must:

7. be standardized
8. have extra features

These criteria provide a nonarbitrary method for evaluating a technology. Kurzweil used audio technology as an example of his stages [and . . .] stated in 1992 that electronic books were at the false pretender stage. . . .

## Quality

For both print books and e-books quality is determined by the display. The print book's display is far superior to either the Cathode Ray Tube (CRT) or Liquid Crystal Display (LCD) used for e-books. Display quality can be measured in terms of display resolution (in units of dots per inch—dpi) and contrast. Most books are printed at a resolution of 1,200 dpi. Commercially available video displays (whether CRT or LCD) have a maximum resolution of 100 dpi. The 1,200 dpi resolution of print is not twelve times the resolution video displays, but 144 times since a display is a two-dimensional surface and print is twelve times the resolution of a video display both horizontally and vertically. . . .

Kurzweil recognized display technology problems . . . but underestimated their magnitude and the time it would take to make improvements. He predicted that video display resolution would catch up to print in three years, but display resolution remains stalled at 100 dpi. As Jacobo Valdés (developer of Clearview, a competitor of ClearType) put it, "Screen resolution hasn't improved much over the past decade. It is still abysmal. Until it increases another 50 percent or so in each direction—which means about twice as many pixels per square inch—things will not get substantially better." Or as Bill Gates put it, "The computer screen is a terrible limitation versus reading the newspaper."

. . . IBM [has] announced a 200 dpi LCD display that has yet to go into production or have a price announcement . . . , and this display will still be only 1/36 the resolution of print. Entirely new electronic display technologies such as electronic ink, which is being developed by MIT and Xerox, are still a minimum of five years from being produced commercially.

In addition to resolution problems, contrast is greater for print than for CRT displays. Contrast is the ratio of maximum brightness to maximum darkness. For CRTs it can be as high as 100:1 and for LCDs 300:1; however, this is only a theoretical maximum. Any display device which emits light (CRT, backlit LCD, projectors, etc.) loses contrast with increased ambient light (hence our darkened electronic classrooms and movie theaters). For LCD, the contrast also decreases if the display is at an angle to the reader. Practical figures for the contrast of CRTs in normal light is 20:1 to 40:1 and for LCD it is approximately 100:1. Ink on paper has a contrast ratio of around 120:1 or three to six times greater than CRT displays and, since paper reflects light, the contrast does not deteriorate with ambient light. Most library patrons still use CRT displays and will continue to use them to read the e-books our libraries purchase. John Dvorak, a columnist for *PC Magazine,* said that for e-books to be practical, "The display needs to be at least 300 dots per inch with a contrast ratio of 40:1 to 50:1 and it must be readable in both the brightest sunlight and the most poorly lit office. Good luck."

The physical problems caused by computer use have been classified by the American Optometric Association as "Computer Vision Syndrome" or CVS. Symptoms of CVS include eyestrain, blurred vision, headaches, back and neck aches, dry eyes, distorted color vision, temporary myopia, double vision, after images, and increased sensitivity to light. A Harris poll called "computer related eyestrain" the number one office-related health complaint. Nearly 10 million people annually seek eye exams because of problems related to computer use, forty times the number of people afflicted with carpal tunnel syndrome and other repetitive stress injuries. Between 50 percent and 75 percent of PC users complain of eye problems associated with computer use. The National Institute of Health and Safety said that 88 percent of the 66 million people in the United States who work at computers for more than three hours a day suffer from eyestrain. All types of computer monitors (color or monochrome) produce these symptoms. Investigations at UC Berkeley indicate that the effects of CVS decrease productivity from 4 percent to 19 percent. The treatment cost for CVS approaches $2 billion annually.

Reading on computer displays is also inherently slower and less accurate. Proofreading experiments showed that reading speed is between 10 percent and 30 percent slower on a CRT and accuracy is 10 percent to 20 percent less. In one experiment, Gould et al. showed that an extremely bad copy of poor quality print deemed unacceptable by test participants could still be read as fast and as accurately as a CRT, even by experienced computer users.

This combination of physical stress and lower reading speed and accuracy is why the "paperless society" envisioned in the 1970s and 1980s never happened. Whenever readers encounter more than a few paragraphs of text, they print them out as an unconscious protection mechanism. Bill Gates acknowledged this in a speech at Harvard in 1996 where he said, "when you get a large document it's very typical to print it out on your local printer and then read it on paper. Many people do this because anything more than about four or five screensful is just easier to read that way." Walt Crawford estimated that, "people will print out anything longer than five hundred words or so." Kurzweil also recognized this: "Until the computer display truly rivals the qualities of paper, computers will increase the use of paper rather than replace it." E-books transfer the cost of printing from publishers to patrons without reducing library expenses and with *increased* environmental damage. Paul Curlander, chairman of printer maker Lexmark, predicted that office consumption of paper worldwide would increase from today's three trillion pages to eight trillion in 2010. . . .

## Durability

The print book is a model of durability. It can be dropped from great heights, exposed to sand and food, and even fully immersed in water for brief periods without losing its information content. As a truly severe test, give a print book and an e-book reader to a six year old and see which one survives longer.

Even if the pages of a print book are ripped out, the information content still remains. Libraries recognize this and rebind books to return them to full usefulness. Print books degrade gradually; the content remains useful even when the pages are yellowed and the binding is worn. Electronic devices, by contrast, tend to fail catastrophically; a single transistor in one chip can turn the entire device and all contents into scrap.

From five-thousand-year-old papyrus scrolls to five-hundred-year-old Gutenberg Bibles, paper has demonstrated durability. Print on nonacid paper can last for five hundred years. No digital storage media are stable for longer than one hundred years and I have found none guaranteed longer than twenty-five years. This is less than the lifespan of acid paper which most libraries prefer not to collect.

Even if a digital medium and its data survive one hundred years, the hardware and software needed to read it will no longer be available. How many computers can read a 5 1/4" inch disk, the standard only a decade ago? The time before magnetic or optical media becomes obsolete is estimated by Van Bogart of National Media Laboratory (NML) to be "ten or twenty years (or less)." As Kodak says on its Web site, after bragging about the projected one-hundred-year lifespan of its CDs:

> The principal fact of life for all digital storage media is the rapid obsolescence of hardware and software. Users of CD technology should be reassured by the long physical life of CD discs, but they must not lose sight of the need to maintain a viable path for migration of data to new hardware and software platforms. Digital storage media impose a strict discipline that human-readable records do not: their rapid evolution creates a continual progression of technology that cannot safely be ignored for too long.

A more serious durability problem is the nature of the Internet, which is used as the primary means of distribution for most e-book systems. Internet companies and sites are notoriously short lived, as recent "dot-com" shakeouts have shown. The Kodak site still exists; however, the information on media durability quoted above was removed from NML's site after it was used in a *U.S. News & World Report* article, which Van Bogart said misrepresented NML's findings. The site itself is no longer open to the public. The only verifiable copies of the Van Bogart data are the print copies from the 1996 conference where he presented the data. A book in the hand is worth a database of books on a shut-down server.

## Initial Cost

No hardware is required to read a print book. All e-books require an expensive reader, whether a $1,000 computer or a $200 SoftBookTM Reader. There is a social aspect to this initial cost: the poor cannot afford computers or e-book readers. Unless we wish to develop an elitist collection, libraries must lend the expensive e-book readers. If they are lost or damaged, the library will also have to assume the replacement expense. It would be unacceptable in most libraries (especially public libraries) either to charge a deposit or to hold poor patrons liable for massive damage expenses. This makes e-book readers a continuing expense for the library.

## Continuing Cost

Electronic books are still as expensive or more expensive than their print counterparts. One of the paradoxes of any new technology is that to become inexpensive, a technology must be ubiquitous, but it will not become ubiquitous until it is inexpensive. To overcome this, most new technologies must be produced at a loss and marketed on a par or at a discount compared to their mature competition until they gain ubiquity. That e-book vendors are not doing this may say something about the lack of confidence they have in their product.

Some continuing costs are unique to each media. Print books have shelving and space costs for libraries. If delivered via the Web, e-books have continuing subscription costs and costs associated with the computers, servers, and networks used to access them. If e-books are stand-alone, then the books must either be periodically repurchased or transferred to new media as they age or their format becomes obsolete. Since these costs are long-term and e-books have only been around for a short time, it is not yet possible to compare them.

## Ease of Use

While technologically savvy people find e-books easy to use, nothing matches the simplicity of a print book—just open it and read. There is no learning curve involved. In addition, print books can be annotated easily with a pencil or highlighter and, while such annotations are the bane of libraries, they usually do not damage the information content. Dedicated e-book readers have some moderately complicated mechanism for annotation, while computer-based e-books have either no mechanism or one which requires significant practice to master and greater time to perform.

## Features

E-books have features comparable to print with the exception of skimming, browsing, and sharing content. A print book can be rapidly flipped through to find a certain text or illustration while the inherent slowness of computer displays, especially LCD displays, along with the inherent difficulty in reading displays makes this task impossible for e-books.

Most dedicated e-book readers tie the purchased book to a specific reader while e-books accessed over the Internet are usually tied to a specific set of IP addresses. This means the book cannot be loaned or given to another person without including the reader. "Paper seems ideally suited for sharing. . . . For the most part, paper provides an easy and inexpensive solution that is unlikely to be bettered by reading appliances."

## Standardization

Most e-books use proprietary formats that cannot be read on different machines. This may change in the near future with the advent of the Open eBook standard (www.openebook.org); however, this standard could make current e-book readers obsolete.

## Added Features

E-books have four added features: text searching, hyperlinking, greater data density, and rapid updating. Text searching provides the ability to find specific sections in an e-book; however, this has limited usefulness since one must search on the exact word or phrase used by the author. By contrast, human-created indexes, often omitted from e-books, index concepts rather than words and cross-reference commonly used alternate terms. Hyperlinking can make electronic indexes very friendly and allow rapid switching between related sections of the text. This feature is most useful in highly cross-referenced texts and not as useful in linear texts such as novels and longer, descriptive works. Increased data density means that many e-books can be stored in one reader, allowing a person, for example, to carry a small reference library in a limited space. Rapid updating can be accomplished via the Internet. This can keep reference works much more up-to-date than their print counterparts.

## Conclusions

E-books fail six of the eight criteria. They are not comparable to print books. As Wildstrom put it, "They're too pricey, hard to read, and offer limited titles." The print book, as the *New York Times* stated in a 1994 editorial "is close to perfect: cheap, durable, portable, and complete unto itself." As Harold Bloom, noted educator and literary critic put it, "Imagine that for the last five hundred years we had nothing but e-books, and then there was some great technological advance that brought us the printed and bound book. We would all be ecstatic. We would be celebrating after the long horror of the e-book."

E-books are still very much in Kurzweil's development stage and not yet advanced enough to be a false pretender. The sales figures show this too; only twenty thousand to fifty thousand dedicated e-book readers have been sold, far fewer than the first day sales of the latest Harry Potter book or the contents of a small branch library. The recent success of Stephen King's e-book, *Riding the Bullet*, does not counter this, since it is estimated that only 1 percent of those who downloaded the book actually read it.

In spite of this, e-books may have a limited place in library collections where their special features outweigh their flaws. If searchability, linking, and currency are highly important and text is in short, discrete segments, e-books may be a useful solution. Such categories of books include:

- indexes
- encyclopedias
- almanacs
- gazetteers

- technical manuals
- handbooks (e.g., *PDR, Merck Index, CRC Handbook of Chemistry and Physics*)

As Gass put it, "Gazetteers, encyclopedias, and dictionaries are scholarly tools, but they are *consulted* rather than *read*" (emphasis mine). E-books do not work well with long segments of linear text such as novels, scholarly research works, most nonfiction, and text books. Even journals with lengthy articles do not lend themselves to electronic reading. These categories still comprise the majority of works in a library's collection.

Some librarians feel "they need to get on the e-book bandwagon now or risk being marginalized." Hage stated, "People want their library to be hip. They want their library to be willing to experiment when something new comes out," and pointed to library collections of VHS and Beta videocassettes as well as eight-track and audio cassettes. These arguments are predicated on the notion that libraries have always been on the cutting edge of technology, but this is not the case. Libraries may have collections of Beta tapes, but how many collected U-Matic videocassettes? We may have collected eight-tracks, but where are the collections of four-track cassettes or quadraphonic records? Libraries may have PCs in storage dating back to the IBM original, but how many of our libraries bought Altairs or IMSAIs? If the reader does not recognize U-Matic, quadraphonic, and Altair, this only emphasizes my point; these technologies were too preliminary and transient to be taken seriously for our collections. Libraries have seldom adopted the earliest, developmental stages of a technology. We are not true "early adopters" but "moderately early adopters." We wait until technologies sort themselves out and reach some level of standardization. This is all that I am suggesting for e-books. John V. Lombardi made a similar point during his speech to the 2000 ALA Annual Conference: "Being first to invent large-scale digital library projects is for those with money to lose, tolerant customers, and tenure. If it will take ten years to deliver value, let someone else invent it." Being the first to invest in a new technology is always expensive and generally unrewarding. The earliest libraries with online catalogs found themselves stuck with a huge investment in mainframe computers and custom software that provided limited, unreliable service for their patrons. Yet they could not afford to scrap these expensive systems and upgrade when smaller, cheaper, more reliable systems with greater functionality became available. Even choosing the most sophisticated new technology is not a guarantee of success as anyone with a Betamax video recorder or the OS/2 computer operating system will attest. Waiting for the market to settle lowers expenses, increases reliability, and reduces the chances that you will be left with rapidly outmoded technology.

Display technology is slowly improving and a standard format for e-books is in the works, but this still does not ensure the final adoption of e-book technology as the successor or even false pretender to the print book. Walt Crawford warns, "perhaps 80 percent of the time, the new technologies simply disappear or fade into specialized use." Other technologies now on the market such as print-on-demand will compete head-to-head with e-books. Print-on-demand stations can download a work from a vendor and provide a properly bound, paper book with all its inherent advantages in as little as five minutes. When the initial cost of this technology drops (as the cost of computer printers has dramatically done), it may be possible for libraries to provide patrons with print copies of any work and change the paradigm for collection development from "just in case" to "just in time."

Kurzweil's stages reassure us that we have no reason to hurry. Even if all of the technological problems with e-books were solved tomorrow and print books reached the stage of obsolescence, they would still be produced and remain useful for 5 percent to 10 percent of their mature lifespan. For print books, which have been produced for over five hundred years, that means we would have twenty-five to fifty years (one or two generations) to transition to the new technology.

If we begin more than limited collection of e-books, we risk alienating patrons who quickly will weary of the eyestrain caused by current e-books. We also risk wasting money on hardware and software that rapidly will become obsolete. As progress is made on e-book development, the eight criteria outlined here can be used to judge whether the technology is finally ready for widespread acceptance.

# POSTSCRIPT

## Will Screens Replace Pages?

Media theorist Paul Levinson, in *Wired, Analog, and Digital Writings* (Pulpless.com, 1999), tries "to disentangle the extent to which our attachment to books is based on real advantages in performance versus rosy nostalgia." Levinson concludes that digital texts have genuine advantages but that books have enough advantages of their own that they will remain with us for the foreseeable future. Wade Roush, in "A Genuine Button-Pusher," *Technology Review* (November/December 1999), asserts that "the electronic book is [already] beginning to give paper some serious competition." But in the July 6, 2002, *Washington Post,* Linton Weeks could title an article "E-Books Not Exactly Flying Off the Shelves." People who read prefer paper.

Yet Web-based e-books are now appearing, and e-reference material is already here; see Mick O'Leary, "Safari/ProQuest Team Boosts E-Book Prospects," *Information Today* (March 2003) and "netLibrary Rolls Out an Online Reference Collection," *Information Today* (May 2003). E-books are also being tested in many libraries; see for instance Marc Langston, "The California State University E-book Pilot Project: Implications for Cooperative Collection Development," *Library Collections, Acquisitions, & Technical Services* (Spring 2003).

To this we can add the impact of two new technologies, one that is already in play and one that is coming soon. The first is "print-on-demand" (POD) publishing. This process uses computer technology, high-quality laser printers, and automated binding equipment to print single copies of books that have been stored in electronic form. Some publishers have used this technology to make large numbers of out-of-print classics available, as well as to publish many books that large, conventional publishers think would not sell enough copies to be worth their effort. Print-on-demand publishing is suffering growing pains at present, but many observers think that its prospects are strong. See Walt Crawford, "Brace Yourselves—It's the Attack of the PoD People," *American Libraries* (January 2002).

The second technology is "electronic paper," one version of which is paper with tiny plastic balls embedded in it. One half of each ball is black, and one half is white. Electronics allows the balls to be turned so the black or the white shows, which means that this paper can behave almost like a computer monitor. The E-Ink company (`http://www.eink.com/`) unveiled "the world's thinnest active-matrix displays" in June 2002 and said that it expected to commercialize the product by 2004. Ultimately, say some, e-books will look just like paper books, except that the text can be changed by displaying different files; indeed, a single "book" may be able to hold the equivalent of a library, just as can a laptop today. See Michael J. Miller, "The Next Step in Electronic Paper," *PC Magazine* (May 7, 2002), David Cameron, "Flexible

Displays Gain Momentum," *Technology Review* (January 2002), and Steve Ditlea, "The Electronic Paper Chase," *Scientific American* (November 2001).

Perhaps the wave of the future is a combination of old and new that blurs the distinction between screen and page and expands the potential of the reading experience. Roxane Farmanfarmaian, in "Beyond E-Books: Glimpses of the Future," *Publishers Weekly* (January 1, 2001), quotes Rich Gold, director of Research on Experimental Documents (RED) at Xerox Parc in Palo Alto, California, as saying, "E-book readers, print-on-demand, these are just passing technologies, like the telex machine was, that do a lousy job of adding high tech to an old medium. What we can expect in the future is a slew of radically new media where the reader reads at all levels, and content and form deeply resonate."

# On the Internet . . .

## Foundation for Biomedical Research

The Foundation for Biomedical Research promotes public understanding and support of the ethical use of animals in scientific and medical research.

http://www.fbresearch.org

## The Nature of Wellness

The Nature of Wellness aims to inform the public about the medical and scientific invalidity of animal experimentation and testing and to demonstrate that reliance on animal experimentation and testing is destroying the health care system, the environment, and the economy.

http://www.animalresearch.org/

## Union of Concerned Scientists

The Union of Concerned Scientists is an independent nonprofit alliance of concerned citizens and scientists committed to building a cleaner, healthier environment and a safer world. Its Web site provides a great deal of information on many issues, including the use of genetic engineering in agriculture.

http://www.ucsusa.org

## Center for Bioethics

The mission of the Center for Bioethics is to advance scholarly and public understanding of ethical, legal, social, and public policy issues in health care.

http://bioethics.net

## National Human Genome Research Institute

The National Human Genome Research Institute directs the Human Genome Project for the National Institutes of Health (NIH).

http://www.genome.gov/

## The U.S. Department of Energy Human Genome Project

This site offers a huge amount of information and links on genetics and cloning research.

http://www.ornl.gov/techresources/Human_Genome/elsi/Cloning.html

# PART 6

## Ethics

*Society's standards of right and wrong have been hammered out over millennia of trial, error, and (sometimes violent) debate. Accordingly, when science and technology offer society new choices to make and new things to do, debates are renewed over whether or not these choices and actions are ethically acceptable. Today there is vigorous debate over such topics as the use of animals in research, genetic engineering, and cloning.*

- Is the Use of Animals in Research Justified?
- Should Genetically Modified Foods Be Banned?
- Is It Ethically Permissible to Clone Human Beings?

# ISSUE 17

## Is the Use of Animals in Research Justified?

**YES: Mark Matfield,** from "Animal Experimentation: The Continuing Debate," *Nature Reviews, Drug Discovery* (February 2002)

**NO: Steven Zak,** from "Ethics and Animals," *The Atlantic Monthly* (March 1989)

### ISSUE SUMMARY

**YES:** Mark Matfield summarizes the history of protests against the use of animals in research and argues that the research community needs to play a greater part in communicating the benefits of animal use and the commitment of the researchers themselves to protecting and regulating the welfare of laboratory animals.

**NO:** Research attorney Steven Zak maintains that current animal protection laws do not adequately protect animals used in medical and other research and that, for society to be virtuous, it must recognize the rights of animals not to be sacrificed for human needs.

Modern biologists and physicians know a great deal about how the human body works. Some of that knowledge has been gained by studying human cadavers and tissue samples acquired during surgery and through "experiments of nature" (strokes, for example, have taught a great deal about what the various parts of the brain do; extensive injuries from car accidents and wars have also been edifying). Some knowledge of human biology has also been gained from experiments on humans, such as when patients agree to let their surgeons and doctors try experimental treatments.

The key word here is *agree*. Today it is widely accepted that people have the right to consent or not to consent to whatever is done to them in the name of research or treatment. In fact, society has determined that research done on humans without their free and informed consent is a form of scientific misconduct. However, this standard does not apply to animals, experimentation on which has produced the most knowledge of the human body.

Although animals have been used in research for at least the last 2,000 years, during most of that time, physicians who thought they had a workable treatment for some illness commonly tried it on their patients before they had any idea whether or not it worked or was even safe. Many patients, of course, died during these untested treatments. In the mid-nineteenth century, the French physiologist Claude Bernard argued that it was sensible to try such treatments first on animals to avoid some human suffering and death. No one then questioned whether or not human lives were more valuable than animal lives. In the twentieth century, Elizabeth Baldwin, in "The Case for Animal Research in Psychology," *Journal of Social Issues* (vol. 49, no. 1, 1993), argued that animals are of immense value in medical, veterinary, and psychological research, and they do not have the same moral rights as humans. Our obligation, she maintains, is to treat them humanely.

Today geneticists generally study fruit flies, roundworms, and zebra fish. Physiologists study mammals, mostly mice and rats but also rabbits, cats, dogs, pigs, sheep, goats, monkeys, and chimpanzees. Experimental animals are often kept in confined quarters, cut open, infected with disease organisms, fed unhealthy diets, and injected with assorted chemicals. Sometimes the animals suffer. Sometimes the animals die. And sometimes they are healed, albeit often of diseases or injuries induced by the researchers in the first place.

Not surprisingly, some observers have reacted with extreme sympathy and have called for better treatment of animals used in research. This "animal welfare" movement has, in turn, spawned the more extreme "animal rights" movement, which asserts that animals—especially mammals—have rights as important and as deserving of regard as those of humans. Thus, to kill an animal, whether for research, food, or fur, is the moral equivalent of murder. See Steven M. Wise and Jane Goodall, *Rattling the Cage: Toward Legal Rights for Animals* (Perseus, 2000) and Roger Scruton and Andrew Tayler, "Do Animals Have Rights?" *The Ecologist* (March 2001).

This attitude has led to important reforms in the treatment of animals, to the development of several alternatives to using animals in research, and to a considerable reduction in the number of animals used in research. See Alan M. Goldberg and John M. Frazier, "Alternatives to Animals in Toxicity Testing," *Scientific American* (August 1989); Wade Roush, "Hunting for Animal Alternatives," *Science* (October 11, 1996); and Erik Stokstad, "Humane Science Finds Sharper and Kinder Tools," *Science* (November 5, 1999). However, it has also led to hysterical objections to in-class animal dissections, terrorist attacks on laboratories, the destruction of research records, and the theft of research materials (including animals).

In the following selections, Mark Matfield argues that public opinion has begun to give more weight to the value of animals in research and to disapprove of the extreme tactics of animal rights groups. The scientific community must continue to stress the benefits of using animals in research and the role of scientists in protecting and regulating the welfare of laboratory animals. Representing the position of many animal rights activists, Stephen Zak states that morality requires society to recognize the rights of animals not to be made to suffer at all for the benefit of humans. Therefore, researchers should always find alternative modes of research.

**Mark Matfield**

**YES**

# Animal Experimentation: The Continuing Debate

The use of animals in research and development has remained a subject of public debate for over a century. Although there is good evidence from opinion surveys that the public accepts the use of animals in research, they are poorly informed about the way in which it is regulated, and are increasingly concerned about laboratory-animal welfare. This article will review how public concerns about animal experimentation developed, the recent activities of animal-rights groups, and the opportunities and challenges facing the scientific community.

## The Historical Context

The origin of public and political debate about animal experimentation throughout the world occurred at the Annual Meeting of the British Medical Association (BMA) that was held in Norwich in 1874. The BMA had invited the French scientist Eugene Magnan to lecture on the physiological effects of alcohol. After the lecture, Dr. Magnan gave a demonstration of the induction of experimental epilepsy in a dog by the intravenous injection of absinthe. At this time, physiological research in continental Europe had a tradition of experimenting on animals that had become firmly established before the introduction of ether and chloroform for general anaesthesia. In the United Kingdom, however, very little animal experimentation was carried out, chiefly because few scientists would contemplate invasive experiments on conscious animals.

There is no accurate record of what happened at the meeting, but it is known that there was considerable protest from some members of the audience and that, after one animal had been injected, an eminent medical figure summoned the magistrates to prevent the demonstration from continuing. The Royal Society for the Prevention of Cruelty to Animals (RSPCA) brought a prosecution for cruelty, and several of the doctors present at the demonstration gave evidence against Magnan, who returned to France to avoid answering the charges. The press followed these events with interest and there was a heated debate about vivisection in the pages of popular magazines. The very first antivivisection pamphlets, calling for legislation to ban animal experimentation, appeared in London only months after the BMA meeting.

From *Drug Recovery,* vol. 1, February 2002, pp. 149–152. 

Over the next two years, the debate continued to escalate. The first antivivisection society was formed, bills were introduced into Parliament, the scientific community fought back, a Royal Commission of Enquiry was held, and compromise legislation was eventually pushed through by the government.

In the United States, the origins of the debate paralleled developments in the United Kingdom. In 1874, Henry Burgh started the first antivivisection campaign under the auspices of The American Society for the Prevention of Cruelty to Animals (ASPCA), and later introduced a bill into the New York legislature to make vivisection a misdemeanour. However, adverse reports from medical societies throughout the country prevented the bill from gaining any real political support. The American Anti-Vivisection Association, founded in 1883, was the first of several organizations that were set up to continue the campaign.

In both the United States and Europe, the debate about animal experimentation waned with the advent of the First World War, only to re-emerge during the 1970s, when antivivisection and animal-welfare organizations joined forces to campaign for new legislation to regulate animal research and testing. In the United States, the public debate re-emerged in a more dramatic fashion in 1980, when an activist infiltrated the laboratory of Dr. Edward Taub of the Institute of Behavioural Research at Silver Spring, Maryland. This attack on Taub's research was organized by a tiny animal-rights group called People for the Ethical Treatment of Animals (PETA), which has since grown to dominate the campaign in the United States.

## The Anatomy of the Campaign

The United Kingdom still remains the country in which the debate is most intense, with some of the antivivisection organizations that were founded in the late 1800s still campaigning actively. The organizations that are opposed to animal experimentation fall into three broad groups. The legitimate animal-welfare organizations, such as the RSPCA, take a pragmatic approach. Although they espouse the long-term objective of ending animal experimentation, they accept that this is not going to happen within the foreseeable future. In the meantime, they seek to work with scientists to improve the welfare of laboratory animals and develop alternative, non-animal, methods.

The mainstream antivivisection and animal-rights groups campaign very actively, but are careful to remain within the law and, in some cases, are respectable enough to have representatives on government committees. Some of these campaigning organizations take a dogmatic line, and argue that animal experimentation is scientifically invalid and has never produced any medical benefit. Others prefer to use the selective presentation of information to suggest that animal research is of questionable value, is conducted poorly and always causes great suffering.

Over the past 30 years, the philosophical idea of animal rights has grown and come to dominate this movement. Perhaps as a result, the movement has also grown a radical edge, composed of activists and loosely knit groups that are willing to go much further than the campaigning antivivisection organizations.

Some of the radicals limit themselves to demonstrating outside laboratories and shouting abuse. However, the extremists, working under the banner of the Animal Liberation Front, are willing to use intimidation, damage to property and even violence to further their aims.

The United States also has its share of animal-rights extremism, which seems to have grown out of radical environmental activism, but has been strongly influenced by UK extremists. Although the actual number of animal-rights extremist attacks in the United States is much smaller than in the United Kingdom, it has included several serious cases of arson.

## Key Issues in the Debate

The historical perspective gives us a clear indication of the main factors that underlie public attitudes towards animal experimentation. In nineteenth-century Britain, the protest was about cruelty to animals in laboratories. In more recent times, the debate has also focused on whether animal research is necessary, what medical progress it has produced and whether alternatives could be used. A careful analysis of the public debate about animal experimentation shows that essentially all of it revolves around two basic arguments: is animal experimentation cruel, and is it necessary? The 'necessity' argument is presented in different ways, such as citing the use of alternative methods, or questioning the 'validity' of animal research, but ultimately they are all arguing about whether there is a need for animal research.

Two recent opinion surveys conducted in the United Kingdom have given an important insight into the nature and origins of the UK public's views on the issue. They revealed that most of the general public accepted that animals should be used in research, but with some very important qualifications. Their acceptance was conditional on the purpose of the experimentation being for important medical research, that the animals should be rodents and that they should not suffer. If any of these three factors were altered, the level of acceptance diminished substantially.

When the respondents were asked about how they thought animal research should be regulated, they spontaneously suggested all the key elements of the existing UK system of regulation. This indicates that, if they were more aware of the existing regulatory system, they might have stronger support for the way animals are used in research in the United Kingdom.

## The Scientific Community's Response

In those countries in which the scientific community has been faced with a vocal campaign against the use of animals in research, they have responded by setting up organizations to represent their perspective in the public and political debate. The first such organization, The Physiological Society, was founded in the United Kingdom in 1876. However, over the years it evolved into a conventional scientific association, and its role in the debate was taken over by the Research Defence Society in 1908. In the same year in the United States, the American Medical Association responded to the growing activity of the antivivisection movement by forming the Council for the Defense of Medical Research.

Pro-research organizations normally enlist the active support of scientists from both academia and the pharmaceutical industry to provide advice and support and to act as spokespersons and advocates for the use of animals in research. In addition, many pharmaceutical trade associations have developed their own pro-research communication resources to engage directly in the debate. A few individual companies have also become directly involved. However, most companies prefer to rely on the skills and experience developed by the dedicated pro-research organizations, rather than having direct corporate involvement. This arrangement works well as long as the debate and campaigning is focused on the issue at hand. However, when a particular company becomes the target of a campaign, they have to develop the skills needed to respond as rapidly as possible. This has recently been seen in the case of Huntingdon Life Sciences.

## The Recent Changes

The past few years have seen a major change in the campaigning activities of the animal-rights movement in the United Kingdom, which is starting to alter the nature of the debate. Until recently, the movement was very fragmented, with numerous groups adopting different targets and different styles of activity. Although there was a significant level of animal-rights activity, it was directed at a range of targets, including universities, breeders and contract research companies, as well as fur shops, butchers and fox hunts. The style of campaigning activity ranged from peaceful and legitimate protests to the sending of letter bombs. However, in 1996, a group of radical activists started to focus on Consort, a small laboratory dog breeder located near Hereford in the United Kingdom. The repeated demonstrations, harassment, intimidation and attacks on staff and suppliers imposed security costs that the firm was unable to afford. When the breeder closed down in 1997, it was greeted as a huge victory by the activists. In 30 years of animal-rights activism, they had never forced a company to close before. Focused campaigns suddenly became the main tactic adopted by activists.

The same tactic of aggressive targeting was then used against several other small breeders, who were relentlessly forced out of business, one by one. Hillgrove Farm, a cat breeder, was forced to close in 1999, followed by the primate supplier Shamrock Farm, and Regal Rabbits in 2000. With each 'victory', focused campaigns gained more support from rank-and-file animal-rights activists. In the face of these campaigns of harassment and intimidation, the mainstream antivivisection organizations adopted a low profile, not wanting to associate themselves with the often illegal activities of these campaigns, but equally reluctant to mount competing campaigns against other targets, which might have failed due to lack of support.

After closing down four small laboratory-animal breeders, the small group of activists that was organizing the focused campaigns decided to attack a much larger target, and launched the current campaign against

Huntingdon Life Sciences (HLS), the largest contract research company in Europe. With the impetus of the previous successes, the HLS campaign soon grew to completely dominate the UK animal-rights movement, and even became a major animal-rights issue in the United States. In addition to attacks on the company and its staff, secondary targets, such as the banks and stockbrokers used by HLS, also received the unwelcome attention of the activists. When they started targeting the pharmaceutical companies that were clients of HLS, there were nervous discussions in boardrooms around the world.

## Reaction to the HLS Campaign

The activists' success in their campaign against HLS finally provoked the UK government into action. In January 2001, the Royal Bank of Scotland gave in to pressure from animal-rights activists and refused to renew a loan of US$20 million that was essential to the survival of HLS. The realization that animal-rights extremism could bring Europe's largest contract testing company to the verge of financial ruin prompted the personal intervention of the Science Minister, Lord Sainsbury, who had a leading role in the negotiations that resulted in the US investment company Stephens, Inc. taking over the loan to HLS in January 2001.

Once the UK government understood that they were dealing with an issue of strategic importance to the future of the country's bioscience-based industries, they moved swiftly to introduce legislation to deal with animal-rights extremists. The police were given powers to prevent activists demonstrating outside people's homes, including the power to arrest protestors who refused to halt such demonstrations. The government strengthened existing legislation against harassment and malicious communications to criminalize other tactics used by the activists. They also made changes to the legislation concerning company directors, permitting them to keep their home addresses out of the public domain.

Perhaps the most radical action taken by the government was to set up a special police squad, which works at a national level and is dedicated to tracking down animal-rights extremists and prosecuting them for their offences. In July 2001, when HLS were unable to find banking facilities, the UK government took the unprecedented step of allowing them to use an account with the Bank of England.

## Public Opinion Starts to Change

The extremist behaviour of the animal-rights activists had also started to swing public opinion, which in the United Kingdom is usually tolerant of protestors, against their campaign. A few days before Christmas 2000, the Marketing Director of HLS was attacked outside his home by masked activists who sprayed a noxious liquid into his eyes. Fortunately, he managed to get inside his house and close the door before they had done more than land a few blows on his back. A far worse incident took place in February 2001, when three masked activists wielding pickaxe handles attacked Brian Cass, the Managing Director of HLS. He sustained a bad head wound and broken ribs before a neighbour intervened and the attackers fled.

These incidents were widely condemned, and the government made several high-profile statements about the importance of animal experimentation for the pharmaceutical and biotechnology industries. Media coverage of the issue shifted significantly, with most of the news focusing on the problems caused by animal-rights activists. This media coverage was based on the premise that animal research was essential for medical research. Some of the longer news items would explain this in detail, whereas the shorter items simply took it for granted as a known fact. This was in marked contrast to the way in which the media had handled animal experimentation as a controversial issue for the previous decade or more, always taking care to present two opposing views about it.

The introduction of measures to tackle the extremism and the shift in public opinion had a noticeable effect on the campaign against HLS. The unwavering tactical focus that had been the hallmark of these campaigns soon began to break down. Some of the leading activists called for a more moderate approach, wanting to win back public support, although others deliberately undermined their attempts to make the protests more peaceful. A third faction started to refocus the protests against environmental targets, such as Shell and Dow Chemicals. Others drifted into campaigns against other targets, such as a proposed primate research facility at Cambridge University. At the time of writing, the campaign against HLS seems to be fragmenting.

## The Challenges Ahead

With the campaign against HLS starting to wane, and increasing evidence of support for the use of animals in biomedical research and development from both the government and the public, the scientific community in the United Kingdom has an excellent opportunity to present their side of this debate to the public more effectively than ever before. Over the past decade, most of the activity by the scientific community on this issue has been directed at the question of the necessity of animal research. The evidence from opinion polling indicates that this message has reached the public. However, the animal-rights movement will always attack that position, so the scientific community will need to continue to reinforce this argument.

The current situation presents an ideal opportunity for the scientific community to extend the debate and begin to address the other main issue: the welfare of laboratory animals. From the perspective of the general public, whether or not animals suffer in experiments is at least as important as the question of the necessity of the experiments. The scientific community seems to have put far less effort into discussing the welfare issue, and one of the probable reasons for this is that it is far less cut and dried. In some experiments, animals do suffer. That cannot be denied.

However, there is a great deal that can, and is, being done to reduce any distress or suffering to a minimum. Almost every country with a significant bioscience research base also has a system to regulate experiments on animals to ensure they are conducted in an ethical and humane manner. There are two different types of regulatory system. Some countries, particularly those with a long history of public debate on the issue, such as the United Kingdom, Germany and Switzerland, opted for government regulation, with the decisions about what experiments could be done and how they should be done being made by government officials. Other countries have adopted the 'ethical committee' approach, in which the decisions are made by an institutional committee. Both scientists and the institute's animal-welfare staff are normally represented on such committees. In some cases, the members also include non-scientific staff, external lay members and representatives of animal-welfare or antivivisection organizations.

There are benefits and risks associated with including external members on such committees. Although including them can promote greater ethical debate and increased public credibility, some antivivisection representatives have used their membership to attempt to delay or block the approval of animal-research projects. Exactly how to strike the balance will depend on a number of factors, including the institutional culture and national attitudes towards animal experimentation.

However, it is also important that the public is made aware of the way in which animal research is regulated and the ethical and welfare standards that are applied. Given the degree of public concern, we have made little effort to inform the public about our contributions to laboratory-animal welfare, particularly in the light of our strong credentials in this area. Essentially, all the main alternative methods (such as methods that either replace the use of animals, reduce the number of animals used in a procedure, or reduce the welfare impact on the animals), and many of the ways in which the welfare of laboratory animals is improved (by using anaesthetics, analgesics, humane end points and environmental enrichment), were developed by scientists.

For more than a century, the scientific community has had a passive role in the public and political debate about animal experimentation. We have responded when criticized and complied when regulated. This passive, reactive role has always left us at a disadvantage, allowing the antivivisection movement to control the debate. Surely, the time has come for us to take some of the initiative and seek to influence the way in which this debate develops in the future. Instead of being cast as 'the bad guys' because we experiment on animals, scientists should be seen as people who seek to improve the well being of both humans and animals.

NO 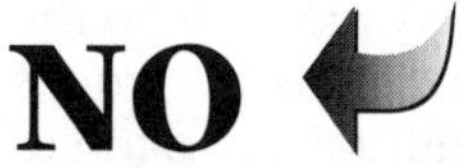

**Steven Zak**

# Ethics and Animals

In December of 1986 members of an "animal-liberation" group called True Friends broke into the Sema, Inc., laboratories in Rockville, Maryland, and took four baby chimpanzees from among the facility's 600 primates. The four animals, part of a group of thirty being used in hepatitis research, had been housed individually in "isolettes"—small stainless-steel chambers with sealed glass doors. A videotape produced by True Friends shows other primates that remained behind. Some sit behind glass on wire floors, staring blankly. One rocks endlessly, banging violently against the side of his cage. Another lies dead on his cage's floor.

The "liberation" action attracted widespread media attention to Sema, which is a contractor for the National Institutes of Health [NIH], the federal agency that funds most of the animal research in this country. Subsequently the NIH conducted an investigation into conditions at the lab and concluded that the use of isolettes is justified to prevent the spread of disease among infected animals. For members of True Friends and other animal-rights groups, however, such a scientific justification is irrelevant to what they see as a moral wrong; these activists remain frustrated over conditions at the laboratory. This conflict between the NIH and animal-rights groups mirrors the tension between animal researchers and animal-rights advocates generally. The researchers' position is that their use of animals is necessary to advance human health care and that liberation actions waste precious resources and impede the progress of science and medicine. The animal-rights advocates' position is that animal research is an ethical travesty that justifies extraordinary, and even illegal, measures.

The Sema action is part of a series that numbers some six dozen to date and that began, in 1979, with a raid on the New York University Medical Center, in which members of a group known as the Animal Liberation Front (ALF) took a cat and two guinea pigs. The trend toward civil disobedience is growing. For example, last April members of animal-rights groups demonstrated at research institutions across the country (and in other countries, including Great Britain and Japan), sometimes blocking entrances to them by forming human chains. In the United States more than 130 activists were arrested, for offenses ranging from blocking a doorway and trespassing to burglary.

To judge by everything from talk-show programs to booming membership enrollment in animal-rights groups (U.S. membership in all groups is estimated at 10 million), the American public is increasingly receptive to the animal-rights position. Even some researchers admit that raids by groups like True Friends and the ALF have exposed egregious conditions in particular labs and have been the catalyst for needed reforms in the law. But many members of animal-rights groups feel that the recent reforms do not go nearly far enough. Through dramatic animal-liberation actions and similar tactics, they hope to force what they fear is a complacent public to confront a difficult philosophical issue: whether animals, who are known to have feelings and psychological lives, ought to be treated as mere instruments of science and other human endeavors. . . .

Animal-rights activists feel acute frustration over a number of issues, including hunting and trapping, the destruction of animals' natural habits, and the raising of animals for food. But for now the ALF considers animal research the most powerful symbol of human dominion over and exploitation of animals, and it devotes most of its energies to that issue. The public has been ambivalent, sometimes cheering the ALF on, at other times denouncing the group as "hooligans." However one chooses to characterize the ALF, it and other groups like it hold an uncompromising "rights view" of ethics toward animals. The rights view distinguishes the animal-protection movement of today from that of the past and is the source of the movement's radicalism.

## "They All Have a Right to Live"

Early animal-protection advocates and groups . . . seldom talked about rights. They condemned cruelty—that is, acts that produce or reveal bad character. In early-nineteenth-century England campaigners against the popular sport of bull-baiting argued that it "fostered every bad and barbarous principle of our nature." Modern activists have abandoned the argument that cruelty is demeaning to human character ("virtue thought") in favor of the idea that the lives of animals have intrinsic value ("rights thought"). Rights thought doesn't necessarily preclude the consideration of virtue, but it mandates that the measure of virtue be the foreseeable consequences to others of one's acts.

"Michele" is thirty-five and works in a bank in the East. She has participated in many of the major ALF actions in the United States. One of the missions involved freeing rats, and she is scornful of the idea that rats aren't worth the effort. "These animals feel pain just like dogs, but abusing them doesn't arouse constituents' ire, so they don't get the same consideration. They all have a right to live their lives. Cuteness should not be a factor."

While most people would agree that animals should not be tortured, there is no consensus about animals' right to live (or, more precisely, their right not to be killed). Even if one can argue, as the British cleric Humphrey Primatt did in 1776, that "pain is pain, whether it be inflicted on man or on beast," it is more difficult to argue that the life of, say, a dog is qualitatively the same as that of a human being. To this, many animal-rights activists would say that every morally relevant characteristic that is lacking in all animals (rationality might be one, according to some ways of defining that term) is also lacking in some "marginal" human beings, such as infants, or the senile, or the severely retarded. Therefore, the activists argue, if marginal human beings have the right to live, it is arbitrary to hold that animals do not. Opponents of this point of view often focus on the differences between animals and "normal" human beings, asserting, for instance, that unlike most human adults, animals do not live by moral rules and therefore are not part of the human "moral community."

The credibility of the animal-rights viewpoint, however, need not stand or fall with the "marginal human beings" argument. Lives don't have to be qualitatively the same to be worthy of equal respect. One's perception that another life has value comes as much from an appreciation of its uniqueness as from the recognition that it has characteristics that are shared by one's own life. (Who would compare the life of a whale to that of a marginal human being?) One can imagine that the lives of various kinds of animals differ radically, even as a result of having dissimilar bodies and environments—that being an octopus feels different from being an orangutan or an oriole. The orangutan cannot be redescribed as the octopus minus, or plus, this or that mental characteristic; conceptually, nothing could be added to or taken from the octopus that would make it the equivalent of the oriole. Likewise, animals are not simply rudimentary human beings, God's false steps, made before He finally got it right with us.

Recognizing differences, however, puts one on tentative moral ground. It is easy to argue that likes ought to be treated alike. Differences bring problems: How do we think about things that are unlike? Against what do we measure and evaluate them? What combinations of likeness and difference lead to what sorts of moral consideration? Such problems may seem unmanageable, and yet in a human context we routinely face ones similar in kind if not quite in degree: our ethics must account for dissimilarities between men and women, citizens and aliens, the autonomous and the helpless, the fully developed and the merely potential, such as children or fetuses. We never solve these problems with finality, but we confront them. . . .

Both advocates and opponents of animal rights also invoke utilitarianism in support of their points of view. Utilitarianism holds that an act or practice is measured by adding up the good and the bad consequences—classically, pleasure and pain—and seeing which come out ahead. There are those who would exclude animals from moral consideration on the grounds that the benefits of exploiting them outweigh the harm. Ironically, though, it was utilitarianism, first formulated by Jeremy Bentham in the eighteenth century, that brought animals squarely into the realm of moral consideration. If an act or practice has good and bad consequences for animals, then these must be entered into the moral arithmetic. And the calculation must be genuinely disinterested. One may not baldly assert that one's own interests count for more. Animal researchers may truly believe that they are impartially weighing all interests when they conclude that human interests overwhelm those of animals. But a skeptical reader will seldom be persuaded that they are in fact doing so. . . .

Even true utilitarianism is incomplete, though, without taking account of rights. For example, suppose a small group of aboriginal tribespeople were captured and bred for experiments that would benefit millions of other people by, say, resulting in more crash-worthy cars. Would the use of such people be morally acceptable? Surely it would not, and that point illustrates an important function of rights thought: to put limits on what can be done to individuals, even for the good of the many. Rights thought dictates that we cannot kill one rights-holder to save another—or even more than one other—whether or not the life of the former is "different" from that of the latter.

Those who seek to justify the exploitation of animals often claim that it comes down to a choice: kill an animal or allow a human being to die. But this claim is misleading, because a choice so posed has already been made. The very act of considering the taking of life X to save life Y reduces X to the status of a mere instrument. Consider the problem in a purely human context. Imagine that if Joe doesn't get a new kidney he will die. Sam, the only known potential donor with a properly matching kidney, himself has only one kidney and has not consented to give it—and his life—up for Joe. Is there really a choice? If the only way to save Joe is to kill Sam, then we would be unable to do so—and no one would say that we chose Sam over Joe. Such a choice would never even be contemplated.

In another kind of situation there *is* a choice. Imagine that Joe and Sam both need a kidney to survive, but we have only one in our kidney bank. It may be that we should give the kidney to Joe, a member of our community, rather than to Sam, who lives in some distant country (though this is far from clear—maybe flipping a coin would be more fair). Sam (or the loser of the coin flip) could not complain that his rights had been violated, because moral claims to some resource—positive claims—must always be dependent on the availability of that resource. But the right not to be treated as if one were a mere resource or instrument—negative, defensive claims—is most fundamentally what it means to say that one has rights. And this is what members of the ALF have in mind when they declare that animals, like human beings, have rights.

Where, one might wonder, should the line be drawn? Must we treat dragonflies the same as dolphins? Surely not. Distinctions must be made, though to judge definitively which animals must be ruled out as holders of rights may be impossible even in principle. In legal or moral discourse we are virtually never able to draw clear lines. This does not mean that drawing a line anywhere, arbitrarily, is as good as drawing one anywhere else.

The line-drawing metaphor, though, implies classifying entities in a binary way: as either above the line, and so entitled to moral consideration, or not. Binary thinking misses nuances of our moral intuition. Entities without rights may still deserve moral consideration on other grounds: one may think that a dragonfly doesn't quite qualify for rights yet believe that it would be wrong to crush one without good reason. And not all entities with rights need be treated in precisely the same way. This is apparent when one compares animals over whom we have assumed custody with wild animals. The former, I think, have rights to our affirmative aid, while the latter have such rights only in certain circumstances. Similar distinctions can be made among human beings, and also between human beings and particular animals. For example, I recently spent $1,000 on medical care for my dog, and I think he had a right to that care, but I have never given such an amount to a needy person on the street. Rights thought, then, implies neither that moral consideration ought to be extended only to the holders of rights nor that all rights-holders must be treated with a rigid equality. It implies only that rights-holders should never be treated as if they, or their kind, didn't matter.

## Animals, Refrigerators, and Can Openers

The question of man's relationship with animals goes back at least to Aristotle, who granted that animals have certain senses—hunger, thirst, a sense of touch—but who held that they lack rationality and therefore as "the lower sort [they] are by nature slaves, and . . . should be under the rule of a master." Seven centuries later Saint Augustine added the authority of the Church, arguing that "Christ himself [teaches] that to refrain from the killing of animals . . . is the height of superstition, for there are no common rights between us and the beasts. . . ." Early in the seventeenth century René Descartes argued that, lacking language, animals cannot have thoughts or souls and thus are machines.

One may be inclined to dismiss such beliefs as archaic oddities, but even today some people act as if animals were unfeeling things. I worked in a research lab for several summers during college, and I remember that it was a natural tendency to lose all empathy with one's animal subjects. My supervisor seemed actually to delight in swinging rats around by their tails and flinging them against a concrete wall as a way of stunning the animals before killing them. Rats and rabbits, to those who injected, weighed, and dissected them, were little different from cultures in a petri dish: they were just things to manipulate and observe. Feelings of what may have been moral revulsion were taken for squeamishness, and for most of my lab mates those feelings subsided with time.

The first animal-welfare law in the United States, passed in New York State in 1828, emphasized the protection of animals useful in agriculture. It also promoted human virtue with a ban on "maliciously and cruelly" beating or torturing horses, sheep, or cattle. Today courts still tend to focus on human character, ruling against human beings only for perpetrating the most shocking and senseless abuse of animals. . . .

Most states leave the regulation of medical research to Washington. In 1966 Congress passed the Laboratory Animal Welfare Act, whose stated purpose was not only to provide humane care for animals but also to protect the owners of dogs and cats from theft by proscribing the use of stolen animals. (Note the vocabulary of property law; animals have long been legally classified as property.) Congress then passed the Animal Welfare Act [AWA] of 1970, which expanded the provisions of the 1966 act to include more species of animals and to regulate more people who handle animals. The AWA was further amended in 1976 and in 1985.

The current version of the AWA mandates that research institutions meet certain minimum requirements for the handling and the housing of animals, and requires the "appropriate" use of pain-killers. But the act does not regulate research or experimentation itself, and allows researchers to withhold anesthetics or tranquilizers "when scientifically necessary." Further, while the act purports to regulate dealers who buy animals at auctions and other markets to sell to laboratories, it does little to protect those animals. . . .

The 1985 amendments to the AWA were an attempt to improve the treatment of animals in laboratories, to improve enforcement, to encourage the consideration of alternative research methods that use fewer or no animals, and to minimize duplication in experiments. One notable change is that for the first time, research institutions using primates must keep them in environments conducive to their psychological well-being; however, some animal-rights activists have expressed skepticism, since the social and psychological needs of primates are complex, and the primary concern of researchers is not the interests of their animal subjects. Last September [1988] a symposium on the psychological well-being of captive primates was held at Harvard University. Some participants contended that we lack data on the needs of the thirty to forty species of primates now used in laboratories. Others suggested that the benefits of companionship and social life are obvious.

The U.S. Department of Agriculture [USDA] is responsible for promulgating regulations under the AWA and enforcing the law. Under current USDA regulations the cages of primates need only have floor space equal to three times the area occupied by the animal "when standing on four feet"—in the words of the USDA, which has apparently forgotten that primates have hands. The 1985 amendments required the USDA to publish final revised regulations, including regulations on the well-being of primates, by December of 1986. At this writing the department has yet to comply, and some activists charge that the NIH and the Office of Management and Budget have delayed the publication of the new regulations and attempted to undermine them.

One may believe that virtue thought—which underlies current law—and rights thought should protect animals equally. After all, wouldn't a virtuous person or society respect the interests of animals? But virtue thought allows the law to disregard these interests, because virtue can be measured by at least two yardsticks: by the foreseeable effects of an act on the interests of an animal or by the social utility of the act. The latter standard was applied in a 1983 case in Maryland in which a researcher appealed his conviction for cruelty to animals after he had performed experiments that resulted in monkeys' mutilating their hands. Overturning the conviction, the Maryland Court of Appeals wrote that "there are certain normal human activities to which the infliction of pain to an animal is purely incidental"—thus the actor is not a sadist—and that the state legislature had intended for these activities to be exempt from the law protecting animals.

The law, of course, is not monolithic. Some judges have expressed great sympathy for animals. On the whole, though, the law doesn't recognize animal rights. Under the Uniform Commercial Code, for instance, animals—along with refrigerators and can openers—constitute "goods."

## Alternatives to Us-Versus-Them

Estimates of the number of animals used each year in laboratories in the United States range from 17 million to 100 million: 200,000 dogs, 50,000 cats, 60,000 primates, 1.5 million guinea pigs, hamsters, and rabbits, 200,000 wild animals, thousands of farm animals and birds, and millions of rats and mice. The conditions in general—lack of exercise, isolation from other animals, lengthy confinement in tiny cages—are stressful. Many experiments are painful or produce fear, anxiety, or depression. For instance, in 1987 researchers at the Armed Forces Radiobiology Research Institute reported that nine monkeys were subjected to whole-body irradiation; as a result, within two hours six of the monkeys were vomiting and hypersalivating. In a proposed experiment at the University of Washington pregnant monkeys, kept in isolation, will be infected with the simian AIDS virus; their offspring, infected or not, will be separated from the mothers at birth.

Not all animals in laboratories, of course, are subjects of medical research. In the United States each year some 10 million animals are used in testing products and for other commercial purposes. For instance, the United States Surgical Corporation, in Norwalk, Connecticut, uses hundreds of dogs each year to train salesmen in the use of the company's surgical staple gun. In 1981 and 1982 a group called Friends of Animals brought two lawsuits against United States Surgical to halt these practices. The company successfully argued in court that Friends of Animals lacked "standing" to sue, since no member of the organization had been injured by the practice; after some further legal maneuvering by Friends of Animals both suits were dropped. Last November [1988] a New York City animal-rights advocate was arrested as she planted a bomb outside United States Surgical's headquarters.

In 1987, according to the USDA, 130,373 animals were subjected to pain or distress unrelieved by drugs for "the purpose of research or testing." This figure, which represents nearly seven percent of the 1,969,123 animals reported to the USDA that year as having been "used in experimentation," ignores members of species not protected by the AWA (cold-blooded animals, mice, rats, birds, and farm animals). Moreover, there is reason to believe that the USDA's figures are low. For example, according to the USDA, no primates were subjected to distress in the state of Maryland, the home of Sema, in any year from 1980 to 1987, the last year for which data are available.

Steps seemingly favorable to animals have been taken in recent years. In addition to the passage of the 1985 amendments to the AWA, the Public Health Service [PHS], which includes the NIH, has revised its "Policy on Humane Care and Use of Laboratory Animals," and new legislation has given legal force to much of this policy. Under the revised policy, institutions receiving NIH or other PHS funds for animal research must have an "institutional animal care and use committee" consisting of at least five members, including one nonscientist and one person not affiliated with the institution.

Many activists are pessimistic about these changes, however. They argue that the NIH has suspended funds at noncompliant research institutions only in response to political pressure, and assert that the suspensions are intended as a token gesture, to help the NIH regain lost credibility. They note that Sema, which continues to keep primates in isolation cages (as regulations permit), is an NIH contractor whose principal investigators are NIH employees. As to the makeup of the animal-care committees, animal-rights advocates say that researchers control who is appointed to them. In the words of one activist, "The brethren get to choose."

However one interprets these changes, much remains the same. For example, the AWA authorizes the USDA to confiscate animals from laboratories not in compliance with regulations, but only if the animal "is no longer required . . . to carry out the research, test or experiment"; the PHS policy mandates pain relief "unless the procedure is justified for scientific reasons." Fundamentally, the underlying attitude that animals may appropriately be used and discarded persists.

If the law is ever to reflect the idea that animals have rights, more drastic steps—such as extending the protection of the Constitution to animals—must be taken. Constitutional protection for animals is not an outlandish proposition. The late U.S. Supreme Court Justice William O. Douglas wrote once, in a dissenting opinion, that the day should come when "all of the forms of life . . . will stand before the court—the pileated woodpecker as well as the coyote and bear, the lemmings as well as the trout in the streams."

Suppose, just suppose, that the AWA were replaced by an animal-rights act, which would prohibit the use by human beings of any animals to their detriment. What would be the effect on medical research, education, and product testing? Microorganisms; tissue, organ, and cell cultures; physical and chemical systems that mimic biological functions; computer programs and mathematical models that simulate biological interactions; epidemiologic data bases; and clinical studies have all been used to reduce the number of animals used in experiments, demonstrations, and tests. A 1988 study by the National Research Council, while finding that researchers lack the means to replace all animals in labs, did conclude that current and prospective alternative techniques could reduce the number of animals—particularly mammals—used in research.

Perhaps the report would have been more optimistic if scientists were as zealous about conducting research to find alternatives as they are about animal research. But we should not be misled by discussions of alternatives into thinking that the issue is merely empirical. It is broader than just whether subject A and procedure X can be replaced by surrogates B and Y. We could undergo a shift in world view: instead of imagining that we have a divine mandate to dominate and make use of everything else in the universe, we could have a sense of belonging to the world and of kinship with the other creatures in it. The us-versus-them thinking that weighs animal suffering against human gain could give way to an appreciation that "us" includes "them." That's an alternative too.

Some researchers may insist that scientists should not be constrained in their quest for knowledge, but this is a romantic notion of scientific freedom that never was and should not be. Science is always constrained, by economic and social priorities and by ethics. Sometimes, paradoxically, it is also freed by these constraints, because a barrier in one direction forces it to cut another path, in an area that might have remained unexplored.

Barriers against the exploitation of animals ought to be erected in the law, because law not only enforces morality but defines it. Until the law protects the interests of animals, the animal-rights movement will by definition be radical. And whether or not one approves of breaking the law to remedy its shortcomings, one can expect such activities to continue. "I believe that you should do for others as you would have done for you," one member of the ALF says. "If you were being used in painful experiments, you'd want someone to come to your rescue."

# POSTSCRIPT

## Is the Use of Animals in Research Justified?

Much debate about the lethal experiments that were conducted on nonconsenting human subjects by the Nazis during World War II, as well as the ensuing trials of the Nazi physicians in Nuremburg, Germany, has established a consensus that no scientist can treat people the way the Nazis did. Informed consent is essential, and research on humans must aim to benefit those same humans.

As these ideas have gained currency, some people have tried to extend them to say that, just as scientists cannot do whatever they wish to humans, they cannot do whatever they wish to animals. Harriet Ritvo, in "Toward a More Peaceable Kingdom," *Technology Review* (April 1992), says that the animal rights movement "challenges the ideology of science itself . . . forcing experimenters to recognize that they are not necessarily carrying out an independent exercise in the pursuit of truth—that their enterprise, in its intellectual as well as its social and financial dimensions, is circumscribed and defined by the culture of which it is an integral part." The result is a continuing debate, driven by the periodic discovery of researchers who seem quite callous (at least to the layperson's eye) in their treatment of animals (see Kathy Snow Guillermo, *Monkey Business: The Disturbing Case That Launched the Animal Rights Movement* [National Press, 1993]) and by the charge that animal rights advocates are misanthropes who just do not understand nature. Steven L. Teitelbaum, in an editorial ("Animal Rights Pressure on Scientists") in the November 22, 2002, *Science*, notes that though one researcher was driven to end his drug-related research by "widespread and prolonged harassment from animal rights activists," his funder, the National Institute on Drug Abuse (part of the National Institutes of Health) found another team to carry on the research.

In the February 1997 issue of *Scientific American,* Andrew N. Rowan presents a debate entitled "The Benefits and Ethics of Animal Research." The opposing articles are Neal D. Barnard and Stephen R. Kaufman, "Animal Research Is Wasteful and Misleading" and Jack H. Botting and Adrian R. Morrison, "Animal Research Is Vital to Medicine." In addition, staff writer Madhusree Mukerjee contributes "Trends in Animal Research." Among books that are pertinent to this issue are F. Barbara Orlans, *In the Name of Science: Issues in Responsible Animal Experimentation* (Oxford University Press, 1993); Rod Strand and Patti Strand, *The Hijacking of the Humane Movement* (Doral, 1993); and Deborah Blum, *The Monkey Wars* (Oxford University Press, 1994). Adrian R. Morrison provides a guide to responsible animal use in "Ethical Principles Guiding the Use of Animals in Research," *American Biology Teacher* (February 2003). Barry Yeoman, "Can We Trust Research Done with Lab Mice," *Discover* (July 2003), notes that the conditions in which animals are kept can make a huge difference in their behavior and in their responses to experimental treatments.

Reviewing recent developments in the animal rights movement, Damon Linker, in "Rights for Rodents," *Commentary* (April 2001), concludes, "Can anyone really doubt that, were the misanthropic agenda of the animal-rights movement actually to succeed, the result would be an increase in man's inhumanity, to man and animal alike? In the end, fostering our age-old 'prejudice' in favor of human dignity may be the best thing we can do for animals, not to mention for ourselves."

Charles Colson and Anne Morse agree that the animal rights movement assaults human dignity in "Taming Beasts," *Christianity Today* (April 2003). Yet the idea that animals have rights too continues to gain ground. Steven M. Wise finds in *Drawing the Line: Science and the Case for Animal Rights* (Perseus, 2002) that there is a spectrum of mental capacities for different species, which supports the argument for rights. Niall Shanks, in "Animal Rights in the Light of Animal Cognition," *Social Alternatives* (Summer 2003) considers the moral/philosophical justifications for animal rights and stresses the question of consciousness. Jim Motavalli, in "Rights from Wrongs," *E Magazine* (March/April 2003), describes with approval the movement toward giving animals legal rights (though not necessarily human rights).

The question of appropriate strategy for the animal rights movement is often of concern, as suggested by Mark Matfield, who is the executive director of the Research Defence Society (`http://www.rds-online.org.uk`). His own discussion referred to demonstrations and physical harassment. In this age of the Internet, other tactics are also available. For instance, a group called "Resist Deadly Surgery" has claimed a Web address (URL) very closely related to that of the Research Defence Society. If you leave off the .uk at the end of the RDS's URL and go to `http://www.rds-online.org`, you find a site that says the Research Defence Society "is the UK organisation representing the interests of vivisectors in the public debate about the use of animals in invasive surgery and testing on animals. It provides misinformation about animal research, the (supposed) controls under which this research is carried out, and the (supposed) benefits to medicine, which it claims, have resulted."

A site with a very different view of the benefits of the use of animals in research is that of Americans for Medical Progress (`http://www.amprogress.org/About/aboutmain.cfm`). For lists of specific benefits, visit Michigan State University at `http://www.msu.edu/unit/ular/benefits.html` and the Pennsylvania Society for Biomedical Research at `http://www.psbr.org/society/ABOUT.htm`. For discussions of many benefits, see `http://www.sciencenet.org.uk/database/Biology/Animals/b00269b.html`.

# ISSUE 18

## Should Genetically Modified Foods Be Banned?

**YES: Martin Teitel and Kimberly A. Wilson,** from *Genetically Engineered Food: Changing the Nature of Nature* (Park Street Press, 2001)

**NO: Ronald Bailey,** from "Dr. Strangelunch," *Reason* (January 2001)

### ISSUE SUMMARY

**YES:** Activists Martin Teitel and Kimberly A. Wilson argue that genetically modified foods should be banned until their safety for human consumption has been demonstrated.

**NO:** Ronald Bailey, science correspondent for *Reason* magazine, argues that because genetically modified foods can save lives, they should be available to those who need them.

In the early 1970s scientists first discovered that it was technically possible to move genes—biological material that determines a living organism's physical makeup—from one organism to another and thus (in principle) to give bacteria, plants, and animals new features and to correct genetic defects of the sort that cause many diseases, such as cystic fibrosis. Most researchers in molecular genetics were excited by the potentialities that suddenly seemed within their grasp. However, a few researchers—as well as many people outside the field—were disturbed by the idea; they thought that genetic mix-and-match games might spawn new diseases, weeds, and pests. Some people even argued that genetic engineering should be banned at the outset, before unforeseeable horrors were unleashed.

Researchers in support of genetic experimentation responded by declaring a moratorium on their own work until suitable safeguards could be devised. Once those safeguards were in place in the form of government regulations, work resumed. James D. Watson and John Tooze document the early years of this research in *The DNA Story: A Documentary History of Gene Cloning* (W. H. Freeman, 1981). For a shorter, more recent review of the story, see Bernard D. Davis, "Genetic Engineering: The Making of Monsters?" *The Public Interest* (Winter 1993).

By 1989 the technology had developed tremendously: researchers could obtain patents for mice with artificially added genes ("transgenic" mice); firefly genes had been added to tobacco plants to make them glow (faintly) in the dark; and growth hormone produced by genetically engineered bacteria was being used to grow low-fat pork and increase milk production by cows. Critics argued that genetic engineering was unnatural and violated the rights of both plants and animals to their "species integrity"; that expensive, high-tech, tinkered animals gave the competitive advantage to big agricultural corporations and drove small farmers out of business; and that putting human genes into animals, plants, or bacteria was downright offensive. See Betsy Hanson and Dorothy Nelkin, "Public Responses to Genetic Engineering," *Society* (November/December 1989).

Thoughts of tinkering with humans themselves have prompted such comments as the following from Richard Hayes, "In the Pipeline: Genetically Modified Humans?" *Multinational Monitor* (January/February 2000): "No one can be sure how the technology will evolve, but a techno-eugenic future appears ever more likely unless an organized citizenry demands such visions be consigned to science fiction dystopias."

Skepticism about the benefits remains, but agricultural genetic engineering has proceeded at a breakneck pace largely because, as Robert Shapiro, CEO of Monsanto Corporation, said in June 1998, it "represents a potentially sustainable solution to the issue of feeding people." Between 1996 and 1998 the area planted with genetically engineered crops jumped from 1.7 million hectares to 27.8 million hectares. Also, sales of genetically engineered crop products are expected to reach $25 billion by 2010. See Brian Halweil, "The Emperor's New Crops," *WorldWatch* (July/August 1999).

Many people are not reassured by such data. They see potential problems in nutrition, toxicity, allergies, and ecology. In protest, some people even destroy research labs and test plots of trees, strawberries, and corn (see, for example, Robert F. Service, "Arson Strikes Research Labs and Tree Farm in Pacific Northwest," *Science* [June 1, 2001]). Other people lobby for stringent regulations and even outright bans on the basis of their fears, while others insist that regulation should be based on sound science. See Karen A. Goldman, "Bioengineered Food—Safety and Labeling," *Science* (October 20, 2000) and Henry I. Miller and Gregory Conko, "The Science of Biotechnology Meets the Politics of Global Regulation," *Issues in Science and Technology* (Fall 2000).

In the following selections, Martin Teitel and Kimberly A. Wilson urge caution. They argue that genetically modified foods have not yet been proven to be safe for human consumption and that, until they are, these foods should be banned. Since they are also not necessary, they maintain, consumers should avoid them. Ronald Bailey, on the other hand, argues that because genetically modified foods can save lives by improving food supply and quality in lands that suffer from drought, famine, and malnutrition—and because they have not been shown to be unsafe—we have no business banning them. They should be available to those who need them.

**Martin Teitel**
**and Kimberly A. Wilson**

# YES

## You Are What You Eat

Throughout history monarchs have employed food tasters. This rather high-risk line of work was invented not for gastronomic reasons, but out of a recognition that when we eat food we are placing a great deal of trust in whomever provides that meal. In societies where people grow their own food one has a pretty good idea of the origins of the food, what was sprayed on the crop as it grew, and how it was cooked. When food is produced locally, just keep the peace with the farmer and the chef and you can eat your dinner with no worries.

In nearly all societies nowadays, even monarchies, most people no longer grow their own food. We eat our meals each day with the assumption that what is sold is safe, both because we choose to trust the farmers and food sellers and because we have some degree of faith in government regulators and food inspectors. If this system of trust breaks down, people would understandably be frightened.

Recently, one of the authors was preparing a huge pot of vegetarian chili for a group of friends. Opening a large can of red kidney beans from a local supermarket, he was surprised to find the can full of peeled, white potatoes. Opening another can of beans from the same store, he found the same unexpected contents. Every person at the chili party had the same reaction: "Don't ever shop at that place again." Even though this one error in labeling some cans of beans produced no illness and was presumably an isolated incident, every person seeing the mislabeled cans had the same unequivocal reaction: their assumptions that food is carefully monitored all the way into their grocery carts were temporarily destroyed.

The genfood industry knows of the tendency of people to have a short fuse when it comes to food safety issues. A Monsanto spokesman told one of the authors that the firestorm of protest over genfoods in Great Britain in 1998 and 1999 was probably strongly propelled by the recent scare over mad-cow disease in that country. This statement recognizes that even though mad cow had little to do with genetically engineered food—any more than a mislabeled can of red beans has anything to do with a store's fish or lettuce—when trust in food purity and safety is shattered, people become *very* conservative.

And so they should. In the United States, up to 80 million people are estimated to become sick from food-caused illness each year. Nine thousand

From Martin Teitel and Kimberly A. Wilson, *Genetically Engineered Food: Changing the Nature of Nature* (Park Street Press, 2001).  Notes omitted.

of them die. Statistics from other countries, when they are available, are comparable. The real incidence of illness is probably much higher: many of us have come home from a barbecue featuring sun-baked potato salad, or tried out a new restaurant that looked a bit seedy, and then attributed that night's sickness to the food we just ate. These relatively minor instances of food-related illness never get reported to the collectors of statistics. We just take some pinkish medicine and wait for the bad time to pass.

Other food-connected illnesses are less benign. So far, more than eighty deaths are attributed to mad-cow disease in Great Britain, and the number of people ultimately affected by this slow-moving disease won't be known for some time. A whole class of deadly illnesses that might be related to some food is cancer, possibly arising from the residue of added chemicals on or in the food. Because studies linking slow-onset diseases that have complex causes are still underway, contradictory, or not readily available, some people choose to ignore the possibility of risk until better information is available. Others decide on a more cautious approach and go to the extra trouble and expense of purchasing foods labeled "organic" to avoid consuming those chemicals. . . .

. . . [W]e are going to look at the human health issues associated with genetically engineered food. Is it safe to eat genfood? Let's look at the information available, and then see what actions a person might take.

## Allergies

As we discussed [elsewhere], each gene contributes a single protein to the genetic "soup" that comprises a living organism. Proteins are crucial substances that play many roles in human physiology. One clear association with proteins involves allergies. When a person exhibits an allergic reaction, what her body is reacting to is a protein, most often a "foreign" or introduced protein.

This leads us to a serious issue that arises in connection to genetically engineered foods. If allergies are associated with introduced proteins, and if genfood is by definition characterized by introduced genes that produce proteins, then we have a situation in which caution about allergies is justified. . . . [A]llergies have already been proved to pass from one type of food into another via gene transfers. The fear of introduced genes triggering dangerous and even fatal allergic reactions is based on sound science.

Allergies are common in people, ranging from extreme reactions to exotic fish to a mild sensitivity to airborne pollen in the springtime. The amount of a given protein that might trigger an allergic reaction is highly variable. Some people are allergic to common foods such as wheat or eggs, while others are able to eat them with no ill effects. Most of us eat peanuts with pleasure, while a few people can find themselves fighting for their lives when they consume even a minuscule quantity of peanut protein. Because of this, most allergy specialists do not advise patients with food allergies to cut down on the food that they are sensitive to. Instead, they sternly admonish their patients to avoid *any* ingestion of that food in even the tiniest, most insignificant-seeming quantity.

The great solace—and safety—for people with food allergies is the labeling of ingredients. In the United States and in many other countries, food producers are obligated to list the ingredients of any prepared or processed food. People with allergies avoid frantic trips to the emergency room by learning to read package labels carefully. Food manufacturers and distributors avoid costly liability by this same disclosure of contents. Our laws tend to say that if an ingredient is revealed, that constitutes fair warning. So if people suffer ill effects from eating something that was properly labeled, they cannot sue the food producer.

This is not so with genetically engineered food. Even in countries that require genfood labeling, the labels will most often just say that genetically modified substances are in the food container. Because there is no requirement to say which gene has been inserted, people must avoid all genfood if they have allergic sensitivities and want to be totally prudent.

It is important to note that, unlike mad-cow disease, there have been no documented cases of deaths due to genfood-caused allergic reactions. However, because an autopsy for a death from allergic shock does not normally test for the presence of genetically engineered food, there is no reliable way of gathering data on genfood allergic reactions.

Genetically modified foods available around the world do not present enhancements to the buyer and consumer of those foods. The foods do not taste better, provide more nutrition, cost less, or look nicer. Why, then, would a person with a food allergy run the risk, however large or small it might be, of a life-threatening reaction when safe alternatives are available?

We just need to make sure that those alternatives *remain* available.

## Nutrition

The assumption that many of us would make is that genfood is nutritionally equivalent to nonmodified food. In 1999 the California-based Center for Ethics and Toxics (CETOS) set out to see if this was the case. The people at the center noticed that the research submitted to, and accepted by, the U.S. government to demonstrate the safety of Monsanto's genetically engineered soybeans had been conducted by Monsanto's own scientists. A conflict of interest doesn't necessarily mean that people with the conflict are dishonest, only that, as in this case, their associations automatically put the objectivity of their work into question. The CETOS staff, Britt Bailey and toxicologist Marc Lappé, observed that the soybeans Monsanto tested were not an accurate representation of the soy that appears in stores as food because they were not treated with the herbicide Roundup, as they would be in real life. So Bailey and Lappé hired a reputable testing firm to conduct tests that would accurately compare Roundup Ready soybeans, treated with Roundup, to conventional soybeans that were identical to the Roundup Ready ones except for the missing engineered gene. The tests were also carefully designed to produce results that reflected real-world conditions. This sort of objectively designed science is what we need to be able to make good decisions about what we buy and eat.

The study was published in a peer-reviewed scientific journal in 1999. The process of peer review is important in science. It means that independent scientists looked at the CETOS study and found it to be based on sound and acceptable methods of scientific investigation. In their study, CETOS found that there was a 12 to 14 percent decline in types of plant-based estrogens called phytoestrogens. Phytoestrogens are associated with protection against heart disease, osteoporosis (bone loss), and breast cancer. A drop in phytoestrogens of 12 to 14 percent is a significant nutritional difference.

The CETOS study was attacked by the American Soybean Association, whose attack was in turn answered by CETOS. Monsanto also conducted new studies that did not show the same changes in phytoestrogens. The new Monsanto study is difficult to compare with the CETOS study, however, because Monsanto inexplicably used a different, older method in some of its research. Meanwhile, CETOS stands by its study, which the researchers point out at the very least raises some important questions about nutritional variances in this particular food.

While scientists sling studies and journal articles at each other, what's a food shopper to do? We can't all be expected to become experts on obscure scientific methods or substances we never knew existed, such as phytoestrogens. The government, which chose to accept the original Monsanto-paid tests as the basis for approval of this food, has been of no use in helping us to make prudent decisions.

Further, we have no way of knowing if differences in plant hormones in soybeans mean much for human health. More important, if CETOS, a non-profit organization, can garner sufficient support to conduct more scientific experiments, we can find out if this study was a fluke.

What can we conclude about nutrition and genfoods from this example?

Soy products appear in many processed and prepared foods. No one knows just how many, but the words *soybean oil, soy flour, soy lecithin, isolated soy protein, textured vegetable protein, functional or nonfunctional soy protein concentrates,* and *textured soy protein concentrates* on the label are good tipoffs. As much as 60 percent of all prepared food in a typical U.S. supermarket contains genetically engineered ingredients. Further, many people who do not eat meat rely heavily on soy-based food for important nutritional components of their diet, including proteins, some fats—and phytoestrogens.

As with allergies and genfood, we are left with more questions than answers. Is genetically modified food more nutritious? There is no evidence for a claim of this type. Is genetically modified food less nutritious? We do not know for certain, yet. Is genetically modified food perhaps more variable in its nutritional value? We have at least one reputable study that suggests yes.

The conclusions we can draw from what is known, and not known, seem to be fairly straightforward. First, there is clearly a great need for many further studies of possible nutritional changes in genetically engineered food, based on the CETOS study. Second, there should be clear, unequivocal labeling of genfood so that people can make their own decisions about their nutrition.

## Pesticides and Herbicides

> *A potential problem arising from herbicide resistant GM crops that is largely being ignored is what is the fate of these chemicals within the plant? Are they stable? If they are degraded, what are the products that are produced? And what health risks do they pose?*
>
> —Michael Antoniou

It should be no surprise to us that in discussing genetically modified food we need to pay attention to chemicals that are designed to kill plants or animals. Many of the significant genfood crops are engineered to either tolerate higher than usual amounts of herbicides or to contain pesticides inside each cell. . . . [M]any of the purveyors of genfood are companies that market agricultural chemicals. Engineering plants to require what a company already sells makes business sense to these corporations.

The pesticide most in question is *Bacillus thuringiensis,* Bt. This bacterium was isolated one hundred years ago, although it did not become commercially available in the United States until 1958. While this bacterium is related to a common bacterium that causes food poisoning and is also a close relative of the organism that causes anthrax, Bt itself is considered relatively safe, especially when compared with synthetic bug-killing chemicals.

Yet Bt *is* a poison. In its purified form it can be extremely toxic to mammals, including humans, and even in its more usual, nonpurified state there are numerous reports of poisonings and various negative health effects. The chemical may be particularly hazardous to people with compromised immune systems. Yet because the EPA has already established that Bt (as a spray *on* crops) is safe, it assumes the toxin is safe to eat *in* crops and does not require testing for human health effects.

When Bt is used by organic growers, it is sprayed on plants. It breaks down rapidly in the environment after killing the target bugs. While there may be health risks to the person applying the pesticide, there is no clear evidence of health problems resulting from people eating food that has been sprayed properly with Bt.

When Bt is engineered into a plant, it may remain present in the plant, and the resulting food, much longer than is the case with conventionally used Bt. There is even evidence that Bt engineered into plants remains after the harvest, so that plant leaves that drop to the ground or plant residue that is plowed under have an effect on the living organisms in the soil.

What we do not have is a series of clear, independent studies on the long- or short-term health effects of eating food containing the pesticide Bt. According to CETOS, from 1987 through 1998, 24 percent of genetically engineered crops released into the environment contained insect-resistant genes. According to this same source, Bt crops are grown in the United States, Brazil, Argentina, China, India, Australia, Canada, South Africa, and Japan. Yet we do not have information in hand to establish the safety of this pesticide for human health. The EPA does not test the plant with Bt in it;

it only tests the bacteria in isolation. Essentially, the EPA is not testing the product that humans will be consuming. The Bt toxin produced by the plant and the toxin produced by the bacteria could be different. Until both are properly tested for human health effects, no one will know the effect of eating Bt food crops.

In a case that gained some notoriety in early 1999, a scientist at the Rowett Research Institute named Arpad Pusztai tested genetically engineered potatoes on rats. After only ten days the animals suffered substantial health effects, including weakened immune systems and changes in the development of their hearts, livers, kidneys, and brains.

When Dr. Pusztai went public with his findings, he was summarily fired and a commission was convened by his former employers to investigate his work. The commission found Dr. Pusztai's work deficient, yet another panel of twenty independent scientists confirmed both his data and his findings. More recent research by another U.K.-based scientist showing enlarged stomach walls in rats fed genetically engineered potatoes seems to support Dr. Pusztai, who has stated publicly that he will not eat genfood.

Aside from Bt crops, the other major genetically engineered plant chemical involves herbicide-tolerant plants, primarily the Roundup Ready series of plants from Monsanto. These genetically modified plants include corn and soy as well as oil-producing canola (rapeseed) and cotton. As we saw, the plants are engineered to withstand the plant-killing effects of the chemical glyphosate, the main ingredient in Roundup. Monsanto claims that this herbicide tolerance means that farmers can spray the plant-killing poison on their fields more precisely and thus use less of it, but there are serious concerns about how much herbicide is actually being sprayed.

What about the health effects of herbicide-tolerant crops? Scientists have already linked the herbicides containing glyphosate to cancer. Non-Hodgkins lymphoma, which is one of the fastest-rising cancers in the Western world, increasing 73 percent since 1973, has been connected to exposure to glyphosate and MCPA, another common herbicide.

Since even proximity to such chemicals has been linked to cancer, what are the health risks of eating crops sprayed with glyphosate or genetically engineered with Roundup resistance? While the maker of Roundup insists that when used properly the herbicide is safe, independent studies raise a long list of questions about the long- and short-term health effects of human ingestion of glyphosate.

Bottom line: Genetically engineered food hasn't been proved safe. Since wholesome alternatives exist, why not suspend production of genfood until *it* is shown to be wholesome? . . .

## Bovine Growth Hormone

Sold in the United States under the Monsanto brand name Posilac, rBGH is injected into cows to increase milk production. Few people would argue that the drug does increase milk production, although in a country that periodically gives away dairy products to deal with the milk surplus it is difficult to understand why we need even more. Aside from well-documented health problems for the cows, including increases in udder infections, there are a series of health issues for humans.

As early as 1995, at a National Institutes for Health conference, the following adverse effects of rBGH were identified:

1. Strong role in breast cancer
2. Special risk of colon cancer due to local effects of rBGH on the GI tract
3. May play a role in osteosarcoma, the most common bone tumor in children, usually occurring during the adolescent growth spurt
4. Implicated in lung cancer
5. Possesses angiogenic properties—important to tumors, some of which secrete their own growth factors to promote angiogenesis
6. Lastly, the 1995 NIH conference recommended that the acute and chronic effects of IGF-1 in the upper GI tract be determined.

Americans have been drinking milk from cows treated with rBGH for several years now. When the hormone was approved by the U.S. government, the approval was based on studies of rats fed rBGH that showed no toxicological changes. Had there been any such changes, further human studies would have been mandated.

In the well-publicized 1998 Canadian Gaps Report . . . , we learn that in fact a large proportion of the rBGH-fed rats, between 20 and 30 percent, showed distinct immunological changes, while some male rats showed the formation of cysts of the thyroid and infiltration of the prostate. These are warning signs for possible immune system effects—and possible carcinogenic effects as well.

The Center for Food Safety and more than two dozen other organizations filed a petition in December of 1998 to reverse FDA approval of rBGH/rBST: "We're going to go to the courts and say—you were lied to," said Andrew Kimbrell of the Center for Food Safety. "Essentially it was fraud by the agency and fraud by Monsanto in telling the court that there were no human health effects possible from consuming these products made with rBGH-treated milk. We now know that not to be true."

The Canadian Gaps Report, the banning of rBGH in many countries around the globe, and the findings of a number of studies in the United States and in Europe all point to real, concrete health concerns about bovine growth hormone.

Estimates are that 15 to 30 percent of the milk supply of the United States comes from rBGH-injected cows. Since rudimentary labeling of rBGH milk exists in some communities, including direct labeling as well as the labeling of some milk as "organic," people can avoid feeding their families dairy products containing genetically engineered growth hormones. When such labeling or alternatives do not exist, there is little choice for people other than . . . becoming active in nationwide efforts to provide people with the option to consume only the food that they feel is safe for their families.

## Is Genetically Engineered Food Safe?

. . . [W]e have examined a number of different possible health issues with genetically modified foods. In some instances, such as phytoestrogen decline in genetically engineered soy, or a variety of health questions arising from animal studies of bovine growth hormone, there are ample reasons for people to decide to avoid genetically modified food. In other instances, such as the health effects of ingesting herbicide-tolerant engineered food, there just isn't enough good science yet to be sure.

If the FDA does not require labels, and safety testing is the exception rather than the rule, just what is the U.S. government doing to protect the public? The Hoover Institute's Henry Miller, a fan of genetic engineering, writes, "The FDA does not routinely subject foods from new plant varieties to premarket review or to extensive scientific safety tests." Later he notes that the FDA only follows "the development of foods made with new biotechnology via noncompulsory informal consultation procedures."

The conclusion to all of this is clear. There is no genetically engineered food product on the market now—not one—that is necessary. Each product, which may confer financial benefit to its producers, can be shown to have an alternative that from the consumer's point of view is at least equivalent if not superior. If genfoods do not provide a benefit to consumers, and may be shown to have health hazards now or in the future, why take any risk with your health or your family's health?

Since safety has not been demonstrated and our health is precious, avoid eating all genfood.

**Ronald Bailey**

# Dr. Strangelunch

Ten thousand people were killed and 10 to 15 million left homeless when a cyclone slammed into India's eastern coastal state of Orissa in October 1999. In the aftermath, CARE and the Catholic Relief Society distributed a high-nutrition mixture of corn and soy meal provided by the U.S. Agency for International Development to thousands of hungry storm victims. Oddly, this humanitarian act elicited cries of outrage.

"We call on the government of India and the state government of Orissa to immediately withdraw the corn-soya blend from distribution," said Vandana Shiva, director of the New Delhi–based Research Foundation for Science, Technology, and Ecology. "The U.S. has been using the Orissa victims as guinea pigs for GM [genetically modified] products which have been rejected by consumers in the North, especially Europe." Shiva's organization had sent a sample of the food to a lab in the U.S. for testing to see if it contained any of the genetically improved corn and soy bean varieties grown by tens of thousands of farmers in the United States. Not surprisingly, it did.

"Vandana Shiva would rather have her people in India starve than eat bioengineered food," says C.S. Prakash, a professor of plant molecular genetics at Tuskegee University in Alabama. Per Pinstrup-Andersen, director general of the International Food Policy Research Institute, observes: "To accuse the U.S. of sending genetically modified food to Orissa in order to use the people there as guinea pigs is not only wrong; it is stupid. Worse than rhetoric, it's false. After all, the U.S. doesn't need to use Indians as guinea pigs, since millions of Americans have been eating genetically modified food for years now with no ill effects."

Shiva not only opposes the food aid but is also against "golden rice," a crop that could prevent blindness in half a million to 3 million poor children a year and alleviate vitamin A deficiency in some 250 million people in the developing world. By inserting three genes, two from daffodils and one from a bacterium, scientists at the Swiss Federal Institute of Technology created a variety of rice that produces the nutrient beta-carotene, the precursor to vitamin A. Agronomists at the International Rice Research Institute in the Philippines plan to crossbreed the variety, called "golden rice" because of the color produced by the beta-carotene, with well-adapted local varieties and distribute the resulting plants to farmers all over the developing world.

[In] June [2000], at a Capitol Hill seminar on biotechnology sponsored by the Congressional Hunger Center, Shiva airily dismissed golden rice by claiming that "just in the state of Bengal 150 greens which are rich in vitamin A are eaten and grown by the women." A visibly angry Martina McGloughlin, director of the biotechnology program at the University of California at Davis, said "Dr. Shiva's response reminds me of . . . Marie Antoinette, [who] suggested the peasants eat cake if they didn't have access to bread." Alexander Avery of the Hudson Institute's Center for Global Food Issues noted that nutritionists at UNICEF doubted it was physically possible to get enough vitamin A from the greens Shiva was recommending. Furthermore, it seems unlikely that poor women living in shanties in the heart of Calcutta could grow greens to feed their children.

The apparent willingness of biotechnology's opponents to sacrifice people for their cause disturbs scientists who are trying to help the world's poor. At the annual meeting of the American Association for the Advancement of Science [in] February, Ismail Serageldin, the director of the Consultative Group on International Agricultural Research, posed a challenge: "I ask opponents of biotechnology, do you want 2 to 3 million children a year to go blind and 1 million to die of vitamin A deficiency, just because you object to the way golden rice was created?"

Vandana Shiva is not alone in her disdain for biotechnology's potential to help the poor. Mae-Wan Ho, a reader in biology at London's Open University who advises another activist group, the Third World Network, also opposes golden rice. And according to a *New York Times* report on a biotechnology meeting held last March by the Organization for Economic Cooperation and Development, Benedikt Haerlin, head of Greenpeace's European anti-biotech campaign, "dismissed the importance of saving African and Asian lives at the risk of spreading a new science that he considered untested."

Shiva, Ho, and Haerlin are leaders in a growing global war against crop biotechnology, sometimes called "green biotech" (to distinguish it from medical biotechnology, known as "red biotech"). Gangs of anti-biotech vandals with cute monikers such as Cropatistas and Seeds of Resistance have ripped up scores of research plots in Europe and the U.S. The so-called Earth Liberation Front burned down a crop biotech lab at Michigan State University on New Year's Eve in 1999, destroying years of work and causing $400,000 in property damage. . . . Anti-biotech lobbying groups have proliferated faster than bacteria in an agar-filled petri dish: In addition to Shiva's organization, the Third World Network, and Greenpeace, they include the Union of Concerned Scientists, the Institute for Agriculture and Trade Policy, the Institute of Science in Society, the Rural Advancement Foundation International, the Ralph Nader–founded Public Citizen, the Council for Responsible Genetics, the Institute for Food and Development Policy, and that venerable fount of biotech misinformation, Jeremy Rifkin's Foundation on Economic Trends. The left hasn't been this energized since the Vietnam War.

But if the anti-biotech movement is successful, its victims will include the downtrodden people on whose behalf it claims to speak.

"We're in a war," said an activist at a protesters' gathering during the November 1999 World Trade Organization meeting in Seattle. "We're going to bury this first wave of biotech." He summed up the basic strategy pretty clearly: "The first battle is labeling. The second battle is banning it."

Later that week, during a standing-room-only "biosafety seminar" in the basement of a Seattle Methodist church, the ubiquitous Mae-Wan Ho declared, "This warfare against nature must end once and for all." Michael Fox, a vegetarian "bioethicist" from the Humane Society of the United States, sneered: "We are very clever little simians, aren't we? Manipulating the bases of life and thinking we're little gods." He added, "The only acceptable application of genetic engineering is to develop a genetically engineered form of birth control for our own species." This creepy declaration garnered rapturous applause from the assembled activists.

Despite its unattractive side, the global campaign against green biotech has had notable successes in recent years. Several leading food companies, including Gerber and Frito-Lay, have been cowed into declaring that they will not use genetically improved crops to make their products. Since 1997, the European Union has all but outlawed the growing and importing of biotech crops and food. Last May some 60 countries signed the Biosafety Protocol, which mandates special labels for biotech foods and requires strict notification, documentation, and risk assessment procedures for biotech crops. Activists have launched a "Five-Year Freeze" campaign that calls for a worldwide moratorium on planting genetically enhanced crops.

For a while, it looked like the United States might resist the growing hysteria, but in December 1999 the Environmental Protection Agency announced that it was reviewing its approvals of biotech corn crops, implying that it might ban the crops in the future. Last May the Food and Drug Administration, which until now has evaluated biotech foods solely on their objective characteristics, not on the basis of how they were produced, said it would formulate special rules for reviewing and approving products with genetically modified ingredients. U.S. Rep. Dennis Kucinich (D-Ohio) has introduced a bill that would require warning labels on all biotech foods.

In October, news that a genetically modified corn variety called StarLink that was approved only for animal feed had been inadvertently used in two brands of taco shells prompted recalls, front-page headlines, and anxious recriminations. Lost in the furor was the fact that there was little reason to believe the corn was unsafe for human consumption—only an implausible, unsubstantiated fear that it might cause allergic reactions. Even Aventis, the company which produced StarLink, agreed that it was a serious mistake to have accepted the EPA's approval for animal use only. Most proponents favor approving biotech crops only if they are determined to be safe for human consumption.

To decide whether the uproar over green biotech is justified, you need to know a bit about how it works. Biologists and crop breeders can now select a specific useful gene from one species and splice it into an unrelated species. Previously plant breeders were limited to introducing new genes through the time-consuming and inexact art of crossbreeding species that were fairly close relatives. For each cross, thousands of unwanted genes would be introduced into a crop species. Years of "backcrossing"—breeding each new generation of hybrids with the original commercial variety over several generations—were needed to eliminate these unwanted genes so that only the useful genes and characteristics remained. The new methods are far more precise and efficient. The plants they produce are variously described as "transgenic," "genetically modified," or "genetically engineered."

Plant breeders using biotechnology have accomplished a great deal in only a few years. For example, they have created a class of highly successful insect-resistant crops by incorporating toxin genes from the soil bacterium *Bacillus thuringiensis*. Farmers have sprayed *B.t.* spores on crops as an effective insecticide for decades. Now, thanks to some clever biotechnology, breeders have produced varieties of corn, cotton, and potatoes that make their own insecticide. *B.t.* is toxic largely to destructive caterpillars such as the European corn borer and the cotton bollworm; it is not harmful to birds, fish, mammals, or people.

Another popular class of biotech crops incorporates an herbicide resistance gene, a technology that has been especially useful in soybeans. Farmers can spray herbicide on their fields to kill weeds without harming the crop plants. The most widely used herbicide is Monsanto's Roundup (glyphosate), which toxicologists regard as an environmentally benign chemical that degrades rapidly, days after being applied. Farmers who use "Roundup Ready" crops don't have to plow for weed control, which means there is far less soil erosion.

Biotech is the most rapidly adopted new farming technology in history. The first generation of biotech crops was approved by the EPA, the FDA, and the U.S. Department of Agriculture in 1995, and by 1999 transgenic varieties accounted for 33 percent of corn acreage, 50 percent of soybean acreage, and 55 percent of cotton acreage in the U.S. Worldwide, nearly 90 million acres of biotech crops were planted in 1999. . . .

One scientific panel after another has concluded that biotech foods are safe to eat, and so has the FDA. Since 1995, tens of millions of Americans have been eating biotech crops. Today it is estimated that 60 percent of the foods on U.S. grocery shelves are produced using ingredients from transgenic crops. In April [2000] a National Research Council panel issued a report that emphasized it could not find "any evidence suggesting that foods on the market today are unsafe to eat as a result of genetic modification." *Transgenic Plants and World Agriculture,* a report issued in July that was prepared under the auspices of seven scientific academies in the U.S. and other countries, strongly endorsed crop biotechnology, especially for poor farmers in the developing world. "To date," the report concluded, "over 30 million hectares of transgenic crops have been grown and no human health problems associated specifically with the ingestion of transgenic crops or their products have been identified." Both reports concurred that genetic engineering poses no more risks to human health or to the natural environment than does conventional plant breeding.

As U.C.-Davis biologist Martina McGloughlin remarked at [a] Congressional Hunger Center seminar, the biotech foods "on our plates have been put through more thorough testing than conventional food ever has been subjected to." According to a report issued in April by the House Subcommittee on Basic Research, "No product of conventional plant breeding . . . could meet the data requirements imposed on biotechnology products by U.S. regulatory agencies. . . . Yet, these foods are widely and properly regarded as safe and beneficial by plant developers, regulators, and consumers." The report concluded that biotech crops are "at least as safe [as] and probably safer" than conventionally bred crops.

In opposition to these scientific conclusions, Mae-Wan Ho points to a study by Arpad Pusztai, a researcher at Scotland's Rowett Research Institute, that was published in the British medical journal *The Lancet* in October 1999. Pusztai found that rats fed one type of genetically modified potatoes (not a variety created for commercial use) developed immune system disorders and organ damage. *The Lancet*'s editors, who published the study even though two of six reviewers rejected it, apparently were anxious to avoid the charge that they were muzzling a prominent biotech critic. But *The Lancet* also published a thorough critique, which concluded that Pusztai's experiments "were incomplete, included too few animals per diet group, and lacked controls such as a standard rodent diet. . . . Therefore the results are difficult to interpret and do not allow the conclusion that the genetic modification of potatoes accounts for adverse effects in animals." The Rowett Institute, which does mainly nutritional research, fired Pusztai on the grounds that he had publicized his results before they had been peer reviewed.

Activists are also fond of noting that the seed company Pioneer Hi-Bred produced a soybean variety that incorporated a gene—for a protein from Brazil nuts—that causes reactions in people who are allergic to nuts. The activists fail to mention that the soybean never got close to commercial release because Pioneer Hi-Bred checked it for allergenicity as part of its regular safety testing and immediately dropped the variety. The other side of the allergy coin is that biotech can remove allergens that naturally occur in foods such as nuts, potatoes, and tomatoes, making these foods safer.

Even if no hazards from genetically improved crops have been demonstrated, don't consumers have a right to know what they're eating? This seductive appeal to consumer rights has been a very effective public relations gambit for anti-biotech activists. If there's nothing wrong with biotech products, they ask, why don't seed companies, farmers, and food manufacturers agree to label them?

The activists are being more than a bit disingenuous here. Their scare tactics, including the use of ominous words such as *frankenfoods,* have created a climate in which many consumers would interpret labels on biotech products to mean that they were somehow more dangerous or less healthy than old-style foods. Biotech opponents hope labels would drive frightened consumers away from genetically modified foods and thus doom them. Then the activists could sit back and smugly declare that biotech products had failed the market test.

The biotech labeling campaign is a red herring anyway, because the U.S. Department of Agriculture plans to issue some 500 pages of regulations outlining what qualifies as "organic" foods by January, 2001. Among other things, the definition will require that organic foods not be produced using genetically modified crops. Thus consumers who want to avoid biotech products need only look for the "organic" label. Furthermore, there is no reason why conventional growers who believe they can sell more by avoiding genetically enhanced crops should not label their products accordingly, so long as they do not imply any health claims. The FDA has begun to solicit public comments on ways to label foods that are not genetically enhanced without implying that they are superior to biotech foods.

It is interesting to note that several crop varieties popular with organic growers were created through mutations deliberately induced by breeders using radiation or chemicals. This method of modifying plant genomes is obviously a far cruder and more imprecise way of creating new varieties. Radiation and chemical mutagenesis is like using a sledgehammer instead of the scalpel of biotechnology. Incidentally, the FDA doesn't review these crop varieties produced by radiation or chemicals for safety, yet no one has dropped dead from eating them.

Labeling nonbiotech foods as such will not satisfy the activists whose goal is to force farmers, grain companies, and food manufacturers to segregate biotech crops from conventional crops. Such segregation would require a great deal of duplication in infrastructure, including separate grain silos, rail cars, ships, and production lines at factories and mills. The StarLink corn problem is just a small taste of how costly and troublesome segregating conventional from biotech crops would be. Some analysts estimate that segregation would add 10 percent to 30 percent to the prices of food without any increase in safety. Activists are fervently hoping that mandatory crop segregation will also lead to novel legal nightmares: If a soybean shipment is inadvertently "contaminated" with biotech soybeans, who is liable? If biotech corn pollen falls on an organic cornfield, can the organic farmer sue the biotech farmer? Trial lawyers must be salivating over the possibilities.

The activists' "pro-consumer" arguments can be turned back on them. Why should the majority of consumers pay for expensive crop segregation that they don't want? It seems reasonable that if some consumers want to avoid biotech crops, they should pay a premium, including the costs of segregation.

As the labeling fight continues in the United States, anti-biotech groups have achieved major successes elsewhere. The Biosafety Protocol negotiated

[in] February [2000] in Montreal requires that all shipments of biotech crops, including grains and fresh foods, carry a label saying they "may contain living modified organisms." This international labeling requirement is clearly intended to force the segregation of conventional and biotech crops. The protocol was hailed by Greenpeace's Benedikt Haerlin as "a historic step towards protecting the environment and consumers from the dangers of genetic engineering."

Activists are demanding that the labeling provisions of the Biosafety Protocol be enforced immediately, even though the agreement says they don't apply until two years after the protocol takes effect. Vandana Shiva claims the food aid sent to Orissa after the October 1999 cyclone violated the Biosafety Protocol because it was unlabeled. Greenpeace cited the unratified Biosafety Protocol as a justification for stopping imports of American agricultural products into Brazil and Britain. "The recent agreement on the Biosafety Protocol in Montreal . . . means that governments can now refuse to accept imports of GM crops on the basis of the 'precautionary principle,'" said a February 2000 press release announcing that Greenpeace activists had boarded an American grain carrier delivering soybeans to Britain.

Under the "precautionary principle," regulators do not need to show scientifically that a biotech crop is unsafe before banning it; they need only assert that it has not been proved harmless. Enshrining the precautionary principle into international law is a major victory for biotech opponents. "They want to err on the side of caution not only when the evidence is not conclusive but when no evidence exists that would indicate harm is possible," observes Frances Smith, executive director of Consumer Alert.

Model biosafety legislation proposed by the Third World Network goes even further than the Biosafety Protocol, covering all biotech organisms and requiring authorization "for all activities and for all GMOs [genetically modified organisms] and derived products." Under the model legislation, "the absence of scientific evidence or certainty does not preclude the decision makers from denying approval of the introduction of the GMO or derived products." Worse, under the model regulations "any adverse socio-economic effects must also be considered." If this provision is adopted, it would give traditional producers a veto over innovative competitors, the moral equivalent of letting candlemakers prevent the introduction of electric lighting.

Concerns about competition are one reason European governments have been so quick to oppose crop biotechnology. "EU countries, with their heavily subsidized farming, view foreign agribusinesses as a competitive threat," Frances Smith writes. "With heavy subsidies and price supports, EU farmers see no need to improve productivity." In fact, biotech-boosted European agricultural productivity would be a fiscal disaster for the E.U., since it would increase already astronomical subsidy payments to European farmers.

The global campaign against green biotech received a public relations windfall on May 20, 1999, when *Nature* published a study by Cornell University researcher John Losey that found that Monarch butterfly caterpillars died when force-fed milkweed dusted with pollen from *B.t.* corn. Since then, at every antibiotech demonstration, the public has been treated to flocks of activist women dressed fetchingly as Monarch butterflies. But when more-realistic field studies were conducted, researchers found that the alleged danger to Monarch caterpillars had been greatly exaggerated. Corn pollen is heavy and doesn't spread very far, and milkweed grows in many places aside from the margins of cornfields. In the wild, Monarch caterpillars apparently know better than to eat corn pollen on milkweed leaves.

Furthermore, *B.t.* crops mean that farmers don't have to indiscriminately spray their fields with insecticides, which kill beneficial as well as harmful insects. In fact, studies show that *B.t.* cornfields harbor higher numbers of beneficial insects such as lacewings and ladybugs than do conventional cornfields. James Cook, a biologist at Washington State University, points out that the population of Monarch butterflies has been increasing in recent years, precisely the time period in which *B.t.* corn has been widely planted. The fact is that pest-resistant crops are harmful mainly to target species—that is, exactly those insects that insist on eating them.

Never mind; we will see Monarchs on parade for a long time to come. Meanwhile, a spooked EPA has changed its rules governing the planting of *B.t.* corn, requiring farmers to plant non-*B.t.* corn near the borders of their fields so that *B.t.* pollen doesn't fall on any milkweed growing there. But even the EPA firmly rejects activist claims about the alleged harms caused by *B.t.* crops. "Prior to registration of the first *B.t.* plant pesticides in 1995," it said in response to a Greenpeace lawsuit, "EPA evaluated studies of potential effects on a wide variety of non-target organisms that might be exposed to the *B.t.* toxin, e.g., birds, fish, honeybees, ladybugs, lacewings, and earthworms. EPA concluded that these species were not harmed."

Another danger highlighted by anti-biotech activists is the possibility that transgenic crops will crossbreed with other plants. At the Congressional Hunger Center seminar, Mae-Wan Ho claimed that "GM-constructs are designed to invade genomes and to overcome natural species barriers." And that's not all. "Because of their highly mixed origins," she added, "GM-constructs tend to be unstable as well as invasive, and may be more likely to spread by horizontal gene transfer."

"Nonsense," says Tuskegee University biologist C.S. Prakash. "There is no scientific evidence at all for Ho's claims." Prakash points out that plant breeders specifically choose transgenic varieties that are highly stable since they want the genes that they've gone to the trouble and expense of introducing into a crop to stay there and do their work.

Ho also suggests that "GM genetic material" when eaten is far more likely to be taken up by human cells and bacteria than is "natural genetic material." Again, there is no scientific evidence for this claim. All genes from whatever source are made up of the same four DNA bases, and all undergo digestive degradation when eaten.

Biotech opponents also sketch scenarios in which transgenic crops foster superpests: weeds bolstered by transgenes for herbicide resistance or pesticide-proof bugs that proliferate in response to crops with enhanced chemical defenses. As McGloughlin notes, "The risk of gene flow is not specific to biotechnology. It applies equally well to herbicide resistant plants that have been developed through traditional breeding techniques." Even if an herbicide resistance gene did get into a weed species, most researchers agree that it would be unlikely to persist unless the weed were subjected to significant and continuing selection pressure—that is, sprayed regularly with a specific herbicide. And if a weed becomes resistant to one herbicide, it can be killed by another.

As for encouraging the evolution of pesticide-resistant insects, that already occurs with conventional spray pesticides. There is no scientific reason for singling out biotech plants. . . .

As one tracks the war against green biotech, it becomes ever clearer that its leaders are not primarily concerned about safety. What they really hate is capitalism and globalization. "It is not inevitable that corporations will control our lives and rule the world," writes Shiva in *Stolen Harvest.* In *Genetic Engineering: Dream or Nightmare?* (1999), Ho warns, "Genetic engineering biotechnology is an unprecedented intimate alliance between bad science and big business which will spell the end of humanity as we know it, and the world at large." The first nefarious step, according to Ho, will occur when the "food giants of the North" gain "control of the food supply of the South through exclusive rights to genetically engineered seeds."

Accordingly, anti-biotech activists oppose genetic patents. Greenpeace is running a "No Patents on Life" campaign that appeals to inchoate notions about the sacredness of life. Knowing that no patents means no investment, biotech opponents declare that corporations should not be able to "own" genes, since they are created by nature.

The exact rules for patenting biotechnology are still being worked out by international negotiators and the U.S. Patent and Trademark Office. But without getting into the arcane details, the fact is that discoverers and inventors don't "own" genes. A patent is a license granted for a limited time to encourage inventors and discoverers to disclose publicly their methods and findings. In exchange for disclosure, they get the right to exploit their discoveries for 20 years, after which anyone may use the knowledge and techniques they have produced. Patents aim to encourage an open system of technical knowledge.

"Biopiracy" is another charge that activists level at biotech seed companies. After prospecting for useful genes in indigenous crop varieties from developing countries, says Shiva, companies want to sell seeds incorporating those genes back to poor farmers. Never mind that the useful genes are stuck in inferior crop varieties, which means that poor farmers have no way of optimizing their benefits. Seed companies liberate the useful genes and put them into high-yielding varieties that can boost poor farmers' productivity.

Amusingly, the same woman who inveighs against "biopiracy" proudly claimed at the Congressional Hunger Center seminar that 160 varieties of kidney beans are grown in India. Shiva is obviously unaware that farmers in India are themselves "biopirates." Kidney beans were domesticated by the Aztecs and Incas in the Americas and brought to the Old World via the Spanish explorers. In response to Shiva, C.S. Prakash pointed out that very few of the crops grown in India today are indigenous. "Wheat, peanuts, and apples and everything else—the chiles that the Indians are so proud of," he noted, "came from outside. I say, thank God for the biopirates." Prakash condemned Shiva's efforts to create "a xenophobic type of mentality within our culture" based on the fear that "everybody is stealing all of our genetic material."

If the activists are successful in their war against green biotech, it's the world's poor who will suffer most. The International Food Policy Research Institute [IFPRI] estimates that global food production must increase by 40 percent in the next 20 years to meet the goal of a better and more varied diet for a world population of some 8 billion people. As biologist Richard Flavell concluded in a 1999 report to the IFPRI, "It would be unethical to condemn future generations to hunger by refusing to develop and apply a technology that can build on what our forefathers provided and can help produce adequate food for a world with almost 2 billion more people by 2020."

One way biotech crops can help poor farmers grow more food is by controlling parasitic weeds, an enormous problem in tropical countries. Cultivation cannot get rid of them, and farmers must abandon fields infested with them after a few growing seasons. Herbicide-resistant crops, which would make it possible to kill the weeds without damaging the cultivated plants, would be a great boon to such farmers.

By incorporating genes for proteins from viruses and bacteria, crops can be immunized against infectious diseases. The papaya mosaic virus had wiped out papaya farmers in Hawaii, but a new biotech variety of papaya incorporating a protein from the virus is immune to the disease. As a result, Hawaiian papaya orchards are producing again, and the virus-resistant variety is being made available to developing countries. Similarly, scientists at the Donald Danforth Plant Science Center in St. Louis are at work on a cassava variety that is immune to cassava mosaic virus, which killed half of Africa's cassava crop two years ago.

Another recent advance with enormous potential is the development of biotech crops that can thrive in acidic soils, a large proportion of which are located in the tropics. Aluminum toxicity in acidic soils reduces crop productivity by as much as 80 percent. Progress is even being made toward the Holy Grail of plant breeding, transferring the ability to fix nitrogen from legumes to grains. That achievement would greatly reduce the need for fertilizer. Biotech crops with genes for drought and salinity tolerance are also being developed. Further down the road, biologist Martina McGloughlin predicts, "we will be able to enhance other characteristics, such as growing seasons, stress tolerance, yields, geographic distribution, disease resistance, [and] shelf life."

Biotech crops can provide medicine as well as food. Biologists at the Boyce Thompson Institute for Plant Research at Cornell University recently reported success in preliminary tests with biotech potatoes that would immunize people against diseases. One protects against Norwalk virus, which causes diarrhea, and another might protect against the hepatitis B virus which afflicts 2 billion people. Plant-based vaccines would be especially useful for poor countries, which could manufacture and distribute medicines simply by having local farmers grow them.

---

Shiva and Ho rightly point to the inequities found in developing countries. They make the valid point that there is enough food today to provide an adequate diet for everyone if it were more equally distributed. They advocate land reform and microcredit to help poor farmers, improved infrastructure so farmers can get their crops to market, and an end to agricultural subsidies in rich countries that undercut the prices that poor farmers can demand.

Addressing these issues is important, but they are not arguments against green biotech. McGloughlin agrees that "the real issue is inequity in food distribution. Politics, culture, regional conflicts all contribute to the problem. Biotechnology isn't going to be a panacea for all the world's ills, but it can go a long way toward addressing the issues of inadequate nutrition and crop losses." Kenyan biologist Florence Wambugu argues that crop biotechnology has great potential to increase agricultural productivity in Africa without demanding big changes in local practices: A drought-tolerant seed will benefit farmers whether they live in Kansas or Kenya.

Yet opponents of crop biotechnology can't stand the fact that it will help developed countries first. New technologies, whether reaping machines in the 19th century or computers today, are always adopted by the rich before they become available to the poor. The fastest way to get a new technology to poor people is to speed up the product cycle so the technology can spread quickly. Slowing it down only means the poor will have to wait longer. If biotech crops catch on in the developed countries, the techniques to make them will become available throughout the world, and more researchers and companies will offer crops that appeal to farmers in developing countries.

Activists like Shiva subscribe to the candlemaker fallacy: If people begin to use electric lights, the candlemakers will go out of business, and they and their families will starve. This is a supremely condescending view of poor people. In order not to exacerbate inequality, Shiva and her allies want to stop technological progress. They romanticize the backbreaking lives that hundreds of millions of people are forced to live as they eke out a meager living off the land.

Per Pinstrup-Andersen of the International Food Policy Research Institute asked participants in the Congressional Hunger Center seminar to think about biotechnology from the perspective of people in developing countries: "We need to talk about the low-income farmer in West Africa who, on half an acre, maybe an acre of land, is trying to feed her five children in the face of recurrent droughts, recurrent insect attacks, recurrent plant diseases. For her, losing a crop may mean losing a child. Now, how can we sit here debating whether she should have access to a drought-tolerant crop variety? None of us at this table or in this room [has] the ethical right to force a particular technology upon anybody, but neither do we have the ethical right to block access to it. The poor farmer in West Africa doesn't have any time for philosophical arguments as to whether it should be organic farming or fertilizers or GM food. She is trying to feed her children. Let's help her by giving her access to all of the options. Let's make the choices available to the people who have to take the consequences."

# POSTSCRIPT

## Should Genetically Modified Foods Be Banned?

Until the last few years, most of the attention aimed at genetic engineering focused first on its use to modify bacteria and other organisms to generate drugs needed to fight human disease, and second on its potential to modify human genes and attack hereditary diseases at their roots. See Eric B. Kmiec, "Gene Therapy," *American Scientist* (May–June 1999).

Despite some successes, gene therapy has not yet become a multimillion-dollar industry. Pharmaceutical applications of genetic engineering have been much more successful. According to Brian Halweil, in "The Emperor's New Crops," *World Watch* (July/August 1999), so have agricultural applications. Halweil is skeptical, saying that genetically modified foods have potential benefits but that they may also have disastrous effects on natural ecosystems and—because high-tech agriculture is controlled by major corporations such as Monsanto—on less-developed societies. He argues that "ecological" agriculture (e.g., using organic fertilizers and natural enemies instead of pesticides) offers much more hope for the future. Similar arguments are made by those who demonstrate against genetically modified foods and lobby for stringent labeling requirements or for outright bans on planting and importing these crops (as in Europe). See Capulalpum, "Risking Corn, Risking Culture," *World-Watch* (November–December 2002).

Many researchers see more hope in genetically modified foods. In July 2000, for example, the Royal Society of London, the U.S. National Academy of Sciences, the Brazilian Academy of Sciences, the Chinese Academy of Sciences, the Indian Academy of Sciences, the Mexican Academy of Sciences, and the Third World Academy of Sciences issued a joint report entitled "Transgenic Plants and World Agriculture" (available at `http://www.royalsoc.ac.uk`). This report stresses that during the twenty-first century, both population and the need for food are going to increase dramatically, especially in developing nations. According to the report, "Foods can be produced through the use of GM [genetic modification] technology that are more nutritious, stable in storage and in principle, health promoting. . . . New public sector efforts are required for creating transgenic crops that benefit poor farmers in developing nations and improve their access to food. . . . Concerted, organised efforts must be undertaken to investigate the potential environmental effects, both positive and negative, of GM technologies [compared to those] from conventional agricultural technologies. . . . Public health regulatory systems need to be put in place in every country to identify and monitor any potential adverse human health effects."

The worries surrounding genetically modified foods and the scientific evidence to support them are summarized by Kathryn Brown, in "Seeds of Concern," and Karen Hopkin, in "The Risks on the Table," both in *Scientific American* (April 2001). In the same issue, Sasha Nemecek poses the question "Does the World Need GM Foods?" to two prominent figures in the debate: Robert B. Horsch, a Monsanto vice president and recipient of the 1998 National Medal of Technology for his work on modifying plant genes, who says yes, and Margaret Mellon, of the Union of Concerned Scientists, who says no, adding that much more work needs to be done on safety. Walter F. Deal and Stephen L. Baird, in "Genetically Modified Foods: A Growing Need," *Technology Teacher* (April 2003), contend that GM foods "can help overcome the world's concern for feeding its ever-growing population."

Is the issue safety? Human welfare? Or economics? When genetically modified corn and other foods were offered as relief supplies to African nations threatened by famine, some accepted the aid. Others, pressured by European activists, turned it down. Robert L. Paarlberg discusses what the U.S. can do to counter resistance to GM foods in "Reinvigorating Genetically Modified Crops," *Issues in Science and Technology* (Spring 2003); he favors addressing the needs of developing countries. Perhaps unfortunately, the Bush Administration chose to address the issue by filing suit against the European Union for imposing restrictions counter to the regulations of the World Trade Organization. See "United States to Challenge EU Moratorium on GMO Imports," *CongressDaily* (May 9, 2003). Some claim this only proves that the real motive behind GM foods is business. See for instance Andy Rowell and Jonathan Matthews, "Strange Bedfellows," *Ecologist* (April 2003).

And is the issue only genetically modified food? The July/August 2002 issue of *WorldWatch* magazine bore the overall title of "Beyond Cloning: The Risks of Rushing into Human Genetic Engineering." The editorial says that human genetic engineering poses "profound and medical social risks." Contributors object to it as unnatural, commercial, a violation of human integrity, potentially racist, and more. Francis Fukuyama, "In Defense of Nature, Human and Non-Human," says, "Anyone who feels strongly about defending non-human nature from technological manipulation should feel equally strongly about defending human nature as well. . . . Nature—both the natural environment around us, and our own—deserves an approach based on respect and stewardship, not domination and mastery."

# ISSUE 19

## Is It Ethically Permissible to Clone Human Beings?

**YES: Julian Savulescu,** from "Should We Clone Human Beings? Cloning as a Source of Tissue for Transplantation," *Journal of Medical Ethics* (April 1, 1999)

**NO: Leon R. Kass,** from "The Wisdom of Repugnance," *The New Republic* (June 2, 1997)

### ISSUE SUMMARY

**YES:** Julian Savulescu, director of the Ethics Program of the Murdoch Institute at the Royal Children's Hospital in Melbourne, Australia, argues that it is not only permissible but morally required to use human cloning to create embryos as a source of tissue for transplantation.

**NO:** Biochemist Leon R. Kass argues that human cloning is "so repulsive to contemplate" that it should be prohibited entirely.

In February 1997 Ian Wilmut and Keith H. S. Campbell of the Roslin Institute in Edinburgh, Scotland, announced that they had cloned a sheep by transferring the gene-containing nucleus from a single cell of an adult sheep's mammary gland into an egg cell whose own nucleus had been removed and discarded. The resulting combination cell then developed into an embryo and eventually a lamb in the same way a normal egg cell does after being fertilized with a sperm cell. That lamb, named Dolly, was a genetic duplicate of the ewe from which the udder cell's nucleus was taken. Similar feats had been accomplished years before with fish and frogs, and mammal embryos had previously been split to produce artificial twins. And in March researchers at the Oregon Regional Primate Research Center announced that they had cloned monkeys by using cells from monkey embryos (not adults). In July the Roslin researchers announced the cloning of lambs from fetal cells—this time cells including human genes. But the reactions of the media, politicians, ethicists, and laypeople have been largely negative. Dr. Donald Bruce, director of the Church of Scotland's Society, Religion and Technology Project, for example, has argued at some length about how "nature is not ours to do exactly what we like with."

Many people seem to agree. In 1994 the U.S. National Advisory Board on Ethics in Reproduction called the whole idea of cloning oneself "bizarre . . . narcissistic and ethically impoverished." Arthur Caplan, director of the Center for Bioethics at the University of Pennsylvania, wonders, "What is the ethical purpose of even trying?" Conservative columnist George Will asks whether humans are now uniquely endangered since "the great given—a human being is the product of the union of a man and a woman—is no longer a given" and "humanity is supposed to be an endless chain, not a series of mirrors."

Others go further. President Bill Clinton asked the National Bioethics Advisory Commission (see `http://bioethics.georgetown.edu/nbac/`), chaired by Harold T. Shapiro, president of Princeton University, to investigate the implications of this "stunning" research and to issue a final report by the end of May 1997. He also barred the use of U.S. funds to support work on human cloning. The commission's report called for extending the ban and called any attempt to clone a human "morally unacceptable" for now. Many countries besides the United States agreed, and bans on cloning research were widely imposed.

Yet, says J. Madeleine Nash in "The Case for Cloning," *Time* (February 9, 1998), "hasty legislation could easily be too restrictive." Cloning could serve a great many useful purposes, and further development of the technology could lead to much less alarming procedures, such as growing replacement organs within a patient's body. See Arlene Judith Klotzko, "We Can Rebuild . . . ," *New Scientist* (February 27, 1999). Some of these benefits were considered when George Washington University researchers, using nonviable embryos, demonstrated that single cells could be removed from human embryos and induced to grow into new embryos. If permitted to develop normally, the cells would grow into genetically identical adults. The resulting adults would be duplicates, but only of each other (like identical twins), not of some preexisting adult.

Did Dolly represent something entirely new? For the very first time, it seemed more than science fiction to say it might soon be possible to duplicate an adult human, not just an embryo. But when ethicist John A. Robertson spoke at the National Bioethics Advisory Commission conference held in Washington, D.C., March 13–14, 1997, he said, "At this early stage in the development of mammalian cloning a ban on all human cloning is both imprudent and unjustified. Enough good uses can be imagined that it would be unwise to ban all cloning and cloning research because of vague and highly speculative fears."

In the following selection, Julian Savulescu argues, in part, that because cloned embryos have no moral value beyond that of the cells from which they are cloned, and because human suffering can be relieved, it is not only permissible but morally required to use human cloning to create embryos as a source of tissue for transplantation.

In the second selection, Leon R. Kass contends that people should trust their initial repugnance about human cloning because it threatens important human values, such as the profundity of sex, the sacredness of the human body, and the value of individuality. Human reproduction must not be debased by turning it into mere willful manufacturing. Kass concludes that human cloning is "so repulsive to contemplate" that it should be prohibited entirely.

Julian Savulescu

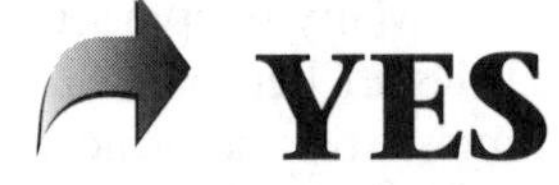

# Should We Clone Human Beings?

## Introduction

When news broke in 1997 that Ian Wilmut and his colleagues had successfully cloned an adult sheep, there was an ill-informed wave of public, professional and bureaucratic fear and rejection of the new technique. Almost universally, human cloning was condemned. Germany, Denmark and Spain have legislation banning cloning; Norway, Slovakia, Sweden and Switzerland have legislation implicitly banning cloning. Some states in Australia, such as Victoria, ban cloning. There are two bills before congress in the US which would comprehensively ban it. There is no explicit or implicit ban on cloning in England, Greece, Ireland or the Netherlands, though in England the Human Embryology and Fertilisation Authority, which issues licences for the use of embryos, has indicated that it would not issue any licence for research into "reproductive cloning". This is understood to be cloning to produce a fetus or live birth. Research into cloning in the first 14 days of life might be possible in England.

There have been several arguments given against human reproductive cloning:

1. It is liable to abuse.
2. It violates a person's right to individuality, autonomy, selfhood, etc.
3. It violates a person's right to genetic individuality (whatever that is—identical twins cannot have such a right).
4. It allows eugenic selection.
5. It uses people as a means.
6. Clones are worse off in terms of wellbeing, especially psychological wellbeing.
7. There are safety concerns, especially an increased risk of serious genetic malformation, cancer or shortened lifespan.

There are, however, a number of arguments in favour of human reproductive cloning. These include:

1. General liberty justifications.
2. Freedom to make personal reproductive choices.

3. Freedom of scientific enquiry.
4. Achieving a sense of immortality.
5. Eugenic selection (with or without gene therapy/enhancement).
6. Social utility—cloning socially important people.
7. Treatment of infertility (with or without gene therapy/enhancement).
8. Replacement of a loved dead relative (with or without gene therapy/enhancement).
9. "Insurance"—freeze a split embryo in case something happens to the first: as a source of tissue or as replacement for the first.
10. Source of human cells or tissue.
11. Research into stem cell differentiation to provide an understanding of aging and oncogenesis.
12. Cloning to prevent a genetic disease.

The arguments against cloning have been critically examined elsewhere and I will not repeat them here. Few people have given arguments in favour of it. Exceptions include arguments in favour of 7–12, with some commentators favouring only 10–11 or 11–12. Justifications 10–12 (and possibly 7) all regard cloning as a way of treating or avoiding disease. These have emerged as arguably the strongest justifications for cloning. This paper examines 10 and to some extent 11.

## Human Cloning as a Source of Cells or Tissue

Cloning is the production of an identical or near-identical genetic copy. Cloning can occur by fission or fusion. Fission is the division of a cell mass into two equal and identical parts, and the development of each into a separate but genetically identical or near-identical individual. This occurs in nature as identical twins.

Cloning by fusion involves taking the nucleus from one cell and transferring it to an egg which has had its nucleus removed. Placing the nucleus in the egg reprogrammes the DNA in the nucleus to replicate the whole individual from which the nucleus was derived: nuclear transfer. It differs from fission in that the offspring has only one genetic parent, whose genome is nearly identical to that of the offspring. In fission, the offspring, like the offspring of normal sexual reproduction, inherits half of its genetic material from each of two parents. Henceforth, by "cloning", I mean cloning by fusion.

Human cloning could be used in several ways to produce cells, tissues or organs for the treatment of human disease.

### Human Cloning as a Source of Multipotent Stem Cells

In this paper I will differentiate between totipotent and multipotent stem cells. Stem cells are cells which are early in developmental lineage and have the ability to differentiate into several different mature cell types. Totipotent stem cells are very immature stem cells with the potential to develop into any of the mature cell types in the adult (liver, lung, skin, blood, etc). Multipotential stem cells are more mature stem cells with the potential to develop into different mature forms of a particular cell lineage, for example, bone marrow stem cells can form either white or red blood cells, but they cannot form liver cells.

Multipotential stem cells can be used as

1. a vector for gene therapy.
2. cells for transplantation, especially in bone marrow.

Attempts have been made to use embryonic stem cells from other animals as vectors for gene therapy and as universal transplantation cells in humans. Problems include limited differentiation and rejection. Somatic cells are differentiated cells of the body, and not sex cells which give rise to sperm and eggs. Cloning of somatic cells from a person who is intended as the recipient of cell therapy would provide a source of multipotential stem cells that are not rejected. These could also be vectors for gene therapy. A gene could be inserted into a somatic cell from the patient, followed by selection, nuclear transfer and the culture of the appropriate clonal population of cells in vitro. These cells could then be returned to the patient as a source of new tissue (for example bone marrow in the case of leukaemia) or as tissue without genetic abnormality (in the case of inherited genetic disease). The major experimental issues which would need to be addressed are developing clonal stability during cell amplification and ensuring differentiation into the cell type needed. It should be noted that this procedure does not necessarily involve the production of a multicellular embryo, nor its implantation in vivo or artificially. (Indeed, cross-species cloning—fusing human cells with cow eggs—produces embryos which will not develop into fetuses, let alone viable offspring.)

A related procedure would produce totipotent stem cells which could differentiate into multipotent cells of a particular line or function, or even into a specific tissue. This is much closer to reproductive cloning. Embryonic stem cells from mice have been directed to differentiate into vascular endothelium, myocardial and skeletal tissue, haemopoietic precursors and neurons. However, it is not known whether the differentiation of human totipotent stem cells can be controlled in vitro. Unlike the previous application, the production of organs could involve reproductive cloning (the production of a totipotent cell which forms a blastomere), but then differentiates into a tissue after some days. Initially, however, all early embryonic cells are identical. Producing totipotent stem cells in this way is equivalent to the creation of an early embryo.

## Production of Embryo/Fetus/Child/ Adult as a Source of Tissue

An embryo, fetus, child or adult could be produced by cloning, and solid organs or differentiated tissue could be extracted from it.

# Cloning as Source of Organs, Tissue and Cells for Transplantation

## The Need for More Organs and Tissues

Jeffrey Platts reports: "So great is the demand that as few as 5% of the organs needed in the United States ever become available". According to David K C Cooper, this is getting worse: "The discrepancy between the number of potential recipients and donor organs is increasing by approximately 10–15% annually". Increasing procurement of cadaveric organs may not be the solution. Anthony Dorling and colleagues write:

> "A study from Seattle, USA, in 1992 identified an annual maximum of only 7,000 brain dead donors in the USA. Assuming 100% consent and suitability, these 14,000 potential kidney grafts would still not match the numbers of new patients commencing dialysis each year. The clear implication is that an alternative source of organs is needed."

Not only is there a shortage of tissue or organs for those with organ failure, but there remain serious problems with the compatibility of tissue or organs used, requiring immunosuppressive therapy with serious side effects. Using cloned tissue would have enormous theoretical advantages, as it could be abundant and there is near perfect immunocompatibility.

There are several ways human cloning could be used to address the shortfall of organs and tissues, and each raises different ethical concerns.

## 1. Production of Tissue or Cells Only by Controlling Differentiation

I will now give an argument to support the use of cloning to produce cells or tissues through control of cellular differentiation.

*The fate of one's own tissue.* Individuals have a strong interest or right in determining the fate of their own body parts, including their own cells and tissues, at least when this affects the length and quality of their own life. A right might be defended in terms of autonomy or property rights in body parts.

This right extends (under some circumstances) both to the proliferation of cells and to their transmutation into other cell types (which I will call the Principle of Tissue Transmutation).

***Defending the Principle of Tissue Transmutation***

Consider the following hypothetical example:

**Lucas I** Lucas is a 22-year-old man with leukaemia. The only effective treatment will be a bone marrow transplant. There is no compatible donor. However, there is a drug which selects a healthy bone marrow cell and causes it to multiply. A doctor would be negligent if he or she did not employ such a drug for the treatment of Lucas's leukaemia. Indeed, there is a moral imperative to develop such drugs if we can and use them. Colony-stimulating factors, which cause blood cells to multiply, are already used in the treatment of leukaemia, and with stored marrow from those in remission in leukaemia before use for reconstitution during relapse.

**Lucas II** In this version of the example, the drug causes Lucas's healthy skin cells to turn into healthy bone marrow stem cells. There is no relevant moral difference between Lucas I and II. We should develop such drugs and doctors would be negligent if they did not use them.

If this is right, there is nothing problematic about cloning to produce cells or tissues for transplantation by controlling differentiation. All we would be doing is taking, say, a skin cell and turning on and off some components of the total genetic complement to cause the cell to divide as a bone marrow cell. We are causing a differentiated cell (skin cell) to turn directly into a multipotent stem cell (bone marrow stem cell).

Are there any objections? The major objection is one of practicality. It is going to be very difficult to cause a skin cell to turn *directly* into a bone marrow cell. There are also safety considerations. Because we are taking a cell which has already undergone many cell divisions during terminal differentiation to give a mature cell such as a skin cell, and accumulated mutations, there is a theoretical concern about an increased likelihood of malignancy in that clonal population. However, the donor cell in these cases is the same age as the recipient (exactly), and a shorter life span would not be expected. There may also be an advantage in some diseases, such as leukaemia, to having a degree of incompatibility between donor and recipient bone marrow so as to enable the donor cells to recognise and destroy malignant recipient cells. This would not apply to non-malignant diseases in which bone marrow transplant is employed, such as the leukodystrophies. Most importantly, all these concerns need to be addressed by further research.

**Lucas IIA** In practice, it is most likely that skin cells will not be able to be turned directly into bone marrow cells: there will need to be a stage of totipotency in between. The most likely way of producing cells to treat Lucas II is via the cloning route, where a skin cell nucleus is passed through an oocyte to give a totipotent cell. The production of a totipotent stem cell is the production of an embryo.

*Production of an embryo as a source of cells or tissues.* There are two ways in which an embryo could be a source of cells and tissues. Firstly, the early embryonic cells could be made to differentiate into cells of one tissue type, for example, bone marrow. Secondly, differentiated cells or tissues from an older embryo could be extracted and used directly.

Are these permissible?

In England, the Royal Society has given limited support to cloning for the purposes of treating human disease. The Human Genetics Advisory Commission (HGAC) defines this as "therapeutic cloning," differentiating it from "reproductive cloning". Both bodies claim that embryo experimentation in the first 14 days is permitted by English law, and question whether cloning in this period would raise any new ethical issues.

Cloning in this circumstance raises few ethical issues. What is produced, at least in the first few days of division after a totipotent cell has been produced from an adult skin cell, is just a skin cell from that person with an altered gene expression profile (some genes turned on and some turned off). In one way, it is just an existing skin cell behaving differently from normal skin cells, perhaps more like a malignant skin cell. The significant processes are ones of *cellular multiplication* and later, *cellular differentiation*.

If this is true, why stop at research at 14 days? Consider the third version of the Lucas case:

**Lucas III** The same as Lucas IIA, but in this case, Lucas also needs a kidney transplant. Therefore, in addition to the skin cell developing blood stem cells (via the embryo), the process is adjusted so that a kidney is produced.

The production of another tissue type or organ does not raise any new relevant ethical consideration. Indeed, if Lucas did not need the kidney, it could be used for someone else who required a kidney (if, of course, in vitro maturation techniques had been developed to the extent that a functioning organ of sufficient size could be produced).

Consider now:

**Lucas IV** In addition to the blood cells, all the tissue of a normal human embryo is produced, organised in the anatomical arrangement of an embryo. This (in principle) might or might not involve development in a womb. For simplicity, let us assume that this occurs in vitro (though this is impossible at present).

Is there any morally relevant difference from the previous versions? It is not relevant that many different tissues are produced rather than one. Nor is the size of these tissues or their arrangement morally relevant. If there is a difference, it must be that a special kind of tissue has been produced, or that some special relationship develops between existing tissues, and that a morally significant entity then exists. When does this special point in embryonic development occur?

The most plausible point is some point during the development of the brain. There are two main candidates:

1. when tissue differentiates and the first identifiable brain structures come into existence as the neural plate around day 19.
2. when the brain supports some morally significant function: consciousness or self-consciousness or rational self-consciousness. The earliest of these, consciousness, does not occur until well into fetal development.

On the first view, utilisation of cloning techniques in the first two weeks to study cellular differentiation is justifiable. The most defensible view, I believe, is that our continued existence only becomes morally relevant when we become self-conscious. (Of course, if a fetus can feel pain at some earlier point, but is not self-conscious, its existence is morally relevant in a different way: we ought not to inflict unnecessary pain on it, though it may be permissible to end its life painlessly.) On this view, we should use the drug to cause Lucas IV's skin cells to transmutate and remove bone marrow from these. What is going on in Lucas IV is no different, morally speaking, from cloning. If this is right, it is justifiable to extract differentiated tissues from young fetuses which have been cloned. . . .

I cannot see any intrinsic morally significant difference between a mature skin cell, the totipotent stem cell derived from it, and a fertilised egg. They are all cells which could give rise to a person if certain conditions obtained. (Thus, to claim that experimentation on cloned embryos is acceptable, but the same experimentation on non-cloned embryos is not acceptable, because the former are not embryos but totipotent stem cells, is sophistry.)

Looking at cloning this way exposes new difficulties for those who appeal to the potential of embryos to become persons and the moral significance of conception as a basis for opposition to abortion. If all our cells could be persons, then we cannot appeal to the fact that an embryo could be a person to justify the special treatment we give it. Cloning forces us to abandon the old arguments supporting special treatment of fertilised eggs.

## Production of a Fetus

If one believes that the morally significant event in development is something related to consciousness, then extracting tissue or organs from a cloned fetus up until that point at which the morally relevant event occurs is acceptable. Indeed, in law, a legal persona does not come into existence until birth. At least in Australia and England, abortion is permissible throughout fetal development.

## Production of a Child or Adult as a Source of Cells or Tissues

Like the production of a self-conscious fetus, the production of a cloned child or adult is liable to all the usual cloning objections, together with the severe limitations on the ways in which tissue can be taken from donors for transplantation.

Many writers support cloning for the purposes of studying cellular differentiation because they argue that cloning does not raise serious new issues above those raised by embryo experimentation. Such support for cloning is too limited. On one view, there is no relevant difference between early embryo research and later embryo/early fetal research. Indeed, the latter stand more chance of providing viable tissue for transplantation, at least in the near future. While producing a cloned live child as a source of tissue for transplantation would raise new and important issues, producing embryos and early fetuses as a source of tissue for transplantation may be morally obligatory.

## Consistency

Is this a significant deviation from existing practice?

### 1. Fetal Tissue Transplantation

In fact, fetal tissue has been widely used in medicine. Human fetal thymus transplantation is standard therapy for thymic aplasia or Di George's syndrome. It has also been used in conjunction with fetal liver for the treatment of subacute combined immunodeficiency.

Human fetal liver and umbilical cord blood have been used as a source of haematopoietic cells in the treatment of acute leukaemia and aplastic anaemia. Liver has also been used for radiation accidents and storage disorders. The main problem has been immune rejection.

One woman with aplastic anaemia received fetal liver from her own 22-week fetus subsequent to elective abortion over 20 years ago.

Fetal brain tissue from aborted fetuses has been used as source of tissue for the treatment of Parkinson's disease. Neural grafts show long term survival and function in patients with Parkinson's disease, though significant problems remain.

Fetal tissue holds promise as treatment for Huntington's disease, spinal cord injuries, demyelinating disorders, retinal degeneration in retinitis pigmentosa, hippocampal lesions associated with temporal lobe epilepsy, cerebral ischaemia, stroke and head injury, and beta thalassemia in utero using fetal liver. Fetal pancreas has also been used in the treatment of diabetes.

## Fetal Tissue Banks

Indeed, in the US and England, fetal tissue banks exist to distribute fetal tissues from abortion clinics for the purposes of medical research and treatment. In the US, the Central Laboratory for Human Embryology in Washington, the National Diseases Research Interchange, and the International Institute for the Advancement of Medicine and the National Abortion Federation, all distribute fetal tissue.

In the UK, the Medical Research Council's fetal tissue bank was established in 1957 and disperses about 5,000 tissues a year.

### 2. Conception of a Non-Cloned Child as a Source of Bone Marrow: Ayala Case

Not only has fetal tissue been used for the treatment of human disease, but human individuals have been deliberately conceived as a source of tissue for transplantation. In the widely discussed Ayala case, a 17-year-old girl, Anissa, had leukaemia. No donor had been found in two years. Her father had his vasectomy reversed with the intention of having another child to serve as a bone marrow donor. There was a one in four chance the child would be compatible with Anissa. The child, Marissa, was born and was a compatible donor and a successful transplant was performed.

A report four years later noted: "Marissa is now a healthy four-year-old, and, by all accounts, as loved and cherished a child as her parents said she would be. The marrow transplant was a success, and Anissa is now a married, leukaemia-free, bank clerk."

Assisted reproduction (IVF) has been used to produce children to serve as bone marrow donors. It is worth noting that had cloning been available, there would have been a 100% chance of perfect tissue compatibility and a live child need not have been produced.

## Objections

While there are some precedents for the proposal to use cloning to produce tissue for transplantation, what is distinctive about this proposal is that human tissue will be: (i) cloned and (ii) deliberately created with abortion in mind. This raises new objections.

### Abortion Is Wrong

Burtchaell, a Catholic theologian, in considering the ethics of fetal tissue research, claims that abortion is morally wrong and that fetal tissue cannot be used for research because no one can give informed consent for its use and to use it would be complicity in wrongful killing. He claims that mothers cannot consent: "The flaw in this claim [that mothers can consent] is that the tissue is from within her body but is the body of another, with distinct genotype, blood, gender, etc." Claims such as those of Burtchaell are more problematic in the case of cloning. If the embryo were cloned from the mother, it would be of the same genotype as her, and, arguably, one of her tissues. Now at some point a cloned tissue is no longer just a tissue from its clone: it exists as an individual in its own right and at some point has interests as other individuals do. But the latter point occurs, I believe, when the cloned individual becomes self-conscious. The presence or absence of a distinct genotype is irrelevant. We are not justified in treating an identical twin differently from a non-identical twin because the latter has a distinct genotype.

In a society that permits abortion on demand, sometimes for little or no reason, it is hard to see how women can justifiably be prevented from aborting a fetus for the purpose of saving someone's life. And surely it is more respectful of the fetus, if the fetus is an object of respect, that its body parts be used for good rather than for no good purpose at all.

### It Is Worse to Be a Clone

Some have argued that it is worse to be a clone. This may be plausible in the sense that a person suffers in virtue of being a clone—living in the shadow of its "parent", feeling less like an individual, treated as a means and not an end, etc. Thus cloning in the Ayala case would raise some new (but I do not believe overwhelming) issues which need consideration. But cloning followed by abortion does not. I can't make any sense of the claim that it is worse to be a cloned cell or tissue. These are not the things we ascribe these kinds of interests to. Cloning is bad when it is bad for a person. Likewise, arguments regarding "instrumentalisation" apply to persons, and not to tissues and cells.

## Creating Life with the Intention of Ending It to Provide Tissue

Using cloning to produce embryos or fetuses as a source of tissue would involve deliberately creating life for the purposes of destroying it. It involves intentionally killing the fetus. This differs from abortion where women do not intend to become pregnant for the purpose of having an abortion.

Is it wrong deliberately to conceive a fetus for the sake of providing tissue? Most of the guidelines on the use of fetal tissue aim to stop women having children just to provide tissues. The reason behind this is some background belief that abortion is itself wrong. These guidelines aim to avoid moral taint objections that we cannot benefit from wrong-doing. More importantly, there is a concern that promoting some good outcome from abortion would encourage abortion. However, in this case, abortion would not be encouraged because this is abortion in a very special context: it is abortion of a *cloned* fetus for medical purposes.

But is it wrong deliberately to use abortion to bring about some good outcome?

In some countries (for example those in the former Eastern bloc), abortion is or was the main available form of birth control. A woman who had intercourse knowing that she might fall pregnant, in which case she would have an abortion, would not necessarily be acting wrongly in such a country, if the alternative was celibacy. When the only way to achieve some worthwhile end—sexual expression—is through abortion, it seems justifiable.

The question is: is the use of cloned fetal tissue the best way of increasing the pool of transplantable tissues and organs?

## An Objection to the Principle of Tissue Transmutation

Another objection to the proposal is that we do not have the right to determine the fate of all our cells. For example, we are limited in what we can do with our sex cells. However, we should only be constrained in using our own cells when that use puts others at risk. This is not so in transmutation until another individual with moral interests comes into existence.

## Surrogacy Concerns

At least at present, later embryonic and fetal development can only occur inside a woman's uterus, so some of the proposals here would require a surrogate. I have assumed that any surrogate would be freely consenting. Concerns with surrogacy have been addressed elsewhere, though cloning for this purpose would raise some different concerns. There would be no surrogacy concerns if the donor cell were derived from the mother (she would be carrying one of her own cells), from the mother's child (she would be carrying her child again) or if an artificial womb were ever developed.

## Should We Give Greater Importance to Somatic Cells?

I have claimed that the totipotent cells of the early embryo, and indeed the embryo, do not have greater moral significance than adult skin cells (or indeed lung or colon or any nucleated cells). I have used this observation to downgrade the importance we attach to embryonic cells. However, it might be argued that we should upgrade the importance which we attach to somatic cells.

This is a *reductio ad absurdum* of the position which gives importance to the embryo, and indeed which gives weight to anatomical structure rather than function. If we should show special respect to all cells, surgeons should be attempting to excise the very minimum tissue (down to the last cell) necessary during operations. We should be doing research into preventing the neuronal loss which occurs normally during childhood. The desquamation of a skin cell should be as monumental, according to those who believe that abortion is killing persons, as the loss of a whole person. These claims are, I think, all absurd.

## Yuk Factor

Many people would find it shocking for a fetus to be created and then destroyed as a source of organs. But many people found artificial insemination abhorrent, IVF shocking and the use of animal organs revolting. Watching an abortion is horrible. However, the fact that people find something repulsive does not settle whether it is wrong. The achievement in applied ethics, if there is one, of the last 50 years has been to get people to rise above their gut feelings and examine the reasons for a practice.

## Permissive and Obstructive Ethics

Many people believe that ethicists should be merely moral watch-dogs, barking when they see something going wrong. However, ethics may also be permissive. Thus ethics may require that we stop interfering, as was the case in the treatment of homosexuals. Ethics should not only be obstructive but constructive. To delay unnecessarily a good piece of research which will result in a life-saving drug is to be responsible for some people's deaths. It is to act wrongly. This debate about cloning illustrates a possible permissive and constructive role for ethics.

# Conclusion

The most justified use of human cloning is arguably to produce stem cells for the treatment of disease. I have argued that it is not only reasonable to produce embryos as a source of multipotent stem cells, but that it is morally required to produce embryos and early fetuses as a source of tissue for transplantation. This argument hinges on:

1. The claim that the moral status of the cloned embryo and early fetus is no different from that of the somatic cell from which they are derived.
2. The claim that there is no morally relevant difference between the fetus and the embryo until some critical point in brain development and function.
3. The fact that the practice is consistent with existing practices of fetal tissue transplantation and conceiving humans as a source of tissue for transplantation (the Ayala case).
4. An argument from beneficence. This practice would achieve much good.
5. An argument from autonomy. This was the principle of tissue transmutation: that we should be able to determine the fate of our own cells, including whether they change into other cell types.

This proposal avoids all the usual objections to cloning. The major concerns are practicality and safety. This requires further study.

The HGAC and The Royal Society have broached the possibility of producing clones for up to 14 days: "therapeutic cloning". Those bodies believe that it is acceptable to produce and destroy an embryo but not a fetus. Women abort fetuses up to 20 weeks and later. We could make it mandatory that women have abortions earlier (with rapid pregnancy testing). However, we do not. Moreover, while the decision for most women to have an abortion is a momentous and considered one, in practice, we allow women to abort fetuses regardless of their reasons, indeed occasionally for no or bad reasons. If a woman could abort a fetus because she wanted a child with a certain horoscope sign, surely a woman should be able to abort a fetus to save a person's life.

I have been discussing cloning for the purposes of saving people's lives or drastically improving their quality. While we beat our breasts about human dignity and the rights of cells of different sorts, people are dying of leukaemia and kidney disease. If a woman wants to carry a clone of her or someone else's child to save a life, it may not be society's place to interfere.

**Leon R. Kass**  **NO**

# The Wisdom of Repugnance

Our habit of delighting in news of scientific and technological breakthroughs has been sorely challenged by the birth announcement of a sheep named Dolly. Though Dolly shares with previous sheep the "softest clothing, woolly, bright," William Blake's question, "Little Lamb, who made thee?" has for her a radically different answer: Dolly was, quite literally, made. She is the work not of nature or nature's God but of man, an Englishman, Ian Wilmut, and his fellow scientists. What's more, Dolly came into being not only asexually—ironically, just like "He [who] calls Himself a Lamb"—but also as the genetically identical copy (and the perfect incarnation of the form or blueprint) of a mature ewe, of whom she is a clone. This long-awaited yet not quite expected success in cloning a mammal raised immediately the prospect—and the specter—of cloning human beings: "I a child and Thou a lamb," despite our differences, have always been equal candidates for creative making, only now, by means of cloning, we may both spring from the hand of man playing at being God.

After an initial flurry of expert comment and public consternation, with opinion polls showing overwhelming opposition to cloning human beings, President Clinton ordered a ban on all federal support for human cloning research (even though none was being supported) and charged the National Bioethics Advisory Commission to report in ninety days on the ethics of human cloning research. The commission (an eighteen-member panel, evenly balanced between scientists and non-scientists, appointed by the president and reporting to the National Science and Technology Council) invited testimony from scientists, religious thinkers and bioethicists, as well as from the general public. It is now deliberating about what it should recommend, both as a matter of ethics and as a matter of public policy.

Congress is awaiting the commission's report, and is poised to act. Bills to prohibit the use of federal funds for human cloning research have been introduced in the House of Representatives and the Senate; and another bill, in the House, would make it illegal "for any person to use a human somatic cell for the process of producing a human clone." A fateful decision is at hand. To clone or not to clone a human being is no longer an academic question.

... [S]ome cautions are in order and some possible misconceptions need correcting. For a start, cloning is not Xeroxing. As has been reassuringly reiterated, the clone of Mel Gibson, though his genetic double, would enter the world hairless, toothless and peeing in his diapers, just like any other human infant. Moreover, the success rate, at least at first, will probably not be very high: the British transferred 277 adult nuclei into enucleated sheep eggs, and implanted twenty-nine clonal embryos, but they achieved the birth of only one live lamb clone. For this reason, among others, it is unlikely that, at least for now, the practice would be very popular, and there is no immediate worry of mass-scale production of multicopies. The need of repeated surgery to obtain eggs and, more crucially, of numerous borrowed wombs for implantation will surely limit use, as will the expense; besides, almost everyone who is able will doubtless prefer nature's sexier way of conceiving.

Still, for the tens of thousands of people already sustaining over 200 assisted-reproduction clinics in the United States and already availing themselves of in vitro fertilization, intracytoplasmic sperm injection and other techniques of assisted reproduction, cloning would be an option with virtually no added fuss (especially when the success rate improves). . . .

In anticipation of human cloning, apologists and proponents have already made clear possible uses of the perfected technology, ranging from the sentimental and compassionate to the grandiose. They include: providing a child for an infertile couple; "replacing" a beloved spouse or child who is dying or has died; avoiding the risk of genetic disease; permitting reproduction for homosexual men and lesbians who want nothing sexual to do with the opposite sex; securing a genetically identical source of organs or tissues perfectly suitable for transplantation; getting a child with a genotype of one's own choosing, not excluding oneself; replicating individuals of great genius, talent or beauty—having a child who really could "be like Mike"; and creating large sets of genetically identical humans suitable for research on, for instance, the question of nature versus nurture, or for special missions in peace and war (not excluding espionage), in which using identical humans would be an advantage. Most people who envision the cloning of human beings, of course, want none of these scenarios. That they cannot say why is not surprising. What is surprising, and welcome, is that, in our cynical age, they are saying anything at all.

## The Wisdom of Repugnance

"Offensive." "Grotesque." "Revolting." "Repugnant." "Repulsive." These are the words most commonly heard regarding the prospect of human cloning. Such reactions come both from the man or woman in the street and from the intellectuals, from believers and atheists, from humanists and scientists. Even Dolly's creator has said he "would find it offensive" to clone a human being.

People are repelled by many aspects of human cloning. They recoil from the prospect of mass production of human beings, with large clones of lookalikes, compromised in their individuality; the idea of father-son or mother-daughter twins; the bizarre prospects of a woman giving birth to and rearing a genetic copy of herself, her spouse or even her deceased father or mother; the grotesqueness of conceiving a child as an exact replacement for another who has died; the utilitarian creation of embryonic genetic duplicates of oneself, to be frozen away or created when necessary, in case of need for homologous tissues or organs for transplantation; the narcissism of those who would clone themselves and the arrogance of others who think they know who deserves to be cloned or which genotype any child-to-be should be thrilled to receive; the Frankensteinian hubris to create human life and increasingly to control its destiny; man playing God. Almost no one finds any of the suggested reasons for human cloning compelling; almost everyone anticipates its possible misuses and abuses. Moreover, many people feel oppressed by the sense that there is probably nothing we can do to prevent it from happening. This makes the prospect all the more revolting.

Revulsion is not an argument; and some of yesterday's repugnances are today calmly accepted—though, one must add, not always for the better. In crucial cases, however, repugnance is the emotional expression of deep wisdom, beyond reason's power fully to articulate it. Can anyone really give an argument fully adequate to the horror which is father-daughter incest (even with consent), or having sex with animals, or mutilating a corpse, or eating human flesh, or even just (just!) raping or murdering another human being? Would anybody's failure to give full rational justification for his or her revulsion at these practices make that revulsion ethically suspect? Not at all. On the contrary, we are suspicious of those who think that they can rationalize away our horror, say, by trying to explain the enormity of incest with arguments only about the genetic risks of inbreeding.

The repugnance at human cloning belongs in this category. We are repelled by the prospect of cloning human beings not because of the strangeness or novelty of the undertaking, but because we intuit and feel, immediately and without argument, the violation of things that we rightfully hold dear. Repugnance, here as elsewhere, revolts against the excesses of human willfulness, warning us not to transgress what is unspeakably profound. . . .

Typically, cloning is discussed in one or more of three familiar contexts, which one might call the technological, the liberal and the meliorist. Under the first, cloning will be seen as an extension of existing techniques for assisting reproduction and determining the genetic makeup of children. Like them, cloning is to be regarded as a neutral technique, with no inherent meaning or goodness, but subject to multiple uses, some good, some bad. The morality of cloning thus depends absolutely on the goodness or badness of the motives and intentions of the cloners. . . .

The liberal (or libertarian or liberationist) perspective sets cloning in the context of rights, freedoms and personal empowerment. Cloning is just a new option for exercising an individual's right to reproduce or to have the kind of child that he or she wants. Alternatively, cloning enhances our liberation (especially women's liberation) from the confines of nature, the vagaries of change, or the necessity for sexual mating. Indeed, it liberates women from the need for men altogether. . . .

The meliorist perspective embraces valetudinarians and also eugenicists. . . . These people see in cloning a new prospect for improving human beings—minimally, by ensuring the perpetuation of healthy individuals by avoiding the risks of genetic disease inherent in the lottery of sex, and maximally, by producing "optimum babies," preserving outstanding genetic material, and (with the help of soon-to-come techniques for precise genetic engineering) enhancing inborn human capacities on many fronts. Here the morality of cloning as a means is justified solely by the excellence of the end. . . .

These three approaches, all quintessentially American and all perfectly fine in their places, are sorely wanting as approaches to human procreation. It is, to say the least, grossly distorting to view the wondrous mysteries of birth, renewal and individuality, and the deep meaning of parent-child relations, largely through the lens of our reductive science and its potent technologies. Similarly, considering reproduction (and the intimate relations of family life!) primarily under the political-legal, adversarial and individualistic notion of rights can only undermine the private yet fundamentally social, cooperative and duty-laden character of child-bearing, child-rearing and their bond to the covenant of marriage. . . .

The technical, liberal and meliorist approaches all ignore the deeper anthropological, social and, indeed, ontological meanings of bringing forth new life. To this more fitting and profound point of view, cloning shows itself to be a major alteration, indeed, a major violation, of our given nature as embodied, gendered and engendering beings—and of the social relations built on this natural ground. Once this perspective is recognized, the ethical judgment on cloning can no longer be reduced to a matter of motives and intentions, rights and freedoms, benefits and harms, or even means and ends. It must be regarded primarily as a matter of meaning: Is cloning a fulfillment of human begetting and belonging? Or is cloning rather, as I contend, their pollution and perversion? To pollution and perversion, the fitting response can only be horror and revulsion; and conversely, generalized horror and revulsion are prima facie evidence of foulness and violation. The burden of moral argument must fall entirely on those who want to declare the widespread repugnances of humankind to be mere timidity or superstition.

Yet repugnance need not stand naked before the bar of reason. The wisdom of our horror at human cloning can be partially articulated, even if this is finally one of those instances about which the heart has its reasons that reason cannot entirely know. . . .

## The Perversities of Cloning

First, an important if formal objection: any attempt to clone a human being would constitute an unethical experiment upon the resulting child-to-be. As . . . animal experiments . . . indicate, there are grave risks of mishaps and deformities. Moreover, because of what cloning means, one cannot presume a future cloned child's consent to be a clone, even a healthy one. Thus, ethically speaking, we cannot even get to know whether or not human cloning is feasible.

I understand, of course, the philosophical difficulty of trying to compare a life with defects against nonexistence. Several bioethicists, proud of their philosophical cleverness, use this conundrum to embarrass claims that one can injure a child in its conception, precisely because it is only thanks to that complained-of conception that the child is alive to complain. But common sense tells us that we have no reason to fear such philosophisms. For we surely know that people can harm and even maim children in the very act of conceiving them, say, by paternal transmission of the AIDS virus, maternal transmission of heroin dependence or, arguably, even by bringing them into being as bastards or with no capacity or willingness to look after them properly. And we believe that to do this intentionally, or even negligently, is inexcusable and clearly unethical. . . .

Cloning creates serious issues of identity and individuality. The cloned person may experience concerns about his distinctive identity not only because he will be in genotype and appearance identical to another human being, but, in this case, because he may also be twin to the person who is his "father" or "mother"—if one can still call them that. What would be the psychic burdens of being the "child" or "parent" of your twin? The cloned individual, moreover, will be saddled with a genotype that has already lived. He will not be fully a surprise to the world. People are likely always to compare his performances in life with that of his alter ego. True, his nurture and his circumstance in life will be different; genotype is not exactly destiny. Still, one must also expect parental and other efforts to shape this new life after the original—or at least to view the child with the original version always firmly in mind. . . .

Since the birth of Dolly, there has been a fair amount of doublespeak on this matter of genetic identity. Experts have rushed in to reassure the public that the clone would in no way be the same person, or have any confusions about his or her identity: as previously noted, they are pleased to point out that the clone of Mel Gibson would not be Mel Gibson. Fair enough. But one is shortchanging the truth by emphasizing the additional importance of the intrauterine environment, rearing and social setting: genotype obviously matters plenty. That, after all, is the only reason to clone, whether human beings or sheep. The odds that clones of Wilt Chamberlain will play in the NBA are, I submit, infinitely greater than they are for clones of Robert Reich. . . .

Genetic distinctiveness not only symbolizes the uniqueness of each human life and the independence of its parents that each human child rightfully attains. It can also be an important support for living a worthy and dignified life. Such arguments apply with great force to any large-scale replication of human individuals. But they are sufficient, in my view, to rebut even the first attempts to clone a human being. One must never forget that these are human beings upon whom our eugenic or merely playful fantasies are to be enacted.

Troubled psychic identity (distinctiveness), based on all-too-evident genetic identity (sameness), will be made much worse by the utter confusion of social identity and kinship ties. . . .

Social identity and social ties of relationship and responsibility are widely connected to, and supported by, biological kinship. Social taboos on incest (and adultery) everywhere serve to keep clear who is related to whom (and especially which child belongs to which parents), as well as to avoid confounding the social identity of parent-and-child (or brother-and-sister) with the social identity of lovers, spouses and co-parents. True, social identity is altered by adoption (but as a matter of the best interest of already living children: we do not deliberately produce children for adoption). True, artificial insemination and in vitro fertilization with donor sperm, or whole embryo donation, are in some way forms of "prenatal adoption"—a not altogether unproblematic practice. Even here, though, there is in each case (as in all sexual reproduction) a known male source of sperm and a known single female source of egg—a genetic father and a genetic mother—should anyone care to know (as adopted children often do) who is genetically related to whom.

In the case of cloning, however, there is but one "parent." The usually sad situation of the "single-parent child" is here deliberately planned, and with a vengeance. In the case of self-cloning, the "offspring" is, in addition, one's twin; and so the dreaded result of incest—to be parent to one's sibling—is here brought about deliberately, albeit without any act of coitus. Moreover, all other relationships will be confounded. . . .

Human cloning would also represent a giant step toward turning begetting into making, procreation into manufacture (literally, something "handmade"), a process already begun with in vitro fertilization and genetic testing of embryos. With cloning, not only is the process in hand, but the total genetic blueprint of the cloned individual is selected and determined by the human artisans. . . . In clonal reproduction, . . . and in the more advanced forms of manufacture to which it leads, we give existence to a being not by what we are but by what we intend and design. As with any product of our making, no matter how excellent, the artificer stands above it, not as an equal but as a superior, transcending it by his will and creative prowess. Scientists who clone animals make it perfectly clear that they are engaged in instrumental making; the animals are, from the start, designed as means to serve rational human purposes. In human cloning, scientists and prospective "parents" would be adopting the same technocratic mentality to human children: human children would be their artifacts.

Such an arrangement is profoundly dehumanizing, no matter how good the product. Mass-scale cloning of the same individual makes the point vividly; but the violation of human equality, freedom and dignity are present even in a single planned clone. . . .

Finally, and perhaps most important, the practice of human cloning by nuclear transfer—like other anticipated forms of genetic engineering of the next generation—would enshrine and aggravate a profound and mischievous misunderstanding of the meaning of having children and of the parent-child relationship. When a couple now chooses to procreate, the partners are saying yes to the emergence of new life in its novelty, saying yes not only to having a child but also, tacitly, to having whatever child this child turns out to be. In accepting our finitude and opening ourselves to our replacement, we are tacitly confessing the limits of our control. In this ubiquitous way of nature, embracing the future by procreating means precisely that we are relinquishing our grip, in the very activity of taking up our own share in what we hope will be the immortality of human life and the human species. This means that our children are not *our* children: they are not our property, not our possessions. Neither are they supposed to live our lives for us, or anyone else's life but their own. To be sure, we seek to guide them on their way, imparting to them not just life but nurturing, love, and a way of life; to be sure, they bear our hopes that they will live fine and flourishing lives, enabling us in small measure to transcend our own limitations. Still, their genetic distinctiveness and independence are the natural foreshadowing of the deep truth that they have their own and never-before-enacted life to live. They are sprung from a past, but they take an uncharted course into the future. . . .

## Meeting Some Objections

The defenders of cloning, of course, are not wittingly friends of despotism. Indeed, they regard themselves mainly as friends of freedom: the freedom of individuals to reproduce, the freedom of scientists and inventors to discover and devise and to foster "progress" in genetic knowledge and technique. They want large-scale cloning only for animals, but they wish to preserve cloning as a human option for exercising our "right to reproduction"—our right to have children, and children with "desirable genes." As law professor John Robertson points out, under our "right to reproduce" we already practice early forms of unnatural, artificial and extramarital reproduction, and we already practice early forms of eugenic choice. For this reason, he argues, cloning is no big deal.

We have here a perfect example of the logic of the slippery slope, and the slippery way in which it already works in this area. Only a few years ago, slippery slope arguments were used to oppose artificial insemination and in vitro fertilization using unrelated sperm donors. Principles used to justify these practices, it was said, will be used to justify more artificial and more eugenic practices, including cloning. Not so, the defenders retorted, since we can make the necessary distinctions. And now, without even a gesture at making the necessary distinctions, the continuity of practice is held by itself to be justificatory.

The principle of reproductive freedom as currently enunciated by the proponents of cloning logically embraces the ethical acceptability of sliding down the entire rest of the slope—to producing children ectogenetically from sperm to term (should it become feasible) and to producing children whose entire genetic makeup will be the product of parental eugenic planning and choice. If reproductive freedom means the right to have a child of one's own choosing, by whatever means, it knows and accepts no limits.

But, far from being legitimated by a "right to reproduce," the emergence of techniques of assisted reproduction and genetic engineering should compel us to reconsider the meaning and limits of such a putative right. In truth, a "right to reproduce" has always been a peculiar and problematic notion. Rights generally belong to individuals, but this is a right which (before cloning) no one can exercise alone. Does the right then inhere only in couples? Only in married couples? Is it a (woman's) right to carry or deliver or a right (of one or more parents) to nurture and rear? Is it a right to have your own biological child? Is it a right only to attempt reproduction, or a right also to succeed? Is it a right to acquire the baby of one's choice? . . .

## Ban the Cloning of Humans

What, then, should we do? We should declare that human cloning is unethical in itself and dangerous in its likely consequences. In so doing, we shall have the backing of the overwhelming majority of our fellow Americans, and of the human race, and (I believe) of most practicing scientists. Next, we should do all that we can to prevent the cloning of human beings. We should do this by means of an international legal ban if possible, and by a unilateral national ban, at a minimum. Scientists may secretly undertake to violate such a law, but they will be deterred by not being able to stand up proudly to claim the credit for their technological bravado and success. Such a ban on clonal baby-making, moreover, will not harm the progress of basic genetic science and technology. On the contrary, it will reassure the public that scientists are happy to proceed without violating the deep ethical norms and intuitions of the human community. . . .

I appreciate the potentially great gains in scientific knowledge and medical treatment available from embryo research, especially with cloned embryos.

At the same time, I have serious reservations about creating human embryos for the sole purpose of experimentation. There is something deeply repugnant and fundamentally transgressive about such a utilitarian treatment of prospective human life. This total, shameless exploitation is worse, in my opinion, than the "mere" destruction of nascent life. But I see no added objections, as a matter of principle, to creating and using *cloned* early embryos for research purposes, beyond the objections that I might raise to doing so with embryos produced sexually.

And yet, as a matter of policy and prudence, any opponent of the manufacture of cloned humans must, I think, in the end oppose also the creating of cloned human embryos. . . . We should allow all cloning research on animals to go forward, but the only safe trench that we can dig across the slippery slope, I suspect, is to insist on the inviolable distinction between animal and human cloning.

Some readers, and certainly most scientists, will not accept such prudent restraints, since they desire the benefits of research. They will prefer, even in fear and trembling, to allow human embryo cloning research to go forward.

Very well. Let us test them. If the scientists want to be taken seriously on ethical grounds, they must at the very least agree that embryonic research may proceed if and only if it is preceded by an absolute and effective ban on all attempts to implant into a uterus a cloned human embryo (cloned from an adult) to produce a living child. Absolutely no permission for the former without the latter.

The National Bioethics Advisory Commission's recommendations regarding this matter should be watched with the greatest care. Yielding to the wishes of the scientists, the commission will almost surely recommend that cloning human embryos for research be permitted. To allay public concern, it will likely also call for a temporary moratorium—not a legislative ban—on implanting cloned embryos to make a child, at least until such time as cloning techniques will have been perfected and rendered "safe" (precisely through the permitted research with cloned embryos). But the call for a moratorium rather than a legal ban would be a moral and a practical failure. Morally, this ethics commission would (at best) be waffling on the main ethical question, by refusing to declare the production of human clones unethical (or ethical). Practically, a moratorium on implantation cannot provide even the minimum protection needed to prevent the production of cloned humans.

Opponents of cloning need therefore to be vigilant. Indeed, no one should be willing even to consider a recommendation to allow the embryo research to proceed unless it is accompanied by a call for *prohibiting* implantation and until steps are taken to make such a prohibition effective.

---

Technically, the National Bioethics Advisory Commission can advise the president only on federal policy, especially federal funding policy. But given the seriousness of the matter at hand, and the grave public concern that goes beyond federal funding, the commission should take a broader view. (If it doesn't, Congress surely will.) . . .

The proposal for such a legislative ban is without American precedent, at least in technological matters, though the British and others have banned cloning of human beings, and we ourselves ban incest, polygamy and other forms of "reproductive freedom." Needless to say, working out the details of such a ban, especially a global one, would be tricky, what with the need to develop appropriate sanctions for violators. Perhaps such a ban will prove ineffective; perhaps it will eventually be shown to have been a mistake. But it would at least place the burden of practical proof where it belongs: on the proponents of this horror, requiring them to show very clearly what great social or medical good can be had only by the cloning of human beings. . . .

The president's call for a moratorium on human cloning has given us an important opportunity. In a truly unprecedented way, we can strike a blow for the human control of the technological project, for wisdom, prudence and human dignity. The prospect of human cloning, so repulsive to contemplate, is the occasion for deciding whether we shall be slaves of unregulated progress, and ultimately its artifacts, or whether we shall remain free human beings who guide our technique toward the enhancement of human dignity.

# POSTSCRIPT

## Is It Ethically Permissible to Clone Human Beings?

Have humans already been cloned? At the end of 2002, Clonaid, founded by members of the Raelian religious cult, announced that it had succeeded. However, it neither produced the so-called clone baby nor permitted it to be tested. Most scientists believe the claims were lies at best.

The cloning technique has been shown to work with sheep, cattle, cats, rabbits, mules, pigs, and other animals. Early in 2003, researchers reported that the technique appears to be impossible in primates (including humans) because of the way certain proteins are arranged in egg cells (Calvin Simerly, et al., "Molecular Correlates of Primate Nuclear Transfer Failures," *Science*, April 11, 2003). However, useful applications of cloning are already being developed (see Ian Wilmut, "Cloning for Medicine," *Scientific American,* December 1998) and the debate over whether we should even try to clone humans and human stem cells continues to rage.

Leon Kass develops his objections further in "Preventing a Brave New World," *The Human Life Review* (July 2001), and *Life, Liberty and the Defense of Dignity: The Challenge for Bioethics* (Encounter, 2002). He gains support from Mary Midgley, who in "Biotechnology and Monstrosity: Why We Should Pay Attention to the 'Yuk Factor'," *Hastings Center Report* (September–October 2000), argues that intuitive, emotional responses to things such as cloning have a significance that must not be dismissed out of hand. In *Our Posthuman Future: Consequences of the Biotechnological Revolution* (Farras, Strauss & Giroux, 2002; paperback Picador, 2003), Francis Fukuyama argues for limits on cloning and genetic engineering in order to protect human nature and dignity. In 2002, the President's Council on Bioethics, chaired by Leon Kass, concluded that the U.S. government should ban reproductive cloning but only impose a 4-year moratorium on cloning for biomedical research; see Stephen S. Hall, "President's Bioethics Council Delivers," *Science* (July 19, 2002). In February 2003, the U.S. House of Representatives passed a bill banning all human cloning, whether for reproduction or research (the Senate version of the bill was expected to have trouble getting passed).

Speaking to the National Bioethics Advisory Commission (whose report was summarized by chair Harold T. Shapiro in the July 11, 1997, issue of *Science*), Ruth Macklin, of the Albert Einstein College of Medicine, said, "It is absurd to maintain that the proposition 'cloning is morally wrong' is self-evident. . . . If I cannot point to any great benefits likely to result from cloning, neither do I foresee any probable great harms, provided that a structure of regulation and oversight is in place. If objectors to cloning can identify no greater harm than a supposed affront to the dignity of the human species, that is a flimsy basis on which to erect barriers to scientific research and its applications." Nathan Myhrvold argues in "Human Clones: Why Not? Opposition to Cloning Isn't Just Luddism—It's Racism," *Slate* (March 13, 1997), that "Calls for a ban on cloning amount to discrimination against people based on another genetic trait—the fact that somebody already has an identical DNA sequence." There are reasons why cloning—at least of embryonic cells—should be permitted. According to Thomas B. Okarma (interviewed by Erika Jonietz, "Cloning, Stem Cells, and Medicine's Future," *Technology Review*, June 2003), they hold great hope for new and useful medical treatments. And according to Robin Marantz Henig, "Pandora's Baby," *Scientific American* (June 2003), when other reproductive technologies such as *in vitro* fertilization were new, they faced similar objections; now they are routine, and it is likely that someday cloning will be too. Daniel J. Kevles agrees; in "Cloning Can't Be Stopped," *Technology Review* (June 2002), he said that if human cloning can but succeed, it will "become commonplace . . . a new commodity in the growing emporium of human reproduction."

# Contributors to This Volume

## EDITOR

**THOMAS A. EASTON** is a professor of life sciences at Thomas College in Waterville, Maine, where he has been teaching since 1983. He received a B.A. in biology from Colby College in 1966 and a Ph.D. in theoretical biology from the University of Chicago in 1971. He has also taught at Unity College, Husson College, and the University of Maine. He is a prolific writer, and his articles on scientific and futuristic issues have appeared in the scholarly journals *Experimental Neurology* and *American Scientist,* as well as in such popular magazines as *Astronomy, Consumer Reports,* and *Robotics Age*. His publications include *Focus on Human Biology,* 2d ed., coauthored with Carl E. Rischer (HarperCollins, 1995), *Careers in Science*, 4th ed. (VGM, 2004), and *Taking Sides: Clashing Views on Controversial Environmental Issues*, 10th ed., coedited with the late Theodore D. Goldfarb (McGraw-Hill Dushkin, 2003). Dr. Easton is also a well-known writer and critic of science fiction.

## STAFF

Larry Loeppke Managing Editor
Jill Peter Senior Developmental Editor
Nichole Altman Developmental Editor
Beth Kundert Production Manager
Jane Mohr Project Manager
Tara McDermott Design Coordinator
Bonnie Coakley Editorial Assistant

## AUTHORS

**RONALD BAILEY** is science correspondent for *Reason Magazine.* A member of the Society of Environmental Journalists, his articles have appeared in many popular publications, including the *Wall Street Journal, The Public Interest,* and *National Review.* He has produced several series and documentaries for PBS television and ABC News. Bailey was the Warren T. Brookes Fellow in Environmental Journalism at the Competitive Enterprise Institute in 1993. He is the editor of *Earth Report 2000: Revisiting the True State of the Planet* (McGraw-Hill, 1999) and the author of *ECOSCAM: The False Prophets of Ecological Apocalypse* (St. Martin's Press, 1993).

**ROGER BATE** is a director of Africa Fighting Malaria, a South African humanitarian group. He is also an adjunct fellow at the Competitive Enterprise Institute.

**ROGER BERNIER** is Associate Director for Science, National Immunization Program, Centers for Disease Control and Prevention, U.S. Department of Health and Human Services.

**LEWIS M. BRANSCOMB** is the Aetna professor of public policy and corporate management emeritus and former director of the Science, Technology, and Public Policy Program in the Center for Science and International Affairs at Harvard University's Kennedy School of Government.

**LESTER R. BROWN** is founder and former president of the Worldwatch Institute. He is the author or coauthor of dozens of books, including *Tough Choices: Facing the Challenge of Food Scarcity* (W. W. Norton, 1996) and *Beyond Malthus: Sixteen Dimensions of the Population Problem,* with Gary Gardner and Brian Halweil (Worldwatch Institute, 1998).

**JOSEPH BURNS, IRVING PORTER** Church Professor of Engineering and Professor of Astronomy at Cornell University, is a member of the National Research Council's Solar System Exploration Survey Committee.

**BRIAN BUTLER** is an assistant professor of business administration at the University of Pittsburgh.

**DANIEL CALLAHAN,** a philosopher, is cofounder and president of the Hastings Center in Briarcliff Manor, New York, where he is also director of International Programs. He is the author or editor of over 30 publications, including *Ethics in Hard Times,* coauthored with Arthur L. Caplan (Plenum Press, 1981); *Setting Limits: Medical Goals in an Aging Society* (Simon & Schuster, 1987); and *The Troubled Dream of Life: In Search of Peaceful Death* (Simon & Schuster, 1993). He received a Ph.D. in philosophy from Harvard University.

**GEORGE CARLO** is a public health scientist, epidemiologist, lawyer, and founder of the Health Risk Management Group. He is chairman of the Carlo Institute and a fellow of the American College of Epidemiology, and he serves on the faculty of the George Washington University School of Medicine. Dr. Carlo has published numerous research articles, commentaries, chapters in books, and health policy papers addressing issues in the health sciences, and he is frequently consulted for television, radio, and newspaper interviews pertaining to public health issues.

**RICHARD J. CLIFFORD** is a professor of biblical studies at Weston Jesuit School of Theology in Cambridge, Massachusetts, and a former president of the Catholic Biblical Association of America. He is the author of *Creation Accounts in the Ancient Near East and in the Bible* (Catholic Biblical Association of America, 1994).

**JONATHAN N. CUMMINGS** is an assistant professor of management at the Massachusetts Institute of Technology.

**RICHARD DAWKINS** is the Charles Simonyi Professor of the Public Understanding of Science at Oxford University and the recipient of the American Humanist Association's 1996 Humanist of the Year Award.

**JOHN DERBYSHIRE** is a conservative critic, commentator, and novelist. His latest book, *Prime Obsession,* is "about a great unsolved mathematical problem, the Riemann Hypothesis."

**STEVE DITLEA**, a journalist based in Spuyten Duyvil, New York, is a contributing writer to *Technology Review.*

**GARY GARDNER** is director of research at the Worldwatch Institute. His research focuses on a wide range of issues, including agricultural resource degradation, materials use, global malnutrition, and the dynamics of social change. He has also developed training materials for the World Bank and for the Millennium Institute in Arlington, Virginia. He holds an M.A. in politics from Brandeis University and an M.A. in public administration from the Monterey Institute of International Studies. He is coauthor, with Brian Halweil, of *Underfed and Overfed: The Global Epidemic of Malnutrition* (Worldwatch Institute, 2000).

**MARJORIE GEORGE** is a professor of political science and director of the Institute of Governmental Studies at the University of California, Berkeley.

**JOHN B. HORRIGAN** is a senior researcher with the Pew Internet & American Life Project. Prior to joining the Project, he was a staff officer for the Board on Science, Technology, and Economic Policy at the National Research Council.

**BRIAN HALWEIL** is a research associate at the Worldwatch Institute, where he focuses on the social and ecological consequences of the way we produce food, examining such topics as organic farming, biotechnology, and water scarcity. He has written editorials and articles for *World Watch* magazine, and his work has been featured in the *L.A. Times, Christian Science Monitor,* and the *New York Times*. He has also been the John Gardner Public Service Fellow at Stanford University. He is coauthor, with Lester R. Brown and Gary Gardner, of *Beyond Malthus: Sixteen Dimensions of the Population Problem* (Worldwatch Institute, 1998).

**INTERGOVERNMENTAL PANEL ON CLIMATE CHANGE** was established by the World Meteorological Organization and the United Nations Environment Programme to assess the scientific, technical, and socioeconomic information relevant to the understanding of the risk of human-induced climate change. It bases its assessments mainly on peer-reviewed and published scientific/technical literature.

**LEON R. KASS** is the Addie Clark Harding Professor in the College and the Committee on Social Thought at the University of Chicago and an adjunct scholar at the American Enterprise Institute. A trained physician and biochemist, he is the author of *Toward a More Natural Science: Biology and Human Affairs* (Free Press, 1985), and *Life Liberty and the Defense of Dignity: The Challenge for Bioethics* (Encounter, 2002).

**DIANE KATZ** is director of science, environment, and technology policy at the Mackinac Center for Public Policy (Michigan).

**MARNIE KO** is a Canadian investigative reporter who specializes in crime and law, human interest stories, society and culture, and controversies.

**ROBERT KRAUT** is the Herbert A. Simon Professor of Human Computer Interaction at Carnegie Mellon University.

**MARK MATFIELD** is the executive director of the Research Defence Society (`http://www.rds-online.org.uk`) in London, England.

**ANNE PLATT McGINN** is a senior researcher at the Worldwatch Institute and the author of "Why Poison Ourselves? A Precautionary Approach to Synthetic Chemicals," *Worldwatch Paper 153* (November 2000).

**JOHN MERCHANT** is an aerospace engineer developing infrared sensors and automatic target recognition based upon human vision. He is president of RPU Technology in Needham, Massachusetts.

**STEPHEN MOORE** is president of the Club for Growth and senior fellow at the Cato Institute, where he has also served as director of fiscal policy studies. He is a contributing editor of *National Review* and coauthor, with Julian L. Simon, of *It's Getting Better All the Time: 100 Greatest Trends of the Past 100 Years* (Cato Institute, 2000). He holds an M.A. in economics from George Mason University.

**TAMAR NORDENBERG**, a former staff writer for *FDA Consumer,* now writes for the Food and Drug Administration's Food Safety Initiative program.

**HENRY PAYNE** is a freelance writer, and an editorial cartoonist for the Detroit News.

**DAVID PIMENTEL**, a professor at Cornell University in Ithaca, New York, holds a joint appointment in the Department of Entomology and the Section of Ecology and Systematics. He has served as consultant to the Executive Office of the President, Office of Science and Technology, and as chairman of various panels, boards (including the Environmental Studies Board), and committees at the National Academy of Sciences, the United States Department of Energy, and the United States Congress.

**JEREMY RIFKIN** is the president of the Foundation on Economic Trends in Washington, D.C., and author of *The Hydrogen Economy: The Creation of the World Wide Energy Web and the Redistribution of Power on Earth* (Tarcher/Putnam, 2002).

**JULIAN SAVULESCU** is director of the Ethics Unit of the Murdoch Institute at the Royal Children's Hospital in Melbourne, Australia, and an associate professor in the Centre for the Study of Health and Society at the

University of Melbourne. He has also worked as a clinical ethicist at the Oxford Radcliffe Hospitals, and he helped set up the Oxford Institute for Ethics and Communication in Health Care Practice.

**MARTIN SCHRAM** is a syndicated columnist, television commentator, and author. His publications include *Mandate for Change,* coedited with Will Marshall (Berkley Books, 1993) and *Speaking Freely: Former Members of Congress Talk About Money in Politics* (Center for Responsive Politics, 1995).

**KEVIN A. SHAPIRO** is a researcher in neuroscience at Harvard University.

**SETH SHOSTAK** is a senior astronomer at the SETI Institute and the author of *Sharing the Universe: Perspectives on Extraterrestrial Life* (Berkeley Hills Books, 1998).

**STEPHEN SOTTONG** is Engineering, Technology, and Computer Science Librarian and Leader of the Library Information Technology Team, California State University, Los Angeles.

**STUART TAYLOR, JR.**, is a senior writer and columnist for *National Journal* and a contributing editor at *Newsweek.*

**MARTIN TEITEL** is executive director of the Council for Responsible Genetics, a nonprofit organization of concerned scientists, doctors, and activists founded in 1983 to foster public debate about the social, ethical, health, economic, and environmental implications of genetic technology. He is the author of *Rain Forest in Your Kitchen: The Hidden Connection Between Extinction and Your Supermarket* (Island Press, 1992).

**CHARLES M. VEST** is president of the Massachusetts Institute of Technology.

**J. MICHAEL WALLER** is a senior writer for *Insight Magazine.*

**EDWARD WEILER** is NASA's Associate Administrator for space science.

**BEN ZUCKERMAN** is Professor of Physics and Astronomy at the University of California, Los Angeles, and coeditor with Michael Hart of *Extraterrestrials: Where Are They?* (Cambridge University Press, 1995).

**KIMBERLY A. WILSON**, former director of the Commercial Biotechnology and the Environment program of the Council for Responsible Genetics, works with the Greenpeace biotechnology campaign.

**STEVEN ZAK** is an attorney in Los Angeles, California. He received a B.A. in psychology from Michigan State University in 1971, an M.S. from the Wayne State University School of Medicine in 1975, and a J.D. from the University of Southern California Law School in 1984. He has written about animals with regard to ethics and the law for numerous publications, including the *Los Angeles Times,* the *New York Times,* and the *Chicago Tribune.*

# Index